Building a Social Science

OXFORD STUDIES IN THE HISTORY OF ECONOMICS

Series Editor:
Steven G. Medema, PhD, University Distinguished
Professor of Economics, University of Colorado Denver

This series publishes leading-edge scholarship by historians of economics and social science, drawing upon approaches from intellectual history, the history of ideas, and the history of the natural and social sciences. It embraces the history of economic thinking from ancient times to the present, the evolution of the discipline itself, the relationship of economics to other fields of inquiry, and the diffusion of economic ideas within the discipline and to the policy realm and broader publics. This enlarged scope affords the possibility of looking anew at the intellectual, social, and professional forces that have surrounded and conditioned economics' continued development.

Building a Social Science

*19th Century British
Cooperative Thought*

Kirsten Madden and Joseph Persky

OXFORD
UNIVERSITY PRESS

OXFORD
UNIVERSITY PRESS

Oxford University Press is a department of the University of Oxford. It furthers
the University's objective of excellence in research, scholarship, and education
by publishing worldwide. Oxford is a registered trade mark of Oxford University
Press in the UK and certain other countries.

Published in the United States of America by Oxford University Press
198 Madison Avenue, New York, NY 10016, United States of America.

Library of Congress Cataloging-in-Publication Data
Names: Madden, Kirsten K. (Kirsten Kara), 1956– author. | Persky, Joseph, author.
Title: Building a social science : 19th century British cooperative thought /
[Kirsten Madden, Joseph Persky].
Description: New York, NY : Oxford University Press, [2024] |
Includes bibliographical references and index.
Identifiers: LCCN 2023056789 (print) | LCCN 2023056790 (ebook) |
ISBN 9780197693735 (hardback) | ISBN 9780197693759 (epub)
Subjects: LCSH: Cooperation—Great Britain—History—19th century. |
Cooperative societies—Great Britain—History—19th century. |
Economics—Great Britain—History—19th century.
Classification: LCC HD3485.A4 M33 2024 (print) | LCC HD3485.A4 (ebook) |
DDC 334.0941—dc23/eng/20240119
LC record available at https://lccn.loc.gov/2023056789
LC ebook record available at https://lccn.loc.gov/2023056790

DOI: 10.1093/oso/9780197693735.001.0001

Printed by Integrated Books International, United States of America

CONTENTS

ACKNOWLEDGMENTS

Arguments in a few chapters in this book draw on our previous work. Chapter 4 builds on Joseph Persky's "Mill's Socialism Re-Examined," *Utilitas*, 32:2 2020, pp. 165–180, as well as Joseph Persky's "Producer Co-operatives in 19th Century British Economic Thought," *European Journal of the History of Economic Thought*, 24:2, 2017, pp. 319–340. Chapter 7 is a major rewrite of Kirsten Madden and Joseph Persky, "The Economic Thought of the Women's Co-operative Guild," in *Routledge Handbook of the History of Women's Economic Thought*, Kirsten Madden and Robert Dimand (eds.), New York: Routledge, 2018, pp. 150–168. Chapter 10 is a major rewrite of Joseph Persky and Kirsten Madden, "The Economic Content of G. D. H. Cole's Guild Socialism: Behavioral Assumptions, Institutional Structure, and Analytic Arguments," *European Journal of the History of Economic Thought*, 26:3, 2019, pp. 427–463.

We are grateful to Edith Kuiper, Ross Emmett, Helen McCabe, Steve Pressman, and Piers Turner for their friendly encouragement. The Chicago Political Economy Group has heard material from this volume twice. The anonymous reviewers from Oxford University Press provided insightful comments. We thank the History of Economics Society, the International Association for Feminist Economics, and the Philosophy, Politics, and Economics Society for including us in conferences (mostly zoomed) that provided feedback on research in progress during the Covid pandemic. We also thank the librarians of Millersville University and the University of Illinois-Chicago for their generous support in tracking down arcane sources. And thanks to Norma Bulman, who searched out references and made copies at the London School of Economics archives.

We benefitted from the helpful advice, experience, and support of Steve Medema, the editor of the Oxford Studies in the History of Economics as well as from James Cook, our editor at Oxford University Press. This project could not have been completed without the thoughtful and diligent attention of the production team including: Sarah Ebel, Dharuman

Bheeman, and Elise Davies. Many, many thanks to them. We thank the art team at Oxford University Press for the cover design; Willam Morris (see Chapter 9) is the originator of the underlying art.

Thanks to Greg and Vicky for their support throughout this project.

We dedicate the book to all those people around the world who are working earnestly to realize the best elements of cooperative economic systems.

CHAPTER 1

⌒⌣⌒

Introduction to the Economics
of Cooperation

WHAT THIS BOOK IS ABOUT

As the Industrial Revolution expanded, a renowned circle of economists including David Ricardo and Thomas Robert Malthus formalized the core of Adam Smith's political economy. They postulated a highly simplified self-centered, indeed frequently selfish, human animal. Ironically, these classical political economists built a science of scarcity, just as the Industrial Revolution promised an awesome abundance. Political economy rationalized production and distribution in a technologically sophisticated, self-organizing market economy. The new discipline provided a dazzling intellectual apology for the emerging capitalist system—its factories and its rush for profits.

This book is about the history of a different set of ideas—a different approach to the economic possibilities of Britain after the Industrial Revolution.[1] We focus on a set of writers, the cooperative theorists, much at odds with the classical dictums. Indeed, the cooperative theorists effectively turn Smith on his head. In a famous passage early in his *Wealth of Nations*, Smith asserts, "It is not from the benevolence of the butcher,

---

1. Revisionist historians disagree about the length of the Industrial Revolution or whether it happened at all. Throughout this volume, we adopt the more traditional view that places the Industrial Revolution in the last quarter of the 18th century.

Building a Social Science. Kirsten Madden and Joseph Persky, Oxford University Press. © Oxford University Press 2024.
DOI: 10.1093/oso/9780197693735.003.0001

the brewer, or the baker that we expect our dinner, but from their regard to their own self-interest" (Smith [1776] 1976, 26–27). For Smith, all benefit when each individual is directed by narrow self-love.[2] In contrast, the cooperative theorists assert that each individual is most likely to prosper and flourish when all are directed by a broader sense of themselves, embracing an appreciation of the common good. Scarcity and selfishness were suitable economic organizing principles for the world before the Industrial Revolution. But the new world encourages a more humane approach.

As one of the most successful early cotton manufacturers, Robert Owen observed firsthand the potential of the new technology. Rather than scarcity, he saw the prospect of a broad abundance for all. He rejected classical political economy. Instead, he projected the need for a social science—a science capable of appreciating not only selfishness under conditions of scarcity, but also cooperation under conditions of abundance.[3] Envisioned as an explicit alternative to classical political economy, Owen's social science initiative advances a very different understanding of humans in society. This new discipline attempts a picture of human nature that includes an awareness of the "social" as well as of the "self." The new social science asserts that humans are more complex and richer in possibilities than the simple actors assumed in classical political economy.

For our purposes, social psychology includes those elements of psychology and sociology that shape how individuals respond to differing social conditions. In the 21st century it is easy to be disillusioned with the narrow social psychology of classical political economy and its cousin Marxian political economy. In this respect, modern neoclassical economics, as its name suggests, builds on much the same ground as the classical schools. Economics still needs a fuller treatment of social psychology and human potential. Reading the cooperative theorists provides one vantage point for explorations in this direction. These writers offer a rich view of human nature and the possibilities opened by an economy of abundance.

2. But note, at least in Smith's *Theory of Moral Sentiments (TMS)*, there is an awareness that social psychology is more complex than simply channeling selfishness in a competitive economy. Indeed, *TMS* even speculates on the advantages of a social system based on benevolence.

3. The prominent Owenite, William Thompson first introduced the term "social science." Owen then adopted the term. John Stuart Mill used it later in a similar sense. Both Thompson and Mill were familiar with French writers, like Condorcet and Comte, who previously made use of the expression "science sociale" (Claeys 1986, 85–89). See also Kaswan (2014, 221n) for a discussion of the history of this term. Throughout the present work we think of a science in its 18th-century meaning as any connected body of knowledge organized together in a coherent manner.

We can only appreciate their contribution (and its implications for a more expansive economics) if we seriously consider their work.

THE HARBINGERS OF COOPERATION

British cooperative theory draws on a broad history of radical tendencies going back to the Middle Ages. Cooperative ideas appear early on in religious thought and popular uprisings. Wat Tyler's rebellion in 1381 advocated the redistribution of land.[4] Thomas More's famous *Utopia* (1516) anticipates common ownership, universal labor, the encouragement of learning, and greater gender equality. In the 17th century English Revolution, the Diggers, popular in Cromwell's army, advanced plans for small-scale, egalitarian agricultural cooperatives with free access to product. Their leader, Gerrard Winstanley, preached a return to Christian principles of property held in common.[5] In the late 18th century, the English radical Thomas Spence advocated common land ownership and universal suffrage for all men and women (Parssinen 1973). Perhaps most important for our writers is the work of the British philosophic anarchist William Godwin, which advances a well-articulated theory of the plasticity of human character, the possibilities of benevolence, and the progress of society toward equality.[6]

These ideas worked in complex ways through religion, the popular press, and political groups to influence the (semi-)consciousness of the working classes. Importantly for our story, these ideas were widely accessible to the educated middle-class cooperative theorists.

WHAT IS COOPERATION?

As the following chapters make clear, writers with middle-class backgrounds and somewhat marginal positions in society constructed the

---

4. For background on Wat Tyler and his movement, see Alastair Dunn (2004) *The Peasants' Revolt: England's Failed Revolution of 1381*. Somewhat curiously, in 1794 Robert Southey penned a drama entitled *Wat Tyler*. Despite the older, more conservative Southey's efforts to suppress it, the play became a favorite piece of the Chartist movement (See Vargo ed. 2020). A featured line is the old adage, "When Adam delved and Eve span, who was then the gentleman."

5. A solid history of radical thinking in the English Revolution is Christopher Hill's *The World Turned Upside Down* (1972).

6. Godwin's major work is *An Enquiry Concerning Political Justice* (1793). Peter Marshall (1984) provides biographical insights. Robert Owen was particularly attracted to Godwin, with whom he developed a close personal relationship.

bulk of 19th-century British cooperative thought. Where most members of the middle class scrambled to prosper from the opportunities created by economic growth, the cooperative theorists were uneasy with this brave new world. As young people, they developed a strong sense of fairness, often with religious overtones. Several rebelled against fathers who were more authoritarian than the norm. Almost instinctively they sympathized with the working classes and looked toward an alliance to enlarge the happiness of all. They rejected the ethics of the nouveau riche and oppressive industrialists. They rejected the political economists' glorification of those new manufacturers. They insisted that in the world of new technologies, the work of accumulation could be better achieved by a cooperative commonwealth.[7] Their sympathetic reading of human nature provides an optimistic foundation for material prosperity, happiness, and human development.

In reviewing cooperative literature, there is no straightforward and common definition of cooperation. While the cooperative theorists differ, a synthesis of their writings might well define cooperation as a working together with cordial benevolence and sharing the common benefit. All recognize that cooperation requires an intentional drawing out and reinforcement of the cooperative consciousness. And all perceive within cooperation the centrality of equality, whether in community standing, resource access, or effort toward a common cause.

These are the commonalities shared across the 19th century, but different cooperative thinkers also introduced unique elements into their approaches to cooperation. For some, cooperation requires a full-fledged, small-scale semi-autarchic community with common possessions. Some narrow the scope of cooperation to specific sectors of the formal economy. And others broaden the scope to consider the household and social services. Other differences stand out as well. For some, cooperation must involve pure voluntarism and self-governance or must emphasize creativity. Others maintain a "friendly rivalry" as central to cooperation, while most see competition as a deadly enemy. Some highlight absolute gender equality. And the religious make cooperation devoutly Christian, an extension of God's command to love one another and sacrifice one's own interest for the commonweal.

---

7. The term "cooperative commonwealth" is not frequently used before the 1870s, but well captures the broader goals of both early and late cooperative thinking.

COOPERATIVE ECONOMIC SYSTEMS

Any analysis of an economic system requires exploring the interaction of social psychology and institutions given a level of technological know-how. A cooperative economic system is no exception.

Social Psychology

Early in his career, the young J. S. Mill laid down the essentials of the classical assumptions about human nature, the homo economicus.[8] In this minimalist statement, humans pursue wealth, desire luxury, seek leisure, and crave sexual gratification (Mill [1844] 1967, 321–323). For the school of classical liberal political economy, that is a sufficient base on which to build. Indeed, they constructed a class analysis of the emerging capitalist economy largely by parceling out this small set of drives among the various major classes. The capitalists are the most eager to accumulate wealth; the landowners focus on luxury and leisure; sex drives the working classes into the Malthusian population trap. This is all there is to the human stuff out of which the mainstream of classical political economy constructed its story.

In explicit opposition, Robert Owen claims that environmental factors completely determine human character. For him, individuals are good or bad, selfish or altruistic depending on experience. Human plasticity generates the possibilities of cooperation. The first serious theorist of British cooperation, William Thompson, argues that self-interest hardly demands selfishness. In the right environment, individuals come to realize that actions oriented to improving the welfare of others best serves personal self-interest. A rich social psychology characterizes cooperative social science. The range of human motives and behaviors is far more complex than homo economicus.

Institutions

Given their emphasis on environment, Owen and Thompson devoted a tremendous amount of energy to envisioning cooperative institutions, both principled (e.g. equality, voluntarism, fellowship, and social responsibility)

---

8. Ironically, Mill and his wife, Harriet Taylor, later elaborated a quite general approach to social psychology.

and concrete (e.g. common property, cooperative education, communal living, and self-governed workshops). They attempted then to describe convincingly the interactions of these institutions and social psychology.

For cooperative theorists, the most fundamental of concrete institutions are the cooperative enterprise, the educational system and common property. Throughout the long 19th century, a number of writers pointed to a range of characteristics that identify such enterprises. Theorists, including Owen, Thompson, J. S. Mill and Harriet Taylor, and G. D. H. Cole, emphasize varying styles of management, pay scales determined by the workforce, and internalization of responsibility. Owen, Thompson, and much later in the century, the artisan William Morris, offer distinct insights into cooperative education. Common property for most all cooperative theorists becomes the bedrock of their new system but with differences about which property to consider—land, industrial capital, retail space, or residential quarters.

Technology

It is ironic that early mainstream economists often accused cooperative theorists of a naïve view of the technological realities of production. The irony stems from the simple fact that Robert Owen, with his deep personal understanding of the material base of the new system of manufacturing, was one of the best-informed participants in the early phase of the Industrial Revolution. Before turning full time to his writing and organizing efforts, Owen managed one of the largest cotton mills at the very center of technological innovation. Moreover, Owen experimented broadly with adapting the labor system of his factories to the new machines in a humane fashion.

TOWARD A THEORY OF COOPERATION

In the pages that follow we describe the thought of the British cooperative theorists. Despite their differences in approach, most of this thought commits to a materialist view of history. Theirs is a materialist history before and after Marx. The cooperative thinkers take the new technological possibilities of 19th-century industrialism as generating widespread opportunities.

The cooperative theorists apply their logic to the combination of social psychology and cooperative institutions on the ground of the new technological base. They deduce then the economic and social consequences of their new economies. Most argue that their cooperative system in full bloom further stimulates technology, erases widespread poverty, and does away with unemployment. Craftsmanship and free service increasingly motivate work. Women are full members of the community with dramatic implications for societal flourishing. Elaborate opportunities abound for whole human development—physically, intellectually, socially. And most importantly, if the theoreticians judge rightly, the cooperative economy empowers each individual to self-develop their own character in a socially positive and responsible manner. For the most part, these claims are not idle speculation, but reasoned conclusions based on well-defined assumptions.

Throughout the book, we consider each writer's approach to enlarged self-interest (i.e. a broader sense of self embracing the common good, expressed in behavior). And we keep in mind that cooperative thinkers are building a theory (and a system) for an age of modern technology, an age launched by the Industrial Revolution. In this context we trace the likely consequences of the interaction of such an enlarged self-interest with cooperative institutions.

While cooperative theorists differ in their proposed institutional structures, they are uniformly optimistic. As we will show, they argue that the interactions of enlarged self-interest and cooperative institutions result in combinations of three broadly attractive outcomes: material superabundance, happiness, and human development. We explore the varieties of these arguments in some detail. Most of the cooperative theorists provide serious and reasoned explanations for the emergence of the three outcomes. We try in subsequent chapters to clarify and explicate the arguments. We find them surprisingly convincing—given an assumption of the feasibility of enlarged self-interest.

All of this may seem to beg the question. One might accept the cooperative logic and still reject the conclusions by asserting the impossibility of the basic assumption. But the cooperative thinkers considered here are more sophisticated than such an assessment suggests. Fundamental to most of their theoretical explorations is the claim of a powerful social psychological feedback mechanism. Experiencing the attractive outcomes of superabundance, happiness, and human development reinforces

and strengthens individuals' enlarged self-interest and institutional commitments.

TRANSITION

Virtually all our writers confound the analysis of a fully cooperative system with the pragmatic need to address the character of transition. How does an individualist competitive economy develop into a cooperative one? For some readers of the present book, this practical question may resonate. Each cooperative theorist sketches at least some angles of a transitional path. These are perhaps the most difficult and incomplete elements of the new social science. Owen and Thompson look to experimental communities to act as examples. They expect the success of those communities to evoke imitation without end. J. S. Mill and Harriet Taylor depict the rise of cooperative enterprises against a background of falling profit rates in a competitive market economy. The advocates of an expanding Cooperative Wholesale Society anticipate that the "Wholesale" grows into a universal provider for consumers while spreading cooperation across productive enterprises through backward linkages. The Women's Cooperative Guild make path-breaking contributions to the development of consciousness-raising civic organizations. Numerous advocates of profit-sharing see significant room for softening the divide between capital and labor. The Guild Socialists outline a theory of "encroaching control," as unions expand their power and influence in the workplace. Each of these paths are thoughtful and historically relevant analysis. In all of them the process is one of evolution and not of sudden revolution. The cooperative theorists look not for a deus ex machina, but for the deep tendency of historical development.

WHAT THIS BOOK DOES

The present volume describes, often restates, and in places reconstructs 19th-century British cooperative thought.[9] The cooperative theorists wrote extensively on all their major subtopics. In places, the material is dense. By

---

9. For background we also provide biographical and historical material, although the current volume is only an introduction to the rich history of 19th-century British cooperation. Furthermore, we present and discuss the most serious contemporary criticisms of cooperative theory, particularly in Chapter 11. Finally, we address the considerable secondary literature that touches on cooperative theory. Most of this interaction with other modern writers occurs in the footnotes.

restatements we simply mean efforts at clarification. Such efforts can also involve reorganization, sometimes using more modern categories. As the reader may notice, some chapters have more depth and detail. Hopefully this reflects the character of the original writings.

There are multiple meanings to the term reconstruction in the history of economic thought. Without engaging in any formal *methodenstreit*, we define a reconstruction as an effort to provide an explicit logical structure for theoretical work originally presented in what today might be considered an informal manner. Central to our efforts are clarifying critical assumptions, describing the structure of proposed institutions, and making precise hypothesized causal connections, including important feedback mechanisms.

While description, restatement, and reconstruction of cooperative theory are central to this work, in the course of the argument we also elaborate on the cooperative writers' critique of classical liberal political economy. For most of the 19th century, classical political economy was the dominant paradigm for discussing serious economic matters. The cooperative theorists found that paradigm woefully inadequate. Hence their insistence on building an alternative.

The 19th century was also one of rampant gender-based discrimination in economics as well as in the British economy. This discrimination had major implications for the ability of people assigned female at birth to create knowledge and to disseminate it. Even so, 19th-century British women did make valuable contributions to cooperative thought. This volume highlights, in particular, the insights from Anna Doyle Wheeler, Harriet Taylor, the Women's Cooperative Guild, and Beatrice Potter Webb.[10]

Nineteenth-century British cooperative economic thought—by women as well as men—is rich in variety. This volume draws across a large number of contributors, opening possibilities for comparative analysis across their thought. Few current writers have compared and contrasted Robert Owen to William Morris, for example, or Anna Doyle Wheeler to the Women's Cooperative Guild. And ultimately, this approach allows us to synthesize and reconstruct the economic thought of 19th-century British cooperative writers.

---

10. In part due to the intentional focus on gender in the history of economic thought, this book does use gender-specific pronouns. We also do so for a second reason. For the most part, social norms on gender were quite strict in 19th-century Britain; the people we write about conformed (at least in public) to gender norms reflected by the then commonly accepted understandings of sex at birth. It seems appropriate in this historical work to reflect the norms imposed by the culture of the time.

A NOTE ON 18TH-CENTURY MORAL PHILOSOPHY

In many ways the personal tie between Robert Owen and William Godwin provided a deep link between cooperative economic thought and 18th-century British moral philosophy. We explore this link in later chapters. But interestingly, classical political economy also grew out of that discipline. Before all, Adam Smith was a moral philosopher. Smith was a student of Francis Hutcheson (who strongly influenced Godwin). Hutcheson's moral philosophy emphasizes benevolence and utility. For that matter, Smith's first major work, *Theory of Moral Sentiments* (*TMS*), develops at length the case for making benevolence a mainspring of social action.[11]

In a vein reminiscent of his teacher, Smith is clear that a society based on malevolent selfishness cannot survive. The "prevalence of injustice must utterly destroy it" ([1790] 2004, 101). And while Smith asserts that a just (non-malevolent) self-interested society is functional and can persist, he argues that such a society is only capable of a lower level of social welfare than one including strong elements of benevolence (100). Indeed, it is possible to read passages of *TMS* as detailing the inner workings of a social psychology in support of virtuous behavior based in benevolence, justice, prudence, and self-command.

Throughout *TMS*, Smith invokes a central assumption: love and respect from others are major sources of happiness.[12] The coupling of this assumption along with a sympathetic imaginary trade of places are the starting points for the mechanism that restrains selfishness and calls up socially virtuous behavior.[13] The psychological development of an internal, impartial spectator arises as a person realizes that not only do they judge others, but others judge them. Smith describes the internalization of this realization: "I divide myself, as it were, into two persons; and that I, the examiner and judge, represent a different character from that other I, the person whose conduct is examined into and judged of" ([1790] 2004, 131). With this psychological division begins the process of self-scrutiny, examining

---

11. This is not to say that in *TMS*, Smith recognizes no useful roles for self-interest. With consciousness of pleasure and pain residing only within the person embodying those feelings, *TMS* declares it prudent to take responsibility for oneself ([1790] 2004, 256–257). And self-interest is appropriate where efforts to relieve the perceived suffering of others is certain to come to naught (161). At one point, *TMS* also recognizes the value of self-interest where it motivates industry and gets people what they need (359–360).

12. See, for example Smith [1790] 2004, 130–131; 132; 135; 136; 149; 194; 249; and 265.

13. Other virtues are also relevant, including self-command (Smith [1790] 2004, 29; 32–33).

one's own conduct "as we imagine any other fair and impartial spectator would examine it" (130–131).

Self-love compels us to prefer our own interests to that of the many, but "The man within immediately calls to us, that we value ourselves too much and other people too little, and that, by doing so, we render ourselves the proper object of the contempt and indignation of our brethren" ([1790] 2004, 159). It is the internal spectator "who shows us the propriety of generosity . . . the propriety of resigning the greatest interests of our own, for the yet greater interests of others" (158). Though preferring oneself, Smith's mechanism stimulates voluntary constraints on personal selfishness. The internal impartial spectator humbles "the arrogance of his self-love," bringing "it down to something which other men can go along with" (97).

The internal impartial spectator assesses personal motivations, behavior, and social outcomes. Out of regular communion with the spectator, a deeper realization dawns that "characters of virtue" deserve love and reward from others. This realization excites virtuous behavior to attract that love and its corresponding reward. Even when there is no external reward, there is a psychological reinforcement: "The consciousness that is the object of such favourable regards, is the source of that inward tranquility and self-satisfaction" ([1790] 2004, 132).

When Smith discusses a fully benevolent society, he includes all the members of that society:

> All the members of human society stand in need of each others assistance, and are likewise exposed to mutual injuries. Where the necessary assistance is reciprocally afforded from love, from gratitude, from friendship, and esteem, the society flourishes and is happy. All the different members of it are bound together by the agreeable bands of love and affection, and are, as it were drawn to one common centre of mutual good offices. ([1790] 2004, 100)

This is not tithing on Sunday for charity, but a society built on a powerful benevolence.

Despite Smith's extensive treatment of the mechanism of benevolence and his assertion that a society based on benevolence could be the most flourishing state, he argues that there are intrinsic limits.[14] Benevolence

14. By contrast, William Godwin explicitly asserts that the "eye of an impartial spectator" dictates a universal benevolence and designs his system on the possibility of achieving a society ruled by such a strong conscience (Godwin 1793, 796). It is unclear how much Smith's *TMS* influenced Godwin, but the usage of the term seems more than coincidental.

tends to manifest in some contexts more than others. Given the frequency of interaction, Smith identifies the capacity for benevolence arising most naturally among members of a household. Benevolence also frequently arises between those who regularly interact in the workplace and the neighborhood. And people tend naturally to return benevolence to the benevolent ([1790] 2004, 263–265). But beyond these realms "though naturally sympathetic," people "feel so little for another, with whom they have no particular connexion, in comparison of what they feel for themselves." Further, Smith explicitly acknowledges the capacity to hurt others and the temptation to succumb (101). The internal, impartial spectator can fail to restrain harmful behavior when anger, fear, pride, or vanity arise. To avoid social dissolution, justice must be "the main pillar that upholds the whole edifice" 101).

Clearly Smith never endorses a cooperative society, but he does deeply consider why and how to constrain self-interest. His rich moral social psychology centers in the four virtues of self-command, prudence, justice, and beneficence (309–310). Smith even suggests that "self-love may frequently be a virtuous motive of action" when it includes the "love of true glory" ([1790] 2004, 365). In the context of an engaged internal impartial spectator, this love invokes the "desire of rendering ourselves the proper objects of honour and esteem" (366).

Classical economists embraced Smith's *Wealth of Nations*. Indeed, it became the foundation of their new discipline. Somewhat surprisingly, their works barely mention Smith's *TMS*. In particular, they did not look there for broader insights into social psychology. Instead for the classical political economists, perhaps starting with Smith's own *Wealth of Nations*, narrow self-interest became an acceptable description of and norm for actions in the competitive economy.[15]

Benevolence was cast into the sociological periphery. A richer social psychology, such as Smith's *TMS* hints at, would require a fuller description of economic behavior and a normative accounting of the social and psychological costs of the new industrial economy.[16] Instead, most

---

15. Historians of economic thought still debate the so-called Adam Smith problem that points to an inconsistency between the Smith of *TMS* and the Smith of the *Wealth of Nations*. Montes (2003) provides a good review of the history of the problem from its 19th-century German roots to the 21st century. As suggested in the text, we find a claim of consistency between *TMS* and the *Wealth of Nations* somewhat strained.

16. To be fair, in Book 5 of *Wealth of Nations*, Smith does elaborate on the costs of excessive specialization: "[T]he understandings of the greater part of men are necessarily formed by their ordinary employment. The man whose whole life is spent in performing a few simple operations, of which the effects too are perhaps always the same, or very nearly the same, has no occasion to exert his understanding or to exercise his

political economists—both in their written tracts and in their occasional testimonies before Parliament—supported unregulated factories and harsh workhouses that predictably dehumanized their charges. The political economists assumed most working people are lazy and unmotivated. The only solution to this perverse character of a working-class homo economicus is the harsh discipline of need and subsistence wages. The classical political economists refused to actively engage in any speculation on what a more universal economy could look like; on what a more democratic and benevolent internal spectator might demand. Most damning, they refused to actively engage in any serious discussion of whether the historical reality of the Industrial Revolution might fundamentally change the character of the possible.[17]

invention in finding out expedients for removing difficulties which never occur. He naturally loses, therefore, the habit of such exertion, and generally becomes as stupid and ignorant as it is possible for a human creature to become" (Smith [1776] 1976, 782).

17. It is not only the classical economists who ignored Smith's *TMS*. As far as we can tell, the cooperative thinkers did not work Smith's insights on possible psychological mechanisms into their contributions. This is odd, as it seems reasonable to speculate that many of the first cooperative theorists might have knowledge of *TMS*. For example, both Jeremy Bentham and James Mill were familiar with *TMS*, and these men interacted socially with and influenced Robert Owen, William Thompson, and Anna Doyle Wheeler. And both men were major influences on J. S. Mill.

PART I

———————◦◇◦———————

The First Theorists

During the Industrial Revolution, Robert Owen, an owner of one of the largest cotton factories in Britain, devoted himself to the construction of a new social science, a science projected to unleash unparalleled returns to material productivity, human development, and happiness. This science is possible because of a new appreciation of social psychology underlying human character and a conscious engineering of institutions. William Thompson, a radical utilitarian philosopher, presents a serious attempt at codifying this new social science. With feminist co-author Anna Doyle Wheeler, these two cooperative thinkers develop deep insights into reinforcing mechanisms that allow for system-wide stability in cooperation. John Stuart Mill and Harriet Taylor place cooperation at the center of a new understanding of social progress.

Photo 1. An 1838 idealized rendering of Thomas Stedman Whitwell's plan for Robert Owen's co-operative village at New Harmony, Indiana. Drawn and engraved by F. Bate for Owen's Association of all Classes of all Nations. (Chronicle / Alamy Stock Photo)

CHAPTER 2

⌒⋁⌒

Robert Owen's Cooperative Vision

THE CHALLENGE OF THE INDUSTRIAL REVOLUTION

In the midst of the Industrial Revolution, Robert Owen became the director of the New Lanark textile mill, near Glasgow, Scotland. Much as he saw the broader world, he described the workforce he inherited as a "very wretched society: every man did that which was right in his own eyes, and vice and immorality prevailed to a monstrous extent. The population lived in idleness, in poverty, in almost every kind of crime . . ." (Owen 1813–1816, 27). Classical political economy only rationalizes this discord. But Owen was certain that under the new conditions made possible by the Industrial Revolution, human society can evolve and prosper.

Robert Owen is best remembered for his reform work at the New Lanark cotton factory and his experimental cooperative community in New Harmony, Indiana. But Owen was also a man of ideas. Admittedly, he was not the most rigorous or formal of thinkers. And his theoretical work is often dismissed as utopian. Even the highly sympathetic G. D. H. Cole, leader of 20th-century Guild Socialists, levels this common criticism: "Herein Owen's Utopianism lies. His own vision of the needs of the new age was so clear that he asked men to proceed directly to their full realisation. But men were still utterly unprepared for the way of living that he prescribed" (G. D. H. Cole [1925] 2019, 7). As discussed in Chapter 10, Guild Socialist thought represents the most sophisticated British effort at theorizing a fully industrialized cooperative economy. But like other assessments of Owen, Cole's charge fails to address the historical-materialist base of

Building a Social Science. Kirsten Madden and Joseph Persky, Oxford University Press. © Oxford University Press 2024.
DOI: 10.1093/oso/9780197693735.003.0002

Owen's argument, its extensive social psychology, and its innovative institutional structure. Together these form the foundations of Owen's new social science. Yes, in New Harmony and several of his later ventures, Owen was far too optimistic. But his practical failures reflect the thorny issues of transition and leadership and not his broader theory of society.

Owen's thought starts with an understanding of social psychology much richer than that of classical political economy. Classical political economy takes selfishness as virtually the only relevant character trait. It then asserts that only the competitive system can create material prosperity because that system channels selfishness to socially useful purpose. In contrast, Owen argues that people are far more complex. Taking account of human potential and human character formation, we can build a much better economy—an economy that does well by all and not by just a few.[1]

According to Owen's new social science, people are plastic. Rational-ethical educational institutions can be designed to gently encourage children to develop a range of socially constructive character traits. As children mature, cooperative institutions organized along similar lines foster these traits to naturally organize around a communal ethic.[2] The resulting broader sense of self in community forms the human base for a cooperative society. Owen argues that only cooperative institutions can develop the potential of this base. The well-designed cooperative village generates material superabundance and human development for all. Over the decades, Owen is steadfast in proselytizing his revolutionary ethical program as a necessary condition for social progress (see for example, [1842a] 1993, 83).

Where does Owen's understanding of society originate? More than any other British thinker or social activist, Owen was the child of the Industrial Revolution. He clearly appreciated the history-shattering significance of the series of seemingly specialized technical improvements in spinning and weaving. For the most part, the men of the Industrial Revolution focused on the personal business opportunities it opens. But Owen saw the possibilities of a new world associated with the emerging reality of superabundance. Historically, material wellbeing was the province of only a small

---

1. Owen repeatedly provides detailed critiques of the system of individual competition. For the most part, this chapter follows the advice of Owen himself to point toward "truth" rather than elaborate on error, emphasizing the positive program underscored by his theories of human nature and social psychology. Critiques of individual competition appear sparsely here and only if those shortcomings elicit deeper insight into the construction of a cooperative system.

2. "Moral philosophy" and "moral" are the terms in common usage in early 19th-century political economy. This work uses the terms "ethical" and "virtuous" as synonyms for moral. Beyond the Victorian era and over the next century, "moral" and "moralism" take on negative connotations for many, which we are not addressing here.

share of the world's population; drudgery and want were the lot of the vast majority. The institutions of competitive society reflect the bitterness of this fundamental fact. On the forefront of an Industrial Revolution driven by technical change, Owen dreamed and worked for a new social order amidst burgeoning superabundance.

After a bit of biographical background, this chapter goes on to distill Owen's social science. For Owen, an appreciation of social psychology and new institutional structures generates a range of theoretical insights. The claim here is that Owen's theory provides a fresh understanding of the potential for human society.

CONTEXT FROM BIOGRAPHY

Owen develops a radical environmental determinism. No one can be blamed or praised for their character or actions, because all is the product of a person's environment. It seems only reasonable to explore Owen's own upbringing, searching for clues to his almost unique reading of the Industrial Revolution and its potentialities. What follows is a brief synopsis of Owen's biography.[3]

Owen was born in Wales in 1771. His father, also Robert, earned a living as a saddler and ironmonger. The senior Owen married into a respectable farm family in the Newton area, where he took up his trade. He also served as postmaster and managed parish affairs.

The younger Owen started school early and picked up reading quickly. He read widely in the libraries of town professionals. In addition to novels and travel books, he read religion. In effect, he educated himself. He even composed a few sermons. His religious upbringing was orthodox, touched with a bit of evangelical Methodism (Davis 2011, 91–93). By ten he declared "there was something fundamentally wrong in all religions" (Owen [1857] 1967, 4).

At seven Owen served as his teacher's assistant, trusted to manage much of the education of his peers. He was a good athlete and a good dancer. He was a favorite in the family and a favorite in town. He found walking in the countryside pleasant. One hot day he and a cousin joined

---

3. A word of warning is in order here. Owen (1857) in his autobiography treats the first ten years of his life in just ten pages. There are few other sources on his early life. While Owen writes extensively on how children should be raised, he recounts only the barest facts of his own childhood. Moreover, his recollections many years later are an imperfect source. We shouldn't expect too much from this exercise.

a group of workpeople and afterward "found ourselves much more comfortable with active employment than when we were idle" (Owen [1857] 1967, 7).

Often corralled into competitions with other children, he wrote in his autobiography, "Such competitions are unjust, because no two organizations are the same, there can be no just comparison between the competing efforts of any two individuals." In such activities "the successful one is taught vanity, and the unsuccessful, jealousy and hatred" (Owen [1857] 1967, 5). This may well be Owen's most characteristic thought from childhood.

At nine he began working full time in a local haberdashery and grocery. He continued to participate in dancing classes, where he again observed that the adults were insensitive to the children's feelings. "I am now conscious there was much real suffering in that dancing room, which, had there been more knowledge of human nature in the dancing master and in the parents of the children, might have been avoided." Finally, his autobiography describes an incident, which he claims unique, when his mother sought his father to whip him. He bore it without wincing, maintaining his position as "the favorite" (Owen [1857] 1967, 10–11). And another whipping never occurred again.

And that is that for childhood. At the age of ten in 1781, Robert Owen traveled to London to enter the world of serious work, his character presumably formed. He was gifted, resourceful, and sensitive. He found major opportunities open to him by the Industrial Revolution. Many possessing similar traits use such opportunities to pursue personal interests, engaging in philanthropy if convenient. And, indeed, that is the path Owen began. But something—something, if we are to believe Owen's own theories, laid down in his early childhood—made his response to the revolutionary situation far different. Something moved him to seek nothing less than the overhaul of the entire society.

Reviewing Owen's early childhood hardly prepares us for what he calls "the greatest discovery ever made by man" (xli). But we can trace the series of events that expose him to the red-hot core of the ongoing Industrial Revolution. He experienced the productivity of the new technology from the very center of the ongoing transformation.

Owen first served as an apprentice to a London draper's shop. From these modest beginnings he moved to Manchester, where his career took a sharp upward climb, moving from an assistant in a wholesaling business to master of a small spinning establishment, to manager of a large Manchester cotton mill. In this boom-town environment, his self-confidence served him well (M. Cole 1953, 16–25; Owen [1857] 1967, 23–28). In Manchester

he mingled with the reform-minded Unitarian elite and participated in the Literary and Philosophical Society (M. Cole 1953, 27).

The Industrial Revolution was vast, and Owen was at its center. He inspired the confidence of partners and others around him. Most importantly he developed a close relationship with David Dale the owner of New Lanark, one of the largest mills in Britain. At the age of twenty-eight Owen took over Dale's expansive cotton works near Glasgow. Within two years he married Dale's daughter (M. Cole 1953, 31–35).

Owen focused full time on improving the business. People already knew Dale's New Lanark for its efforts at reform, such as softening the treatment of child labor. But Owen saw the need for deeper changes. He gave up the apprentice system and its use of child labor. He employed families and concentrated on community building. Never humble in his aspirations, Owen proceeded "to commence the most important experiment for the happiness of the human race that had yet been instituted at any time in any part of the world" (Owen [1857] 1967, 59–60). The experiment was undertaken with the sponsorship of several prominent investors/philanthropists, including the philosopher Jeremy Bentham (60).[4] Anticipating a thrust of his future work, the new community centered on an experimental school of his own design. For Owen, the school's success proved "the truth of the principle that the character is formed *for* and not *by* the individual" (62).

Owen developed his theory with surprisingly little influence from political economists or philosophers. As several biographers note, Owen was largely self-taught. Despite building a substantial library in New Lanark, he was not widely read.[5] Cole suggests that the only book Owen took seriously is William Godwin's (1793) *An Enquiry Concerning Political Justice* (M. Cole 1953, 27).[6] Very likely Owen was strongly influenced by Godwin's proto-utilitarianism and his associationist psychology.[7]

4. Although Owen was clearly utilitarian in outlook, he and Bentham did not much care for each other (Trincado & Santos-Redondo 2019, 16).

5. See for example Donnachie (2000, 9).

6. Claeys reports that Owen and Godwin met over fifty times from 1813 to 1818 (1989, 33).

7. David Hartley influences Godwin's thought. In his 1878 commentary on his father James' contributions to psychology, J. S. Mill points to Thomas Hobbes (1588–1679) and John Locke (1632–1704) as providing the basis of a materialist psychology: that is, Hobbes and Locke suggest the mind builds out of sensory experience. From that foundation David Hartley, in 1749, identifies that "the great fundamental law of Association of Ideas" applies broadly to mental phenomena. That law can explain how "experience operates in moulding our thoughts and forming our thinking powers" (J. S. Mill, ed. 1878, x). Concerning Hartley's influence on Godwin, see (Jakalski 2017).

Anticipating Owen's emphasis on plasticity of character, Godwin asserts, "The actions and dispositions of mankind are the offspring of circumstances and events, and not of any original determination that they bring into the world" ([1798] 1976, 97). Over time, Godwin recognizes people as becoming more capable of constructive reasoning, more committed to disinterested benevolence, and more engaged in human development. On these tendencies Godwin projects an intellectual movement toward equality. Owen is clearly attracted to Godwin's thought. The two men were in "almost weekly contact for a decade."[8] Among other ideas, Godwin may well have passed on his thoughts about the formation of sympathy: its roots begin in an infant's associating the cries of another with their own experience of pain, but then develops into a benevolence based on rationality and a deep appreciation that others are very much like ourselves.[9] According to Godwin's biographer Peter Marshall, Godwin claimed, "one evening he converted Owen from the doctrine of 'self-love' to that of benevolence" (Marshall 2017, 310).[10] But Godwin was at root a philosophical anarchist, and he offers almost no institutional or structural details of this new world. Indeed Godwin asserts "every thing that is usually understood by the term co-operation is in some degree an evil" (Godwin 1793, 844) and deeply hostile to most organized forms of cooperation. In contrast, Owen articulates the institutional detail of cooperation as a necessary complement to his understanding of human nature.

Not the least of Owen's institutional concerns is to build a new system of rational-ethical education. Although Owen engaged on good terms with the well-known Quaker education reformer, Joseph Lancaster, he considered Lancaster's monitorial approach but a "mite" of instruction for the poor. Similarly, he held a low view of the reformer Andrew Bell and his National Schools: "It must be evident to common observers, that children may be taught, by either Dr. Bell's or Mr. Lancaster's system, to read, write,

---

8. The quote is from Stedman Jones (2020, 96) who, on this matter, cites Claeys (1993) and Marshall ([1984] 1967). Stedman Jones (2020) also traces a famous debate beginning between Thomas Robert Malthus and Godwin and later extending to Owen. See Chapter 11 for the Malthusian critique of Owenite thinking.

9. This mechanism is emphasized in Godwin as the connection between early associations of sympathy and mature appreciation of universal benevolence (Godwin 1793, 348–350).

10. Peter Marshall goes on to note that the next time the two men met "Owen admitted that he had been too precipitate." Despite this recantation, Marshall concludes Owen's "attempt to derive benevolence from a desire for happiness is not very different from Godwin's" (Marshall 2017, 310). Donnachie writes "Owen certainly never acknowledged a direct debt to *Political Justice*, perhaps because he never properly read it. Yet many of the fundamental ideas, and sometimes the actual phrasing of Owen's works, resemble the doctrines of *Political Justice*" (Donnachie 2000, 115).

account, and sew, and yet acquire the worst habits and have their minds rendered irrational for life" (Owen 1813–1816, Essay IV, quoted in G. D. H. Cole [1925] 2019, 130).

Owen intends to shape new human materials for a new age. Unchecked, the poverty and anarchy of the Industrial Revolution left the working class with a "ferocity of character" which does not suffice to build a new society (quoted in O'Hagan 2011, 80). At New Lanark, Owen applied proceeds from new technology toward education and amenities for all in the community. And at New Lanark, his experiment was a success: "Those employed became industrious, temperate, healthy, faithful to their employers, and kind to each other" (Owen 1813–1816, 33). And he goes on, "[t]he community exhibits the general appearance of industry, temperance, comfort, health, and happiness" (35).

While Owen emphasizes the importance of developing ethics, throughout his life he maintained a hostile attitude toward organized religions. For Owen, virtually all historical religions only divide people. His morality is that of reason rather than divine commandments. At times his writing reflects Deism, at others he puts forth a new religion of nature or life spirit (Davis 2011, passim). Repeatedly his religious unorthodoxy alienated partners and coworkers.[11] After a quarter century of success at New Lanark, he lost control of the mill and its school to a group of religious, conservative partners (Trincado & Santos-Redondo 2019, 4).

Perhaps on the rebound, he committed to building a more-or-less complete socialist-cooperative on the banks of the Wabash in Indiana. In this new world he intended to realize greatly expanded social plans. America of 1825 was replete with religious communal societies, including the Rappites with whom Owen was in contact and from whom he purchased the town of New Harmony (Donnachie 2011, 17).[12] And who held more aspirational rights than Owen to build the definitive workers' cooperative?

The atmosphere was heady. Visiting the United States, Congress and the President entertained Owen. He partnered with William Maclure, a

---

11. As early as 1817 Owen engaged in a harangue about religion. This is the first of many diatribes promoting discord among like-minded thinkers. (See the introduction of Claeys (1993 xxxii); also see Morris and Bax (1893, 209)). Morris and Bax date the tirade to August 1816. G. D. H. Cole goes so far as to suggest that, at this point, "Owen went a little mad . . . and he went on getting madder to the end of his days" ([1925] 1965, 197). Owen's attitude toward religion also caused tensions for his children since Owen's wife remained a devout Presbyterian.

12. The Rappites were reasonably successful in their town of Harmony but sought a new beginning. On the Rappites see (Pitzer & Elliott 1979).

self-made man and geographer of note. For almost unexplainable reasons, Owen brought to New Harmony an odd collection of

> lawyers, physicians, political economists, musicians, dancing-masters, young la-
> dies just transplanted from the hot-bed of artificial life, learned men and literati
> of every grade and description, with as many of their domestics probably as they
> could induce to accompany them, and as many labourers as could at that time be
> obtained from the scanty market of American labour. (*New Moral World*, July 22,
> 1837, quoted in M. Cole 1953, 152–153)

Owen wrote and rewrote the town's constitution, never getting it right.[13] He plunged money into the enterprise only to waste away much of his fortune. In the end, and the end came quickly, Owen concludes,

> This last experiment has made it evident that families trained in the individual
> system, founded as it is upon superstition, have not acquired those moral
> qualities of forbearance and charity for each other which are necessary to pro-
> mote full confidence and harmony among all the members, and without which
> Communities cannot exist. (quoted in M. Cole 1953, 159)

While Owen was in America, Abram Combe (brother of the phrenologists George and Andrew Combe) and Archibald James Hamilton attempted to realize Owen's cooperative vision in Lanarkshire, Scotland. They established the cooperative community, Orbiston just southeast of Glasgow and not far from New Lanark. Like New Harmony, Orbiston accepted all wishing to join. As contemporaries note, it lacked a clear plan. Plagued by managerial ineptness, Orbiston lasted from 1825 to 1827. It fell apart shortly after Combe's death (Garnett 1972, 65–99).

On returning to Britain in 1829, Owen somewhat reluctantly moved toward the leadership of its burgeoning cooperative movement. However, he did not immediately launch another cooperative community. That waited until 1839, when he actively led community efforts at Queenwood in Hampshire. With grandiose capital commitments, Owen initially overinvested in extravagant technology, such as air conditioning. He effectively

---

13. The problem of writing a constitution is symptomatic of Owen's uncertainty concerning the status of the residents of the village. "Incomprehensible as it seems, Owen still had no clear idea if the communitarians were to be regarded as employees, almsmen, partners or tenants of his as lord proprietor of New Harmony" (Donnachie 2000, 219).

drove the project into the ground. Others forced his exit by 1844, and Queenwood fell apart shortly afterward (Garnett 1972, 166–208).

G. D. H. Cole traces Owen's falling influence in the upper classes, which was matched by his rising influence among the working classes. The former might be ascribed to his unconventional approach to religion and his broad social criticism. The latter reflects a widely felt "need of the new working-class movement for a gospel of hope" (G. D. H. Cole [1925] 2019, 25). Owen became the recognized head of a truly working-class movement. "The New Society was to be based, said these pioneers, on the free association of producers in guilds and manufacturing societies strong enough to dispense with employers and with the exploitation of labour for private profit" (29).[14]

Between 1829 and 1839, and in quick succession, Owen engaged in two closely related movements—his National Equitable Labour Exchange ([1832] 1993) and the Grand National Consolidated Trades Union ([1834] 1993). Both launched at massive scale due to Owen's considerable prestige. Both promised to completely revolutionize the economy. And both quickly disintegrated.

The cooperative movement widely discussed the underlying idea of an "exchange" during this time. The intention behind the Labour Exchange was to establish a system of labor notes facilitating direct trade between workers or between cooperatives and customers. Labor notes might serve as a solution to the persistent problem of middlemen (M. Cole 1953, 183). After an exciting start, the Exchange disappeared by 1834. The National Union fared no better. As the name suggests, the Consolidated sought the widest possible base for its membership. Following a meteoritic expansion to over half a million members, the Consolidated engaged in several disastrous strikes and quickly dissolved (G. D. H. Cole 1944, 28).

After New Lanark, Owen's record in the real world is not impressive. It is easy to dismiss his various ventures as poorly executed. He was a man at the center of a whirlwind. Clearly enjoying the attention, he moved from one undertaking to another, trying to realize his vision, but without ever managing to build lasting institutions. Under the circumstances, many find

---

14. Notice Owen's approach to exploitation is close to that of Marx and Engels, while differing fundamentally from the radical position of the advocates of the People's Charter. The latter emphasized using broader political participation to end high taxation. Owen and his followers thought lower taxes would simply lead to lower wages (See Claeys 1989, 150–152 and Ch. 6).

it tempting to also conclude that Owen's efforts were ill-conceived, that his theoretical foundations are insubstantial. As previously noted, Owen was not a formal thinker. Nevertheless, his insights fueled the radical imagination of the 19th century. Learned firsthand, his appreciation of the superabundance created by the Industrial Revolution provides a new perspective for understanding society's possibilities as suggested by Godwin and other Enlightenment thinkers. Whatever his practical mistakes, his ideas are substantial and worth modern attention. Owen, first among British cooperative thinkers, brings together a serious social psychology and creative institutional analysis. More important than his practical achievements or failures, is his new way of thinking about human development. Owen in effect initiates the foundations of a social science. We turn now from recounting the man's life and attempt a serious description and restatement of his thought.

SOCIAL PSYCHOLOGY

Like Jeremy Bentham and Adam Smith, Owen holds the Enlightenment belief that people are born with a desire for happiness. But Owen aligns his utilitarianism with a very different take on social psychology, including human nature and character formation.

Human Nature and Character Formation

For Owen each person is a compound of three interrelated parts: physical, intellectual, and moral (Owen 1836, 27). In turn, each part evidences a basic inclination. As to the physical, the person seeks wellbeing. With respect to intellectual capacity, all begin with a "natural love for truth." Perhaps more controversial, Owen assumes an inclination toward a morality of fellow feeling—"the desire to benefit others to the greatest possible extent" (Owen [1825a] 1993, 10). Owen emphasizes a harmonious coexistence of these three, each part in "subserviency" to the others (Owen 1836, 73).

While sharing these common inclinations, each human being evolves a unique character, or a specific set of feelings, preferences, beliefs, morality, will, intelligence, and talents. "None are or can be bad by nature; their education is always the business of work of society, and not of the individual. The individual is thus, evidently, a material of nature, finished and fashioned by the society in which it lives" (Owen 1836, 75). Echoing William

Godwin, Owen holds plasticity as central to that character.[15] Character forms for a person—not by a person—through social forces unwittingly cultivated over generations. Socialization shapes preferences, beliefs, intelligence, talents, etc. Some forms of socialization generate social weal better than others (Owen 1813–1816).

For most of history, socialization distorts human experience and disconnects people from their basic inclinations (Owen [1825a] 1993, 10). In the world as it is, contact with dominant social institutions necessarily degrades character. In a talk he gave in 1817, Owen identifies how four social affiliations cause the person to acquire "peculiar notions," which muddle thought and generate feelings of ill will. The four institutional affiliations are religious, economic, political, and national. They create "dense atmospheres of error and prejudice." Viewed through these atmospheres, "each object becomes distorted or indistinct . . . and in consequence nature has hitherto been hidden from man." From this fog, each individual creates a different world.[16]

The Social System (Owen [1826] 1993) develops at great length the idea that character is formed for the person, not by the person. We give here an extended quote to suggest its flavor. Take as A the organization at birth which includes a person's basic inclinations.

> Then the first circumstance acting upon it to be represented by B. A and B unite, and make a compound, represented, we will suppose by C. The second circumstance which influences the organization shall be called D, which then unites with the last compound C, making a new compound of character, which we will call E. The next external influence, which we will call F, must now make another compound—not however by uniting A or C (which peculiar compounds have been lost for ever)—but with the last new compound E; making, together the fourth compound, which we will denominate G. And in this manner the character of each individual undergoes a continued change, or makes a constant advance towards maturity, and afterwards to old age. (Owen 1836, 6–7)

15. To the best of our knowledge, Owen does not explicitly base his proposition of plasticity on the formal associationist psychology available to him through Hartley and Godwin, and later, through James Mill. A deeper exploration of plasticity along these lines might have provided a more intellectually acceptable mechanism for Owen's claims among political economists of the time. More discussion of associationism follows in Chapters 4 and 12.

16. When people meet, "they soon discover that they do not see objects alike; and wholly unconscious of the real cause of difference between them" they create "an opposition of feeling, as well as of seeing." This opposition can extend from "a slight degree of dislike to anger, hatred, revenge, death, and destruction" (Owen [1817] 1993, 176).

External circumstances B, D, and F integrate into the clay, shaping and re-shaping a new compound from A to C to E to G in a dynamic process that can neither be replicated nor undone.

The argument is not that nature plays no role in character development. After all, individuals are born with basic inclinations. Instead, the argument is that character formation is largely a social process with no role for self-creation or free-will. The human compound does not create itself, has no control over the circumstances which shape it or how it is shaped, and therefore has no claim to the results emanating from it, whether beneficial, neutral, or detrimental (Owen [1826] 1993, 57).

Owen offers a powerful, hypothetical example to make his point:

> [The human character] may be made so humane, and be so directed, that the matured man shall be compelled to feel considerable horror at accidentally injuring the limb of the smallest insect, or be made to experience the greatest pleasure and delight in first killing, afterwards roasting, and then eating, one of his fellow-men; and be made equally, in either case, to think that he is acting right. (Owen 1836, 62)

The character formation hypothesis has a major implication. If individual character forms through a long chain of events, the resulting individual is not responsible for their character whether good or bad. In short:

Character formation hypothesis   →   no responsibility

A person is "not, nor ever can become responsible" for any peculiar (person-)compound. In rebuking the mainstay belief in personal responsibility, Owen writes, "nothing created can form any part of itself; . . . it must exist, think, will or act, according to the qualities given to it" (Owen [1826] 1993, 59).

Character Formation and Rational-Ethical Education

The character formation hypothesis leads directly to Owen's deep interest in education. The core idea is to shape character in alignment with original inclinations. While those inclinations include concern for an individual's own wellbeing, they also include a love of truth and a benevolent concern for others. Notice, the assumption is not that people are born saintlike. Only that, in addition to self-love, there are two important margins that a healthy education can and should address.

The basic elements of Owen's education program appear early, in *New View* (Owen 1813–1816).[17] The program involves training in rationality and ethics. The rational component develops reasoning to accurately distinguish truth from falsehood. The ethical component stresses experiential training that encourages children to systematically explore and learn to do right by others. Assuming humankind is built with the original inclinations of fellow feeling and a love of truth, this education program simply invigorates instinct into daily experience.

In school, the teacher's charge is to use every opportunity to link the "inseparable connection which exists between the interest and happiness of each individual and the interest and happiness of every other individual" with the student exploring outcomes of various behaviors (Owen 1813–1816, 49).[18] For Owen, this approach is one of reasoning based on experiential education that emphasizes natural consequences, not indoctrination.[19]

Owen intends this education program to begin at infancy. If training consistently and correctly conveys the truths of interdependence, people learn to promote strongly the happiness of others. Activity directed to the benefit of others tends to support one's own health, strength and vigor of body, and peace of mind. And as people learn that circumstances beyond personal control form human character, they develop a sense of charity for all—forgiving flaws and accepting others even when grievous wrongdoings occur.

Since no one is exempt, Owen infers as general policy that there can be no exclusion in the training to truth. "Good habits must be given to all, or the best cannot be given to any" (Owen 1836, 51). Owen also argues that it is an error to force truth—this can actually reduce intelligence. People come to experience the validity underlying the logic of consistently caring for others, including enemies. In response to an irrational act (generating harm to others), the rational person looks for the social sources of

---

17. *New View* makes Owen's reputation as a reform thinker. Donnachie observes that it was probably edited by James Mill and Francis Place. He goes on to speculate that their editing "gave the essays the clarity that is missing from most of his later works" (Donnachie 2000, 116–117).

18. When Suzy hits Johnny, the teacher encourages Suzy to consciously attend to the natural consequences: Johnny cries and lashes out, returning discomfort to Suzy. When Suzy shares her sandwich with Johnny, the teacher encourages Suzy to consciously attend to the natural consequences, perhaps a friendly rapport arising between the two.

19. William Thompson continues in this vein, making an important distinction between natural and factitious rewards and punishments. Thompson's educational vision is also distinguished by emphasizing various pleasures that arise through education. See Chapter 3.

	Elementary Aspects of Character	Complex Social Attitude
Plasticity (No Responsibility)	Good Judgement (Reasoning to truth)	Trust, Mutual Confidence
+ →		→ Respect for Diversity
Institution of Rational-Ethical Education	Benevolence (Charity, Forgiveness, Compassion)	Support for Equal Access

Figure 2.1 The Development of Social Psychology in the Context of Rational-Ethical Education
Combining the character formation hypothesis—that people are not responsible for their actions due to plasticity—with the institution of rational-ethical education, Owen infers broad emergence of reasoned judgment, altruism, and norms of trust and respect across human interactions. He also argues that people will develop a strong preference for equality including equal access to inputs and output.

irrationality. Empathy (instead of anger) arises. And empathy encourages the rational person to seek to undo the miseries that underly irrationality in order to bring about social weal. Owen is sure that rational-ethical education works in this way to dissolve hatred, revenge, insincerity, ambition, personal distinction, and envy (Owen 1813–1816, 53).

As people apperceive that no one is responsible for the development of their own personal character, they become more charitable toward others, more willing to forgive, more ready to exercise compassion. Kindness and benevolence predominate with a "pure charity and sincere affection for the whole family of mankind" (Owen 1836, 36). This charity "suffereth long and is kind, . . . envieth not, . . . vaunteth not itself, and is not puffed up" (Owen [1826] 1993, 74). Mutual confidence develops from sincere efforts to promote one another's interests (Owen [1834] 1993, 233–234).

Understanding the complexity of the character-shaping process, people develop a deepening respect for human diversity and uniqueness (Owen 1836, 31–33; see also 100–101). And people come to support the call for a "perfect equality of rights, privileges, and happiness, among all of the human race" (30–31). For a schematic overview see Figure 2.1.

INSTITUTIONS

Where classical political economy relies on narrow selfishness, Owen describes a much richer social psychology. This broader human social psychology is not well-served by competitive institutions. Indeed, the competitive system brings out the very worst in people. In contrast, Owen argues

that well designed cooperative institutions are fundamentally consistent with human nature and character formation. He is confident that such institutions, building on the base of rational-ethical education, generate whole human development—the cultivation "with equal care" of physical, intellectual, and moral character for every individual (Owen [1826] 1993, 76; [1842b] 1993 Pt 3, 135).

The organizing principle of Owen's system is cooperation, a cordial, other-centered working together. Cooperation starts from the following rule of conduct: "There is but one mode by which man can possess, in perpetuity, all the happiness which his nature is capable of enjoying—that is, by the union and the cooperation of ALL for the benefit of EACH" (Owen [1826] 1993, 63). Beyond serving as an organizing principle for institutions, cooperation also serves as inspirational ideation for individuals. The motivating factor for cooperative activity in Owen's work is central—genuine reflection about and activism toward the general welfare of others. Cooperation is Owen's fundamental premise for human flourishing.

Perhaps the most radical concrete institution of the evolved cooperative is that inputs are public property. There is no privately held capital or land. Private property, by its nature, is exclusive (Owen [1826] 1993, 63). Inequality of wealth is a deep source of social conflict. The excluded act out harmfully. They minimize their contributions to the common good and may even lash out.[20] Property held in common guarantees a sense of inclusion and encourages all to participate. And common capital is invested not with the aim of making profit, but with an overriding concern for enhancing the quality of work and life.

Owen devotes hundreds of pages to elaborating a range of concrete institutions rooted in the cooperative principle and common property. At base is a semi-autarchic cooperative village of 500–2000 people (Owen 1835, 210). The physical form of the village reflects the cooperative concern to achieve the happiness of all (Owen [1817] 1993, 177; [1832] 1993). The village takes the shape of a parallelogram. Housing along the sides provides people with private rooms, one for sleeping, another for sitting. Public buildings—community kitchen, community space, childcare, a library, etc—occupy the center (Owen [1826] 1993, 69). There are public gardens and pathways for leisurely strolls.[21]

---

20. This acting out by the excluded can even undermine the happiness of those initially included (Owen 1813–1816, 19).

21. Leopold provides a detailed elaboration of Owen's "grand design" for a cooperative village as depicted in an architectural blueprint from circa 1826. The design includes four large buildings for educational activities; multiple public rooms for various

In this environment Owen plans the cooperative around four departments. In addition to a department focusing on schooling and the formation of character, Owen envisions departments devoted to production, distribution, and government (Owen [1842a] 1993, 97). All community members come "to understand the principles and practices of the four departments" (97). Multi-tasking for full human development is the norm in these villages. Age rather than class is the basis for labor organization, with each age cohort assuming a major responsibility. Youth attend school for the formation of character and assist with domestic labor. Those in their early teens learn agricultural and industrial skills. Production, preservation, and distribution occupy the efforts of people until their early 30s. Governance and conduct of foreign affairs are a primary concern of those over 30 (Claeys 1993, liv). Thus, across the life span, each human being unites "a due proportion of agriculture, manufactures, commerce, education, and government" (Owen [1833] 1993, 231).

The Production Department starts from the contemplation of human need. Intrinsic usefulness determining value, the "most necessary wealth is air, water, food, clothes, shelter, instruction, amusement, the affections of our associates, and good society" (Owen [1842a] 1993, 90). The cooperative aims to discover and adopt "the best means by which a redundant supply . . . may be produced, and be accessible to all" (Owen [1826] 1993, 72).

Perhaps most central to Owen's design for the Production Department is his insistence that it exclude extreme divisions of labor and intense specialization. "In a rational state of society there will not be any mere physical, or mental, or moral, or practical beings, or mere imperfect parts of humanity; but all will be trained, from birth, to become at maturity full formed men and women" (Owen [1842b] 1993 Pt 3, 147). Owen's concerns about division of labor stem from his belief that health and happiness require the daily temperate exercise of body, intellect, and morals. That mix in work is central to whole human development.

In defense of his position on the division of labor, Owen makes a deep argument rooted in his own informal historical materialism. He does not reject Adam Smith out of hand, for when Smith wrote the *Wealth of Nations*, "men were struggling against a deficiency of the powers of production in

purposes such as concerts, artists' studios, and places of worship; dwelling houses, apartments, and dormitories for children; communal kitchens and bathhouses; and even an underground railway running below all four sides of the complex (Leopold 2019, 63–69). As Leopold points out, the "built environment of the new moral world reflects and reinforces certain threads in Owen's social theory," including education, science, and the family (69).

society to supply all their reasonable wants; and the principle of division of labour which he [Smith] ably advocated, was well calculated by its practice to lessen the difficulty." But the Industrial Revolution fundamentally changed the capacity to produce. Owen continues, "[Smith] could not then imagine that in less than half a century the improvements effected by the combined sciences of mechanism and chemistry should set aside the necessity for the division of human labour to create the requisite wealth for happiness" (Owen [1827] 1993, 108). These are not the observations of an ivory-towered academic or some wild-eyed utopian, but rather of a man intimately involved in the construction and application of machinery to the textile industry at the very height of the Industrial Revolution. Now "a minute division of human labour, for the creation of wealth, [is] as unnecessary as experience has proved it to be deteriorating to the physical and mental faculties of man, and therefore, always opposed to his happiness" (109).

In this same vein, Owen (1836) applies the principle of diminishing returns to all pleasure-generating stimuli, be these of the physical, intellectual, or moral faculties (67–69). An activity should be continued only to "the point of temperance" (68). The contrast with production under the competitive system is striking. According to Owen, the only "slaves" of the cooperative village are machines and chemistry (Owen [1826] 1993, 70–71; [1842b] 1993 Pt 3, 147). Rather than producers being the slaves of the machines, the intent is to introduce the most advanced new technologies with the purpose of elevating and enriching work processes.

The community Distribution Department includes an absolute minimum number of distributors. The work of the distributors is preservation, storage, and conveyance. Owen foresees minimal inter-village trade due to the self-sufficiency of each based on "their numbers and union" (Owen [1826] 1993, 72).

Within the village, the only relevant banks are "banks of real wealth"—warehouses engineered to store product in top condition. There is no medium of exchange and no pricing. People may take as they need from the banks of real wealth (Owen [1826] 1993, 72–73). Under these conditions there is no need for extrinsic compensation: no wages, profits, or interest. And there are no rewards based on performance or achievement. Any such rewards are inconsistent with Owen's theory of character formation and social cohesion. Recall that in his view, it is irrational to infer that individuals deserve reward or punishment, praise or blame, for individuals merely reflect socialization.

Every community member participates in the Government Department when they reach the appropriate age cohort (Owen [1832] 1993, 220).

Table 2.1. OWEN'S EVOLVED COOPERATIVE SYSTEM: INSTITUTIONS

Rational-Ethical Education
Production: Moderation/Self-Regulation
Participatory Governance
Common Ownership
Production: Labor-Complementing Technology
Distribution: Banks of Real Wealth

The age of participation is somewhere in the 30s or early 40s, presumably to guarantee maturity, experience, and competence (Owen [1826] 1993, 80).

The organization of the Government Department has deep implications for freedom. Village governance presumes "the natural right of all men to act conscientiously, according to their convictions, as long as their conduct shall be beneficial to the public and not injurious to others" (Owen [1833] 1993, 225). All have the "utmost individual freedom of action, compatible with the permanent good of society" (Owen [1842b] 1993 Pt 3, 182; [1833] 1993, 230).[22] Freedoms extend fully to religious and to intellectual liberty (see, for example Owen [1825a] 1993, 13). Always against the use of force, villager participation in village governance for those over 16 years of age is fully voluntary (Owen [1832] 1993, 220).

Table 2.1 summarizes the institutional structure of Owen's cooperative system. Keep in mind, the social psychological development sketched in Figure 2.1 is not restricted to rational-ethical education. It suffuses across and gains strength from all the institutions of the cooperative.

Owen's cooperation institutionalizes moderation in labor processes, including workday length and task variety across physical, intellectual, and moral spheres. Cooperation also reinforces self-moderation over personal desires. The evolved village normalizes participatory governance. Common ownership and publicly available inputs extend to capital, land, and raw materials. Labor-complementary technology enhances the experience of work, and its product is available in public warehouses, or "banks of real wealth." These warehouses hold sufficient stores for the taking among a civic-minded population with each moderating personal claims.

22. The obviously reasonable, yet also problematic, clause being that this freedom extends only to that which is compatible with the social good. More on the problems in this thinking concerning freedom in the following discussion section.

THE THEORETICAL CLAIMS FOR COOPERATION

Owen's system presumes the character formation hypothesis and application of rational-ethical education to stimulate socially healthy character development. In turn, the evolved village institutions provide a structure for working and living in a cooperative setting. These are the elements underlying the theoretical base. Building off this base, Owen puts forth a set of broad claims for the resulting cooperative society. He argues that the cooperative village generates superabundance and human development for all.[23] In the process it deepens social cohesion within the community. This section draws together that material and elaborates its logic.

Superabundance

The Industrial Revolution altered once and for all the productive possibilities of human labor. Owen argues that the new cooperative system generates superabundance.[24] Material wealth is no longer "an object of contest . . . any more than water or air is at present" (Owen [1826] 1993, 68). The sources of this cooperative superabundance are manifold. Though Owen's thought predates the formalization of the production function, he clearly understands that output is a function of the quantity and quality of labor and the quantity and technological sophistication of capital.[25] These categories provide a useful way to approach Owen's claims of superabundance.

Cooperative thinkers of the early 19th century tend to identify redundant capitalists, retailers, and other middlemen in the capitalist economy as unproductive (Owen [1842a] 1993, 102) as well as "bankers, professional

23. Beatrice Potter [Webb] emphasizes the centrality of human development in Owen's thought: "the one legitimate object of society is the improvement of the physical, moral, and intellectual character of man. The wealth of the nation was no longer the goal of political and economic action; it was simply a means to an end—the formation of a noble character in the citizen" (Potter [Webb] 1891, 20). See Chapter 11 for more on Webb's critically constructive commentary on cooperative thought.

24. As Claeys points out, Owen's emphasis on the superabundance made possible by the Industrial Revolution set his movement apart from "contemporary radicalism" which looked to political solutions such as Parliamentary reform and tax reduction (Claeys 1989, 147). Claeys (1989) goes on to extensively explore the political implications of Owen's anti-political stance.

25. A German contemporary of Owen, Johann Heinrich von Thünen, most often receives credit for the production function. Interestingly, in von Thünen's writing there is also a search for cooperative solutions to the misery associated with 19th-century competition (Dempsey [1850] 1960; Persky 2019).

characters, or idlers, . . . [who] endeavor to buy cheap and sell dear" (Owen 1844a2, Pt V2, 262). Owen highlights the tremendous unnecessary waste associated with unproductive labor. In contrast to individual competition, cooperative villages exhibit substantial levels of total product in part due to the high ratio of productive to unproductive workers. In addition, Owen advocates an end to the professions of law, religion, and medicine (Owen [1841] 1993, 347–351), and any military beyond defense ([1842a] 1993, 93–94). None of these professions return "good air and water, superior food, clothes, shelter, furniture, instruments, implements, complicated valuable machinery, instruction, amusement, the affections of our associates and good society" (93–94).[26] From a system point of view, the institutional elaboration of the four departments releases labor from these unnecessary and unproductive positions.

The cooperatives translate surpluses once directed to the profits of a mere 1/10th of the population into general consumer abundance. Because the cooperative institutions direct output to provisioning basic human needs across the population, workers achieve better housing and nutrition, more leisure time, and generally a higher standard of living. This high standard of living supports a healthy workforce, which then tends to experience higher productivity. The cooperative workplace emphasis on worker welfare further enhances productivity. Owen advocates treating "living machines" on par with the care given technology in the manufacturing system. Based on his New Lanark experience, Owen claims that organization along these lines easily increase returns by 50% (Owen 1813–1816, 9).

The cooperative intentionally structures its workplaces to intrinsically incentivize participation and effort. In the fully developed cooperative village "[work] will be a moderate exercise of an elevating and pleasurable character, in which all will ardently desire to have their full share, and be at all times ready to take more" (Owen [1842a] 1993 Pt 2, 99).[27]

Turn now to the contributions of capital. In his early career through New Lanark, Owen experiences firsthand the potential of modern industrial technology. He insists that the cooperative village is a groundswell

---

26. Like Owen, classical political economy divides labor into productive and unproductive. However, the classical definition of productive is based on whether a certain class of labor generates a vendable product. The classical writers define as necessary a subclass of unproductive labor including some of the professions listed above. In contrast, Owen's definition of productive relates to the satisfaction of human needs, including social needs. Owen treats activities that he judges unproductive as also unnecessary.

27. See also (Owen [1827] 1993, 108) for a similar claim. Owen's views about worker welfare are a harbinger of William Morris' contributions on pleasure in labor covered in Chapter 9.

for the "latest and best machinery." As a result, it produces "the greatest amount of the most valuable wealth, in the shortest time and best manner" (Owen [1842a] 1993 Pt 2, 99). Owen is a leading advocate for technological innovations across work and home life. Of course, all inventions must be "wisely directed" to maximize peace and wealth (251; 252).

Human Development

The superabundance of the cooperative economy is the material base for human development. Owen insists that the cooperative economy makes possible the impressive development of each of its members. An insistence on equality in an environment of superabundance guarantees this outcome. Thus, superabundance allows individuals to explore and develop deep inclinations for wellbeing, truth, and benevolence.

The Realization of Wellbeing

Superabundance in the cooperative setting supports the realization of wellbeing of all through equal access to the village's substantial stores of consumer goods. Because the system produces to satisfy human needs, quality products dominate. Superabundance also provides a base for much improved workplace organization, with task variety, labor complementing machinery, and intentional moderation in work time and intensity.[28] And cooperatives tend to dedicate a substantial portion of the surplus to public goods such as walkways and public gardens, enhancing the quality of life for all.

Intellectual Development

With superabundance the labor of all "will be converted into healthy, pleasant, and desirable occupation, while each individual will possess ample leisure for intellectual improvement and social enjoyment" (Owen [1826] 1993, 71). A modest workday frees time and energy for the pursuit of truth and to extend its margin. People have time to read and discuss. People have time to attend meetings and lectures. People have time to explore the world. People have time to think. Building on their rational-ethical

---

28. Notice that Owen here may be drawing on Charles Fourier. Anna Doyle Wheeler is an important conduit of cooperative ideas across the channel (see Chapter 3).

education, adults apply and continue to develop reasoning skills with an emphasis on discerning truth.

Realization of Fellow Feeling

There is an obvious intention in Robert Owen's educational program to underscore the rationality of benevolence and to extend its margin. Beyond formal education, as an individual moves through the departments of production, distribution, and governance, there is "gain of illimitable amount" in the development of "natural, physical, mental, moral and practical powers" (Owen [1842b] 1993 Pt 3, 255). Throughout the cooperative career, the individual's commitment to the community deepens and matures.

Underlying economic factors reinforce these benevolent inclinations. As discussed above, superabundance means that community members can obtain what they need from village warehouses and from public works. The obvious point is that it is relatively easy to share and to do right by others in a post-scarcity environment. But that superabundance also provides each with the security to develop community conscientiousness and internal discipline. The institutions of moderation in the workplace and self-regulation in production reinforce sensitivity to the gains from personal discipline. Owen predicts, for example, that "all will rejoice when they arrive at the age for distribution" (Owen [1842a] 1993, 106) because under thoughtful arrangement, it is simple, easy, pleasant work involving moderate, healthy exercise. Importantly from a character development perspective, the distribution phase of work returns pleasure from giving (106).

When shortages of desirable products arise, this provides opportunities to test personal discipline and further internalize limits. When "demand" exceeds "supply," cooperators re-evaluate their own claims on product and reduce the demand to correspond to supply.[29] For example, during the strawberry harvest, each villager moderates their personal strawberry claim, knowing that what each takes personally reduces that available for others. When scarcity does arise, cooperation internalizes that scarcity, providing opportunities to extend the margin of benevolence.

---

29. Beatrice Potter [Webb] also recognizes the importance of normalizing control of personal desires in Owen's system. She specifically identifies the diversion of desire "into channels of social welfare" (Potter [Webb] 1891, 24–25).

Social Cohesion

The members of the cooperative observe every day the superabundance and experience opportunities for human development created by themselves as a group. Given the cooperative institutions, the typical cooperator both creates and responds to the social cohesion in the community. Cooperators grow up with rational-ethical education, which helps shape their character. Cooperative mindsets tend not to fuel personal ambition, hatred, or revenge. At the individual level, this frees up energy for constructive engagement. In the workplace, there is less interpersonal conflict and a general appreciation that minor, pilfered gains amount only to a distraction. Finally, cooperation aligns with the basic inclinations: wellbeing, love of truth, and fellow feeling. Hence, there are intrinsic rewards of producing well for others. As we clarify in Chapter 3, these impressive outcomes naturally reinforce each cooperator's commitment to their fellows. Superabundance and opportunities for human development provide a base for social cohesion. Social cohesion contributes to superabundance and human development. Thompson and Wheeler's approach to cooperation expands and formalizes this theme.

High levels of social cohesion contribute to the falling away of major social ills—poverty, murder, theft, betrayal, and extreme inequality. Such outcomes are largely traceable to the malignant forces that erode human character. Widespread comprehension of those causes leads people away from blame and punishment and toward the building of institutions to reshape society in socially uplifting ways. In the absence of self-serving acts, there is less likelihood that any individual directly experiences socially induced harm. And empathetic individuals benefit because of little exposure to vice-induced misery for others.

The deeper argument addresses interdependence. A lack of control in shaping character means there must be system-wide improvement. Only such improvement can reduce the probability of negative effects reverberating across people from one department to another.

In sum, the education system rationally trains people toward cooperative mindsets. Institutions are consistent with and reinforce cooperative character. Congenial behavior follows. Owen envisions remarkable returns for individual and social welfare. Cooperation makes superabundance possible. Cooperation generates whole human development across physical, intellectual, and moral dimensions. Internal harmony results as people's behavior aligns with their original inclinations. Owen's cooperative economic system consistently enhances social cohesion.

COOPERATIVE VILLAGE INSTITUTIONS
FOR TRANSITION

Owen's social science provides confidence about the potential of the well-designed cooperative society. Still, the new society can only emerge after a period of transition. The central question is how quickly people raised in the old competitive system can adapt to the new social forms. The early experiments in New Lanark encouraged Owen. The changes in worker behavior there and the successes in the educational program made him optimistic. The time for a full transition seemed imminent. Owen began to advocate the immediate construction of transitional villages. Much of his writing attempts to draw the path from these transitional structures to a full cooperative system. Because competition nurtures selfishness, the transitional cooperative village begins with selective inclusion of those who more fully exhibit its social psychology.

Education in Transition

The transitional villages start training children at young ages in the cooperative social psychology. Not long after birth, children move into socialized dormitories (with regular parental visitation), run by those who exhibit cooperative social psychology. The organization of schools in transitional villages closely reflects plans for the fully matured cooperative. The basic principle is to sharpen abilities toward rationality by experientially reinforcing the truth that benevolent interactions maximize happiness. Before wisdom may dawn, the mind "must be discharged of all the inconsistent associations which have been formed within it; the foundation must be laid anew" (Owen [1817] 1993, 177).

Beyond its formal educational institutions, the transitional village emphasizes reforming character through reflective processing of human interactions. Owen started some of this in his directorship at New Lanark. In the workplace, mill workers referred unresolvable quarrels to management (e.g. Owen), who pointed out errors on both sides, advocated forgiveness and friendship, and promoted one principle to repeat and live by: "In future they should endeavour to use the same active exertions to make each other happy and comfortable, as they had hitherto done to make each other miserable" (Owen 1813–1816, 31). Owen reports that disputes slowly fizzled away.[30]

30. Unfortunately, in the post-New Lanark, transitional villages adult education did not work so smoothly. Lacking a clear benevolent authority, cooperators without this

Production in Transition

Production processes in transition center on the quality of the work process for workers, while maintaining productivity. The transition villages emphasize the introduction of labor complementing technology, either to improve the quality of the work experience or reduce the quantity of human labor necessary in production. There is a movement toward collective provisioning, including in the domestic economy. While productivity advances can be substantial, there can be noteworthy tendencies toward slacking depending on the shallowness of the cooperative mindset in the village. Although Owen advocates the socialization of most work traditionally completed in the household, he curiously maintains a gender-based division of labor, with women attending to most of the domestic economy tasks.[31]

Class Structure and Distribution in Transition

In the transition stage, the village maintains a class system based on capital infusion. Both those who bring capital and those who do not may join a village (Owen [1825c] 1993, 30). The advanced capital pays for rent, interest, taxes, the purchase of raw materials and physical capital, and other expenses. Voluntary provisioners of capital receive financial returns, with 5% the norm.[32] Capital provisioners have no work requirement in transition and have the option to serve on governing committees.

Those who work receive housing, food, clothing, and health care of "the best . . . that the circumstances of the establishment will afford" (Owen [1825c] 1993, 30). And the system institutionalizes social services and amenities so that all villagers have a secure standard of living to satisfy a wide variety of human needs.

Throughout Owen's career, he advocated and practiced full accounting transparency (Owen [1825c] 1993, 32). Beyond the returns to capital and the workforce, village surpluses initially apply to liquidate debt from

cooperative education often failed to appreciate the needs and rewards of altruism. And they lacked a cooperative spirit in reaching democratic decisions through consensus (See Dos Passos & Shay (1940) for brief accounts of New Harmony's demise).

31. For a gendered analysis of the American Owenite Communities from 1824–1828, see Kolmerten (1981). For deeper insights into linkages between cooperation and gender equality, see Chapter 3 of this volume.

32. In contrast, Owen treats the New Harmony funding he provides for physical capital as public property (Owen [1825b] 1993, 28).

establishing the village. After paying off all debt, Owen suggests two options. First, surpluses may fund additional villages depending upon the level of population growth (34). Second, Owen suggests a form of profit sharing across villagers, based upon some combination of productive contribution and consumer expenditure (30–31).[33]

Distribution in transitional stages involves labor as the foundation for exchange value.[34] Where trade is necessary, quantity of labor is the recommended unit to express intrinsic value, to be agreed upon and fixed (Owen [1826] 1993, 72) at "a fair exchange among yourselves, of value for value, or the amount of labour in one article, against the same amount in another" (Owen [1827] 1993, 110).[35] The labor note is an "intermediate and temporary arrangement only" for transition, based on equal exchanges of labor (Owen [1833] 1993, 228).[36]

Freedom and Governance in Transition

Major political revolutions during Owen's lifetime centered on freedom, and while Owen reflects the thought of his day in advocating freedom, in practice he is a conflicted advocate. In his writing and his practical experience running New Lanark, Owen exhibits a penchant toward benevolent authority. At least in part, this is likely in response to concerns about whether people, raised in a competitive context, are unready for cooperation ([1842b] 1993, 183–184). Owen's dominant paternalistic impulse appears in *The New Moral World* as well, where he explicitly links directing rights to ethical insight (92–93).[37]

Owen does support full freedom regarding village entry and exit. Cooperators have freedom to exit their villages, with the expectation that

33. The idea of profit sharing appeared at least four years earlier, in 1821, in the cooperative periodical, *The Economist*. Chapter 8 in this volume provides fuller treatment of profit sharing as a transition strategy.

34. Extending to the middle of the 19th century, Owen continually rejected gold, silver, paper money, and credit as media of exchange (Owen [1842a] 1993 Pt 2, 104).

35. The major qualifications being that "as one person will take more time than another to perfect the same kind of article, the time required by a workman possessing an average degree of skill and industry, should be the principle by which the calculation should be made" (Owen [1827] 1993, 111).

36. As noted in the biography above, Owen made a major effort to establish a labor exchange outside of the transitional villages between 1832 and 1834.

37. Leopold (2015) distinguishes between Owen's views on governance in transition versus fully transitioned cooperatives (in which all beginning at birth receive rational training). Leopold argues that non-democratic, paternalistic authority-based governance only appears in Owen's consideration of transitional communities.

the community cordially support those who decide to leave. For example, the exit plan in New Harmony required only one week's notice to quit a village. The person leaving takes the value brought in as well as any outstanding credit in the village books from the prior year (Owen [1825c] 1993).

Owen's penchant for authority does ultimately diffuse in favor of somewhat broader participation in decision making as he anticipates members of the community maturing over time. Owen brainstorms different appointment processes to the transitional village governing committee, with all these schemes at least initially limiting appointing powers and appointments to a subgroup within the village. When Owen is not the primary financier, he initially rests majority decision-making authority with the capital provisioners until full repayment of capital and sufficient character formation among villagers (Owen [1825c] 1993). In this plan, there is an election of eight of twelve overseeing committee members from those who advance capital of at least £100, the other four elected from the general community (32–33). Elsewhere, before education processes inculcate the desired value set and reasoning skills, Owen gives directing power to the middle class, with the lower class (presumably enthusiastically) following directions (Owen [1844b] 1993 Pt 7, 395).

However formed, Owen's plans vest the governing committee with substantial responsibilities. One key responsibility is a committee charge to assign and regulate employment across villagers, giving "every regard to the inclinations of each, consistent with the general good" ([1825c] 1993, 33). So it seems that Robert Owen's transitional village emphasizes a less than fully democratic coordinating committee of decision-makers.[38]

The Historic Villages

As discussed in the biography section, Owen participated closely in two transitional villages, New Harmony in Indiana and Queenwood in Hampshire. Both were major failures, declaring bankruptcy after only a few years. In both cases, Owen could not fit the pieces together. It is difficult to determine the extent to which these disappointments are the result

---

38. In his analysis of Owen's views on governance, Leopold conveys: "Owen maintains that governing a transitional settlement is *'the most difficult task* that man will ever have to perform.' It is analogous to superintending 'a great lunatic asylum,' except that in the communitarian case . . . the 'patients' (i.e. the members of the settlements) are 'armed'—they have the 'power of life and death' in a thousand different ways—and the 'physicians' (i.e. the communal governors) have no weapon aside from reason, truth, and kindness" (Leopold 2015, 198, quoting Owen from *The New Moral World*).

of Owen's theories. The next section considers elements of this question. Alternatively, a lack of the type of thoughtful attention and judgment characteristic in Owen's management of the New Lanark venture may be the cause of the two later community failures.

DISCUSSION

The intention of this chapter is to present the logic—even if incomplete—and the seriousness of Owen's efforts to build a social science.[39] His first application of this social science is to demonstrate the attractiveness and feasibility of a broad system of cooperative villages. Chapter 11 considers leading 19th-century critiques of Owen and the other cooperative theorists. Here we raise four concerns that strike us as particularly central for the unfolding of the book.

1. Even if Owen's logic is plausible, the structure ultimately rests on a key assumption. Owen considers human nature as building on a set of original inclinations including fellow feeling. Owen explicitly proposes that antipathy is not an original faculty. Rather, it is a conditioned response arising in societies which falsely attribute personal responsibility to individual behavior. The issue is whether he misses deep sources of antipathy in human nature. Such a possibility appears in many 19th- and 20th-century philosophers, such as Schopenhauer, Nietzsche, and Freud. Owen gives no suggestion as to how to test his position. In tracing the development of cooperative thought, we want to be particularly attentive to the treatment of this fundamental question.

2. Trends driving major political revolutions in the late 18th century raised the centrality of individual freedom, and Owen certainly provides lip service toward this ideal. But there are major contradictions, especially when he discusses transition. Owen qualifies that cooperators' freedom is only "as long as their conduct shall be beneficial to the public and not injurious to others" (Owen [1833] 1993, 225). Elsewhere, Owen raises an important qualification to freedom: until education trains all toward rational character, "man cannot be permitted to have full freedom of action, without creating constant collisions and injurious contests" (Owen 1842b

---

39. Not all agree. Critics often claim that Owen makes assertions rather than builds arguments. Even a strong supporter, writing to *The Economist* under the pseudonym Philadelphus, echoes this position, but does not worry. Likening Owen to Christ, Philadelphus suggests the role of Owenite disciples is precisely to build the analytical system justifying his assertions (Owen Vol. II, 40).

Pt 3, 183–184). In practice these problematic clauses imply the villages only extend freedom to those whose actions are compatible with the social good. A relevant concern is the validity of perceptions about what is in the social interest and who in the community has the power to determine social interest. Owen does provide a consistent response: have patience until people are fully trained to be rational and ethical (183). But this position gives little guidance in practice. Owen's ideas about freedom contradictorily coexist with Owen's penchant for paternalistic benevolent authority.

Similarly, Owen consistently delegates decision-making to a small group of patrons with alleged deep rational-ethical insight. While he does promise broader participation in the future, he shows little concern for the possibility that genuine human development may require villagers and workers to be sovereign. William Thompson, a major philosopher of cooperation and supporter of Owenite communities, takes serious issue with Owen's approach. In Thompson's view, patronage from a large group of idlers is no other than patronage from

> the Leagued Oppressors of their Fellow-creatures: leagued by a community of supposed, though really false interests . . . . Truth cannot be served, but may be fearfully injured by patronage. Their patronage converts knowledge, which demands of them nothing but free discussion, into an instrument of mischief, the ally and support of their selfish short-sighted interests. (Thompson 1827, 98)

Instead, Thompson argues for a more democratic transitional structure (see the next chapter).

3. Owen is clear as early as 1813–1816 about the detrimental social outcomes resulting from exclusionary processes. But like later cooperators, Owen does sometimes advocate selective entry into the villages. Related to the issue of exclusion, in the case of New Harmony, Owen explicitly and problematically excludes "persons of color" from start-up villages, suggesting migration to other continents, such as Africa, for those with cooperative inclinations (Owen [1825d] 1993, 42).[40] These segregationist policies are in gross contradiction with Owen's professed doctrine of equal access and inclusion. Racism among cooperative theorists reappears

---

40. Owen does leave open that "persons of color" might serve the New Harmony cooperative as "helpers" (Owen [1825d] 1993, 42). Owen also demonstrates his insensitivity to the exploitation of African slaves on a visit to Jamaica. He reflects the common radical Tory trope, "The West Indian 'slave,' as he is called, is greatly more comfortable and happy than the British or Irish operative manufacturer or day-laborer" (*British Co-Operator*, 1830, 93 quoted in G. D. H. Cole [1925] 2019, 249).

throughout the 19th century as does antisemitism and sexism. Some cooperative thinkers are at the forefront of the anti-slavery movement as well as the movement for full gender equality. But some are not. As much as we consider a broader equality necessary for the success of cooperative economics, the 19th-century cooperative theorists do not reach such a consensus.

4. Another set of transition questions concerns motivation and incentives. In the mature cooperative society, reasoned insight about the benefits of altruism is the major community incentive. But does a transitioning cooperative system require additional incentives? One of the commonly perceived causes of the New Harmony failure is that many participants, however attracted by the ideals of cooperation, proved unwilling to do the hard manual labor in building a new community. Perhaps, in this sense, the selection of community members is not exclusive enough. Individual competition relies heavily on incentive strategies powered by greed (the "carrot") or aversion (the "stick"). The common good, much touted by Owen, may not provide sufficient motivation for the first or second generations of cooperative workers. Each cooperative theorist must come to grips with this fundamental question.

These are obviously major issues. As a practical instigator of transition, Owen may well have feet of clay. But our observations here do not undermine Owen's deep contribution to both social science and cooperative theory. Later British cooperative theorists address some of these problems. For example, William Thompson develops Owen's analysis of the semi-autarchic cooperative community in a more formal manner. Thompson and Anna Doyle Wheeler also expand the theory regarding gender equality. We turn to their contributions in the next chapter. More generally, the remainder of this book is an analysis of the elaborations and responses to Owen's foundations for a social science and his claims for cooperation.

CHAPTER 3

⌒

To Owen's Left

William Thompson and Anna Doyle Wheeler

BENTHAMITE ROOTS, OWENITE PLANS

Owen's vision of the possibilities created by the Industrial Revolution widely appealed to people of goodwill from a range of social backgrounds and political perspectives. Of all of these, the most serious were William Thompson and Anna Doyle Wheeler. Thompson was an Anglo-Irish landowner from a prosperous merchant family in Cork. In 1821, he enmeshed himself in the intellectual milieu of utilitarians and cooperators—most notably Jeremy Bentham and Robert Owen. Anna Doyle Wheeler, also from Ireland, was fresh from exploring cooperative thought in France. She landed in London in the early 1820s and made contact with Bentham and Owen. Together Thompson and Wheeler provided an expanded and more rigorous foundation for Owen's new social science.

Thompson set to work on his magnum opus, *An Inquiry into the Principles of the Distribution of Wealth* ([1824] 1963), which is an ambitious Benthamite work in political economy.[1] Thompson's approach is radical.[2]

---

1. Thompson was a deep thinker often putting forth complex arguments. Throughout this chapter, we use (sometimes lengthy) footnotes. The intention is to keep the main argument flowing while doing justice to Thompson's more involved insights.
2. Utilitarians use the term "philosophical radicals" to indicate their emphasis on going to root causes. While Thompson, like Wheeler, clearly accepts that concern, their writings embody a much more extensive radicalism including an insistence on voluntarism, self-governance, and complete gender equality.

Building a Social Science. Kirsten Madden and Joseph Persky, Oxford University Press. © Oxford University Press 2024.
DOI: 10.1093/oso/9780197693735.003.0003

Much more explicitly than Owen, Thompson wishes to demonstrate that Bentham underestimates the ability of common people to construct a good society. The point is to organize the economy so as to make the happiness of the greatest number as great as possible.[3] Thompson formulates his problem in terms of three alternative economic systems or what Marx will call "modes of production." Specifically, he considers the coercive system, the competitive system, and the cooperative system. Which of the three systems achieves the greatest happiness of the greatest number?

According to Thompson, the competitive system generates security which strengthens the incentives for accumulation.[4] He also argues that the competitive system results in a much higher level of equality than earlier coercive systems of "force and fraud."[5] But the guarantee of perfect security in the system of competition substantially constrains that level of equality.[6] Competition gives up much happiness to guarantee freedom of voluntary individual exchange.[7]

3. Thompson mentions Helvetius, Priestly, and Paley as advocating much the same objective (Thompson [1824] 1963, 1). Thompson explicitly identifies the greatest number with the poorest 90%.

4. Thompson spends chapter after chapter elaborating the advantages of competition over compulsion. As suggested by Claeys, Thompson was very much one of those Enlightenment "radicals who were brought up to understand the system of free competition as a more just, fair, and meritocratic alternative to aristocratic monopoly and parliamentary corruption" (Claeys 1987, 109). In this vein Claeys, like Foxwell, singles out William Godwin as the source of much of Thompson's enthusiasm for voluntary exchanges (Claeys 1987, 94; see also Foxwell 1899, xxxix). Kaswan questions Claeys' emphasis on Thompson's affinity to competition (1996, 247). This seems reasonable since his later works fully advance the cooperative agenda.

5. Thompson is one of the first in England to call the budding industrial system the "competitive system," drawing on Sismondi and Saint Simon (Pankhurst [1954] 1991, 38).

6. In a discussion deep in the tangle of his argument, Thompson considers the share of product that falls to capitalists in the system of competition. Thompson's capitalists are not so much leaders of industry as rentiers who receive payment from individual laborers for the use of their accumulated capital. He writes of a fundamental wedge between the price the worker considers appropriate for the use of the capital and the price the capitalist considers appropriate. The first is based on replacing the depreciation of the capital and a small supplement that is sufficient to allow the capitalist to live in the style of a skilled worker. The second demands the entire surplus value (Thompson is the first to use the term), i.e. the difference between the actual product and what the worker could produce without capital. Both these figures represent serious thought about the capital market and demonstrate Thompson's ability to handle the mechanics of classical political economy. Thompson concludes that in the real world the actual payment for capital will be somewhere between these two extremes. While he does not make a formal argument here, he recognizes that the payment to the capitalist will be considerably greater than cost and will create a fund for accumulation. At the same time, these market prices for capital will inevitably generate a substantial level of overall inequality ([1824] 1963, 167).

7. Bentham offers four "subordinate ends": security, equality, subsistence, and abundance. Kaswan (2014, 107) argues that Thompson's and Bentham's understandings of

Thompson's acknowledgment that competition is necessarily characterized by much inequality sets the stage for a fundamental expansion of his argument. There is now a third mode of human labor—mutual cooperation, that is, "the voluntary yielding the products of individual labor to a common fund, on condition of enjoying equally the products of all other associated labor" ([1824] 1963, 391–392). Thompson's version of mutual cooperation promises virtually complete equality and maintains the condition of perfect security. Just as individual competition produces substantially more happiness than compulsion, Thompson concludes that mutual cooperation produces substantially more happiness than competition (xviii).

Thompson's argument for the superiority of cooperation gains a second dimension from his work with Anna Doyle Wheeler. In 1825 Thompson and Wheeler published *Appeal of One Half the Human Race*.[8] Wheeler fundamentally expands the argument: cooperation is necessary for gender equality and gender equality is necessary for high levels of human welfare.

Bringing their thoughts together, Thompson and Wheeler elaborate a rich cooperative social psychology with Benthamite roots, construct relevant institutions, and justify cooperation in terms of superabundance and happiness. This chapter restates and in places reconstructs their social science, deriving what we call the "Thompson-Wheeler" theorem. The theorem captures the underlying, self-reinforcing mechanism of successful cooperation. Before turning to questions of social psychology and institutional structure of this cooperative economy, a few words about Thompson and Wheeler.

---

happiness while overlapping, differ substantially. Thompson is sure that in Owenite cooperation he finds a resolution of a conflict Bentham thinks unavoidable—the conflict between equality and security. Later in the chapter, we return to this question in detail.

8. The full title is *Appeal of One Half the Human Race, Women, Against the Pretensions of the Other Half, Men, to Retain them in Political, and Hence in Civil and Domestic, Slavery* (1825). Although formal authorship in 1825 only recognizes Thompson, Thompson and Wheeler are coauthors, writing this piece as a critical response to James Mill's thesis that men can effectively serve as women's political voice in his *Britannica* article "On Government." The introduction to *Appeal* acknowledges Wheeler as the central thinker behind this work with Thompson primarily serving as Wheeler's "interpreter and the scribe of your sentiments" (1825, iv). Dooley (1995, 31) and Cory (2004, 114–118) report linguistic analysis of the text to identify specific sections that reflect Thompson's writing style versus Wheeler's writing style. They argue that the final section entitled "Concluding Address" reflects Wheeler's writing style. Dooley (1997) argues that the utilitarians (among others) assist in burying *Appeal* because of its direct challenge to James Mill's hypothesis (1997, 19).

THOMPSON AND WHEELER: LIFE STORIES

Unlike Robert Owen, William Thompson (1775–1833) was not a self-made man of the Industrial Revolution. His family was not from the marginal middle class. His father, John Thompson, served as Mayor and High Sheriff.[9] When John died in 1814, he left William with a large, landed estate and considerable merchant capital. It remains mysterious why William derived a strong commitment to progressive ideas. His grandfather was a "Protestant divine." It is possible that despite Thompson's agnosticism he drew on a family background of religiosity for his broader social activism. In any case, once in possession of the family property, he introduced a range of agricultural innovations as well as a broad reform of his tenant farms, dividing the land into relatively large, viable allotments devoted to new methods (Pankhurst [1954] 1991, 2–4).

Even then, Thompson did not take an active role in political matters until 1818, when he became involved in a dispute over the curriculum of the Cork Institution of which he was a proprietor. He asserted misuse of the public funds available to the Institution and advocated a liberal secondary education for the middle class, both young men and women (Pankhurst [1954] 1991, 8).

Thompson's interest in educational reform brought him into contact with Jeremy Bentham and, through Bentham, with James Mill. At the same time, he came under the influence of Robert Owen. In 1824 he published *Inquiry*. It is this theory of cooperation that he famously debated with the young John Stuart Mill in 1825 (Cinelli & Arthmar 2018). Mill, at this early stage of his development, took a position strongly opposed to cooperatives.

Esther Lowenthal, in her canonical survey of early British Socialists, concludes that Thompson ultimately bases his argument on "the old Utopian faith in human perfectionism . . . .The economic analysis is incidental and almost overlaid" (Lowenthal [1911] 1972, 30). Perhaps, given his pedantic style, Thompson's work does give the impression of being "overlaid." But Lowenthal misses the scope and significance of his contribution.[10] Thompson in the *Inquiry* and two later works, *Labour Rewarded* (1827) and *Practical Directions* (1830) puts forward a serious defense of the social science of cooperation along with an empirical and institutional strategy for its implementation.[11] Rather than an "old Utopian faith, in

---

9. Dooley (1996, Chs. 1 and 2) provides extensive biographical information on both Thompson and Wheeler.

10. A similar criticism of Lowenthal is made by Dooley (1996, 405n).

11. Thompson is the first to use the term "social science" in its British 19th-century meaning.

human perfectionism," Thompson operationalizes Owen's social psychology using utilitarian philosophy, while challenging Owen's failure to insist on genuine participatory equality.[12] He develops serious arguments about the productivity of cooperative production. More generally, Thompson argues for the ability of cooperation to maximize happiness, broadly defined.[13]

While he was in London, Thompson expanded his circle of intellectual friends. Most importantly he met Anna Doyle Wheeler (1785–1848).[14] Although they were both from prosperous Protestant Irish backgrounds, Wheeler brought a far broader experience to their joint effort, *Appeal*. Wheeler's father was a prominent clergyman. She married Francis Massey Wheeler when she was only 15. Of her six pregnancies, only two daughters survived. In response to "on-going marital abuse and neglect," by age 27 she took her daughters and left her husband (Dooley 1995, 20). In 1816, she lived in Caen, France where she interacted with Saint Simonians. It is during her four-year stay in France that she became the "Goddess of Reason," considered by some "'the most gifted woman of the age'" (21). In the 1820s, she resided in London, in Dublin, and also spent more time in France. In the early 1820s, while in London, she developed a collegial acquaintance with the utilitarian philosopher Jeremy Bentham, became a "close ally and co-worker" with Robert Owen, befriended cooperator, feminist, and abolitionist Frances (Fanny) Wright, and most importantly, began an intellectual collaboration and close friendship with William Thompson. While in Paris from 1823–1825, she met the French philosopher Charles Fourier, who became "'a regular visitor to her salon'" (Dooley 1995, 22–23).[15] Wheeler made more accessible Fourier's ideas through written and verbal correspondence, and she facilitated the flow of cooperative ideas as a translator.[16] In 1825 Thompson and Wheeler produced the *Appeal*.

---

12. Although both men held each other in high esteem, the disagreements between Owen and Thompson are deep: there are differences about philanthropy in cooperative start-ups (Dooley 1996, 24; 48), differences over appropriate community governance (1996, 50), and differences over the role of charisma as potentially undermining reason (1996, 25).

13. Claeys argues that Thompson's concerns are more questions of morality than economics and that any economic benefits of cooperation are largely secondary (1987, 97). Our treatment considers both morality and economic benefits as central and mutually reinforcing.

14. The *Oxford Dictionary of National Biography* is the only source to identify a specific death date for Wheeler, giving May 7, 1848.

15. The *Appeal* credits Fourier with a concern that cooperation achieves for women as well as for men "equal means of happiness from all sources" (Dooley 1995, 205).

16. Fourier himself was aware of Thompson. In a letter dated 1825, he wrote: "I know that a person of the name of Thompson, who is studying Association, and to whom my book has been communicated, has translated some parts of it into English, and has

For the rest of his life, Thompson contributed steadily to the cooperative movement writing two other major works, *Labor Rewarded. The Claims of Labour and Capital Conciliated: or How to Secure to Labor the Whole Products of Its Exertions* (1827) and *Practical Directions for the Speedy and Economical Establishment of Communities on the Principles of Mutual Co-operation, United Possessions and Equality of Exertions and the Means of Enjoyments* (1830). Thompson actively contributed to cooperative magazines and newspapers. He played a critical role in two early cooperative congresses as well. At those meetings the tension between him and Owen became manifest. Owen, smarting from the failure at New Harmony, insisted on the need for centralized, paternalistic control of any new cooperative communities, while Thompson advocated for broad principles of self-governance. Thompson carried the day against Owen, but he died before any application of his plans could materialize (Pankhurst [1954] 1991, 109–128).

Wheeler's later life was less straightforward. Likely a result of marital abuse, other major losses, and health problems, Wheeler fluctuated between periods of seclusion and activism after 1825. During her active periods, she held salons, a norm for intellectual social women of this era. More unusual is that there is at least one record of Wheeler giving a public lecture on cooperation and gender equality. Wheeler wrote three other known publications on gender equality and cooperation. These are all in the form of letters. Two of the letters (1830, 1833) were published in cooperative magazines. The letter of (1834) is one she wrote to Lord Hampden as a eulogy after William Thompson's death. This eulogy also covers some main ideas of their thought on gender and cooperation. Common for women during this timeframe, Wheeler adopted a pseudonym (Vlasta) in her letters of 1833 and 1834.[17]

SOCIAL PSYCHOLOGY

Thompson was a Benthamite. At root, people desire happiness (Thompson 1827, 100).[18] Every human being is equally capable of experiencing

---

conferred with competent persons on the subject . . ." (Pellarin 1848, 150). Most likely, it "had been communicated" by Wheeler.

17. Vlasta is the name of a legendary woman leading an army of women for seven years to free women of subordination to men (Dooley 1996, 79; story taken from (Wheeler 1834, 326)).

18. Similarly, Thompson and Wheeler state, "The original principle of human nature . . . is simply the desire of happiness and aversion to misery, without any wish, kindly or malignant to others. As men acquire knowledge . . . they pursue to a greater

happiness (Thompson [1824] 1963, 4). Thompson agrees with economists that this pursuit of happiness is a reflection of self-interest. But people do not have to degenerate into mere selfishness. The outcome depends on the social psychological capacities of human beings interacting with institutions. One of Thompson's most original contributions to Owen's new social science centers on his development of a theory of self-interest. Key to that theory is the distinction between self-interest and selfishness (446). Classical political economists translate self-interest into selfish motives toward arbitrary goals within the competitive system. The economists pitch these motives as "the only ones by which energetic and permanent exertion can be produced" (442). They do not appreciate the broader range of possible human responses to different institutional environments.

When coupled with destructive education and/or extreme scarcity, self-interest degenerates into selfish behavior. Selfishness seeks happiness "by direct, short-sighted means, ignorantly disregarding the surrounding interests of other sentient beings," a particularly likely response in an unsupportive environment ([1824] 1963, 446). And the selfish tend to pursue false pleasures from power and distinction, from superiority, domination, and antipathy (461).

In seeking such false pleasures, selfish people create "factitious" or artificial rewards and punishments to induce others to ignore their deeper interests. Over and above natural painful consequences of an antisocial act, factitious punishments rely on compulsion and restraint as well as any "arbitrary addition to the natural evils, mental or physical" ([1824] 1963, 452). Problematically, factitious punishments and rewards "divert the mind of the agent from the contemplation of the natural consequences of . . . actions, the real tests of their value, to the contemplation of arbitrary lots of pleasure and pain" (449–450).

Factitious rewards and punishments are common in gender relations. Wheeler is particularly sensitive to the power relations within marriage. Husbands seeking false pleasures use arbitrary and capricious incentives. Women too often internalize the message of this oppression. They far too often support the worldview and actions of their oppressors. More generally, the mechanics of oppression appear in all extant economic systems.[19]

---

or less extent their own individual happiness in connexion with, or to the exclusion of, that of others" (Thompson & Wheeler 1825, 13).

19. Thompson finds this true even for superficially cooperative societies. Previous "schemes of equality," such as the Shakers in North America rest on "compulsion, or delusion, religious or otherwise" ([1824] 1963, 443).

Self-interest does not have to degenerate in this manner. When coupled with a supportive environment, an enlarged self-interest can emerge in which individuals see their happiness tied to the broader happiness of the community. Selfishness is only one possible realization of self-interest. Thompson points to a human capability of conducting "an enlarged calculation, estimating the interests of all human beings within the sphere of its influence" ([1824] 1963, 446).[20] Happiness still drives behavior, but people recognize interdependence. Actions can lead to complicated reactions. An enlarged calculation takes into account "the good and evil, immediate and remote, physical, social and intellectual." From repeat life experiences in a cooperative environment, the recognition dawns that the greatest happiness for oneself results from "principles of benevolence or enlightened self-interest" (1827, 19).[21] For radical cooperators, benevolence is central to rationality (Dooley 1996, 137).

Reasoning in large part includes the skill of tracing natural consequences. When natural punishments and rewards are apparent, they serve as valid indicators for action and motivate virtue (Thompson [1824] 1963, 255). Thompson clarifies that where there are mixed consequences to both the agent and others, wisdom is necessary to determine optimal choice (456).[22]

PRINCIPLED AND CONCRETE INSTITUTIONS

For Thompson and Wheeler, achieving happiness is irreducible to a simple mental activity. Thompson teases William Godwin for proclaiming "man as capable of attaining happiness by his mental powers alone, almost independent of material subordinate agency." Such flights of fancy come easily to Godwin with all "his animal wants comfortably supplied" ([1824] 1963,

20. Notice the idea was clearly in the air at the time. In 1821, correspondent "The Dog Under the Table" wrote on the concept of enlarged self-interest as fundamental to cooperation: "As, by the law of nature, each individual's interest is essentially and constantly that of his neighbor, it follows, that being himself but one interest compared with many others, he must always (when he clearly perceives his own advantage) be much more occupied in promoting those of others, which are numerous, while his is but one" (see Mudie Vol. I, 249). Thompson's treatment develops these ideas in far more detail.

21. This enlightened self-interest arises when there is no coercion. It assumes that most others are rational and do this enlarged calculation as well. Thompson does accommodate irrationality by suggesting that the rational person accounts for any irrationality in the calculus and acts "to guard calmly against evil" (1827, 19).

22. Thompson also notes that natural returns are to be "obeyed in proportion to the magnitude of the pains or pleasures attached to them" ([1824] 1963, 456). Basically, he is willing to accept small imperfections in his rational calculus.

2). For the rest of us, material conditions matter. In practice, real-world outcomes depend on the interaction of human social psychology and institutional structures.

What structures do Thompson and Wheeler put forth to shape and reinforce an enlarged self-interest, bringing greater happiness to the community? These institutions are of two general types, principled and concrete. Concrete institutions are specific procedures, conventions, and arrangements and are often required by principled institutions.[23] Principled institutions are broad social guidelines establishing presumptive expectations within a community. Central to Thompson and Wheeler's radical thought about any truly effective economic system are Bentham's principles of equality and security. Thompson and Wheeler assert that equality and security, although incompatible in the competitive system, are fully compatible in the cooperative system.[24] Indeed this is the deep puzzle that cooperation solves.

Thompson and Wheeler make the principled institution of equality fundamental to cooperation. Equality applies to all community members, women as well as men. In Thompson's blueprint of a cooperative community, the principled institution of equality carried to its logical limits requires the concrete institutions of "equal voluntary effort, equal proprietorship, and equal means of enjoyment to all" (1830, 23). In addition, the cooperative system makes concrete equal access to education and capital and equal freedoms (1827, 53; see also Wheeler 1834, 322; and Wheeler 1830, 35–36).[25]

In practice, these radical ideas on equality reinforce the social psychology of enlarged self-interest. Experiencing the reality of equality, cooperators come to recognize and accept the logic that each count as one and only one among equals. And thus, the cooperative may sacrifice no individual, no minority—or effective majority—to maximize the happiness of others.

---

23. We take the concepts of procedures, conventions, and arrangements from Hamilton's definition of "institution" (1932, 84). The distinction between principled and concrete institutions is our own.

24. Bentham holds that for achieving the greatest happiness equality must defer to security when they are in conflict. Thompson also sees these two as lexicographic. However, he and Wheeler design institutions of cooperation to maximize both simultaneously.

25. Assuming equality of exertion holds, Thompson qualifies the distribution of output based on whether the output is a basic necessity or a comfort/convenience. Thompson advocates proportioning the distribution of necessities to physical need (for example, a pregnant woman might receive more potatoes and milk), whereas the distribution of comforts requires rigidly equal distribution across cooperators, particularly when in limited supply (1830, 5).

Most importantly, interacting with the centrality of equality is a principle of benevolence, which redefines each cooperator's self-interest and brings social cohesion.

Thompson formalizes his version of Bentham's security as three "natural laws of distribution:"[26]

> i. All labor is free and voluntary, where freedom in this context requires no external compulsion and voluntariness requires full labor consent;[27]
> ii. Laborers collectively claim all product;[28]
> iii. All exchange is free and voluntary (Thompson [1824] 1963, 6; 382).[29]

26. Thompson absorbs this term in reading James Mill's *Elements of Political Economy*. Thompson critiques Mill for declaring the centrality of "natural laws of distribution" without explaining it and then using the term to justify inequality. Thompson turns what he sees as an ambiguity in Mill's analysis to his advantage—Thompson defines the natural laws and uses them to justify equality and security as fundamental institutions of the cooperative economic system ([1824] 1963, xi).

27. Thompson distinguishes between genuine and artificial voluntarism. He qualifies that "want," common in all other economic systems, serves as a form of "indirect compulsion . . . extorting a species of voluntary acquiescence" ([1824] 1963, 165). Also relevant to voluntariness, Thompson is aware that people may be ignorant of their true interest, but "Delusion is still voluntariness, and knowledge is its appropriate cure" (174). The community must continually promote self-education.

28. The actual wording of the second law is: "All the products of labor ought to be secured to the producers of them." In this context, security requires non-coercion. Security requires the protection of laborers from forcible and fraudulent attempts to appropriate the product (Thompson [1824] 1963, 176). The wording of Thompson's second law reflects the individualism of major thinkers such as John Locke, Thomas Paine, and Jeremy Bentham. But such an individualist interpretation is not what Thompson means. He (1827) explains that the second law does not translate as individual claim to individually produced product, because, even in competition, product is the result of many hands. As Thompson works through the implications, he comes to understand that it is "impractible to award to the individual, separately, the products of his labor" (Thompson 1827, 37; see also 99, 115). When product is the joint production of multiple laborers, it is infeasible to award precise individual product to each laborer given the difficulty in determining individual contributions. But it is certainly possible to lay a claim of "joint possession" to the entire product among a community of voluntarily associated workers. In a system based on "[e]very man for every man (himself included)" (1827, 18), where "every adult person shall possess every thing . . . ," Thompson advocates equal distribution (1830, 6). We rephrase the second natural law to convey Thompson's broader meaning.

29. A few clarifications are necessary on exchange in cooperation. Within the cooperative, the main "exchange" is that of physical and intellectual exertion for claim to capital, education, and to output in the common store (Thompson 1830, 135). There is also inter-cooperative trade where "exchange" is of product for product (see, for example, 1830, 3). In external exchange, Thompson argues that outsiders or middlemen cannot dictate trades because full information is only available to the potential trading partners; only they can correctly judge their own net benefits from trade. But even among traders themselves, Thompson identifies welfare losses if the trade is forced. Forced trade generates ill will. If a resistant potential trader does not correctly perceive that

Thompson initially outlines the natural laws of distribution in *Inquiry* while comparing forced labor to the ideal competitive system; but even at this early stage, he suggests the natural laws hold for cooperation as well. Although Thompson is a strong advocate of equality, following Bentham, he is clear throughout his writing that security outweighs equality—that is, any distribution, equal or otherwise, of joint possessions must result from free and voluntary agreement among all affected parties (Thompson [1824] 1963, 145). In her published letter eulogizing Thompson, Wheeler clarifies the centrality of voluntariness across people and action: "Liberty becomes a tyrant unless possessed by all" (1834, 317).

For Thompson and Wheeler the concrete institutions of the cooperative system allow the full and simultaneous realization of both equality and security. In addition, like any society, a cooperative system must have institutions of justice to guarantee that it lives up to its principles. As a consistent advocate for women's liberation, Wheeler's writing emphasizes the need for impartial justice. For both Wheeler and Thompson, the reading of impartiality is literal and all-encompassing. It addresses privilege, voluntarism, and access. At the concrete level, all privileges impose unacceptable expense on the non-privileged (Thompson [1824] 1963, 103). In a just system, there can be no exception to voluntarism, every exchange must be voluntary.[30]

Heavily influenced by Owen in the concrete details of institutional structure, Thompson starts with a group of two hundred and up to two thousand or more who voluntarily produce for themselves the greatest output possible with "all the aids of science and art" ([1824] 1963, 387).[31] All adults participate in the labor of the community. Except for illness or infirmity of age, no one remains idle, and none are overworked, as moderate labor is necessary for health and wellbeing (528).

a trade would actually return personal net benefits, the trade should not go through. Education and the diffusion of knowledge are necessary conditions for voluntary exchange ([1824] 1963, 52–56).

30. For Thompson, the voluntariness of exchange holds for accumulated land and capital appropriated by previous generations. The only option for the redistribution of previously appropriated land and capital is voluntary trade: "We must not rob one . . . to encourage another. Security in the entire use must be administered impartially to all" because the "violation of one person's security annihilates all claims for security" ([1824] 1963, 40). Equal security does not undo accumulation from past force or fraud but shields future production from force and fraud (589–590).

31. Thompson provides elaborate justification for a community of 2000 inhabitants, emphasizing positive outcomes for health, individual independence, and social and intellectual happiness and improvement (1830, 26–46).

The cooperative cultivates land for its own needs. Thompson reckons land requirements of somewhere from half an acre per person to an acre and a half. Useful labor is the mental or physical exertion "which affords more pleasure in the use of its products than pain in their production" (1830, 1). There are three categories of goods. Necessaries cover basic needs that return health for longest life expectancy. Comforts are not necessary but "give so much pleasure in the use as more than to counter-balance the trouble of producing them" (2). And superfluities are articles of net loss in utility.[32] Self-supplying the community's basic necessities, all cooperators alternate between agriculture and manufacturing of useful clothing, housing, furniture, and other desired articles ([1824] 1963, 387–388). Thompson emphasizes careful selection of parcels on which to construct housing and gardens needed "for health, economy, personal independence, and social pleasures" (1827, 111).

Thompson (1830) provides elaborate detail on three-story co-housing. Communal living includes private sitting rooms and sleeping quarters for adults with the third-story attics serving as space for youth. Food preparation occurs in communal kitchens, and clothing is available from the common store.

Women see to their own children until the age of two, after which the cooperative educates children in common (Thompson [1824] 1963, 389). Thompson's approach to education draws heavily on Owen and the character formation hypothesis. Cooperative educational systems teach skills of observation, reason, and sympathy. Thompson, more than Owen, links education to utilitarian philosophy (1830, 207; 214; 219). Thompson's instructional program highlights teaching through stimulation of the pleasures of activity, novelty, curiosity, discovery, invention, and planning; of imitation; and particularly of the pleasure of sympathy (214–218). Central to Thompson's educational program is that *"every child should be guaranteed the free development of its powers, and the free exercise of its judgment"* (italics original, 219–220). And ultimately this education serves the commonweal.

The objectives of the united labor are to ensure community independence with the production of necessities for internal use (Thompson 1830, 3): abundant, wholesome foods with reserves for lean harvests; clothing; and construction and maintenance of community infrastructure. After meeting necessities through local production, additional labor may produce

---

32. Interestingly, Thompson also distinguishes "embelishments or elegancies." As long as these return net utility, they may serve to adorn necessaries as well as comforts or superfluities (1830, 2).

comforts and conveniences. Alternatively, the community may acquire such goods through external trade (Thompson [1824] 1963, 525).[33] Artists and scientists are not artificially separated from the community. Instead, their surplus hours attend to education and other useful work (390). The arts and sciences help to stimulate originality and individuality (522).[34]

Cooperatives in the spirit of Thompson and Wheeler are self-governed, with each working member serving as a joint proprietor. Governance must be by those being governed (Thompson 1827, 15). Self-governance is an important source of happiness as well as expediency (1830, 228).[35] Community agreement determines the specific form this self-governance takes, be it democratic election, rotation, or seniority ([1824] 1963, 390).

Thompson and Wheeler consider public opinion as central to any economic system. A well- functioning cooperative builds public opinion along lines of mutual esteem (Thompson 1827, 66). Cooperative public opinion operates without factitious rewards or punishments ([1824] 1963, 506). Social norms reinforce reason and kindness in that public opinion. Cooperators are attentive to smiles, frowns, and the "averted eye" (395), small signals of community feedback, devoid of "suspicion of sinister interest" (507).

In the cooperative context, Thompson sees little to fear from slander, gossip, and "prying curiosity," as there is nothing to be gained in the system constantly reflecting and reinforcing "mutual kindness and forbearance" ([1824] 1963, 499). The more seriously problematic issue is when public opinion works to compel all to bend to it, scrutinizing and judging community members (497). Hopefully the institutionalization of freedom of opinion and free discussion greatly limits the scope of such outcomes. However, even in a cooperative, Thompson recognizes that public opinion can be misdirected.

---

33. The just equivalent of "labor for labor, equal amounts for equal amounts" serves as pricing for inter-cooperative trade—with the expectation of fair pricing as an external check on labor exploitation (Thompson [1824] 1963, 526).

34. Notice in this chapter, we use the term "community" rather than the commonly used term "village" because Thompson, himself, takes exception to the latter: "I do not like the terms, villages, and villagers, as applied to the establishments of Communities of Mutual Co-operation. With these terms are always associated the ideas of poverty, want of knowledge, uncouthness of manners, and dependence. Wealth, knowledge, real refinement, and independence will be the most striking characteristics of Co-operative Communities. They will be as much unlike modern or antique villages and their inhabitants as they will be unlike cities and those who now inhabit them" (Thompson 1826, 232).

35. Self-governance requires sufficient education among the population to guarantee that "none but equal laws to be made" (Thompson 1827, 15).

The community is also responsible for arbitrating conflict and bringing reconciliation. If someone commits a serious injury within the community, the community does hold the power to remove that person. In these cases, the community pays the exiting member their share of joint property (Thompson [1824] 1963, 390–391). All community members are also at perfect liberty to leave and claim their share of joint property.

THE SELF-REINFORCING NATURE OF COOPERATION

Given the social psychology and institutional base of the radical cooperative, perhaps the prime question is whether the cooperative structure is self-sustaining. Thompson is clear: "[T]here is nothing in the known and ordinary motives that influence human conduct incompatible with the formation and progress of these co-operating communities" ([1824] 1963, 473). This is not a simple assertion. It suggests self-reinforcing stability. It greatly expands on Owen's concept of social cohesion. In this section we reconstruct a theorem around this theme. In our view, it lies at the very center of Thompson and Wheeler's effort to build a radical social science. The reconstruction makes explicit that the cooperative's material superabundance and high levels of happiness support the individuals' identification of their self-interest with the broader success of the community. At the same time, the strong commitment to the community becomes the continuing foundation of its superabundance and high levels of happiness.

Unparalleled Superabundance

One striking element in the radical social science is its heavy use of material arguments. More than simply economically viable, the cooperative system enjoys superabundant material returns. The abundance and security of co-operation undergirds the active economic participation of its members. A system of mutual cooperation, based not on compulsion or delusion but on voluntary participation, dramatically increases the state of comfort of its members by "three to four times" in the short run and by potentially far more in the long run (Thompson [1824] 1963, 444). Thompson's discussion of superabundance expands on Owen's early statement of the theme (Owen 1813–1816). For Thompson, superabundance originates from four sources: unique cooperative incentives, expanded labor force participation, enhanced efficiency, and technological advancement.

Incentives

The satisfaction of "real wants" (e.g. physical necessities) motivates productive activity irrespective of economic system. Having satisfied basic needs, all economic systems must condition habit to generate "persevering industry" (Thompson [1824] 1963, 33). The question is how to incentivize habitual productive activity. Incentives to produce reflect dominant characteristics of the economic system in which those incentives are imbedded. With force on their side, slaveholders incentivize via the manipulation of fear and avoidance of physical pain. In the selfish-serving version of individual competition, the withholding of product from the industrious also elicits fear of deprivation to motivate effort. When labor is fully voluntary, there must be stimuli for habitual effort (Thompson [1824] 1963, 34). The second law of distribution—laborers' claim to product—provides noteworthy stimulus in funneling the entire benefit of the product to the producers (36). The fundamental exchange that every cooperator makes is their personal effort for a full share of community product. The promise of a full share in the community's product works as a powerful incentive.

Beyond security, happiness from physical, intellectual, and social pleasures of work stimulates further productivity (Thompson1827, 66; [1824] 1963, 465–467). The cooperative disentangles and eliminates factitious rewards and punishments from natural pleasures and pains. Equal access to education and a shared base of knowledge guarantees personal interest in production and sensitivity to its pleasures (1827, 21). Moreover, self-governance has its effect; it is one of the social pleasures of work. Where there exists social encouragement for equal participation as decision-makers, managers, and overseers, such empowerment further fuels participation.

Public sympathy and public opinion enhance all these incentives. While public opinion matters for all, Thompson recognizes the import behind social esteem and praise that naturally returns to those exhibiting superior effort, skill, or innovative capacities ([1824] 1963, 468–469). Indeed, "the regret will be on the part of those, whose powers of co-operation and usefulness will be the least" (470–471).

The mechanics of incentives—security and the hierarchy of pleasures from work—make work in the cooperative attractive. They push the cooperative toward superabundance. They guarantee general participation by all. They put an end to widespread freeriding.[36]

---

36. Thompson himself asserts, "if in these communities the arrangement were such that the idle could eat the bread of the industrious, that error would be fatal to them" ([1824] 1963, 500).

Expanded Labor Force Participation

The "lopping off of the excrescences of wealth and poverty" expands meaningful labor force participation at both ends (Thompson [1824] 1963, 444). The formerly rich are no longer idle. The formerly poor now have access to education, innovations, land, and capital, enabling full contribution. Both groups are ready to respond given the cooperative incentives. Their participation leads to greater production.

Gender equality drives the other major expansion in labor force participation. Writing in a period of unabashed social acceptance of women's perceived inferiority, Thompson and Anna Doyle Wheeler are women's rights radicals.[37] For Wheeler and Thompson, cooperation is "[l]arge numbers of men *and women* co-operating together for mutual happiness, all their possessions and means of enjoyment being the equal property of all" (Thompson & Wheeler 1825, 199). They go further than simply acknowledging women in their definition of cooperation; they ultimately argue that cooperation is necessary for gender equality.

Thompson and Wheeler identify a significant contribution that women can make to the cooperative labor force, once free from "domestic drudgery" (Thompson [1824] 1963, 401–402).[38] In providing free and equal access to land, capital, and output, the community serves as social insurance for women. Add to this the equal access to education and the non-gendered diffusion of knowledge, and all women cooperators can develop talents to participate in any sector of the economy. The institutions of equality and impartial justice reinforce social respect toward women's contributions to the community. Such social respect is important for psychological health; psychological health is necessary for their effective participation in social and economic activities.

---

37. There are other exceptions to the socialized perception of women's inferior position by the early 19th century. See, for example, Mary Wollstonecraft's *Vindication of the Rights of Woman* (1792). Rostek (2021) provides insight into women's economic thought about marriage, women working for pay, and "moral economics" during this period. Taylor (1983, 1–16) considers the early history of socialist feminism. Also see Kuiper (2022).

38. While recognizing and applauding the radical feminism of Thompson and Wheeler, particularly given the time period, Dooley (1996) provides a critique of "male bias" underlying Thompson's thought as well as Wheeler's. Dooley highlights that their writing shows bias in its elevation of the market over the "drudgery" of the domestic sphere (see, for example, pp. 222–223; 340). See Folbre (1998) for historical insight into the gendered nature of these spheres. Despite this clear bias, the basic argument for greater occupational opportunity in a cooperative setting still suggests higher levels of aggregate productivity. Addressing this bias could only enhance the argument.

Thompson ([1824] 1963) estimates the waste of women's productive time inherent in the system of individual production at "more than a fourth of human effort."[39] With advances in technology, machinery can make women as productive as men in previously male-dominated spheres (372). The institutional structure of cooperation also makes domestic work more efficient. Education of children is a major concern for the entire community, while cooking takes place in a common kitchen. Thus, cooperation "relieves" women from much of childcare and household "drudgery" (389). And women, like men, fully participate in agriculture and manufacturing as each takes on work suited to their abilities (389).

Efficiency Claims

After considering incentives and labor force expansion, Thompson turns to other efficiencies. He offers no less than six specific claims that reinforce superabundance in a cooperative community ([1824] 1963, 442).

(i) To begin, efficiency results from rational consumption standards. The community emphasizes production that generates net natural pleasures, focusing on physical necessities for all, intellectual and social needs fulfillment, and more ornamental pursuits. Rational consumption curtails waste. As the community shifts to higher pleasures, it rethinks demand for intoxicants, harmful outputs, and superfluities. Thompson believes the cooperative community will voluntarily embrace temperance, reckoning a gain of between 10% and 30% in labor productivity from this reform alone. Thompson doubts that the cooperative requires substantial resources to intervene in internal disputes. Most disputes concern property and these fizzle away when the community shares equal access. The semi-autarchic form of the cooperative economy also promises major savings in transportation costs (399–400).

(ii) The very structure of the cooperative greatly reduces unemployment and related inefficiencies. Thompson highlights the stabilizing nature of cooperative demand where workers-as-consumers self-produce to satisfy needs. Free of factitiousness, focusing on usefulness and the extension of happiness, demand tends to be relatively stable. Unknown in the cooperative is the withholding of supply

---

39. Elsewhere he estimates the loss as 5/12ths of human labor (Thompson [1824] 1963, 402).

to drive up returns for the privileged few. The stabilizing nature of demand and the lack of profit-driven supply shocks means there is no tendency toward cyclical unemployment.[40] Seasonal unemployment is also unlikely. The tendency to involve every adult in both manufacturing and agriculture offers options for productive activity in the agricultural off-season (400–401).

(iii) Efficiency results from the saving of labor and of profits in wholesale and retail activities. Like some other cooperative thinkers, Thompson assigns no worthwhile social purpose to the bulk of retail and wholesale activities, and thus no claim to profit.[41] Concerning shopkeeping, "[w]ants being supplied in common, there would be nothing to retail" (404). Thompson imagines one central consumer storehouse. The retail work that remains in the cooperative is a social task that serves "a source of amusement as well as universal utility" (405). There is no wasted activity on bargaining and pilfering (405–406).

(iv) Efficiency results from a focus on cooperator health.[42] Thompson reflects his own lifelong struggle with physical ailments in establishing human health as central to happiness. Cooperative education includes substantial training on human physiology, nutrition, etc. to facilitate self-diagnosis and self-care (414). Thompson stresses health in the choice of building sites, food, and clothing. He conveys real health advantages in individuals mixing manufacturing with agricultural labor. This combination exercises the full range of physical and mental capabilities (411–412). The emphasis on health raises worker productivity.[43]

(v) Efficiency results from substituting mutual sympathy, benevolence, and virtue for the "contentions, animosities and cruelties" associated with insecurity. Insecurity encourages the selfish pursuit of wealth which in turn prompts the entire panoply of "deceits, perjuries, forgeries . . . violence and fraud that desolate human life"

40. According to Pankhurst, Thompson studies the works of Sismondi, who has early insights into business crises ([1954] 1991, 3; 38–39).

41. This topic of retail is central in Chapter 6 on consumer cooperatives. That chapter includes coverage of John Gray—Thompson's contemporary—on this issue.

42. Thompson (1830) continues to emphasize the theme of cooperator health in his blueprint for a cooperative community; see, for example, pp. 21, 26, 32–33, 52, 70, 113, 174, 179, and an entire chapter on health (193–204).

43. Where health and productivity are incompatible, health takes precedence (Thompson [1824] 1963, 413). And where such trade-offs exist, Thompson argues that the other returns to efficiency generated by cooperatives more than counterbalance productivity losses (414).

(415). In a society which does not experience insecurity, this range of wasteful crimes simply does not exist.

(vi) And finally, efficiency flows from the matching of supply with demand. The "system of equal security, of the natural laws of distribution, and the simple institutions compatible with them" tend to quickly re-balance shortages and surpluses. Generally, producers who are also consumers are well aware of community desires. With demand for necessities known and supplied locally, any surplus labor diverts into procuring comforts and conveniences or to produce for external trade (424). If demand falls for a product the cooperative sells externally, the varied skillsets of each laborer and shared technological knowledge allow flexibility to redirect labor to other productive activity.[44] If external supply fails for an import, the same labor and technological flexibility allows innovation to produce substitutes. And since the cooperative only purchases non-necessities from external sources, if unable to create substitutes, the cooperative reduces demand.

In considering imbalances of supply and demand, Thompson also tackles the question of Malthusian over-supply of population. Malthusian population theory is central to the classical political economy of the day. Thompson doesn't question Malthus's logic applied to the competitive system. However, he strongly denies that a system of cooperatives would suffer from overpopulation. Such growth is the result of poverty, misery, and gender inequality, not abundance. Improved material conditions and gender equality lead to greater prudence in families. And improved material conditions accommodate a modest increase in population with no dire consequences (425–426).

Technology

With equal access to education, capital, and land, all who are so inclined in the community have the ability to invent and publicize their ideas. "[W]hen our own interests are identified with the interests of those around us" there is motivation to innovate (Thompson 1827, 27). Enlarged calculations of self-interest lead to the diffusion of innovations and skill. More talented cooperators experience pain rather than pleasure in the lesser skill of their

---

44. Thompson anticipates trades with other communities will use labor content as their standard of value. Gains in productivity, which he broadly expects, lead to appropriate rescheduling of trading ratios ([1824] 1963, 524–526).

compatriots. So there is a heightened tendency to share knowledge and skills across all members of the community (65). This diffusion of knowledge and sharing of innovations have the obvious economic effects of increasing labor productivity (25–26).

One stimulus to innovation is to reduce costs in the grossly unpleasant side of work (Thompson 1827, 15). Cooperators design and implement technological substitutes for work that over-stresses muscular systems, that brings illness, or reduces life expectancy (28). Innovation, itself, returns substantial "pleasures of public opinion, of sympathy and of beneficence," enhancing the reputation of inventors (27; 15; 114; see also [1824] 1963, 530).

As the cooperatives leave behind the "factitious importance given to articles of wealth as mere sources of distinction," they assess innovations for their real contribution to utility. If, for example, there is innovation in style or materials, the question becomes one of usefulness ([1824] 1963, 533). Thompson is clear, however, that "embellishments and elegancies" can often pass the test of utility (1830, 2).

The drive to innovate and produce capital is not an end but a means of production and enjoyment (Thompson [1824] 1963, 528). Thompson recognizes that mechanization may generate overproduction relative to demand. If so, cooperators redirect labor from that over-supplied economic activity into other areas. Innovation in a cooperative is not to generate material growth for growth's sake. At some point, the cooperative experiences material satiation, and the benefits of technologically induced growth diffuse more generally to the quality of the work experience, leisure, and human development (531).

All told, equal distribution is more productive than any mode of unequal distribution (Thompson 1830, 4). The basic argument is that when there is a guarantee to each cooperator of equal shares, they appreciate the incentives, they fully participate in the labor force, they build efficiencies, and encourage the diffusion of technology. These result from the institutions of cooperation and the feedbacks of enlarged self-interest on production.

Unparalleled Levels of Happiness

Thompson and Wheeler are clear that in addition to material superabundance, the cooperative generates unparalleled levels of happiness. Despite Thompson and Wheeler's extensive use of the Benthamite term "happiness," their understanding of happiness overlaps significantly with the

concept of human development we discussed in the last chapter. They trace this broad happiness to three major sources: expanded self-interest, workplace norms, and gender equality. Along with superabundance, happiness is a prerequisite for self-reinforcing stability.

Enlarged Self-Interest

Thompson conveys his strongly held belief that cooperation supplants the more troubling outcomes deriving from selfishness (1827, 100–101). And though he predicts "gardens, pleasure-grounds, and palaces" for all, he asserts that material comforts are not "the end of life; they will serve but as a theatre on which the new course of human existence, the development of the physical and intellectual powers of the human race, will proceed unrestrained." At the same time, cooperation generates unparalleled levels of social pleasures (118).[45] Likewise, Wheeler (1834) considers the scope of cooperation to extend far beyond the sphere of material production to "the full development and free exercise of all the faculties of human beings" (317).

As identified above, an expanded sense of benevolence is key to broader self-interest. "[I]n every minor pursuit" people seek "happiness of all by mutual kindness and good offices." Thompson portrays this happiness as reflective and contagious (Thompson [1824] 1963, 421). This reflected happiness works in reverse as well: in enlarged calculations of self-interest, distress among others returns further distress to those who perceive it.

The everyday business of the community requires a benevolent worldview that treats each with sincere respect. An Owenite form of education—including the development of sympathy and effective reasoning—points toward such a view.[46] People learn that their highest levels of happiness occur when they include in their calculations the welfare of others across their sphere of influence.[47] These calculations serve as the most fundamental check on pain-generating behaviors. From experience, the rational sympathetic person infers that domination, while providing short-term pleasure, has neutral or negative effects on happiness over the longer haul.

---

45. Similarly, taking a lead from Owen, Thompson predicts that full and impartial application of the natural laws of distribution stimulates "the development of all human faculties physical and intellectual, the continual increase in knowledge, and the acquisition of moral habits," particularly sympathy and benevolence (103).

46. Thompson (1830) provides a detailed and insightful discussion about the "pleasure of sympathy" in a chapter on education (214–218).

47. Recall that these enlarged self-interest calculations include estimating reactive behavior.

Education is the start. Building on their shared education, cooperative members internalize a respect for the "security and comfort of others" (Thompson [1824] 1963, 263). The continuing experience of the cooperative system brings benevolence to full fruition. Voluntarism and equality support benevolence, while virtually eliminating false pleasures, such as domination and antipathy.[48] In place of the false, people find "pleasures of sense, sympathy and intelligence" (1827, 65). Moreover, the cooperators' comfortable social and economic position allows the processing of long-term consequences of actions. They investigate "the effect on happiness of every habit" and acquire "dispositions of fortitude, self-command, and universal sympathy" ([1824] 1963, 263). Voluntarism is instrumental toward the stimulus to benevolence in this system. With every act of voluntary association, "every member loses the mere selfish individuality of his character: he acknowledges that his interest is united with that of numbers: his benevolence is drawn forth towards them." Cooperative equality leads to shared employments and concerns with "larger circles" until each individual "shall ultimately feel an interest in the happiness of all the industrious" (1827, 86).

The Workplace

An expanded "sphere of benevolence" creates much happiness. That sphere includes relations at work. At the same time, the very conditions of work generate happiness. In a system of voluntary equality with labor claiming all output, good work conditions become the norm. These contribute to quality of life, including health, leisure-work balance, and longevity (Thompson 1827; 22; 25; 29; see also 108–109). The cooperative community dedicates resources to engineer technological substitutes for harmful but necessary work (28). Pleasures of the sensory and muscular systems result directly from improved work processes. More leisure hours

---

48. "Where all are afforded amply, by their own united exertions, all the means of happiness which wealth can supply, no pleasures of superiority, false and vicious as such pleasures are, can be derived from the aspect of surrounding misery; no stimulus to exertion can be derived from the hope of acquiring the pleasures of domination or corruptive influence . . . .[F]or the treacherous and false pleasures of antipathy, the cheap, the real, the enduring pleasures of sympathy will be substituted. The inferiority of others in wealth, talents, refinement, kindly dispositions, and consequently happiness, is necessarily, to a well-constituted mind, a source of pain rather than of pleasure . . ." (Thompson 1827, 65). Although Thompson does not explicitly mention self-governance in this argument, we suspect the experience of self-governance is necessary for elimination of the false pleasures.

enhance intellectual and social pleasures depending on choices people make about the use of free time—across educational, innovative, artistic, and/or social pursuits. Moreover, the lack of free riding, the norm of industriousness, and equal access to rational-ethical education enhance social respect (113).

The Gender Dimension

All of this discussion of happiness extends to women as well as men. Strikingly for their time and place, Thompson and Wheeler see gender equality as necessary for the greatest community happiness. In the competitive system of early industrialization, women carry major disadvantages. Physically, women of this era have less strength than men and they must lose time in the "gestation and rearing of infants" (Thompson & Wheeler 1825, x).[49] Moreover, in the "domestic slavery" of marriage, men withhold knowledge, land, and capital (1825, xi).[50] In addition, Thompson and Wheeler explain the internalized oppression of women, women's collusion with that oppression (192–196) and their resulting antisocial behaviors (Wheeler 1833, 35; see also Dooley 1996, 101). A central argument across Wheeler's published writing involves two claims: (a) gender equality is necessary for high levels of happiness; and (b) cooperation is necessary for gender equality.[51]

The radical cooperators offer an argument in three parts to support the hypothesis that high levels of happiness require gender equality. The first of the arguments is the utilitarian position that each individual counts for one in the calculation of happiness. Women's happiness must be counted. Second the fundamental utilitarian proposition of diminishing marginal utility implies that as men lose their advantage and as women gain, the

---

49. Wheeler references Chateaubriand to clarify that "deficiency of strength in Woman, is nothing but a civilized disease" (1830, 15).

50. Modern socialist feminist thought, including the work of social reproduction feminist such as Susan Ferguson, supports this conclusion about the incompatibility of full-gender equality and capitalism. Ferguson (2020) explicitly credits Wheeler and her coauthor William Thompson with being the first to recognize that reproductive labor plays an unacknowledged role in support of the capitalist economy. In this view, gender equality requires recognizing that under capitalism, the devaluation of reproductive labor is central to sustained exploitation and higher profits (48).

51. In a forthcoming paper in *Feminist Economics*, we develop Wheeler's argument in more detail. Renee Prendergast also picks up on the idea that cooperation is necessary for gender equality (2021, 28).

overall level of utility must rise with equality.[52] Finally, the total happiness achieved with equality is even greater if as Thompson and Wheeler assume the utility functions of men and women are interdependent. In their words, a call for rights of women is a call for "the cause of men by showing the mighty influence Women hold over the happiness or misery of men" (; Wheeler 1830, 13). Gender equality for women—including education, liberties, self-respect, and access to social relations—indirectly but powerfully affect the utility of men.

Historically, gender inequality is the outcome of a complex entanglement of institutional and socioeconomic factors. How to undo it? Thompson and Wheeler claim that full gender equality can only be realized in a cooperative community. The social psychology and the institutions of cooperation are key. Access to communal property—land and capital— frees women from men's traditional monopoly. The equal duty to work enhances the respect women receive socially and from themselves.[53] Equal access to enjoyments and equal rights—including to justice and medical aid—institutionalizes claims to a share of the bounty. Apartment-style living in large buildings with internal hallways and communal kitchens, along with a broadened sense of community orientation reduces the potential for tyranny within interpersonal relationships. And the cooperative nurturing of an enlarged self-interest elicits community rejection of exploitation (Wheeler 1833, 279).

This level playing field generates a full restructuring of relations between men and women. The community, as a whole, comes to recognize that whoever "wishes, man or woman . . . to be esteemed or loved, must deserve to be esteemed or loved." Each now knows they lose if they neglect "those good qualities which called esteem or love into existence" (Thompson & Wheeler 1825, 204). Under cooperative conditions, men also develop other-serving qualities because to be loved he "must learn the art of pleasing, of benevolence, of deserving love" (200–201). Assuming liberty to leave harmful relationships, these higher expectations generate improved behavior by men. The radical cooperators even dare to proclaim: "Such men, in such an Association might love themselves!" (202).

52. Wheeler is likely aware of diminishing marginal utility as Thompson uses the concept ([1824] 1963, 104; 118).

53. Thompson and Wheeler argue: "To enjoy equal happiness with men, to associate with them on terms of perfect equality, you must be equally useful to the common good by an equal improvement and equally useful application of all your faculties of mind and body . . ." (1825, 204).

The Self-Reinforcing Mechanism

We claim a self-reinforcing mechanism is more or less fully realized in Thompson and Wheeler's social science.[54] Given the insights of the last two subsections, a reconstruction of this mechanism is now a relatively straightforward matter. We start with a lemma and proceed to a theorem.

> Lemma: In the cooperative system, superabundance supports happiness and happiness supports superabundance.
> Proof: The arguments of Thompson and Wheeler for this point are clearly stated above.
> A Theorem: The cooperative system and its outcomes are mutually reinforcing.
> Heuristic Proof: Once the cooperative system achieves the outcomes of superabundance and high levels of happiness, they support the alignment of personal self-interest with the common good. But a broad self-interest in the common good, interacting with cooperative institutions, reproduces those very outcomes. Thus, the cooperative has a self-reinforcing mechanism.

In the cooperative, individuals are surrounded by abundant material goods and widespread happiness. Cooperators appreciate that their highest self-interest is in maintaining the commonweal. Their broad self-interest reinforces the community's superabundance and happiness. For example, as we noted above, efficiency is enhanced by beneficent behavior, and broad self-interest builds morality, contributing to greater happiness. The self-reinforcing mechanism is the substance of the Thompson-Wheeler theorem.

Recall Adam Smith's treatment in *Theory of Moral Sentiments* of the mechanism of benevolence within the human psyche. There Smith asserts that a society based on benevolence could be the most flourishing state.[55] But even at its broadest, Smith's analysis does not approach that of these cooperative theorists. Smith provides no detail on the mechanics of the interaction between benevolence and institutions. He nowhere estimates the likely material outcomes of such interactions.

And finally, Smith in no way anticipates the reinforcing influences so central to Thompson and Wheeler.

---

54. Notice the theme here is similar to that of social cohesion discussed in the last chapter.
55. See Chapter 1 of this work.

Of course, the Thompson-Wheeler theorem, itself, doesn't tell us how to get from here to there. It doesn't tell us how to achieve the transition from individual competition to a full cooperative commonwealth.

THOMPSON AND WHEELER ON TRANSITION

Most of the cooperative theorists are concerned not only with the ulti-mate cooperative commonwealth, but also with constructing a transitional road. In the *Inquiry* ([1824] 1963, 386–391) and in elaborate empirical detail in *Practical Directions* (1830), Thompson puts forth his version of the transitional cooperative community. These communities emerge in the midst of the capitalist economy, drawing together 200 to 2000 individuals committed to voluntary cooperation (*Inquiry*, 387).[56] Start-up capital may not derive from force, fraud, or philanthropic gifts (*Practical Directions* 1830, 11). A member "having the means" invests £40 (£160 for a family) for housing and machinery.[57] Where members lack such savings, the new cooperative may resort to nonresident subscribers, borrowing and repaying both interest and principal from production surpluses. If a member can afford it, another £40 of investment serves to purchase land. If funds for land purchases are unavailable, the community can rent land ([1824] 1963, 388). Thompson is careful to advocate site selection based on considerations of community health and safety from environmental problems such as flooding (1830, 52). It is unclear whether members making basic contributions receive interest credits. In any case, the actual distribution of wealth in these transitional cooperatives (as opposed to the distribution of consumption) can be quite unequal.

There are alternative paths toward establishing a cooperative commu-nity. Taking encouragement from the early union movement and its ability to raise wages, Thompson suggests that unions might act as a major in-stitutional mechanism for facilitating worker savings. These savings might underwrite cooperative workshops. The workshops might then ac-quire agricultural land. In time, workshops and farms come together as a

56. While acknowledging the influence of Owen on Thompson's architectural designs of a small-scale cooperative, Leopold (2019) points to substantial differences. Owen's vision is far more extravagant. For example, Owen's vision includes a small under-ground railway. In contrast, Thompson's vision aims at feasibility given limited start-up capital. And Thompson puts more emphasis on ideas concerning manufacturing that he adapts from Fourier (Leopold 2019, 73–74).

57. *Practical Directions* reduces this initial investment to 20 pounds per member (1830, 14).

cooperative community, expanding to include a range of small producers, a school, and dwellings for members. In this way, worker savings alone finance the entire community (Dooley 1996, 323; Thompson 1827, 90–94).

Concerns arise regarding the skill composition of the transitional cooperative labor force. Thompson advocates taking care to guarantee the participation of workers skilled in all fundamental occupations. However, the community may hire workers from the outside for training purposes when an early cooperative lacks needed skills (Thompson [1824] 1963, 389).

Thompson (1830) encourages the initial production of basic necessities. If the cooperative begins with 200 people, he recommends the following manufacturing activities: linen, cottons, and woolen cloth, iron and other metal fabrications, and flour (138; 155). Every cooperator participates in both agricultural and manufacturing activities. Goods are consumed in common, and cooking is a community responsibility. Women take care of their infant children.[58] Once the children enter schools at the age of two, their mothers work in a variety of other productive roles.

But the situation for women in the transitional cooperative must also remediate the historical oppression of women. These historical forces derive from patriarchal norms demanding women's submission and subservience within the household, reinforced by legal and religious institutions that withhold education, capital, and access to income-creating forms of employment. As noted above, oppressive forces tend to internalize in women's psyches. And women often perceive and portray themselves as inferior to gratify the vanity of the men in their lives (Thompson & Wheeler 1825, 192–196). Given the challenges of this transformation, the communities must intentionally attend to the reversal of gendered oppression. The *Appeal* provides numerous clues to this reversal. That process includes raising awareness of the negative effects on human character of sexism; coming together to commune over the wrongs done women; and ending all willing submission to men's caprices. The *Appeal* calls for women to stop enabling bad behavior, to challenge oppression, and to encourage rational-ethical morality (208–213).

Thompson is careful to distinguish the organization of the transitional community from that of Owen's New Lanark. Whatever its social goals, at root New Lanark always remains a profit-making organization. It "is necessarily governed . . . [by] the proprietors of that establishment" ([1824] 1963, 386). Being completely voluntary, the transitional cooperative community

---

58. Notice, despite the radical nature of the proposal, Thompson still limits men's participation in the earliest stages of childcare.

must from the start be "freed from any . . . arbitrary regulations and involuntary obedience." The community is self-governed. Every working member ultimately becomes a joint proprietor (387). The direction of the community is by "adult, male and female, members" (390). There are specific managers to direct labor.[59] Key is that management must be accountable to and removable by the workers in their respective departments (Dooley 1996, 336). Any member of a cooperative can exit the community "with claim on the society for whatever proportion of joint property, or of stock lent, the retiring member may be entitled to" (Thompson [1824] 1963, 391).

Thompson is confident that the transitional cooperatives can make widespread the material gains ushered in by New Lanark and the Industrial Revolution. This is not a zero-sum game. Thompson does argue that more rapid growth occurs in transitional cooperatives which produce all the various necessities across industries for cooperative use. Production of basic necessities eliminates the diversion of surplus for wage advances, profits, and payments to middlemen and eliminates negative shocks from market fluctuations (1830, 186–187; also see 1827, 115–116). The initial goal is to "accumulate gradually . . . an independence, if not a fortune" (1830, 187).

However formed, Thompson is sure that transitional cooperative communities are far more productive than their traditional competitors. The key point is that cooperative members are both laborers and owners of capital. Still, to maintain long-run success the cooperatives must be protected from the unnecessary and unproductive taxation rampant in the Britain of the day. Reform of the national government plays a major role in the transition period. Thompson estimates the "power of public plunder" absorbs a third of total product ([1824] 1963, 596). The nation requires a new government built on a set of representative institutions which give power to the majority. These institutions must avoid "the restraints of insecurity (entail, primogeniture, combination local and general, wages-regulation direct or indirect, monopolies, . . . [and] public plunder)" (600). At root these institutions must also work to dissolve "the league between capitalists and the holders of political power" (595). Rebuilding the government plays a central role in rebuilding the economy.[60]

---

59. Early on, if the community funds derive from subscribers, those subscribers have appointing power subject to agreement of the cooperators. Later, a management appointment is likely to come from the workers within a given department.

60. For Thompson, the establishment of representative institutions and full security are so central that parallel to the development of cooperatives they may break the power of the capitalists and lead to a system of "labor with equal individual competition," with workers coming into ownership of their own capital ([1824] 1963, 592).

In establishing these representative institutions and throughout his argument, Thompson holds that all the benefits of mutual cooperation can be achieved without any violent redistribution or revolution. The potential for growth and improvement are so great that allowing capitalists their current wealth will have only a slight slowing effect on progress, while seizing that wealth achieves little and sets a precedent not easily erased ([1824] 1963, 589).

Starting with Owen's insights, Thompson and Wheeler continue to build the foundations for an ambitious social science. That science points toward the necessary conditions for transition. That science introduces a social psychology and explores a range of socioeconomic institutions. That science provides informal logic through what we call the Thompson-Wheeler theorem. The theorem—the reinforcing nature of superabundance and happiness with an enlarged self-interest and cooperative institutions—explains the fundamental cooperative feedback mechanism. While still somewhat rough, the new science presents a deep and coherent approach to social possibilities. At points, the argument may be overdetermined, but that is the perennial problem of social science. At the same time the argument is open to serious critiques. We return to these matters in Chapter 11.

Still, Thompson expects that a healthy competition between such production and cooperatives will ultimately favor the latter.

CHAPTER 4

cᴧɔ

The Cooperative Socialism of J. S. Mill and Harriet Taylor

THE ARC OF HISTORY

Through the first half of the 19th century, cooperators formed an audience for their own theoreticians, Owen, Thompson, Wheeler, and others. Such writers commanded only modest curiosity from the mainstream of political economy.[1] But by the middle of the century, cooperation attracted the attention of the most accomplished political economist in Britain, John Stuart Mill. More than a passing interest, Mill, working closely with his wife Harriet Taylor, placed cooperation at the very center of his new political economy of progress (Persky 2016, Ch. 5).[2] He and Taylor built up nothing less than a socialism of cooperation. Mill, with his central role in political economy, cannot be ignored. His work lays out a theoretical forecast that challenges the very core of the economy of the day. Anticipating

---

1. See Chapter 11 for the views on cooperation of Malthus, Ricardo, Torrens, and McCulloch.

2. On the collaboration of Mill and Taylor, see Mill's *Autobiography* ([1873] 1981) and *Hayek on Mill: The Mill-Taylor Friendship* (2015). Throughout the chapter we refer to "Mill and Taylor" when quoting or discussing materials on which Mill acknowledges Taylor's major contributions. These are *On Liberty* and the famous chapter on the "Future of Laboring Classes" in *Principles*. The only exception to this rule is that we cite only Mill when discussing the need for competition among cooperatives because we are unsure that Taylor subscribes to that position. Admittedly, such a procedure is somewhat ad hoc, but it serves to validate Taylor's active participation in their work most relevant to cooperation.

Building a Social Science. Kirsten Madden and Joseph Persky, Oxford University Press. © Oxford University Press 2024.
DOI: 10.1093/oso/9780197693735.003.0004

elements of Marxian historical materialism, Mill and Taylor identify co-operation as the key to a revolutionary transformation of the economy, a transformation toward a more humane and social base. Younger liberal economists, such as Henry Fawcett and J. E. Cairnes, necessarily took this work seriously.

Like Thompson and Wheeler, Mill and Taylor's cooperative socialism merges seamlessly with the fundamental commitment to utilitarian evaluation in their work. In particular, Mill fully endorses the proposition to organize society in a manner conducive to the greatest happiness for the greatest number.[3] Like the utilitarian Bentham, Mill is certain that attempts at direct redistribution on any substantial scale would prove disastrous to the economy. From such an observation Bentham's triumphalist liberalism concludes that the status quo with its security and subsistence is essentially the best that one can hope for. Mill and Taylor, like the Benthamite Thompson, strongly differ. Rejecting both the status quo and immediate revolution, their work suggests that through the progress of producer cooperatives, coupled with other essential reforms, society might achieve a genuine improvement in the welfare of the greatest number. While Mill anticipates serious struggle to achieve such an outcome, he sees the arc of history undergirding the course of progress.

Mill anchors his work with Taylor in the very depths of classical economics. Drawing on Smith, Malthus, and Ricardo, he lays out a version of the evolution of capitalist accumulation resulting ultimately in a stationary state (see Persky 2016, Ch. 5). Ricardo links the falling rate of profit to population growth. But Mill outlines another path. Prudent family planning can avoid the Malthusian population problem. The result then is rising wages. High wages will bring on a very different stationary state. For Mill and Taylor, the stationary state of high wages promises a meaningful social transformation.

On this theoretical base Mill and Taylor anticipate the very suppression of the employer/employee relations of the factory. In effect, they question the viability of a defining institution of capitalist production. For Mill and

---

3. Mill devotes Chapter 2 of his essay, *Utilitarianism* ([1863] 1987), to elucidating the utilitarian formula and Chapter 4 to offering his "proof" of that formula. Early on in his career, Mill is clear about exactly who counts in the "greatest number": "the working people being the majority of the whole population, the interests of all the other classes are of no importance compared with theirs . . . . [I]f it were necessary I would willingly suffer every other person in the community to starve, rather than that they should be inadequately provided with the necessaries of life" (Mill 1988, 312). Interestingly, Mill made this statement in his famous debates with Thompson where, as a young man, he argued against the cooperative system. For more on the debates, see the "Mill and Taylor" section.

Taylor the capitalist's firm does not represent a certain end-of-history but rather an admittedly useful, but unattractive and transitional, structure. As profit rates fall, the factories evolve toward worker-owned cooperatives making possible a far more equal economy. Mill ultimately refers to Taylor and himself as socialists, but he remains highly critical of attempts to centralize planning in the economy.[4] Mill's vision is fundamentally different from that of Owen, Thompson, Wheeler and many of the later cooperative theorists. Mill enmeshes workers associations in a competitive system. Where most other cooperative writers reject competition as a destructive facet of a market economy, Mill argues that competition is useful, even vital, to the success of cooperation.

Mill and Taylor strongly endorsed cooperation. As we will see, they might have gone further in developing the theory of cooperation as they envisioned it. For example, Mill doesn't attempt to construct a full theory of cooperation under competition. At the same time, it is curious that Mill and Taylor don't fully address how workers might adapt psychologically to a cooperative mindset of enlarged self-interest, despite Mill's broader understanding of the psychology of associationism.

Nevertheless, Mill and Taylor make a major contribution. More clearly than any of the earlier cooperative theorists, they develop a materialist theory of the historically defined and limited role of capitalist production. Rather than an aside or curiosum, a belief in the transformation of the capitalist's firm into a softer, more democratic cooperative structure stands as a fundamental tenet of their socialism.

MILL AND TAYLOR LIFE STORIES

John Stuart Mill, born in 1806, experienced a childhood without warmth. In the first draft of his lucid *Autobiography* he labels it loveless. He related only superficially with his mother, whom he considered "kind" but lacking in "tenderness and affection." Somewhat oddly for a feminist, the adult J. S. Mill went so far as to blame his mother's dullness for his father's dearth of "feeling."[5]

---

4. In his *Autobiography*, Mill explicitly refers to Taylor and himself as socialists. Famously Friedrich Hayek claims such socialist ideas are really Taylor's and that Mill only flirts with them. A recent book by McCabe (2021) concludes that indeed, it is reasonable to consider Mill as an advocate of socialism. Also see Persky (2019).

5. Persky (2018, 55–56) is the basis for this biographical snapshot. The published version of the *Autobiography* excises virtually all of Mill's discussion of his mother.

If Mill was negative concerning his parents' emotional makeup, he gave much praise to his father James Mill for laying out an aggressive curriculum of home schooling. Greek and Latin studies commenced at an early age. Much Plato, history, and arithmetic as well as the classics of poetry. At fourteen the young Mill took on Ricardo and Smith. In the end he credited his father with providing an excellent education, stimulating his interest in logic and inspiring his understanding of morality.

In 1823 James Mill wangled a position for John Stuart as his assistant in the East India Company. J. S. Mill continued with the company after his father's death in 1830. In 1856 he earned a promotion to the major position of Examiner of Indian Correspondence. In his *Autobiography*, Mill suggested the work at the East India Company left him considerable time for his own interests. Be that as it may, Mill left the company when the Indian Rebellion of 1857 resulted in India's formal merger into the British Empire.

From early in his career, Mill participated in the Utilitarian Society, where members intensively discussed Bentham's works. Mill's first substantive interaction with advocates of cooperation emerged from a debate between the members of the Utilitarian Society and the London Cooperative Society. Given our interest in Mill's eventual championing of cooperation, it is worth a little space here to review his views on the topic as a young man. It is especially interesting to consider his opinions before he met Harriet Taylor. In 1825, Mill aggressively argued the shortcomings of cooperatives in a major dispute with William Thompson. Mill held that the pool of profits promises little in wage gains even if shared (Mill 1988, 315); that cooperatives very likely reduce the level of worker effort; that cooperative management is at best perfunctory; and that it is reasonable to expect a proliferation of regulations of various types (320).

In the debate with Thompson, Mill took great exception to the cooperators' hostilities toward competition. In his notes for his concluding speech, Mill observes that any prosperous system of cooperatives almost necessarily involves competition. "[W]ould there be trade, would there be interchange of commodities, or would there not? If not you are reduced almost to primitive barbarism. But if one Community trades, and exchanges its commodities with other communities, there would still be competition." Rejecting the emphasis on autarchy in much of Owen's and Thompson's writings, Mill in effect argues that cooperatives must necessarily create a new type of competition, not one in which each man is the rival of every other, but rather one in which "one community would be the rival of another community" (Mill 1988, 318). Such thoughts on competition among cooperatives, although delivered as part of an attack on the Owenites,

anticipate elements of Mill's later endorsement of competition in a cooperative mode.[6]

It is the year after the debates that Mill suffered a deep and extended depression.[7] The *Autobiography* poignantly describes his experience: "I was in a dull state of nerves, such as everybody is occasionally liable to: unsusceptible to enjoyment or pleasurable excitement: one of those moods when what is pleasure at other times, becomes insipid or indifferent." He asked himself whether achieving his goals for reforming institutions and opinion would actually make him happy. "And an irrepressible self-consciousness distinctly answered 'No!'" The episode left him fearful that he "has nothing left to live for" (Mill [1873] 1981, 137–139).

Mill was only about twenty years old. He struggled with his demons. He turned to the poetry of Wordsworth. Over the next several years he started to read Coleridge and, perhaps most oddly, became friends with the romantic conservative Thomas Carlyle. Taken with Comte and the Saint-Simonians, he searched for new more humanistic influences. And of these by far the most important was Harriet Taylor, whom he met in 1830.

At that time, Harriet, one year younger than John Stuart, was married to John Taylor and actively parenting their two sons. She was 23 (Jacobs 1998, xii). At a dinner party at their home, the intellectual Mill stood in sharp contrast to her rather dull husband, "a prosperous pharmacist and supporter of radical causes, and a particular patron of political refugees" (Reeves 2007, 80–81). Harriet and John Stuart developed a close relation almost immediately. John Taylor reluctantly accepted the new reality, supporting Harriet in a country residence where she often entertained John Stuart. Biographers generally doubt that the affair had a sexual side. Some doubt that sex was part of the couple's life even after they married in 1851.[8] The possibility that Taylor may have had syphilis, presumably acquired from her first husband, further complicated the Mill–Taylor relationship.[9] As Jacobs points out, a diagnosis of syphilis, at the same time that Harriet became pregnant with her daughter Helen and set out on her relationship with Mill, might explain both her turning away from Taylor

---

6. For a more extensive discussion of the Thompson-Mill debate, see Cinelli and Arthmar (2018).

7. Mill acknowledged more than one episode of depression in his life, but this was the most serious (Mill [1873] 1981, 145).

8. For a review of the opinions of both contemporaries and biographers see Reeves (2007, 149–154).

9. Jacobs discusses the question of syphilis (1998, xxx–xxxii). Jacobs gives evidence in support of the hypothesis but acknowledges that evidence is not conclusive. Still, she writes "we are left with an intriguing proposal that could radically change the way readers see HTM's life and work" (xxxii).

and his generous treatment of her for the rest of his life (Jacobs 1998, xxxii).

Whatever the details of their private life, John Stuart and Harriet were intellectual soulmates. Most pointedly, they both strongly supported the expansion of women's rights. Together and alone, they wrote extensively on the topic. Harriet Taylor's most powerful writing is her essay "Enfranchisement of Women" (Taylor [1851] 1998).[10] Her worldview, here, is clearly that of the Wollstonecraft school of equality feminism.[11] Taylor argues that European society trains women for dependence and drudgery. Under the circumstances, "[h]igh mental powers in women will be but an exceptional accident, until every career is open to them, and until they as well as men, are educated for themselves for the world—not one for the other" (Taylor [1851] 1998, 66).[12] And Taylor, with Mill, writes extensively on domestic violence. She also may have influenced Mill's *Utilitarianism*.[13] Mill in his *Autobiography* ([1873] 1981, 249) asserts that *On Liberty* is virtually a joint product, placing Taylor at the very font of liberalism.[14] Most importantly for our concerns, by Mills' own account, she played the central role in writing the chapter on the future of the laboring classes and cooperation in Mill's *Principles*.[15]

By 1848, in the first edition of *The Principles of Political Economy*, Mill and Taylor adopt a cautious attitude toward producer cooperatives. By 1852,

---

10. Originally published in the *Westminster Review* under Mill's name, there is now common recognition that this piece is Taylor's work (Bodkin 1999, 50; Rossi 1970, 41). Bodkin favorably reviews the case that "Enfranchisement" is superior to Mill's later feminist work, *The Subjection of Women* ([1869] 1984, 49).

11. See Ferguson 2020, 30–39.

12. It is somewhat odd that Taylor does not allude here to the connection between feminism and cooperation, that is social reproduction feminism (Ferguson 2019, 41). But she and Mill include the idea in their famous chapter, "On the Probable Futurity of the Labouring Classes" (Mill [1848] 1965).

13. Jacobs draws attention to the similarities between Mill's discussion of higher and lower pleasures in *Utilitarianism* and Taylor's use of the concept (1998, 17).

14. For an extended discussion of Taylor and Mill's coauthorship of *On Liberty*, see McCabe (2021, 252–255). McCabe suggests Mill and Taylor can be profitably viewed as Rawlsian liberal socialists.

15. From Mill: "The chapter of the *Political Economy* which has had a greater influence on opinion than all the rest, that on the 'Probable Future of the Labouring Classes' is entirely due to her: in the first draft of the book, that chapter did not exist. She pointed out the need of such a chapter, and the extreme imperfection of the book without it . . ." ([1873] 1981, 255). Mill goes on to credit Taylor with contributing the *Principles'* fundamental distinction between "laws of the Production of Wealth" and "the modes of its Distribution" which depend largely on human will. Bodkin makes a case that, by modern standards, Taylor deserves coauthorship of the *Principles*, estimating she contributed about 35% of the volume (1999, 48).

Mill and Taylor are champions of cooperation. There is now a new certainty and pungency to their perspective. The causes of the shift are multilayered and overdetermined.[16]

By the late 1840s, Mill was already in touch with George Jacob Holyoake, the activist-historian of the British cooperative movement and a strong supporter of producer cooperatives. Later editions of the *Principles* quote from Holyoake's work at length. It remains unclear, whether the 1852 revision of the chapter reflects conversations with Holyoake.[17]

More surely, the dramatic events of the 1848 revolution in France impacted Mill and Taylor.[18] The attempts to establish a *droit a travail* (a right to work) in cooperative workshops struck them as the logical extension of the drive for more democratic institutions. While undermined by conservative forces, the record of the revolution's cooperative ventures captured Mill and Taylor's attention. This history takes a permanent place in the *Principles*.

A theoretical base for cooperation is already there in the 1848 edition: Mill's description of the stationary state with its falling rate of profit (Mill [1848] 1965, Vol. IV, Chs. 4–6). Perhaps Mill, reflecting on that theory, increasingly saw it as providing a formal rationale for capital's willingness, even eagerness, to lend to cooperatives. At the same time, by 1852, Mill was married to Harriet, and she potentially played a stronger role in shaping the argument. Taylor was a long-time admirer of Robert Owen's work. In any case, Mill and Taylor came to a new appreciation of the social psychological development of the working classes. Workers' expanding access to both the formal education of the school room and the informal education of the press and politics sets in motion an increasing hostility to the employer-employee relationship.

In the first edition of the *Principles* in 1848, Mill and Taylor strongly endorse systems of profit sharing as discussed by Charles Babbage (1846, Ch. 26).[19] But the ideas on full cooperation remain somewhat sketchy. By

---

16. Throughout the current volume, Mill [1848] 1965 is used to cite the eight editions of *Principles*. It is a variorum edition including all variations on the text over time. Where helpful, we identify the specific edition cited.

17. Mill's correspondence for 1847–1848 includes two letters to Holyoake, but neither concerns cooperatives (Mill 1963, 707 and 741).

18. As discussed in Chapter 5, the events of 1848 in France also stimulated the efforts of Ludlow and the Christian Socialists. Their activities in the early 1850s supporting producer cooperatives win Mill and Taylor's warm praise (Mill [1848] 1965, Vol. II, 786).

19. See Chapter 8 for a discussion of Babbage.

the 1852 edition, however, Mill and Taylor clarify their position, adding a paean to the efforts of the French revolutionaries' cooperative workshops. In this edition and for all the subsequent editions, Mill and Taylor commit to the expansion of worker cooperatives. They now expect profit sharing with its "association of the labourer with the capitalist" to be only a "temporary" expedient. They look forward "finally" to "associations of labourers among themselves" running most all production facilities (Mill [1848] 1965, 769).[20]

Starting in the 1852 edition of the *Principles*, Mill and Taylor quote at length from French works on the cooperative establishments set up in the 1848 revolution and afterwards.[21] It isn't until four years after Taylor's death, in 1862, that Mill recognizes the efforts of British cooperatives in any detail, drawing on Holyoake's history of the Rochdale pioneers (786–788).[22] While broadly supportive of the Rochdale movement, there is concern that its manufacturing society "degenerated" and employed "hired labourers without any interest in the profits" (792). The promise of cooperation rests in its mobilizing "the common interest of all the workers in the work" (792). There is a concern that the more traditionally organized workshops of the Cooperative Wholesale Society, where workers share in neither management nor profits, would be bested by "capitalists" using profit sharing (792).[23] Thus, there is a strong endorsement of producer cooperation vis a vis consumer cooperation. Here, their view aligns with the Christian Socialists.[24] When it comes to producer cooperatives, Mill and Taylor's point is precisely that this institution represents an achievable, indeed necessary, advance on the existing system, by replacing the central employer–employee relationship. For Mill and Taylor, producer cooperatives simultaneously address the alienation of work and the expansion of democracy, while preserving the roles of decentralization and competition in the economy.

20. Starting with the 1862 edition, there is a slight alteration to the wording, substituting "perhaps finally" for "finally."

21. Most notable here is a long quotation from Feugueray, *L'Association Ouvriere Industrielle et Agricole* (1851).

22. Holyoake suggests that Mill's use of his material "did more than any one else to call attention to the proceedings of the Rochdale Pioneers" (Holyoake, 1893, viii). Also see Chapter 6 on the Rochdale movement.

23. Again, see Chapter 6 on the consumer cooperative movement and its wholesaling arm, the Cooperative Wholesale Society.

24. Surprisingly, the vast secondary literature on Mill pays relatively scant attention to his position on producer cooperatives. An exception is Claeys (2013); also see McCabe (2021).

TRANSITION TO A COOPERATIVE ECONOMY

A number of 21st-century scholars explore the character of Mill and Taylor's socialism.[25] There is much in that socialism to attract the attention of modern philosophers, political scientists, and economists. The vision of the current chapter puts particular emphasis on the centrality of coopera- tion to the Mill and Taylor understanding of socialism. At the same time, we underscore the persistent influence of the logic of Mill's classical political economy even as he and Taylor endorse a system designed to do away with the central role of private property. While their vision includes strong nor- mative judgments presumably based on utilitarian morality or ethics, most every element of that vision includes positive propositions about the na- ture of the economic world and or its tendencies for development.[26] We do not say that Mill and Taylor's cooperative socialism can only be considered in this manner, but rather that this mixing of the positive and normative highlights the deeper political economy of progress that Mill constructs.

A Social Psychology of Transition

At the most fundamental level of human social psychology, Mill and Taylor perceive an inclination toward independent self-direction. While fol- lowing classical economists in recognizing a natural indolence in people (Mill [1848] 1965, 795), Mill and Taylor explain much indolence arises as a response to authority-centered social relations that deleteriously tamper with the inclination of self-direction. In reducing workers to mere cogs, the capitalist's firm particularly undermines motivation and initiative. These firms destroy liberty, and the worker's job is poorly done. No wonder workers seek alternatives.

While Mill and Taylor clearly sympathize with such a search, their remarks here are not simply value judgments; rather they are empirical observations of deep historical trends. The social psychology of labor is

---

25. See, for example, Baum (2007), McCabe (2019; 2021), Miller (2003), and Turner (2019).

26. We use the term "positive proposition" here in the sense common in economics, that is as descriptive, whether theoretical or empirical, as distinct from a normative (or judgmental or value-laden) proposition. McCabe (2020) speaks of Mill's normative critique of capitalism, and certainly he has one. That system does not do as well on utilitarian grounds as possible alternatives. But as we argue throughout the current chapter, the cooperative socialist alternative, to which Mill and Taylor look forward, draws heavily on positive theory and empirics.

changing. Moving beyond mere slacking, workers exhibit increasing hostility to the old lines of authority. They are more literate and more capable of independent action. But at the same time, they are not eager to turn backward to an economy of independence based on the inefficiencies of peasant proprietorship and craft production. While such producers might achieve a good deal of independence in a market context, Mill and Taylor believe that modern workers find unappealing a reactionary reversal to the explosion in productivity made possible through economies of scale and modern technologies. Small-scale production is not the tendency of the future ([1848] 1965, 767–768).

In seeking an alternative to the hierarchical and exploitative factory, workers increasingly contemplate a new mode of production: the democratic and self-managed cooperative. In the real world, Mill and Taylor point to possible prototypes in the worker cooperatives of the 1848 French Revolution stimulated by the writings of Louis Blanc (1840). They are glad to see workers energetically exploring the possibilities of the worker-managed cooperative and the "association of labourers themselves on terms of equality, collectively owning the capital with which they carry on their operations, and working under managers elected and removable by themselves" ([1848] 1965, 775). This is the direction of labor's aspirations. This is the direction of progress. The cooperative is promising on moral grounds, and at the same time it looks toward a continuing expansion of productivity.

There are Owenite aspects to Mill's emphasis on cooperation. Owen also considers cooperation as the source of a new efficiency. But Mill and Taylor, like Thompson, put greater weight on the productive promise of democratic cooperation. For them the employment relationship that emerges out of the Industrial Revolution destroys the work life of the laborers while it undermines their motivation. Individuals who necessarily follow the strict authoritarian rule of the manufactory lose control over the construction of their very being and lose interest in production itself. The democracy of the worker-managed cooperative is central to the progress of both productivity and worker self-definition. The new cooperatives are likely to "increase the productiveness of labour . . . by placing the labourers, as a mass, in a relation to their work which would make it their principle and their interest— at present it is neither—to do the utmost, instead of the least possible, in exchange for their remuneration" ([1848] 1965, 791–792). This motivation is to come from being part of an active association, one which normalizes "voluntary obedience" to democratically determined decisions (781). And while building a deeper material base, workers participate in a "moral revolution in society," a revolution that elevates "the dignity of labour" and

renders "each human being's daily occupation into a school of the social sympathies and the practical intelligence." Recall here Mill's broader emphasis on the importance of agency (Donner 1991, Ch. 6).

Not the least of the psychological changes already underway is greater care and prudence in workers' attitudes toward their families. Mill, always fearful of Malthusian pressures on population growth, very much hopes that the new independence of the laboring classes includes limiting population growth. Such a historical development plays a key role in the transition from the wage system to the cooperative mode.

The Institutional Character of Transition

Mill and Taylor clearly identify the democratic cooperative as the institutional base of what they call socialism. It is what Mill has in mind when he says: "I agree with the Socialist writers in their conception of the form which industrial operations tend to assume in the advance of improvement; and I entirely share their opinion that the time is ripe for commencing this transformation, and that it should by all just and effectual means be aided and encouraged" (Mill [1848] 1965, 794). At the time, there was certainly justification for Mill and Taylor's identification of democratic producer cooperatives as the central institutional innovation advocated by the early socialists. Thompson writes of it and Blanc also.

As a contrast, consider the later views of those supporting a national, centrally planned economy. Thus while both Marx and Lenin offer positive commentary about cooperatives, neither man places cooperatives at the center of the socialist struggle.[27] Perhaps nationalization does away with the capitalists, but central planning hardly brings about the type of workers Mill and Taylor anticipate. Lacking any pride of ownership and missing the engagement of self-direction and democracy, workers in the centrally planned firm are almost the antithesis of cooperative workers.[28] National planning creates a huge bureaucracy and massive centralization of power. Mill and Taylor, as classic liberals, fear the social psychology implications from the concentration of power in the state.

As a political economist, Mill also holds a low opinion of the efficiency of the state as producer. The government is "hardly ever able to maintain

27. See Chapter 11 for a discussion of Marx and Lenin's views.
28. The broad 20th-century literature on contradictions and worker alienation in centrally planned economies would be no surprise to Mill and Taylor. See, for example, Lebowitz (2012) and Burawoy (1985, Ch. 4).

itself in equal competition with individual agency." Despite government's wide access to resources, it suffers under "one great disadvantage—an inferior interest in the result."[29] Finally, Mill also argues that state control of every type "partakes, either in great or in small degree, of the degradation of slavery" ([1848] 1965, 938). Nationalized production is no basis for socialism.

In opposition to a range of later socialists, Mill and Taylor side with the early cooperators and strongly endorse the internal structure of the cooperative workplace. But the external institutional structure imagined for such producers is fundamentally different from that anticipated by Owen or Thompson. Most of the major advocates of cooperation in the 19th century see competition in the marketplace as a major negative of the capitalist system. Owen looks to a new system of child-rearing to reduce competitive attitudes and enhance cooperative ones. The Christian Socialists too express deep hostility to competition. The British consumer cooperative movement (see Chapter 6) looks forward to a cooperative commonwealth which largely supersedes competition. And while there is not full agreement among Guild Socialists, their leading system architect, G. D. H. Cole also builds arguments against competition (see Chapter 10). But Mill (and Taylor?) dissents strongly from this broad cooperative consensus. Mill writes that while he supports the expansion of cooperatives, "I utterly dissent from the most conspicuous and vehement part of their [Socialist] teaching, their declamations against competition" ([1848] 1965, 794).

According to Mill, socialists blame competition for "all the economical evils which at present exist." While strongly agreeing with "socialists" on "the form which industrial operations tend to assume in the advance of improvement," the same socialists seem to forget "that wherever competition

---

29. Mill does not explicitly compare state management to cooperative management. Interestingly, though, and despite his broad suspicion of government management, in most cases he ranks the state more efficient than the emerging joint-stock companies. While Mill is sure that the state's bureaucracy is less efficient than the individual proprietor, he is doubtful that such bureaucracy is much worse than the similar bureaucracies of the joint-stock company. He asserts, "Whatever, if left to spontaneous agency, can only be done by joint-stock associations, will often be as well, and sometimes better done, as far as the actual work is concerned, by the state." And Mill goes on, "Government management is, indeed, proverbially jobbing, careless, and ineffective, but so likewise has generally been joint-stock management" ([1848] 1965, 954).

In many ways Mill makes clear his low opinion of joint-stock management. For example, in situations in which small gains or losses depend on vigilantly enforcing a system on the workers, a large capitalist can generally be expected to move decisively. "But the managers of a joint stock concern seldom devote themselves sufficiently to the work to enforce unremittingly, even if introduced, through every detail of the business, a really economical system" (138).

is not, monopoly is; and that monopoly, in all its forms, is the taxation of the industrious for the support of indolence, if not of 'plunder.'" He is sure that "with the exception of competition among labourers, all other competition is for the benefit of the labourers, by cheapening the articles they consume" ([1848] 1965, 794). Here, the young Mill of the debates with Thompson and the mature Mill are one.[30]

Mill is aware, of course, that competition among workers in the labor market offends socialists the most. But he searches behind the market for an explanation of low wages and unemployment. As a good Malthusian, Mill argues the problem is not the market itself, but the high birth rates among British laborers' families. Hence, the importance of a change in worker attitudes toward child-raising. "[I]f the supply of labourers is excessive, not even Socialism can prevent their remuneration from being low" ([1848] 1965, 794–795).[31]

In any case, if cooperatives are the standard form of industrial organization, there would be no competition between "labourer and labourer" only between "association and association" (Mill [1848] 1965, 795).[32] And this type of inter-cooperative competition ultimately benefits all the "industrious classes" in their roles as consumers.

Inter-cooperative competition is a key source of motivation for labor in an economy of transitional cooperatives. Many socialists, according to Mill, fail to take account of the "natural indolence of mankind." Workers achieving "any state of existence which they consider tolerable . . . will not exert themselves to improve . . . . Competition may not be the best conceivable stimulus, but it is at present a necessary one, and no one can foresee the time which it will be indispensable to progress" (795).

Ignoring the arguments of Thompson and Owen, Mill considers competition as central to technological change. It would be difficult to convince "the general assembly of an association" to take the trouble to explore an invention unless they know that "rival associations" are also exploring it (795). It would be unfortunate if the move toward cooperatives results in the reassertion of custom over competitive dynamism. While anticipating much from the revolution in worker social psychology, Mill still holds a central role for the competitive market in the cooperative economy. The important issue not addressed is whether competition undermines the

30. The argument resembles that of Greg in his debate with Ludlow. (See Chapter 5). Most likely Greg borrows Mill's ideas.

31. Mill notes that in 19th-century America where demand for labor exceeds supply, competition among producers tends to raise wages.

32. Mill and Taylor here, as throughout, remain vague on exactly how cooperatives recruit their membership.

enlarged self-interest that most cooperative theorists emphasize as central to cooperation.

The Analytics of Transition

Mill and Taylor describe the rising expectations of the working classes as fundamental to the emergence of democratic cooperatives. But these social psychological changes amount to little if not encouraged by a deterioration of the capitalist economy. Like most classical economists, Mill is reasonably sure that as an empirical matter the rate of return on capital is falling, indeed falling toward zero. This piece of empiricism plays a central role in Mill's hopes for a new cooperative economy. Then capitalists may retire from the scene, ultimately leaving most of their capital in the hands of worker associations. While the cooperatives may not be as adventurous with respect to technology as individual owners, the combination of rising wages, falling profit rates, and the attractiveness of working in the expanding cooperatives will leave capitalists on the sidelines.

Profits decline for several likely reasons. First the accumulation of capital proceeds apace, as capitalists continue to save. Second, if better educated workers begin to exercise control over their family size, then a slower growth of population puts upward pressure on wage rates. Finally, the new producer cooperatives increasingly attract the best workers, leaving only those with "little understanding" and "little virtue" for the more traditional factories.[33]

Mill identifies the economy with close to zero profits as a stationary state. In a country like Britain, "the rate of profit is habitually within, as it were, a hand's breadth of the minimum, and the country therefore on the very verge of the stationary state." While the stationary state will not come "soon" it will "require but a short time to reduce profits to the minimum," if no counter-tendencies come into play ([1848] 1965, 738). Mill, anticipating Marx, provides an insightful discussion of the counter-tendencies to a falling rate of profit (Persky 2016, 84). While the argument is perceptive, it remains a bit vague on just how strong the counter-tendencies are likely to be.

In any case, the early experiments with cooperatives face serious problems in obtaining capital. Mill and Taylor express uncertainty about

---

33. See Persky, *The Political Economy of Progress*, pp. 81–88 and 145–148; Mill [1848] 1965, 793.

the wisdom of turning to the national government in such circumstances. More impressive are the efforts of the workers themselves to generate capital from pooling their tools and their modest savings. In the case of France in 1848, the long-term viability of those associations which obtain loans from the government seems dubious, given the poorer track record of such enterprises compared to those that self-finance.

Still, Mill and Taylor are optimistic of the possibilities of private borrowing by cooperatives. If traditional capitalist enterprises find a world of low profits unsupportive, such an environment suits cooperatives well. Almost by definition, capital is abundant and relatively easy to find. And with profits low, borrowing capital is cheap. In the future "instead of maintaining the struggle of the old system with work-people of only the worst description" capitalists might "lend their capital to the associations." Over time the loan rates decrease, reflecting the falling profit rate. In the end, many capitalists simply "exchange their capital for terminable annuities" (Mill [1848] 1965, 793).[34]

Thus, at least in Britain, Mill and Taylor anticipate the capitalist will peacefully give up the stage to the new system of cooperatives.[35] As the above discussion of the falling rate of profit demonstrates, the times are auspicious for a peaceful transition from a capitalist to a cooperative economy without any need for expropriation or violence. Mill and Taylor look for justice, but they take as primary the need for rectification not by violence, but along peaceful and evolutionary lines.[36] Whatever

---

34. While generally sympathetic to Mill's insights on cooperation, Henry Fawcett offers a different view on lending. (See the section on the Mill School in this chapter.)

35. Miller (2003) emphasizes the peacefulness of the transition in "Mill's 'Socialism.'"

36. The emphasis on peaceful evolution as opposed to violent revolution is a common theme among a range of other early socialists. William Thompson is clear about voluntariness of exchange and non-expropriation of land and capital as early as 1824 (see Chapter 3). The Christian Socialists commit to a cooperative economy and see the movement in that direction as fundamentally peaceful (see Chapter 5). Later in the century, the British Fabians follow Mill and Taylor and take an essentially evolutionary approach. But they largely reject cooperative production. The Fabian socialists emphasize working through the political sphere, trade union expansion, and nationalization of industries. Simply committing to an evolutionary approach does not mean taking cooperation and the employment relation as a primary focus. (See Chapter 11 for the critique of producer cooperatives by the Fabian Beatrice Potter (1891) and the later assessment of cooperation coauthored with her husband, Sidney Webb (1921)). Nonviolence also plays a central role for many German Social Democrats including Eduard Bernstein. Note his discussion of cooperatives in *Evolutionary Socialism* ([1899] 1967), 109–134). Of course, other 19th-century socialists, especially those who emphasize nationalization of industry, anticipate the central role of violence and expropriation in their understanding of socialist transformation. Mill and Taylor certainly defer. One could hardly imagine them endorsing Marx and Engels' dictatorship of the proletariat.

provocation in the experiences of the French workers, many do peacefully take up cooperation. Justice is "not by robbing the capitalists of what they or their predecessors had acquired by labour and preserved by economy, but by honestly acquiring capital for themselves" (775).[37] British workers do well to imitate the example.

Mill and Taylor summarize their understanding of transition as follows:

> In this or some such mode, the existing accumulations of capital might honestly, and by a kind of spontaneous process, become in the end the joint property of all who participate in their productive employment: a transformation, which thus effected (and assuming of course that both sexes participate equally in the rights and in the government of the association), would be the nearest approach to social justice and the most beneficial ordering of industrial affairs for the universal good, which it is possible at present to foresee. (Mill [1848] 1965, 793–794)

Finally notice in the above quote, that while they don't develop the theme, Mill and Taylor insist on gender equality among workers in cooperatives. Both rights and governing involve both sexes. It is not clear how such a position relates to Mill's later discussion of the division of labor in the family, *Subjection of Women* (Mill [1869] 1984, 298). There Mill, with only minor qualifications, endorses the traditional arrangement with husbands in the labor force and their wives staying at home.[38] In the *Subjection of Women*, Mill makes no reference to the trend toward cooperative production hypothesized in *Principles*. Perhaps, the two statements can be reconciled if only single women participate in cooperative production. But that leaves married women outside the cooperative orbit. The resulting gender (in)equality falls far short of what Thompson and Wheeler envisioned.

THE LONG RUN: AN INCOMPLETE THEORY

It remains unclear precisely how Mill and Taylor envision the final steps of transition. Mill's sketch of the economics of cooperative competition

37. Mill and Taylor note that the confiscation of existing capital is "imagined by many persons and pretended by more to be the meaning and purpose of Socialism" ([1848] 1965, 775).

38. Mill holds a position that largely excludes married women from work outside the home. His position has led to an extensive literature on whether such a stand is consistent with a utilitarianism that supports justice. See Sigot and Beaurain (2011).

remains unfinished. As an accomplished classical economist, Mill was certainly aware that in the classical view the central role of competition is to equalize profits and thus allocate capital to the most profitable employments. Mill's endorsement of some competition among cooperatives is painfully incomplete. How will failing cooperatives be disassembled? Will workers from those associations be moved to new units or into old units? Will they keep some rights in the community's capital? How in the long run will capital be transferred to the more effective cooperatives? The lack of a full theory of competition under a cooperative regime seems surprising for an economist of Mill's stature and ability. Mill does acknowledge that in some important sense the stimulus provided by competition may not be the best ([1848] 1965, 795). Over time does this mean the cooperative system might be able to lessen the structural role of competition? Mill doesn't tell us. Through the *Principles'* several editions, Mill continued to rework the chapter on the probable future of laboring classes, but he added little serious theory to the presentation.

A closely related issue arises from a speculation on wage payments. Elsewhere in the *Principles*, Mill asserts that "proportioning of remuneration to work done is really just, only in so far as more or less of the work is a matter of choice . . . ." Proportional remuneration is a "compromise with the selfish type of character formed by the present standard of morality, and fostered by the existing institutions, it is highly expedient; and until education shall have been entirely regenerated, is far more likely to prove immediately successful, than an attempt at a higher ideal" (Mill [1848] 1965, 210).

It would be a small step to endorse the ideas of Owen and Thompson and Wheeler on the long-term development of character in the cooperative setting. J. S. Mill is, after all, an adherent of association psychology. The chapter on cooperation in the *Principles* only highlights profit sharing as an intermediate institutional arrangement to accommodate selfishness and provide a training ground to enlarge self-interest. That chapter seems to cry out for a discussion of how cooperative institutions further develop an expanded sense of self as one in a community.

It is not hard to address this lacuna in very Millean terms. James Mill published *Phenomena of the Mind* in 1829.[39] J. S. carefully studied James' work as well as the antecedent by David Hartley (1749). J. S. Mill republished *Phenomena* with detailed commentary.

---

39. J. S. describes James as the "second founder of the Association psychology" with this 1829 publication (J. S. Mill, ed. 1878, xii).

Phenomena begins with a detailed examination of the basic elements of mental experience: sensations arising through the senses. The law of association explains how ideas of external objects form from such sensory experiences. Simple ideas, or copies of sensation, appear in the mind and can reappear even after a sensation ends (J. S. Mill 1878, 52). Complex ideas then arise from series of sensations, as combinations of simple ideas, or other complex ideas (115). The strength of the mental associations depends on (a) the extent to which pain or pleasure arise with the sensory experiences and (b) the frequency of experience (83–88). The edition with commentary covers the nuances of the psychology of association as both Mills understand it, including the law of recognition, false association, and the "law of Oblivescence" (102).[40] In both sensation and in ideas are feelings, and James Mill suggests the word "conscious" as a synonym for the feeling state that corresponds either to a sensation or to an idea (224–225).

In Volume II of *Phenomena of the Mind*, James Mill identifies feelings of pleasure and pain resulting from sensory experiences as "the springs of human action" (J.S. Mill (ed.) 1878 Vol. II, 143–144). In the case of a sensation associated with a pleasurable feeling (or state of consciousness), the mind forms a copy of the experience and marks that state with the name "pleasure." When the ideas of a class of pleasurable sensations arise, these might be called "Desire" (151). Sympathy or love are the names for states of consciousness arising with thoughts of the causes of past pleasant sensations (161). Conversely, antipathy and hatred are names of states of consciousness associated with remembrances of painful past sensations (159–160). Here James Mill effectively reduces love to pleasure and hate to pain. Now for the utilitarian James Mill, "the grand cause of all our pleasures are the services of our fellow-creatures" (165).[41] It is across repeated experiences that the association of a train of pleasure (or the removal of pain) cements bonds among people. While a person only feels their own pains and pleasures, it is possible to associate those ideas of pain and pleasure with others (175).[42] The more attention one person gives to the

---

40. The law of oblivescence describes situations in which the consequences of a series of sensations capture so much attention that there is missing awareness of the antecedents, whether they be sensory experiences or ideas. James Mill explains the idea; J. S. both names and further explores the law.

41. But typically people misconstrue the causes of happiness as deriving from the wealth, power, or dignity that can procure services (see J.S. Mill. ed. 1878 Vol. II, 165–172).

42. As William Godwin highlights much earlier on, sympathetic associations begin in infancy (see Chapter 2).

pains or pleasures of another, the greater the association (177). Conversely, "where there is not a habit of forming the associations, the Affection does not exist" (182). James Mill provides an extensive discussion of prudence, fortitude, justice, and beneficence, all of which tend to elicit a stream of pleasures and call up the feelings of sympathy and love (233–250).

Given the philosophical adherence to associationism, from a Millean perspective how might cooperation generate and reinforce the enlarged self-interest so central to its understanding of social psychology? As Thompson understood, cooperative institutions must frequently stimulate pleasurable sensory experiences.[43] If James Mill is correct, this would include building institutional structures that reflect the specific virtues of prudence, fortitude, justice, and beneficence. Cooperative institutions encourage a habit of sensitivity to the pains and pleasures of others along with the desire to serve the wellbeing of others. And cooperative institutional antecedents to the pleasurable experiences must be obviously recognizable to evade false associations and "oblivescence."

In *Utilitarianism* J. S. Mill (and Taylor?) make quite clear the ideal evolved character among the population at large. Consider Mill's famous comparison of the ethics of utility to Jesus' golden rule:

> In the golden rule of Jesus of Nazareth, we read the complete spirit of the ethics of utility. To do as one would be done by, and to love one's neighbour as oneself, constitute the ideal perfection of utilitarian morality. As the means of making the nearest approach to this ideal, utility would enjoin, first, that laws and social arrangements should place the happiness, or (as speaking practically it may be called) the interest, of every individual, as nearly as possible in harmony with the interest of the whole; and secondly, that education and opinion, which have so vast a power over human character, should so use that power as to establish in the mind of every individual an indissoluble association between his own happiness and the good of the whole; especially between his own happiness and the practice of such modes of conduct, negative and positive, as regard for the universal happiness prescribes: so that not only he may be unable to conceive the possibility of happiness to himself, consistently with conduct opposed to the general good, but also that a direct impulse to promote the general good may be in every individual one of the habitual motives of action, and the sentiments connected therewith may fill a large and prominent place in every human being's sentient existence. (Mill [1863] 1987, 288)

---

43. Early on in transition, it might be sufficient that the pre-cooperative institutions (like profit sharing) significantly reduce painful experiences associated with participation in competitive institutions.

Elsewhere *Utilitarianism* asserts that experience with cooperation encourages a broadening of self-interest: "[People] are also familiar with the fact of co-operating with others, and proposing to themselves a collective, not an individual, interest, as the aim (at least for the time being) of their actions" (304). It is odd that *Utilitarianism* does not explicitly invoke a system of cooperative organization as the framework for these developments. Owen and Thompson and Wheeler precisely highlight this type of enlarged self-interest emerging in their cooperatives. As discussed in Chapters 2 and 3, those authors go further and assert that only a cooperative system can create such an individual. And *Utilitarianism* anticipates that society reaches a point where a "feeling of unity [is] taught as a religion." Then "the whole force of education, of institutions, and of opinion . . . make every person grow up from infancy surrounded on all sides both by the profession and by the practice of it" (305). Although there is no citation of Owen here, this passage has a strong Owenite flavor. It is hard to imagine any social context other than cooperation underlying such passages.

THE MILL SCHOOL
William Thornton

By the 1860s, Mill's position on cooperative production was well known. It gave rise to a cooperative school of thought that for a period attracted the interest of British economists. In 1869, his former colleague in the East India Company and close friend William Thornton (1813–1880) published a monograph, *On Labour: Its Wrongful Claims and Rightful Dues, Its Actual Present and Possible Future* (1869).[44] Mill and Thornton disagreed on many subjects, but on the question of cooperatives, Thornton strongly supported Mill's position.

Thornton starts his section on "Labour and Capital in Alliance" with a chapter on profit sharing, or "industrial partnerships." Citing Mill, the section expands on Mill's treatment while using many of Mill's sources. As apparent in Mill's thought, the section concludes that there is ultimately limited scope for profit sharing, leaving the bulk of workers unaffected.[45] But his work is much more optimistic about "Cooperative Societies." The societies are clearly producer cooperatives since there is a separate chapter

44. It is at least in part in response to this volume that Mill changes his mind on the wage-fund theory. For a discussion of Thornton's influence on Mill, see Kurer (1998).
45. See Chapter 8 for a broader discussion of profit sharing.

on "Cooperative Stores." The most original contribution is to suggest that while groups of relatively unskilled workers cannot split up the management function among themselves, they are "quite competent to provide for their own government. It does not follow that because they cannot directly manage their own affairs, they cannot procure or devise proper machinery of management" (Thornton 1869, 416).

Only a few highly capital-intensive industries are likely to remain noncooperative in form (Thornton 1869, 431). Admittedly, the full spread of cooperation "will be reached only by gradual steps, but arrival at it is to all appearance certain" (432). Once achieved, the cooperative system is likely to greatly curtail poverty. Mill explicitly states that he fully agrees with Thornton's treatment of cooperation.[46]

As for cooperative stores, Thornton chides them. While cooperation broadly "means working together," this chapter reverts to a narrow definition of industrial cooperation as "not simply working together, but working together with a common object, in which all the workers are interested in proportion to the shares they severally take in the work." The "only fault" of the cooperative stores "is their assuming a title that does not rightly belong to them, and thereby professing to do something which is not within their province, and which they consequently leave undone. They call themselves 'cooperative,' while there is really nothing cooperative about them." Store members do no work, "they only trade together." And as to their treatment of workers, the stores fail here as well in their complete disregard for the sharing of profits (389). Nonetheless, his aptly renamed "associative" stores are instrumental in the overall movement. The stores assist in a broader diffusion of capital, and they provide the "special training" for the cooperative workforce in "patience, self-denial, conscientiousness, and public spirit—on which mutual confidence most firmly rests" ([1869] 1967, 390).

Despite his influence on Mill, Thornton remained something of an amateur political economist. More central to the discipline were Henry Fawcett and J. E. Cairnes, both clearly Millean in outlook. While neither achieved the highest rank of success in the profession, they each wrote an influential textbook in the Millean spirit. Each included endorsements of cooperative production.

---

46. Toward the end of his famous essay, "Thornton on Labour and Its Claims," Mill writes, "The reader may be referred to Mr. Thornton for a conclusive answer to the hesitations concerning the probabilities of success of this great movement [i.e. cooperative production], as well as for an inspiring picture of the blessings to human society which may rationally be expected from its progressive realization" (Mill [1869] 1967, 667).

Henry Fawcett

Adapting to blindness in his twenties, Henry Fawcett (1833–1884) demonstrated substantial talents in a range of fields. In academics, he attained the rank of Professor of Political Economy at Cambridge in 1863, where he remained until 1884, publishing widely and distinguishing himself politically as a Liberal MP and as Postmaster-General under Prime Minister William Gladstone (Stephen 1885). Fawcett married the suffragist Millicent Garrett Fawcett (1847–1929) who made contributions to economic thought in her own right.[47] The two of them were an active radical-liberal couple, very much in the Mill–Taylor tradition.[48]

In his political economy, Fawcett served as a devoted disciple of John Stuart Mill. Fawcett's coverage of profit sharing and cooperatives in an 1860 *Westminster Review* article reflects Mill's influence. And Fawcett identifies his textbook, *Manual of Political Economy* (1863) as simply an introduction to Mill's *Principles*.[49] Like Mill's *Principles*, Fawcett's *Manual* includes a substantial chapter on cooperatives. Stronger than Mill in his adherence to laissez-faire, Fawcett conveys all endorsements of cooperatives as consistent with his traditional liberal views.

In 1871, Fawcett published *Pauperism: Its Causes and Remedies*.[50] The volume offers a "strictly scientific" definition of cooperation as "a union between capital and labour" (1871, 184).[51] That is, any truly cooperative enterprise requires that all the workers and only the workers within the enterprise supply the capital. For Fawcett, worker-supplied capital is the central requirement of cooperation.

---

47. See, for example, Millicent Garrett Fawcett's *Political Economy for Beginners* (1870), "The Position of Women in Economic Life" (1917) and "Equal Pay for Equal Work," published in *Economic Journal* (1918).

48. After Henry Fawcett's death in 1884, Millicent becomes a leader of the moderate suffragists.

49. There are eight editions of *Manual* through 1907, with Millicent Garrett taking sole responsibility for preparing the editions after Fawcett's death in 1884. This review of Fawcett's thought about cooperation from *Manual* focuses on the first edition.

50. This book draws from his lectures on poverty at the University of Cambridge. Millicent Garrett was the stimulus for the lecture series, and she served as editor facilitating formal publication. In *Pauperism*, Fawcett takes a classical liberal stance. For example, as a form of "indiscriminate almsgiving," the poor laws are the cause of voluntary poverty, with "leniency and want of firmness" demoralizing inclinations to work (1871, 9). Following Mill, Chapter 4 advocates universal public education as one relevant remedy for poverty.

51. Fawcett presented the definition at least as early as 1860 in "Strikes: their Tendencies and their Remedies" (1860, 11).

Fawcett anticipates the shift to full cooperatives thus: as the intelligence of workers grows, that "[i]ntelligence induces combinations" (1860, 13). Initially, the combinations arise contentiously as strikes, with large costs for all. The costs stimulate employers and workers to realize they are better off amicably negotiating higher wages in good times when business "can afford to make the advance" (8). To Fawcett, such voluntary and amicable negotiations are evidence of partnerships arising between employer and employed (8). More intentional partnerships appear when employers with no direct experience of striking workers nonetheless voluntarily establish co-partnerships by sharing profits with their workers (9). Either way, "combination tends to create a partnership" (13). And such partnerships "inevitably lead the labourer to . . . higher forms of co-operation, in which the labourer and capitalist are combined as one individual" (11). There are two central requirements for the shift to full cooperation with workers serving as their own capitalists: (i) to dissolve dependence on financiers, workers must acquire "habits of prudence which would induce the accumulation of the necessary funds"; and (ii) effective management must be in place (12).

Going beyond mere repetition of the French cooperative experiences elaborated on by Mill and Taylor, Fawcett (1860) relays glowing accounts of three British producer cooperatives, including the Rochdale cooperative cotton mill. Initially established in 1855, high returns inspired Rochdale to construct a second mill in 1859 (12).

Fawcett later updates readers on the experience of the Rochdale cotton mill, which relied on capital from its own workers as well as from outside the manufactory. When the U. S. Civil War reduced cotton supplies in the early 1860s, the old capital–labor conflict reasserted itself across the two groups of capital provisioners, with the non-laboring claimants of profit prevailing. As Fawcett describes it, the Rochdale cotton manufactory devolved into a joint stock business paying dividends to capital (1871, 197). Beyond advocating labor as the sole source of capital, from this example Fawcett generally discourages cooperative production in industries that are subject to erratic returns and speculation.

The first editions of *Manual* and *Pauperism* both offer cautionary encouragement toward cooperative production. *Manual* argues for careful selectivity: "[T]he cooperative principle can be most advantageously applied to those branches of industry whose success is mainly determined by the skill, care and energy of the individual workman" (1863, 293). Where intelligent and moral worker-owners run cooperatives, there is enhanced productivity. Feeling "that the entire results of their labour will be their own" worker-owners become thrifty, self-denying, and energetic (1871, 185). Perhaps in part reflecting Mill and Taylor's focus on independent

self-direction, Fawcett cannot overstate the importance of the "sentiment of self-reliance" (190). And worker-centered infusions of capital provide the escape from capital–labor conflict.

While Fawcett is cautiously optimistic about producer cooperatives under specific circumstances, he expresses reservations about the organization of "communistic society" as reflected in early 19th-century cooperative thought (1871, 203). Fawcett refers vaguely to great future advantages from such cooperative organization, but he warns "that the people are not yet sufficiently advanced for its general adoption" (205).

Thus qualified, Fawcett does speculate about the evolution of economic systems toward communistic cooperation. The first stage of profit sharing more fully unifies capital and labor.[52] This stage requires "higher intellectual and moral training" among the workforce (1871, 198). The next stage involves the provisioning of all capital by all the workers within an enterprise. In order to succeed here, the cooperators must embody the following "essential qualities": mutual confidence; the knowledge to select from among themselves the best managers; the "moral courage to submit to" the orders of those managers; and a capacity to save in years of prosperity (200). Cooperative success is most likely in nonagricultural industries that are relatively stable and nonspeculative, relatively labor intensive, and relatively small scale so it is easier for workers to raise the necessary capital (200–202).

Fawcett finds it "hazardous to venture a prediction" as to the rate of progress toward "the general adoption of co-operation" (1871, 199). Beyond the substandard level of education among the working class, Fawcett criticizes "indiscriminate almsgiving" as misperceived support for cooperation. All such philanthropic gestures misguide workers, who "must rely upon their own efforts for success" (194).

While rejecting philanthropy and remaining generally critical of British cooperative history, over time in the revisions of *Manual*, Fawcett moves to a stronger endorsement of producer cooperatives, taking a position more like that of Mill. It seems that the shift reflects Fawcett's heightened concern over the expanding popularity of centralizing "socialistic schemes" dependent on the "direct intervention of the state" (1888, 281). Fawcett finds such schemes fundamentally destructive. In contrast, cooperatives "place their chief reliance in union of effort, in prudence, and in self-denial." Fawcett eagerly endorses such virtues in contrast to the shortcomings of nationalization. Under the circumstances, he suggests, "[w]e may look with

---

52. Chapter 8 details Fawcett's ideas on profit sharing.

more confidence to cooperation than to any other economic agency to improve the industrial condition of the country" (280).

John Elliott Cairnes

Like Fawcett, Mill's other major disciple, J. E. Cairnes (1823–1875) made a strong endorsement of producer cooperatives as a solution to the capital–labor conflict. In his lifetime, most associate Cairnes with his 1862 study *The Slave Power*. Over a century-and-a-half later, Cairnes retains a reputation for his development of the theory of noncompeting groups. In 1874 (one year after Mill's death and one year before his own), Cairnes published an overview of economics entitled *Some Leading Principles of Political Economy, Newly Expounded*. This volume contains an extended discussion of cooperatives.

Cairnes starts with a defense of private property, much more aggressive than any offered by Mill. Based on the private property defense Cairnes, like Fawcett, rejects any socialist proposals for nationalization or direct redistribution of capital. Cairnes also opposes any favorable financial terms for worker cooperatives. Instead, he insists that progress depends on the establishment of worker cooperatives financed through the savings of workers. "If the laborer is to emerge from his present position and become a sharer in the gains of capital, he must in the first instance learn to save" (1874, 288). Cairnes is cautiously optimistic that reductions in working-class expenditures on alcohol can provide a major source of funds. Beyond that, workers need to develop "habits of saving . . . intelligence, and still more the moral qualifications, required for effective cooperation" (290). Like Fawcett, Cairnes also looks forward to the improvements in workers' capacities through the establishment of government-funded universal education.

Cairnes doubts any significant increase in workers' material conditions via wage increases. The "general capital" of a country grows far faster than the "wages-capital." The "emancipation of labor" ultimately results only through the path of cooperatives. "If workmen do not rise from dependence upon capital by the path of cooperation, then they must remain in dependence upon capital" (1874, 291).

In the end, Cairnes looks forward to a "regime of cooperative industry." He hypothesizes that such a regime strengthens the moral and prudential character of the working classes. Workers participating in cooperatives become more like peasant proprietors, clearer about the fund available for support of the household. Under such circumstances, Cairnes is optimistic

about the blunting of Malthusian overpopulation, as workers take more responsibility for their own welfare.

While Cairnes clearly pins great hopes on the cooperative movement, he provides little in the way of serious analysis of the efficiency or the long-term prospects of cooperative production. There are a couple of passing references to Fawcett's discussion of particular cooperative enterprises, but no theoretical argument for the efficiency of producer cooperatives. Following the Mill school understanding of social psychology, for Cairnes the driving question concerns the potential for worker independence and self-direction.

A LEGACY

What are we to make of Mill's endorsement of socialism? Certainly it is socialism but, just as certainly, this vision builds on democratic worker cooperatives engaged in competitive production. More explicitly than any of the other radical reforms endorsed by Mill, the projected progress toward cooperative production underscores the conviction that the economic system of the mid-19th century is ultimately a transitory formation. From a perspective anticipating Marx's historical materialism, the very progress of accumulating capital and expanding the outlook of workers sets the stage for a more humane and participatory system. Material conditions lay the groundwork for the transition. The employer–employee relation of the wage system is still a hindrance to the growth of productivity, while producer cooperatives result in much higher productivity.

It is unfortunate that Mill didn't construct a more complete theory of the cooperative economy. Nevertheless, John Stuart Mill became the first prominent British political economist to embrace the possibilities of cooperatives, seeing them as both normatively attractive and economically efficient. Among mainstream British economists, the possible evolution of the employment relation loomed large at mid-century. For a moment, with Mill's endorsement, it occupied a central place. The mainstream first seemed to move with Mill and Taylor but, toward the end of the century, opted at most for a modest program of profit sharing. Ironically, by this time, much of the left, which historically championed cooperative production, rejected the popular socialism of Owen and turned toward nationalization and central planning. By the early 20th century, the Mill–Taylor message resonated only with the Guild Socialists who kept the radical argument for producer cooperatives alive.

PART II

Paths

Workshops, Stores, and the Domestic Economy

Mill and Taylor present an analysis of the arc of history. They forecast the organic transformation of the economy into a cooperative mode of production. And indeed, cooperation in Britain was no longer about villages and small communities. It arose from inside the workshops, factories, and stores of the capitalist system. The analysis of the new social science turns toward the problems of cooperatives emerging in direct competition with profit-making enterprises. How in practice can cooperation address the broad selfishness of the economy surrounding them? The Christian Socialists debate hierarchy in cooperative theory. Advocates of profit sharing analyze its implications for productivity, conflict mitigation, and broader human development. At the same time, the Women's Cooperative Guild identifies and challenges the patriarchy and business mentality endemic in the movement. In the process of facing these challenges, the social science continues to develop its rich social psychology even as proposing critical institutional structures. The result is a set of piecemeal, but not yet fully integrated theoretical insights. Most interesting is what we call the consumer cooperators' federalist theorem which identifies the flow of economic surplus in their version of the cooperative commonwealth.

CHAPTER 5

⌒∿⌒

Cooperation in Christ's Kingdom

THE CHRISTIAN SOCIALISTS

As the cooperative movement picked up steam in mid-century Great Britain, an eccentric combination of Christian men recognized the potential synergy between their faith and the budding socioeconomic system. The leaders of what comes to be known as Christian socialism effectively promoted the idea that cooperation can harness religiosity to energize its social psychology. In the context of their specific religious beliefs, these men advocated the mature decision to accept, or more accurately, to embrace Christ. A deep internal drive for union with God operates as the motivating force of their social psychology. The result is selflessness, sacrifice, forgiveness, and fellowship. In practical terms, realization of that union with God requires daily engagement to establish Christ Kingdom's on Earth, beginning with cooperative associations of workers. One of the group's lawyers, John Ludlow, made an important empirical observation that even among the fiercest of competitive firms, concert and coordination govern internal operations, not competition. For the Christian Socialists, the partial application was insufficient. They based concert on a deeper cooperative fellowship that fully replaces competition.

As an effective group, the Christian Socialists lasted only a few years. A major unresolved difference arose concerning industrial organization. E. V. Neale, the group's chief financial backer, promoted concert through centralized hierarchy. He made some headway within the consumer cooperative movement. The theologian and leader of the group, F. D. Maurice resigned. He feared that hierarchy and system, like all efforts to draw good

Building a Social Science. Kirsten Madden and Joseph Persky, Oxford University Press. © Oxford University Press 2024.
DOI: 10.1093/oso/9780197693735.003.0005

from evil, must fail. The effort to move in such a direction demonstrated that everyday people were not yet "ready" for true cooperation. Maurice's understanding of cooperation stands in sharp contrast to the more authoritarian transitional approach of Robert Owen. While several of the Christian Socialists continued to play important roles in the cooperative movement, they gave up the explicitly religious ideology of the group. Maurice abandoned cooperation and shifted his energies to Christian-centered human development in the context of a working men's college.

BEFORE THE 19TH CENTURY

Across the historical record, building a defense of private property challenged religious writers. Western religions are replete with strong suggestions that some other form of economic organization is more in keeping with the moral teachings of the Holy Book. It does not require much religious imagination to conclude that the aggressive, often deceptive, and sometimes violent competition of the marketplace is inconsistent with God's hopes for those made in God's image. From the Hebrew prophets to the Apostolic community, from the Franciscan orders to the Anabaptists, many religious questioned the roles of private property and competition, turning instead to various cooperative structures.

Most telling in preindustrial Britain were claims for sharing land. Several dissenting sects looked toward establishing cooperatives. In English history the Diggers of the Cromwellian period (1649) harkened to their leader Gerrard Winstanley's call:

> Not Inclosing any part into any particular hand, but all as one man, working together, and feeding together as Sons of one Father, members of one Family; not one Lording over another, but all looking upon each other, as equals in the Creation; so that our Maker may be glorified in the work of his own hands, and that every one may see, he is no respecter of Persons, but equally loves his whole Creation (Winstanley, 1649).

Rich in biblical references, Winstanley's claim for cooperation is that it cultivates common work as the completion of God's will.

In the 18th century, various British dissenting religious groups promoted a range of economic reforms. One that survived by emigrating to America was the Shakers, who eventually established a number of communities after the American Revolution. The Shakers followed Revelations' demand that they avoid all contact between the sexes and hold their property in common (Stein 1992).

The potential for religiosity to sway opinion should not be understated. A religious grounding elicits a particular social value system, thus lending moral status to a movement. Religious argumentation also draws upon an authority commonly ascribed to religious presuppositions, historical events and people, illustrations, and parables. The mid-century Christian Socialists were not the first of the 19th-century British cooperators to invoke religion in their quest to build a better society. Lucas (2019) identifies many within the Owenite movement of the 1820s and 1830s who made religious arguments to critique capitalist norms, such as property relations and inequality. Other Owenites applied their religious imaginations to envision and argue for a cooperative future of bread labor and communal living.

None of these groups were recognized contributors to the mainstream Anglican theology. But in the middle of the 19th century the Christian Socialists burst on the scene. They tied their arguments for cooperative production to the cutting-edge Anglican theology of F. D. Maurice. The religion of the Christian Socialists de-emphasizes sin and punishment while seeking union with God through human fellowship.

For the most part originating on the margins of the upper and middle classes, Maurice and his Christian Socialist colleagues found appalling the venal and un-Christian behavior of the new capitalists created by the Industrial Revolution. Their version of social science built on an Anglican understanding of social psychology. And working from that base, they concluded that Christianity and cooperation are two sides of the same coin. Acceptance of Christ's Kingdom necessarily implies a rejection of selfishness and a commitment to communal production (Raven 1920, 307). Beyond their leading theologian Maurice, the most notable of the Christian Socialists were two lawyers, John Ludlow and E. V. Neale, and the clergyman-author Charles Kingsley.[1]

Like the Owenites, their sincere experiments at cooperation ended in abject failure. Unlike Owen and Thompson, they did not construct compelling blueprints for cooperative communities. The worker associations they helped found lasted only a few years. Nevertheless, their theoretical work uncovered a major cooperative issue. They brought to the forefront of cooperative thought a fundamental debate concerning the extent to which structures of institutional hierarchy must complement individual goodness. Indeed, their practical cooperative efforts ran aground on the

---

1. Thomas Hughes, later the author of *Tom Brown's School Days* and an MP is often mentioned as part of the group's inner circle.

fundamental question. But nonetheless, they strongly influenced two central cooperative institutions: working-class education and a parallel movement in consumer cooperation.

CLASS ORIGINS

Whatever their doubts about the logic of British agrarian and commercial society, the religious faced a range of new challenges stemming from the Industrial Revolution of the late 18th century. Fundamental to the new society was a major shift in class structure. Where the bulk of the labor force previously worked in agriculture, now the new class of capitalists in mechanized factories directly employed a larger and larger share. Like Robert Owen himself, the new capitalists started with virtually none of the traditional historic trappings of English landowners. Many began as workers themselves. Many were nonconformists. As a group they seemed unwilling to acknowledge their complicity in the spread of urban poverty that was regularly intensified by cyclical downturns. Not a few gushed the newly minted (soon to be classical) liberal ideology of competition. For the religious of all classes, such self-made parvenus appeared highly suspect.

Under the circumstances, it is not surprising that the sincerely religious should explore the possibilities inherent in an alternative cooperative organization of production. Indeed, of all the advocates of cooperation the religious are perhaps the most obvious. A gospel of cooperation is a straightforward extension of a religious point of view which holds the conviction that God intends something of a heaven on earth.

Nor is it surprising that among the religious in Britain, the strongest theorists, propagandists, and promoters of cooperation arrived from the complex and heterogeneous social groupings that generated the literate middle classes of the 19th century. Their economic base was nothing if not diverse: the orthodox church, the dissenting churches, the law, the second sons of the landed gentry, and imperial adventurers from India and the Caribbean. Such were the origins of the tight-knit group that took the name Christian Socialists. For several, their middle-class positions suggested elements of downward mobility as these men often lived off the earnings of previous generations. But somehow out of the marginal social position of their upbringing and their turn toward religious sincerity, they emerged with a positive conception of the possibilities open to the normal run of people.

Consider first John Ludlow (1821–1911), the man who introduced the Christian Socialists to French cooperative thought. He served as the major

theorist of the group. John Ludlow's grandfather was "born heir to a good landed estate," but was "very extravagant" and "virtually fiddled away the most of his property" (Ludlow 1981, 2–3.) Ludlow's father, also John, made his career in the private army of the East India Company, where he rose to the position of Lieutenant Colonel. John senior married Maria Brown, the eldest daughter of Murdoch Brown, a Scottish adventurer who eventually emerged (according to J. M. Ludlow) as "one of the merchant princes of India" (Ludlow 1981, 4; Masterman 1963, 12). When the younger Ludlow was only two, his father died. The family then moved to France (1981, 4–6). In his autobiography, Ludlow is vague as to why they did not settle back in England. Ludlow's family lived in a middle-class, but certainly not lavish, manner. He acquired a solid French education. He described himself then and throughout his life as a liberal. In 1839 Ludlow, with his mother's encouragement, moved permanently to England when he was a young man of 18. There he studied law and became a "conveyancer," a specialist in handling deeds and other aspects of property transfers. The profession was respectable, but not highly remunerative. A few years later, when his brother-in-law experienced a major financial crisis, Ludlow arranged a substantial loan, but in doing so left his own family severely strapped (Ludlow 1981, Chs. 4–7).[2] While Ludlow was clearly a "gentleman," it seems fair to assign him to the ranks of the reasonably well-educated, but not well-placed.

Ludlow absorbed much of Fourierist French socialism including a respect for cooperative production (1981, 153). He also showed an early interest in religious work among the less advantaged and specifically the *Amis des Pauvres*, a society established by Louis Meyer, a French Lutheran (98–99). In England he eventually made contact with the Christian socialist group gathering around Frederick Denison Maurice. A history of the group credits Ludlow with bringing cooperative ideas into the Christian socialist orbit (Raven 1920, 55).

Frederick Denison Maurice (1805–1872), an accomplished theologian, ultimately served as the leading architect of the social psychology underlying Christian socialism. Maurice, like Ludlow, came from a complex middle-class background with hints of downward mobility. His father, Michael Maurice was from a dissenting Puritan/Presbyterian tradition and

---

2. The career of Ludlow's brother-in-law, Charles Liot, underscores the role colonial activities in the 19th century played in establishing some to an upper-middle class position. Liot's father was from "one of richest St. Domingo planter families." But a revolution there brought the family to ruin. Liot's mother came back to Paris where he met Maria Ludlow, Ludlow's sister. His father returned to the Caribbean as the treasurer for Martinique (Ludlow 1981, 31). Charles and his new wife soon followed. Charles at first prospered, but faced accusal (most likely false) of misallocating funds (Ch. 7).

became a Unitarian minister. His mother, Priscilla Hurry, was the daughter of a Yarmouth merchant. Her son described Priscilla as "having had a far clearer intellect than my father" (Frederick Maurice 1884a, 14).[3] Priscilla's family was likely well off since her eldest brother gave Michael and Priscilla a "handsome manorhouse" of Normanstone near Lowestoft in Sussex on the shore. There, Michael took pupils and earned a reputation for tolerance and scholarship. Michael was a close friend of Joseph Priestley, a founder of Unitarianism. At one point Michael gave up an attractive position to stay true to his Unitarian beliefs (1–11). Michael was not able to keep up Normanstone and removed the family to a much smaller home in Frenchay near Bristol. By the time Maurice was in college, he was clearly aware of the family's somewhat strained circumstances. In a letter to his mother, he indicated that he greatly enjoyed life at Cambridge, but regretted the expense. At Cambridge he was one of the first group of Apostles, the intellectual society that later included the utilitarian Henry Sidgwick and J. M. Keynes. Maurice started out on a legal education but then turned to the Anglican Church and ordination.

The other well-known churchman among the Christian Socialists is Charles Kingsley, who eventually established a reputation as a writer of fiction.[4] His colonial ties were even more complex than Ludlow's. Kingsley's father, also named Charles, was from an upper-class background. The elder Charles received a solid education from Harrow and Oxford. But left an orphan at an early age, much of his fortune dissipated. And so he turned to the Church. And then there is Charles' mother's background. Mary Lucas was born in the West Indies. Her family owned slave plantations on the sugar island of Barbados. Her father Nathan also owned property in British Guiana.[5] Ultimately, these properties yielded little to the Kingsley family because of black emancipation in 1833.

Perhaps the most effective in organizing and financing the Christian Socialists is Edward Vansittart Neale (1810–1892), who contributed considerable capital to the early producer cooperatives. Neale's father, also Edward, was the second son of a rich family. He turned to the church and became a committed Evangelical. Neale's grandfather, George Vanisittart

3. Frederick Maurice, F. D. Maurice's son, compiled this volume, drawing heavily on his father's letters.

4. Newell (1981, 1983) builds the case that the theologian, Alexander John Scott (1805–1866) is, from its inception, "the other Christian Socialist."

5. For documentation see "Legacies of British Slave Ownership," University College London, https://www.ucl.ac.uk/lbs/person/view/2146632191.

came from a line of highly successful Dutch merchant adventurers. George bought Bisham Abbey and served as an MP and was related by marriage to the greatest reform Evangelical, William Wilberforce. Through his mother's family, the elder Edward was heir of the Neale property on the condition he take the Neale name. Serious religious doubts haunted E. V. Neale, doubts encouraged by his reading of the new German Biblical scholarship. He turned from religion to law, a career at which he, like Ludlow, was never a major success. Neale went on to make an advantageous, but apparently loveless marriage (Backstrom 1974, 19–20). Backstrom's excellent biography, *Christian Socialism and Cooperation in Victorian England*, speculates that Neale, guilty over "impure thoughts," took solace in rejecting the rigidities of Evangelicalism and accepting a more liberal Christianity (20). He looked to focus his still considerable religious energy on working to establish a heaven on earth. He read German philosophy; he read French Socialists and was particularly drawn to Fourier (23). He developed an increasingly radical outlook and began to search for a practical avocation addressing both his religion and his widening social commitments.

Neale was wealthy. But his birth family was that of a second son whose evangelical religiosity and lack of achievement left him in a confusing class position. In this respect he held much in common with the other Christian Socialists. Neale, like many of the Christian Socialists, seemed uncomfortable with his class position.

Thus, the Christian Socialists built the leadership of their cooperative effort out of the complex and imperfect social materials available to literate protest. Their first publication, *Politics for the People*, addresses the working classes. While *Politics* clarifies that its founders do not "properly speaking, belong" to the working classes, it distinguishes these men from "idlers in the land" whose "interests" are not "in common with either" (Maurice 2007, 125; Maurice & Ludlow, eds. 1848, 2).

Several of the Christian Socialists were from downwardly mobile families. Some held backgrounds that intertwined with the colonial periphery. Thus, their class positions were ambiguous. Conceivably, they might have regularized those positions by seeking out the opportunities deriving from the Industrial Revolution. But they instinctively balked at the bourgeois glorification of striving. At root, they viewed themselves as too good to follow such a path. They turned instead toward the truths of religion. And chief among the truths is the dignity of a community of grace and cooperation.

CHRISTIAN SOCIALISTS IN THE WORLD

In 1846 Maurice became the chaplain of Lincoln's Inn where Ludlow practiced. Ludlow envisioned a scheme to aid the poor in the immediate neighborhood of the inn. It is natural that he approached Maurice about his plan. Little came of it in the short run, but in 1848 the Revolution became personal for Ludlow, his sisters still living in Paris. Impressed by the work of Louis Blanc in spreading the hope of cooperation, Ludlow wrote to Maurice. The letter was a major influence on Maurice and bound the two men together in their search for meaningful reform (Raven 1920, 71–74).

The first venture was the paper *Politics for the People*, Maurice and Ludlow serving as editors. Here Kingsley, writing under the name of Parson Lot, makes clear the economics of the Christian Socialists. The Bible "instead of being a book to keep the poor in order, is a book, from beginning to end, written *to keep the rich in order* . . . it is full of the most awful warnings and restrictions to the rich . . . . [I]t is the poor man's comfort and the rich man's warning" (Maurice & Ludlow eds. 1848, 59).[6]

Although *Politics* lasted only three months, it brought together the band of Christian Socialists who aggressively promoted concrete schemes of association with the goal of a full-scale reform of the employment relationship. Ludlow organized a meeting of the middle class Christian Socialists with a smattering of working-class activists headed by Walter Cooper, a tailor, a Chartist and reader of *Politics*. The group continued to meet on a regular basis. Later Lloyd Jones joined them, whom Ludlow describes as "evidently well-educated, professedly an Owenite Socialist, a master-tailor in Oxford Street, and editor of a weekly newspaper" (Raven 1920, 140). Ludlow, returning from another trip to Paris and the associations inspired by Louis Blanc, began to plan, with his working-class recruits, the launch of actual workers' associations in England. By early 1850, some two dozen tailors formed the Working Tailors' Association (151). At about the same time, the group decided on establishing a Needlewomen's Association.

The Christian Socialists formally organized The Society for Promoting Working Men's Associations. Maurice reluctantly took the presidency of the Society's Council. He appointed Neale as one of the Treasurers

---

6. Ludlow expands on the theme, advocating as the aim of society: "to make no rich man poorer, but all poor men richer. Richer, not in wealth alone, but in intelligence; not in intelligence only, but in love. Richer by the consciousness that they are fulfilling God's law, by eating their bread in the sweat of their brow, and enriching others by their labour" (1848, 221).

and Kingsley and Ludlow among the members.[7] Meeting regularly with Associates and their Central Board, the Promoters continued their efforts to build understanding between middle class and working-class elements. The demise of Chartism left a considerable opening for the expansion of cooperatives among reform-minded workers. And the early reaction to the Christian Socialist message was enthusiastic. The Society appointed a paid secretary and put together a constitution. By June of 1850, in addition to the two associations mentioned above, there were some six other associations including three of shoemakers (eventually combined into one), one of printers, one of bakers and a builders' association. The opening of associations continued apace (Raven 1920, Ch. VI).

The Society sponsored lecturing tours by the Owenite tailor Lloyd Jones and the Chartist tailor Walter Cooper that further promoted the creation of new associations. Later tours involved Ludlow. The Society also published widely. It puts out eight *Tracts on Christian Socialism* and a journal, the *Christian Socialist* (later the *Journal of Association*), edited by Ludlow. And in 1850 Kingsley published his novel, *Alton Locke*, about a tailor in the Chartist movement (158–159; 166–174).

During this period, Ludlow led the effort to give a new legal status to workers' associations. Up until 1850, the law treated associations as partnerships with unlimited liability for each member. The strategy was to gain limited liability for the associations by including them under the Friendly Societies Acts. Ludlow and Neale gave evidence to the Parliamentary select committee on the "Savings and Investments of the Middle and Working Classes." John Stuart Mill also testified, "there is no way in which the working classes can make so beneficial a use of their savings both to themselves and to society, as by the formation of associations to carry on the business with which they are acquainted and in which they are engaged as workpeople" (Ludlow 1981, 193–196). The Industrial and Provident Societies Bill passed in 1852, but only limited a member's liability after that member withdraws from an association. Ultimately (1862) the same group of Christian Socialists achieved full limited liability.

All such activities required financial outlays, and the Society depended heavily on Neale's funding. In Ludlow's view, the development was "less a help than a hindrance," since "Neale's purse gave a premature and factitious expansion to the movement." The situation gave rise to "mushroom

7. Ludlow was somewhat jealous of Neale's rapid movement toward influence in the Council, undoubtedly the product of the considerable wealth he brought to the group (Backstrom 1974, 32). Although Ludlow respected Neale, at this time they often differed on policy.

bodies devoid of all self-reliance" (Ludlow 1981, 207). Ludlow also feared the associations "instead of containing the pick of the trades, as they should have done, tended often at least to be made up of what the French call the *declasses*" (208). Much to the chagrin of the Society's Council, several associations fell to internal quarreling, while the managers of two disappeared with association funds. Ludlow contrasts the English workers with the French from 1848–1849, faulting the English for an "absence of sufficient perseverance, discipline," and "self-reliance" (208). Promising efforts to encourage cooperation among the members of the Amalgamated Society of Engineers, the strongest of English unions at the time, came to naught (Backstrom 1974, 42–43).

Here considerable tension developed between the Society for Promoting Working Men's Associations and a new organization, the Central Cooperative Agency, which among its main backers boasted the wealthy Neale.[8] The chief difference between the two organizations: instead of workers' associations, the Central Agency supported the creation of consumer cooperative stores. In an extensive published exchange with Neale, Ludlow argues: "production is essentially an unselfish act, consumption a selfish one. The producer begins by giving his labour . . . the consumer takes . . . instead of giving" (*Christian Socialist* 1851, 241). It is not selfless brotherhood but rather a superficial foundation of partnership which serves as the base of cooperative stores. Christian Socialists should work for a deeper change. In the published exchange, Neale replies that, at least for the time being, the cooperative store system is the more important cooperative institution because the store allows the poor to "most easily help themselves, and pave the way for advancing to higher forms of associative life." Stores require little capital. Moreover, they stimulate the home market for cooperative production (262). Ludlow concludes the debate with Neale on a mostly conciliatory note.[9] But Ludlow nonetheless attempts to block members of the Central Agency from the Council of the Society, in part because the Central Agency makes no explicit Christian commitment. His efforts to draw a clear line fail (Raven 1920, 267–268).

The Society launched a series of annual conferences with the purpose of bringing together all the tendencies in the cooperative movement. Highly successful at first, the conferences underscored the shift toward Neale's Central Agency and the declining influence of the Christian Socialists'

---

8. G. D. H. Cole (1944, 103–104) gives 1851 as the starting date for the Agency.

9. The full interchange between Ludlow and Neale in 1851 appears across the following pages of *Christian Socialist*: pp. 201 and 241–242 (both by Ludlow); 261–263 (Neale); 265–266 and 273–275 (Ludlow's response).

Society (now renamed the Association for Promoting Industrial and Provident Societies) (Backstrom 1974, 46–47).

At the same time, Maurice faced serious professional difficulties as the result of his leadership of the Christian Socialists as well as his unorthodox religious ideas. King's College dismissed Maurice in 1853. Discouraged by the setbacks to most of the workers' associations and recognizing them as premature, Maurice pulled away from the worker cooperatives. The English working class was not yet ready or capable of taking up the challenge of producer cooperation. Maurice turned toward workers' education. Drawing on his allies in the Christian Socialist movement, he founded the Working Men's College in 1854, where he served as the principal. The Association for Promoting Industrial and Provident Societies officially disbanded, leaving Neale's Central Agency and consumer cooperative groups to dominate the field. Although Ludlow continued to idolize Maurice and actively participated in the Working Men's College, these developments particularly disappointed him (Backstrom 1974, 44).

HUMAN NATURE, SOCIAL PSYCHOLOGY, AND INSTITUTIONS

The Christian Socialist assumptions about human nature differ from those of Owen. Maurice explicitly rejects Owen's key assumption that circumstances fully shape a person's character (Maurice [1850] 1995, 198). Starting with his theology, Maurice's understanding of human nature is dualistic. Individuals do have free will and are responsible for their actions. "Christ is in every man" (Maurice 1854, xxiv). But at the same time each person struggles internally with the attraction of sin, with a willful alienation from and rejection of both God and our fellow human beings.[10]

A key characteristic of rebellious alienation is its glorification of selfishness. "Selfish rivalry" is the "deadly opponent" of Christian love (Maurice [1850] 1995, 201). In Jeremy Morris's reading of Maurice, "separation, isolation, extreme individualism and selfishness [are] social sins." Maurice therefore preaches a "social theology" (J. Morris 2007, 13–14).

Each individual carries a deep responsibility for their own decisions and character. But even so, Christian Socialists do not hold that environment has no effect. In particular, Maurice argues that the system of competition

---

10. "I find Hell set before me . . . as separation from God." God leads "men to fly from the darkness and turn to the light; . . . they are resisting His will when they prefer Hell to Heaven" (Maurice 1854, xlvi).

is built on a vain attempt to channel the evils of jealousy and greed for social purposes. Participating in such an economy reinforces one's alienation and destroys one's character with damning results for the soul. The institutions of the competitive system encourage the most negative aspects of our make-up.

Hence the Christian Socialists focus on cooperative institutions.[11] It is from this perspective that Maurice's son characterized Maurice's conviction "that there were great truths involved in the principle of co-operation which were essentially Christian truths" (Frederick Maurice 1884b, 41). Society requires new economic institutions, institutions that do not encourage selfishness but rather encourage fellowship and the Christ in every person. Fellowship must infuse everyday life. In *Politics for the People*, Maurice writes that expanding fellowship and accepting Christ's kingdom are not just material for sermons. "We cannot believe these to be good pulpit doctrines without believing them to be as good for the business of every-day life, for every shop and every hovel" (Maurice & Ludlow eds. 1848, 177–178). More generally, the Christian Socialists define their socialism as the "practical application of Christianity to the purposes of trade and industry" (*Christian Socialist* 1851, 161).[12]

For the Christian Socialists, the core concrete institutions, the institutions meant to replace the competitive system, are worker associations.[13] The deep associative principle of fellowship is the

---

11. From Maurice's view, it is ironic that while cooperative Socialists like Owen denied Christianity, the wealthy promoters of economic competition professed Christianity. Owen belittled Christian preachers as purveyors of a system of punishments and rewards used to tame and confuse the working classes. Maurice considered such interpretations as understandable, given the nature of much preaching (Maurice 1855, 8–9).

12. In the same spirit, while Neale expresses doubt over the pure version of Owen's character formation hypothesis, he sees much room for institutional influence, particularly when based on Christian principles (*Christian Socialist* 1851, 138).

13. Maurice recognizes that association underlies many concrete institutions of the competitive system as well. But in this context, the anchor of association is self-interest. Christian cooperative associations must be different, built on "a state of fellowship." Only as "a member of a divinely constituted body" can man obtain "his highest development, be blessed and saved." Maurice continues,

How then does co-operation become truly Christian?—by recognizing the fact that those principles which enable men to work together as brothers are those which enable them to perform the highest acts of worship together—trust in God, love to one another. For what does worshipping together imply? . . . the laying aside of that selfishness which keeps men apart, the being animated by the same spirit. (*Christian Socialist* 1851, 178).

Also see below, Ludlow's discussion of the role of "concert" in modern business.

anchor.[14] In such associations, cooperation "implies a working together, under the belief that the benefit of the body is the benefit of the individual member of that body, and that there must be a sacrifice of whatever tends to separate the members from each other" (*Christian Socialist* 1851, 178).

As E. V. Neale puts it:

> Association is the outward expression of a certain inward feeling, or tendency, the expression of this feeling or tendency . . . . The feeling out of which association arises, is that of the existence of a common brotherhood, a real union among mankind . . . . The value of association, as a means of promoting the spiritual and moral welfare of men, depends upon the extent to which the operation of the system, which grows out of the associative feeling, will reproduce the feeling out of which it arises. (Neale in *Christian Socialist* 1851, 146)

Echoing Thompson and Wheeler, such is the core Christian Socialist claim with respect to social psychology. Where the competitive system reinforces selfishness and alienation, the cooperative association reinforces fellowship and Christian feeling. Participating in a workers' association draws forth and strengthens the individual's commitment to their fellows.[15]

Maurice's rejection of Owen's view of human nature left him cool to Owen's progressive approach to schooling. Such an institution is no foundation for cooperative socialism. Maurice looked instead to an education based on an equality defined in Christian terms. Some stress equality of treatment under the law, others stress equal property or equal rank. Not Maurice. His major concern was equality in education. In particular, the moral and religious dimension of education—available to all—and founded in the "common relation to Him." Such is "the real secret of equality." It is these elements of education that most prepare children for participating in the fellowship of the cooperative. At the same time, Maurice accepted that there are appropriate differences in practical training: the accountant receives a different education from the carpenter. It is education that calls "forth the Man who is to do the work" (Maurice & Ludlow eds. 1848, 100).

---

14. Notice that the Christian Socialist conception of fellowship is not a submergence of identity in the common mass. Maurice explains: "I cease to recognise the distinctness or worth of my neighbour, if I do not recognise my own; I cease to recognise my own distinctness and worth, if I do not recognise his" (Maurice 1869, 128).

15. These comments by Neale draw attention to the major feedback mechanism invoked by cooperative theorists. See Chapter 12 for our reconstruction.

Maurice remained silent as to how such selection is to be made or what implications it might have for the social psychology of the workers associations.[16]

The Christian Socialist approach to institutions differs in other ways from Owen's vision of cooperative villages. They are antithetical to Owen's proposals for a fundamental restructuring of the institution of the family. For example, Neale writes that Christian Socialists are against absorbing "the family in the commune . . . because we believe that the family life is a divinely appointed and most important part of human society." He highlights the bonds of parent and child and advocates an extension of "that feeling of common interest" beyond the home (*Christian Socialist* 1851, 131). The traditional family, not gender equality, provides the foundation for building a new economy and society.

And the Christian Socialists reject, for the time being, Owen's core institution of common property. Here is Ludlow's public response to an invitation to attend a meeting advocating communal property. Christian Socialists, Ludlow writes, are glad there are pure Communists, "But Communists we are not." Before there can be large-scale community of property, there must be a "diffusion of Socialist principles and practice." Men must first learn to be "partners in thought and feeling, before they can become partners in the outward concerns of life, partners in labour before they can become partners in property" (*Christian Socialist* 1851, 245). The timing of this fundamental reform remains highly uncertain.

16. Maurice was not silent in his criticism of the professional classes of his day. The true calling of those in the professions is "to bear witness to all the other classes and see how the people are doing—healthy minds, bodies, lives based in truth, justice, beauty" (Maurice 1855, 8–9). But instead, the common professional practices in a competitive system diffuses falsehoods. In particular, "[w]e teach the middle-class to make the acquisition of money the object of their lives, and to value all skill, talent, strength, just so far as they are serviceable for that object" (10). The professions promote and wrongly link honor to "thoughts of position, of circumstances, of wealth." And those holding professional positions succumb to their own false rhetoric, pretending to be honorable. The attractions of monetary payment for professional services encourages such corruption. The result is one of impoverishment for all (9–10). Many such Christian professionals fundamentally misconceive Christianity. For Maurice, its message is the fulfillment of Christ's Kingdom here on earth. Christ's Kingdom is not only a union with God, but also with our fellow human beings—particularly "with the best and noblest men that your country has produced—with the men who worked for her, starved for her, died for her" (Maurice 1855, 14). Hence, Christ's Kingdom must necessarily be one of cooperation, cooperation based on fellowship as the primary principled institution. In Maurice's view, a mature acceptance of God brings forth the human material for concrete cooperative institutions such as workers' associations.

THE ECONOMICS OF CHRISTIAN
SOCIALIST COOPERATION

Although F. D. Maurice was the undisputed leader of the spirit behind the Christian Socialists, it was John Ludlow who turned the group to socialism, in general, and cooperation, in particular. It was Ludlow, with his French education who knew something of socialist thinking. Maurice himself suggested as much. Ludlow brought a familiarity with Fourier, Blanc, and Proudhon.

Perhaps the most extensive effort to theorize Christian Socialism is in Ludlow's lecture/essay, "Christian Socialism and Its Opponents" (1851). Ludlow writes his essay as a response to a long review of Kingsley's novel, *Alton Locke*. The review, "English Socialism and Communistic Association" is the work of William Rathbone Greg (Greg 1851, 1–17). Greg proclaims himself a defender of the "political economists" and the manufacturers. He identifies the efforts of Kingsley and his Christian Socialists as amateurish and potentially harmful.

The Greg family was the product of the Industrial Revolution. Though actively managing his family's manufacturing firm, by 1851 Greg was living the life of an English gentleman. Samuel Greg, William's father, was originally from Belfast, the son of a ship owner/merchant with land in the West Indies (Rose 1986, 13). Samuel was the founder and owner of the Quarry Bank Mill established in 1784. A paternalistic approach dominated at the Quarry Bank Mill. Samuel Greg constructed a village for his workers. Hannah, his wife and daughter of a prominent Unitarian merchant family, built up an "apprentice" system at Quarry Bank that took children from workhouses and housed and educated them while the children worked in the factory.[17] In the 1830s, William Rathbone's brother, the younger Samuel Rathbone, Jr., experimented with a paternalist plan reminiscent of New Lanark, but gave it up when it proved unprofitable (120–122). Thus William Rathbone Greg was familiar with the realities of British manufacturing at mid-century and perhaps a bit defensive of his family's approach to the new industrial world.

William Rathbone Greg launches his essay with a paean to the creativity of science and engineering and a nod to John Stuart Mill. Society must address the "vast amount of unrelieved misery." The point is that society

---

17. Known at the time as progressive mill owners, the Gregs and their apprentice system were the target of considerable criticism over the years, not the least of which is the recent television series, "The Mill" which deals graphically with life in this brave new world.

cannot trust the problem to "feelers" like the Christian Socialists but must rather invoke the "thinkers," philanthropists who devote their lives to the "systematic" and "laborious research" into the "remote and hidden causes" of that misery. The thinkers attack "the source rather than the symptoms." Ultimately the thinkers eradicate "social evils rather than alleviating them" (Greg 1851, 4). It is not hard to believe Greg included his own family among the thinkers. Quite simply, Greg asserts, "All schemes of social amelioration which violate the principles of economic science must come to naught . . . . Providence makes no shortcuts" (10–11). Greg attacks, in particular, the Christian Socialists because these "clergymen of high literary reputation" threaten to make socialism respectable (12).

Greg holds that the Christian Socialists trace the bulk of the laborer's misery to the dominance of "*competition* instead of combination." As he paraphrases their position, "The antagonistic and regenerative principle which must be introduced, is *association.* Let workmen associate with one another, instead of competing with one another, and there will be work and wages enough for all. Competition is a cruel and unchristian system: Association breathes the very spirit of our divine Master" (1851, 7). Greg goes on to fault the Christian Socialists for asserting that political economy has "had it all its own way." In fact, he argues economic policy repeatedly took the wrong turn, violating most every principle of political economy. Most crucially for the poor, Greg faults the expensive public support of the indolent and criminal in workhouses and prisons (14).

At root, the Christian Socialists have nothing to offer the poor but a return to a system of medieval guilds. They laud that long gone system as being based on "concert" rather than "competition." Behind any such system must be a mechanism to replace the market in matching supply to demand. But this flies in the face of the most central principle of political economy. According to Greg the only way to match supply and demand is through trial and error of the competitive marketplace. Sectors that yield high profits expand, and those that return little or no profit contract. Any effort to interfere with the fundamental competitive process leads to inefficiency and economic retrogression. He writes:

> Concert, then, as an opponent to or substitute for competition, in solving the problem of the wisest distribution of labour, is either a *chimera* or a tyranny. So applied, it delegates to a few men sitting in committee the decisions as to the number of workmen required in each department and the right of warning all others off the ground; while it expects from these men a wisdom and omniscience which neither individuals nor corporations could by possibility possess. (Greg 1851, 9)

At this point Greg redirects the attack. The Christian Socialists engage in much rhetorical bluster. But in their practice, they create nothing approaching a full-scale system of concert. Rather they build only co-partnerships of workers. Greg writes this is no more than what that "sound economist," Mr. Mill advises or what the *Edinburgh Review* itself "advocated two years ago." "In this Association the labourers work under a directing head for wages fixed by him, and as they themselves own the capital they naturally divide among themselves the capitalist's profit" (1851, 10).

Greg runs on. The Christian Socialists in creating these cooperatives fail to solve the basic problem of unemployment. There are simply too many tailors for the business available. At most the cooperatives erase the profits of middlemen, but only redirect much of these funds to pay the skilled supervisor. Such associations do nothing to rid the market of competition, they can only grow through competition.

But what do the Christian Socialists look forward to as the mature new system? Here, Greg quotes Kingsley, "our work will be incomplete till we have blended all these associations into one vast guild. Competition will then be out of the question." And here Greg delivers his coup de grace: "Yes! but it [competition] will be replaced by *monopoly*; and we all know what monopoly means—artificial prices, a restricted market, a gigantic job, a final and inevitable smash" (1851, 10–11).

In sum, Greg's most original piece of economics is: "The advocates of association as a cure for competition are caught between two horns of a dilemma . . . in case you have many Associations, you retain all the evils of competition; in case you merge them all into one, you encounter all the evils of monopoly" (1851, 11). And for the clergymen, he rubs the point in. The only possible escape from the dilemma is "a remodeling of human nature by divine or Christian influences." But if such a remodeling is achievable, "All systems will become indifferent, for the evils of all systems will be wiped away" (12).

While Greg clearly mixes simple calumny into his argument, it is hard not to see here a serious theoretical attack on the plans of the Christian Socialists.[18] By the same token, although it too includes a good dose of rhetoric, Ludlow's response to Greg, "Christian Socialism and Its Opponents," presents the start of a serious theoretical defense of the Christian Socialist program.

---

18. Perhaps the first accomplished economist to appreciate the significance of the argument by Greg was Edwin R. A. Seligman writing in the *Political Science Quarterly* (1886). Raven ([1920] 1968) also discusses it.

Ludlow opens with some broad matters of defining socialism and communism. He also emphasizes that the Christian Socialists, including Kingsley whom Greg particularly attacks, are not hostile to political economy. Ludlow quotes Kingsley's demurring from "the vulgar outcry against political economy in general," an outcry Kingsley labels "as absurd and inhuman." Kingsley goes on to assert "to be a sound and scientific Socialist, a man must be first a sound and scientific political economist" (Ludlow 1851, 22). That said, Ludlow does suggest that Smith with his emphasis on a narrow definition of wealth loses sight of a wider concept of "weal" or "welfare." This broader concept lies behind the historical concern for the "commonwealth" which means not "a common stock of riches, but common welfare, common good." And the term political economy as used by the economists again focuses too narrowly on "mere money-prudence." In seeking laws to govern the nation's households it leaves aside "all those human qualities of justice, and patience, and forbearance, and forgiveness, and ever much more abounding love" so necessary to the happiness of the household. These are the concerns that Greg's political economy must take up if, as Greg claims he desires, it is to actually be "benevolence under the guidance of science" (22–25). Thus Ludlow asserts that while Christian Socialists like the political economists "study and apply the laws of production and distribution," they also attend to "other laws which you neglect" (25).[19]

Now this broad charge against political economy and its narrow focus on selfishness is common among cooperators of all stripes. In Ludlow's presentation, it reaches a crescendo in an anti-Semitic outburst: "we will contemn, and we will scorn, and we will scoff at the pretensions of those who assert that England is to be ruled by the same base competitive selfishness which regulates, to his own damnation, the dealings of a Jew slopseller with his wretched slaves" (Ludlow 1851, 26).[20]

So socialists should pay attention to the political economists' "competitive Plutonomy" when it puts forth scientific findings about wealth, but as "soon it attempts that which outlies its province—to govern society, or, in other words, men—to become a social power—we deny and reject it" (26). Socialists particularly cannot accept political economy's injunction to

19. Likewise Maurice argues "the law of God is not that every man ought to make the most of his position for his own selfish ends; but that a mutual dependence exists between man and man; and that the interest of the body is the interest of the individual" (*Christian Socialist* 1851, 162).

20. A slopseller is a producer of cheap apparel. Ludlow uses the term repeatedly in his contributions to the *Christian Socialist*. See, for example, pp. 3, 27, and 107.

"starve the pauper and maltreat the prisoner." Instead, socialism proposes "the labourer and the artisan should be raised above misery and want" (30).

Moving on toward the central thrust of Greg's challenge, Ludlow asserts that "concert" is far from "tyranny." Its practical success demonstrates its workability "in those branches of labour which constitute the most *social* elements of society—the government and the public services" (Ludlow 1851, 33). Imagine a military led by the forces of competition. Far from such chaos, the public sphere relies on concert and even extends it back into the various military colleges and training schools.

More broadly, Ludlow argues that, peering inside productive organizations, in all of them, whether public office, private factory, shop, or farm, the "internal working of all depends throughout upon concert—upon the adjustment of the demand for labour and its supply, often in the minutest and nicest manner" (Ludlow 1851, 35). Ludlow has hold of something here. The suppression of the competitive market in favor of some approach to concert occurs not only inside the public office, but in all productive entities.[21] Inside firms, "competition is seen in its true light, as mere discord and disorder" (35). Two carters on the same farm don't compete for the use of the same cart. Two spinners in a factory don't compete over who tends which spinning jenny. Such competition destroys the very work contested.

The moral is clear: "If we could learn to look upon a whole trade as we do upon a single establishment, we should find that free competition mars everywhere, instead of making, the wisest distribution of labour" (Ludlow 1851, 35). Throughout history to the extent concert does not regulate the distribution of labor, "that distribution is tyrannical and contradictory, and the whole state of things in which this is allowed to take place, disorganized and anti-social" (36).

Ludlow builds on his theme. Competitors far from sharing their knowledge of the conditions of supply and demand make every effort to hide their private knowledge. "It is of the very essence of competition among employers to conceal which branches of labour are least, and which are most remunerative, to falsify returns, to exaggerate labourer's wages and conceal the trader's profits" (1851, 37). And even when it is patently clear that a given line of work like slop-tailoring cannot, under competitive conditions, support all those engaged, competition in no way insures abandonment of that line of work. The worker knows no other skill, nothing else

---

21. Not until the mid-20th century did economists make this central observation in the work of Coase (1937), Simon (1993), and Williamson (1993).

to turn to. Competition chains down each worker to "some single function" despite his "manifold God-given faculties." Now he turns to his wife and children for aid since his labor alone cannot support them.

In contrast, there is no excess supply of labor once a trade reorganizes under cooperatives. When the worker-organized firms exclude the middlemen of the trade, they garner the resources to provide both living wages and lower prices. Ludlow speculates, "The actual demand for clothes in the metropolis would be sufficient, if those middlemen and masters, who constitute economically but useless wheels in the machinery of production, were suppressed" (1851, 43). More generally he takes exception to Mill's presentation of the wage fund theory—that wages are simply the ratio of the portion of circulating capital extended for wages to the number of available laborers. Ex post this is a tautology, but ex ante Ludlow doubts its relevance. Both the consumer, in choosing how much to pay for goods, and the employer, in deciding how much to pay for labor, have important degrees of freedom. Ludlow suspects that the first is the more important of the two since "between the necessities of the workman and our [consumers'] exactions, the humane employer is often crushed against his will into a heartless taskmaster" (45).[22]

Focusing on the micro-structure of the cooperative association, Ludlow takes exception to Greg's claim that as individual firms they are no different from capitalist firms. He emphasizes two points in particular. First, cooperative enterprises share profits among workers less any interest. There is a striking difference between this arrangement and one in which the firm's promoter claims profits.[23] And, yes, there is need for skilled supervision in the cooperative enterprise. Second, and fundamentally, "the whole question is how shall the manager be appointed? How shall authority be exercised? Shall it be freedom or despotism? Shall it be the authority of a Russian czar or of a constitutional minister?" (Ludlow 1851, 42).

---

22. Again, it is Seligman (1886, 236) who first recognizes that, in these passages, Ludlow "met the economists on their own ground. Here for the first time do we find a successful refutation of the wages-fund theory." Mill himself famously renounced the wage fund theory in 1869. His argument emphasizes not the consumer discretion but that of the employers. As Reeves (2007, 453) puts it, Mill came to think "the amount available for wages was a product of the division between the capitalist's personal profit and the claims of his workers, rather than any 'inexorable limits of the wage-fund.'" (Reeves is here quoting Mill (1869, 645)).

23. While Ludlow, elsewhere, explicitly argues for equal profits in associations, he advocates differential weekly allowances "according to skill and industry." The concern is that equal wages disincentivize workers (*Christian Socialist* 1851, 235).

While cooperative firms are internally different than typical private firms, Ludlow acknowledges that where they act separately, they may compromise themselves and make worse the miseries generated by competition. If there are "many associations in one trade, *and those associations do not agree as to the apportioning of the work either in respect of quantity or description, or as to the prices to be charged for it*, we retain all the evils of competition, and retain them even intensified" (1851, 53–54). Ludlow insists that the various associations must work in concert through a "Central Board, composed of representatives of all the associations." And the regulations of the Board aim "to prevent either monopoly or unfair competition" (54). Ludlow does not clarify exactly what constitutes "unfair competition," but he does admit such a Board may have an aura of monopoly.

Ludlow offers a parable of a small, isolated town in which a single craftsperson represents each trade. Each of these then holds a monopoly in their trade, but Ludlow argues the potential or actual combination of all his fellows constrain each. Even better, the various craftsmen might through concert set the terms of trade among themselves. In a spirit of Christian fellowship, each works for all. In the same spirit, the Christian Socialists look to an association of associations to achieve a harmonious balance among the various trades.[24] Yes, "it is a monopoly, but it is the monopoly of all order and justice against all iniquity and disorder. It is the monopoly of fair prices and living wages against false prices and starvation wages" (1851, 56).[25] It is the realization of Christ's Kingdom.

24. Elsewhere Ludlow claims a system of cooperation produces not only a balance but an expansion of production in "the home-market of association" (*Christian Socialist* 1851, 195).

25. Ludlow ends his response to Greg with several quotes from John Stuart Mill, whom he describes as "the great living master of political economy" (1851, 62). Mill concludes in *Principles* "We are as yet too ignorant of what individual agency in its best form, or Socialism in its best form, can accomplish to be qualified to decide *which of the two will be the ultimate form of human society*" (quoted in Ludlow 1851, 63). Ludlow encourages the critics of Christian Socialism to take an equally open mindset. Perhaps Ludlow's arguments had some real effect, since a couple years later Greg (1852) supports the efforts to include associations under governmental protections. But Greg in taking this view warns, "Some of our Christian Socialist friends will imagine they can trace, in certain passages and expressions of this Article, indications of an approaching conversion to their views. We can encourage no such hopes . . . . We are as far as ever from conceiving that working men's associations and co-operative stores will prove the agencies they are expected to be for the regeneration of our social state" (Greg 1852, 452).

THE DEBATE OVER CHRISTIAN INSTITUTIONS

In his elaboration of "the monopoly of all order and justice," Ludlow's vision of Christian Socialist institutions differs dramatically from that of Maurice. Ludlow argues that a centralized hierarchy can replace the market. Maurice doesn't doubt the claim but considers Ludlow's glorification of a centralizing structure as a virtual denial of the Christian ethos of the movement. It is not too much to claim that this fundamental difference in their theoretical viewpoints ultimately destroyed the Christian Socialist movement.

Ludlow anticipates a hierarchical institutional structure providing coordination to the various workers associations. Ludlow sees the central board and related institutions balancing the system. Ludlow's claim is that a plan must be made, a plan that allows the replacement of competition with concert. Cooperators might argue about the explicit character of the planning process, but a central authority is key.[26]

Maurice maintains that such centralized planning is neither desirable nor necessary. Yes, it is important to eradicate competition, but do not replace it with a hierarchical institutional system. At root, such controlling systems attempt to harness evil for good purposes. They build hierarchy and inequality. Both Maurice and Ludlow hold it is chimerical to think the competitive system can bring good from evil. That is the central lie of classical political economy. But Maurice goes further. The cooperative movement must be cautious not to fall into the trap of thinking that, with its good intentions, it can bring good from evil. Maurice makes his clearest statement of this fundamental point in a letter to Ludlow. There he recounts his rejection of plans for a central cooperative board put to him by Charles Sully (Secretary of the Christian Socialists' Society for Promoting Working Men's Associations). Sully warns Maurice the fully independent cooperative "associations were actuated by a thoroughly mercenary, selfish, competitive spirit; that they aimed merely at a more successful rivalship than is possible on the present system" (Frederick Maurice 1884b, 42). Sully holds that only a central board can keep them in line. Maurice sees Sully's request as asking him to say, "My purpose is to turn a number of warring forces, each seeking the other's destruction, into harmony, by certain scientific

---

26. For Ludlow, each worker cooperative must stay involved and engaged with the Central Board. The Central Board is to "exercise an effective control over the Associations" via "real common management through the representatives of the various united bodies" not devolving into "irksome routine and red-tapery, or the scene of personal squabbles" (Ludlow 1851, 195).

arrangements of mine concerning production and consumption" (43). But Maurice holds

> I acknowledge in these warring creatures an element of peace and harmony, the work of God's spirit. To that I speak in each of them. I can speak to nothing else. . . . I have no hope of entering into terms of peace with the devil. I have no notion that I can make him my servant by a mere ingenious and extensive combination. I believe the more skillful and large the combination of such elements, the worse and the more deadly will be the result. (43)

In the letter to Ludlow, Maurice goes on: "Talk as you like about my system-phobia. It is this which I mean by system, it is this which I have hated in the Church, the State, the family, the heart, and which I see coming out more fearfully every day—the organisation of evil powers for the sake of producing good effects." And he ends in a telling flourish, "But I do say that neither the Council nor the Central Board can make the fraternity, or establish the law or principle of it, and that if we build churches upon the decrees of councils, or associations upon decrees of central boards, we build upon the sand, and that when the rain comes our houses will fall, and that great will be the fall of them" (45).[27]

In an unexpected sense Maurice's position agrees with Greg, that attempting to manipulate a socialist monopoly ends not in building Christ's Kingdom, but in a fall into evil. For Maurice, the moral core of horizontal associations emerges directly from Christ's Kingdom, and if the human material is solid it should require no larger system. Maurice's answer to Greg is not a political economy of planning, but a vague spontaneous system of just trade and social virtue. In its own way, it embodies a deeply anarchistic view. Maurice, at least, sees no need for transitional institutional strategy. A move from the here and now to Christ's Kingdom requires only the internal readiness of the working classes. It is quite understandable at this junction that he turns away from building cooperatives and toward worker education.

Despite his respect for Maurice, Ludlow thinks a central board is the only pragmatic institutional structure for cooperation. He is deeply disappointed at Maurice's rejection of his preliminary blueprint for cooperative organization. Like several of the other Christian Socialists, he remained

---

27. For Maurice, in the long run, system or hierarchy is not the basis for the good of Christ's Kingdom. Good cannot come from evil. Rather, good derives from the concerted interaction of individuals, as children of God working in fellowship for the common weal (Maurice 1848, 3).

active in the cooperative movement but never again occupied the place of major theoretician.

A NOTE ON CLASS AND RACE IN CHRISTIAN SOCIALIST THOUGHT

For a few years in the early 1850s, Christian Socialists found themselves at the vanguard of the cooperative movement. Tentative in their own class identities, they played with the possibilities cooperatives opened for potentially restructuring the meaning of class in industrial Britain. The situation invigorated even as it frightened. As biographers and historians comment, several of the Christian Socialists, like Neale, Kingsley, and Maurice, were fundamentally conservative in their world outlook and even antidemocratic in their political views.[28] Others, like Ludlow, were more liberal in their political outlook.[29] But whatever their politics, they shared a deep dislike for the emerging bourgeoisie, with its path to riches and position that they all explicitly rejected. Instead, they dreamed of rebuilding the economic world along what they perceived as much better lines, explicitly Christian lines.

To an extent, Christian Socialist thought contains an almost reactionary quality with its echoes of the Medieval guilds. But in holding up cooperation against competition, they meant to radically recast the meaning of the Industrial Revolution. Cooperation would not ultimately herald the emergence of the new bourgeois capitalists as the central economic force, but rather the center of the new economy would be the great mass of cooperating and Christian workers. This is a vision both reactionary and radical. This was a point in time when those two outlooks sat together in a surprisingly easy manner. This was the time of Carlyle and Disraeli.

While acknowledging their own shortcomings as organizers and institution builders, the Christian Socialists placed much of the blame for their

---

28. Concerning antidemocratic views, for Neale, for example, see *Christian Socialist* 1851, p. 262; for Kingsley, the same source, p. 50; and for Maurice, see discussion of his political theory in Raven ([1920] 1968, 90–92).

29. For Ludlow, democracy, or "government of the people" is "not the letting loose all the accumulated selfishness of the many, but the giant self-control of a nation, ruling itself as one man, in wisdom and righteousness, beneath the eye of God." The "truest Democracy"? Socialism. He continues: "Let each man only do his duty, and the whole People does its own. Let each man learn to govern himself, not in solitude, but in fellowship with others, and from fellowship to fellowship, from circle to circle, the privilege of the few ever-widening to admit the many, the collective self-government of English Democracy is achieved" (*Christian Socialist* 1851, 49–50).

failure to create transitional cooperatives on the lack of discipline in the less skilled elements of the working classes and the lack of vision in the more skilled higher elements (Raven 1920, 335–337). Individual workers might be capable of much, but the laboring classes as potential economic actors were simply not yet up to the challenge. The bourgeoisie was not going to be kept in check by such a ragtag army. From this perspective, the logic in Maurice's turn toward workers' education makes eminent sense.

The Christian Socialist commitment to the English working class does not imply that all of them took a progressive view with respect to race. Among the Christian Socialists, there was Charles Kingsley, who throughout adulthood remained disappointed over his family's effective dispossession due to emancipation. In a famous letter to Thomas Hughes who, after the American Civil War, asked Kingsley to contribute to the National Freedman's Aid Union, Kingsley writes:

> I am very glad these slaves are freed, at whatever cost of blood and treasure. But now—what do they want from us? . . . What do they ask our money for, over and above? I am personally shy of giving mine. The negro has had all I ever possessed; for emancipation ruined me. And yet I would be mined a second time, if emancipation had to be done over again. I am no slave holder at heart. But I have paid my share of the great bill, in Barbadoes and Demerara, with a vengeance; and don't see myself called on to pay other men's! (Kingsley 1894, 382)

Kingsley's Caribbean connections left him open to racism. In the same letter to Hughes, Kingsley wonders if the fund in question will be "spent in turning the south into a big Hayti of savage squatters?" (382).

In 1865 Jamaican governor Edward John Eyre brutally suppressed an uprising. There were numerous executions of people innocent of the rebellion. In England, liberals, led by John Stuart Mill, formed the Jamaica Committee with the purpose of bringing Eyre to account for his actions. Ludlow joined the Committee and encouraged his fellow Christian Socialists to do likewise. Kingsley surprised them by endorsing the opposing Governor Eyre Defense and Aid Committee with Carlyle at its head (Persky 1990).[30] Most all the Christian Socialists were radical with respect to cooperation and the destruction of the competitive system. But, deeply problematic from a modern perspective, some excluded the black population of the Caribbean (and elsewhere) in their affective world.

---

30. John Ruskin, who at times participated in Christian Socialist activities also joined the Defense Committee. The writing of both Ruskin and Carlyle clearly reflect sincere concerns for the plight of British workers, but that does not carry over to black Jamaicans.

CONCLUSION

The historian and cooperative activist George Holyoake offers a general summary of the Christian Socialist movement at the end of the 19th century. Holyoake certainly sympathizes with their efforts, but honestly criticizes their lack of concrete accomplishment:

> The "Christian Socialists," inspired by eloquent rectors, and directed by transcendent professors, aided by the lawyer mind and the merchant mind, and what was no small importance, the very purse of Fortunatus himself, have made but poor work of association. They have hardly drawn a single tooth from the dragon of competition. So far from having scotched that ponderous snake, they appear to have added to its vitality, and to have convinced parliamentary political economists that competitive strife is the eternal and only self-acting principle of society. (Holyoake 1900, 1)

There is a ring of truth to this harsh overview. But it fails to acknowledge the serious and thoughtful additions of Ludlow and Maurice to the emerging social science.

The Christian Socialists drew much of their critique of the competitive system from the Owenites and other early socialists. More original were their constructive arguments for worker cooperatives. They stood out among the 19th-century cooperative theorists covered in this book in drawing upon religiosity as the foundation for their understanding of cooperative social psychology and the principled institution of fellowship. Perhaps the deepest of their economic insights is an appreciation of the role of concert that governs most of the internal activities of public and private workplaces. As Ludlow makes clear, such an understanding opens a question that classical political economy fails to address: which interactions do competitive markets best conduct, and which do concert of some kind best address? Ludlow answers the question by claiming virtually the entire economic space for concert. In the process, he mounts a spirited defense of cooperatives against the charge that they will descend into monopoly exploitation.

On this key point Ludlow and Maurice differ, and the difference is central to the dissolution of their movement. Maurice argues that an infusion of Christian fellowship and morality should be sufficient to lead workers and their associations to arrange fair and just exchanges. Ludlow argues that balancing the system requires a central board or some other central planning mechanism. Maurice deeply fears that such efforts at external regulation and hierarchy take cooperative organizations down the path

of corrupting power. Coming to cooperation through their mature acceptance of Christ's Kingdom, associations require no coercion. Ludlow greatly
admires and respects Maurice, and Maurice is very fond of Ludlow, but
their inability to find a creative way out of the dilemma brings down their
heady dream.[31]

The failure of the Society is in part the result of Neale and other Christian
Socialists searching outside the group's structure for a path to broader acceptance. If the working classes were not ready for producer cooperatives,
perhaps a fruitful alternative existed through the consumer cooperatives
mushrooming up around England and Scotland at that time. A turn toward
consumer cooperatives is effectively a turn toward the more prosperous
and stable upper working classes. Their social science is the focus of the
next chapter.

31. Several of the Christian Socialists, after the failure of their own Society, continued to search for viable approaches to cooperation. At least one Christian Socialist
actively pursued the possibility of building cooperation on an alternative class basis.
This is the core idea behind a scheme of Thomas Hughes. Hughes never gave up his
commitment to the cooperative goal. In 1880, he played the central part in setting
up a cooperative community in the United States to be populated by younger sons
of the gentry. Hughes staked much of his own resources on the project. He named
the chosen community in Tennessee "Rugby" after Hughes' (and Tom Brown's) much-
loved school. Early on the town's settlers concentrated on the tourism business with
mixed results and then failed to make a go of a tomato cannery. By 1891, the venture
failed (Backstrom 1974, 144).

MANCHESTER.
CENTRAL GROCERY AND PROVISION AND BOOT AND SHOE WAREHOUSES, BALLOON STREET AND GARDEN STREET.
(See pages 14 to 16, 56, and 86.)

Plate 2. The Co-operative Wholesale Society (CWS) warehouses on Balloon Street, Manchester, England, 1896. From *The Co-operative Wholesale Societies, Limited, England and Scotland : annual, 1896*. Manchester: Co-operative Wholesale Society Limited; Glasgow: The Scottish Co-operative Wholesale Society Limited. p. 6.

CHAPTER 6

ᴄᴧᴊ

Redirecting the Surplus through Consumer Cooperation

THE ROCHDALE SOCIETY AND FEDERALISM

Where most Owenite cooperative villages failed, and self-managed workshops favored by the Christian Socialists and John Stuart Mill gained little traction, one element of the traditional cooperative agenda experienced dramatic success. In the second half of the 19th century, the focus of the British cooperative movement shifted from an emphasis on workers to organizing consumers.[1] The network of retail consumer cooperatives grew rapidly after the Rochdale Society of Equitable Pioneers establishes the most famous British cooperative store in 1844.[2] The store the Pioneers built along Rochdale's Toad Lane became the prototype for hundreds more across the country. Over time, these cooperative stores joined together in a "Federalist" system to provide themselves wholesale and manufactured goods as a transition mechanism to the cooperative commonwealth. The resulting consumer cooperative movement evolved a vision of a cooperative commonwealth that Owen would not recognize, and the Christian Socialists would not accept. To support that movement, a small group of

---

1. As early as 1821, "A Journeyman Gilder" wrote to George Mudie's *The Economist* suggesting consumer organization as an expedited mechanism to assist the working class while others detail plans for full-fledged cooperative villages (see Issue #12 4/14/ 1821, 190–191).
2. In fact, co-op stores were popular as early as the 1820s. In 1830, some 300 "co-operative trading associations" were active (Gurney 1996, 13–14).

Building a Social Science. Kirsten Madden and Joseph Persky, Oxford University Press. © Oxford University Press 2024. DOI: 10.1093/oso/9780197693735.003.0006

"Federalists," including J. T. W. Mitchell, William Nuttall and John Watts, advanced a new vision of a consumer-dominated economy.[3] The Federalists anticipated a cooperative commonwealth. But they projected a path to that commonwealth laid out, not through village communities or workshops, but rather through the development of a modern retail and wholesale co-operative corporation.[4]

The central principle of the Federalist theory holds that communities do best when consumer cooperatives obtain and distribute goods and services at, or close to, cost of production. It stands in sharp contrast to visions of cooperation like Mill's, which were based on worker control. In particular, the Federalist understanding of social psychology generated arguments against direct sharing of profits or management with workers. Households in their roles as consumers experience broadly shared interests. Workers, qua workers, have much more narrow concerns. Producer cooperation encourages monopolistic practices. But every worker is part of a consumer household, and that role best represents their socially legitimate interests. Workers as members of consumer cooperatives can democratically participate in guiding their own store and in setting broader policy for cooperative enterprises in wholesale and manufactures. Such policies include enacting fair wages with disciplined and service-oriented production. Such is the Federalist vision for the cooperative commonwealth.

The Federalists were not profuse writers. They produced no lengthy tomes. Nevertheless, they developed a serious and well thought out rationale for their program. Advocates of producer cooperatives attempted to dismiss the Federalists as superficial, conservative, and even soulless. But most often such attacks did not fully engage Federalist thought, its social psychology, and its history. Here we provide a restatement of the Federalist position.

Federalism developed in response to the practical challenges facing co-operative stores like the Rochdale Society of Equitable Pioneers. As such, there is a compelling bloodline. The initial scope of the Rochdale Society reflected Robert Owen's vision. It was nothing if not ambitious. The Pioneers intended not only a retail store, but also a building society, manufacturing facilities, cooperative farms, a domestic cooperative, and ultimately a co-operative village.[5]

---

3. The term "Federalist" strictly applies only to the period after 1872 and the founding of the Cooperative Wholesale Society. However, the Federalist spirit originated in the dividend policy of the Rochdale Pioneers. At the risk of being anachronistic, we use this convenient term to refer to the main line of consumer cooperative thinking.

4. See, for example, Redfern (1924, 52–53).

5. The objects and plans of this Society are to form arrangements for the pecuniary benefit and the improvement of the social and domestic condition of its members, by

The reflection of Owen's thought in the initial Rochdale plan is likely a result of the participation of several of the Pioneers in Owenite activities. Chief among them were James Daly, "a fervent follower of Robert Owen" and Charles Howarth, the "local leader of the 'Owenites'" in Rochdale (Davidson 2016, 59 and 72). In his cooperative history, George Holyoake asserts, "The Socialists [i.e. the Owenites] were the persons who first thought of starting co-operation, who counselled it, who originated and organized it, kept it going and carried it out" (Holyoake 1900, 80).

The plan was grand. And eventually, the Rochdale cooperators accomplished much. But their actual beginnings were modest. With the help of a raised subscription, the Society amassed some £28.[6] The Society then leased the first floor of a warehouse in Toad Lane and stocked it with "flour, butter, sugar, and oatmeal" (Holyoake 1900, 13). With some success and expansion of their capital the Society added tobacco and tea to their wares. The Rochdale Store prospered. It became the model for a host of imitators around the country. While the Society's initial plan was clearly rooted in the old Owenite–Thompson social science, the success of their cooperative stores powerfully influenced their thinking. The original Rochdale plan fell away as the Federalists constructed a new model of consumer cooperation. That model starts with a variant of Owenite social psychology, projects a different set of institutional structures, and follows a distinctive line of argument.

raising a sufficient amount of capital in shares of £1 each, to bring into operation the following arrangements:

- The establishment of a Store for the sale of provisions, clothing, etc.
- The building, purchasing, or erecting a number of houses, in which those members, desiring to assist each other in improving their domestic and social condition, may reside.
- To commence the manufacture of such articles as the Society may determine upon, for the employment of such members as may be without employment, or who may be suffering in consequence of repeated reduction in their wages.
- As a further benefit and security to the members of this Society, the Society shall purchase or rent an *estate or estates of land*, which shall be cultivated by the members who may be out of employment or whose labour may be badly remunerated.
- That, as soon as practicable, this Society shall proceed *to arrange the powers of production, distribution, education and government*; or in other words to establish a self-supporting home-colony of united, interests, or assist other societies in establishing such colonies.
- That for the promotion of sobriety, a Temperance Hotel be opened in one of the Society's houses as soon as convenient. (Quoted in Holyoake 1900, 12)

6. This figure as well as the claim of exactly £1 for each of 28 original members of the Society are likely myths. The initial membership was probably closer to £55 (Davidson 2016, 10, 153).

THE SOCIAL PSYCHOLOGY OF THE
CONSUMER COOPERATIVES

The Federalists, unlike Owen, did not write at length about their basic psychological assumptions. But it is easy enough to draw out their understanding of human nature. Character development can be the product of circumstances. But in contrast to the social psychological optimism driving the various cooperative village experiments or the almost chiliastic spirit of the Christian Socialist enterprises, the Federalist view anticipates that the working class cannot quickly shed the self-interested psychological traits inherited from the past. For example in 1892, J. T. W. Mitchell, the most prominent leader of the consumer cooperative movement, declared in his presidential speech to the Rochdale Congress that the "struggle of the industrious classes" over centuries is to overcome selfishness: "We have had selfishness in centuries past, there is selfishness in our own day, and there is selfishness even amongst us . . . that most unholy quality." Mitchell anticipated a long struggle within cooperation to achieve unselfishness ([1892] 2020, 214).

Like Thompson and Wheeler, the consumer cooperators understood how easily self-interest can translate into selfishness. And thus, the Federalist view assumes a suspicious, almost pessimistic, understanding of the basic human material available in transition to the movement. Particularly where individuals see advantage for themselves—even at a cost to others—they are likely to seize the opportunity.

In response to Mitchell's argument, Federalists encourage young people to develop self-discipline and moral character. Mitchell holds, "The three great forces for the improvement of mankind are religion, temperance, and [consumer] co-operation; and as a commercial force, supported and sustained by the other two, co-operation is the grandest, the noblest, and the most likely to be successful in the redemption of the industrious classes" ([1892] 2020, 218). The cooperative must educate the youth in the practice of community values and the logic of consumer cooperation. The historian Peter Gurney sums the matter neatly: Mitchell is an educationalist because for him " 'intellectual' and 'economic' reform were two sides of the same coin, both equally necessary to assure full emancipation" (Gurney 1996, 46). In 1877, Mitchell enjoined cooperators to promote a cooperative education that " 'would extinguish superstition and jealousy. . . . [T]hey can make for themselves a heaven upon earth'" (Mitchell, as quoted in Gurney 1996, 29).[7]

---

7. As early as 1869, William Thornton identified the co-op store as a major step in transition. Through the dividend it makes possible worker savings. And the co-op store

While the Federalist vision recognizes multiple opportunities for building character in cooperative stores and associated educational institutions, there is no short-cut for the reorganization of the workplace. At least in early transition, the workers seem primarily to respond to self-serving incentives. Workers with limited vision seek out opportunities for slacking. Workers with better character and energy pursue rewards. In either case, it is necessary to manage and motivate workers. William Nuttall, an accomplished accountant for the cooperative movement, suggests that when labor has control over an enterprise they "command it by electing men who would give largely to labour, little to capital, and little or nothing to the consumer."[8] Not unlike Owen, such transitional thinking seems to reflect an underlying belief in the power of management when grounded in intelligence, cooperative service-orientation, and self-denial.[9] A more basic rebuilding of the workplace is a future project.

While reform of worker psychology promises to be difficult, one common sphere of working-class activity lends itself to restructuring. In their roles as consumers, working-class households have much the same interests. The consumer cooperative builds on this basic reality. In the context of consumer cooperation, households become aware of their common interests in lower prices and higher quality. In response to adversity, consumer cooperators must "rise en masse and determine to bind yourselves together as one united force." For, "if you want your great work to proceed it will have to proceed on corporate and not on individual lines" (Mitchell [1892] 2020, 220).

The positive traits of consumer cooperators stand in direct opposition to the longstanding cooperative perception of nastiness of the retail industry. There is little doubt as to the psychology of private retail merchants from the Federalist perspective. The store owners reflect the worst elements of competition.[10] Establishing cooperative stores is a creative community response.

---

provides "special training" in "patience, self-denial, conscientiousness, and public spirit—on which mutual confidence most firmly rests" (1869, 390). Co-ops fund libraries and newsrooms (391); their business and social gatherings grant to all the freedom to speak. Thornton goes on to quote Frederic Harrison: the co-op store "'if not itself a moral and social movement, possesses many high moral and social tendencies'" (392).

8. *Cooperative News* II, 1872, 495, as quoted in (Backstrom 1974, 105).

9. Beyond Robert Owen and Mitchell, John Gray's *Social System* (1831) requires wise and virtuous managers, a problematic requirement as Janet Kimball also acknowledges (Kimball 1948, Ch. 10).

10. Mitchell distinguishes the Rochdale Pioneers who "started on honourable lines to do themselves good, not advertising themselves to do other people an injury." For example, "They never put misleading tickets in their window" ([1892] 2020, 220).

As the retail cooperative stores expanded, most of their customers and members came from the better paid and more skilled elements of the working classes. While strongly emphasizing community, the social psychology of the consumer movement maintained a conservative spirit. Despite William Thompson's and Anna Doyle Wheeler's insistence on the equality of the sexes, patriarchy dominated the cooperative household's self-image.[11] The shops attracted large numbers of evangelical families, which reinforce their conservative tendencies (Cole 1944, 72).

THE COOPERATIVE STORE AND THE DIV

From the Federalist perspective, the evolution of the transitional social psychology rests on uniting the mass of consumers. Institutions are central in the shift toward meaningful cooperation. While early cooperative stores resembled in many ways the small private retailers of the mid-19th century, they held to a set of core practices that defined them as unique institutions and shaped the cooperative character of their membership. Such general practices, developed under Charles Howarth's leadership, made up the day-to-day essence of the consumer cooperative movement (Cole 1944, 64). The cooperative is open and democratic with one vote per household, typically exercised by the male head. The store pays subscribed capital at fixed interest rates. The store never sells adulterated goods. The store conducts its business on a cash-only basis.[12] The Society helps educate its membership in unselfish cooperative principles. The Society is neutral as to religion and politics. All of these rules remain central, but one further institutional practice becomes the virtual defining characteristic of consumer cooperation: the payment of member dividends.

The dividend or "div," often credited to Howarth, becomes the hallmark of the Rochdale movement (Holyoake 1906, 47).[13] Under this plan, after paying interest, making desired investments, and devoting a fraction to education, cooperative stores distribute the rest of earned profits as dividends

11. It is not until later that the Women's Cooperative Guild advanced a new more feminist psychology for the movement. See the next chapter.

12. From the start the Pioneers insisted on cash transactions with the hope to keep stores solvent and the membership out of debt. Despite a strong ideological commitment, the rule was often honored in the breach. In 1898 a report credited to Mrs. Deans of the Women's Cooperative Guild problematically identifies credit trades in cooperative stores.

13. Citing William Nuttall, Holyoake notes that a cooperative society at Meltham Mills began quietly paying a dividend in 1827. Alexander Campbell claimed proposing the system to the Rochdale Pioneers (Holyoake 1906, 278).

in proportion to member purchases.[14] Ironically, a dividend on purchase is much at odds with Owenite principles. Here, for example, is Owen's view of a group of early cooperative stores in Carlisle:

> I found there six or seven Co-operative Societies in different parts of the town, doing well, as they think, that is, making some profit by joint stock retail trading. It is, however, high time to put an end to the notion very prevalent in the public mind that this is the social system which we contemplate or that it will form any part of the arrangements in the New Moral World. (quoted in Cole 1944, 68, from *The New Moral World*, Vol. III, 26)

Despite its Owenite roots and commitments, the Rochdale movement, from the start, built around the non-Owenite institution of the div.

FEDERALIST THEORY

Retail Profits, Classical Economics, and the Federalists

On an economic level, the div represents an innocuous incentive to encourage consumer participation in cooperative stores. And historically the div was a major financial incentive motivating customer participation. If cooperative prices are roughly the same or even a bit higher than those offered by profit making outlets, the div gives the cooperatives a competitive advantage. Serving as a form of quiet savings, the div is a welcome path to modest accumulation for more prosperous working-class households. But the div raises serious theoretical issues for the consumer cooperative movement, questions which circle around the nature and meaning of retail profits in the cooperative economy. Identifying the origins of that surplus lies at the core of Federalist theory—its understanding of reality and the logic of its central institution, the div.

Criticism of retailers has a long populist history—a history that precedes the cooperative movement. In reaction to such attacks, classical political economy early on mounted a theoretical defense of retail profits, developing an extensive position on the character of retailing. Take for an example Adam Smith's *Wealth of Nations*, which is quite explicit on the subject. Retailing, like agriculture, manufacturing, and wholesaling is a

---

14. Writing about the "machinery" of cooperation, Catherine Webb identifies a "large majority of societies" in 1895 with rules or resolutions to place 1–2.5% of net profits into educational funds (1895, 11).

productive activity. Thus, the "persons whose capitals are employed in any of those four ways are themselves productive labourers. Their labour, when properly directed, fixes and realizes itself in the subject or vendible commodity upon which it is bestowed" ([1776] 1976, 362). In short, it is a justification for retail prices based on labor embodied.

Smith's *Wealth of Nations* presents many complaints against retail merchants. But concludes that the "prejudices of some political writers . . . are altogether without foundation." In a competitive setting, "the quantity of grocery goods, which can be sold in a particular town, is limited by the demand of that town and its neighborhood. The capital, therefore, which can be employed in the grocery trade cannot exceed what is sufficient to purchase that quantity." The competition among retailers may ruin some of them, but "can never hurt either the consumer, or the producer." It is their own concern. As to sharp dealing, Smith recognizes that some retailers "perhaps, may sometimes decoy a weak customer to buy what he has no occasion for. This evil, however, is of too little importance to deserve the publick attention, nor would it necessarily be prevented by restricting their numbers." With something of a dramatic flourish, Smith wryly suggests "It is not the multitude of ale-houses, to give the most suspicious example, that occasions a general disposition to drunkenness among the common people; but that disposition arising from other causes necessarily gives employment to a multitude of ale-houses" (361–362).

Smith's general argument dominated early 19th-century political economy. For instance, David Ricardo's *Principles* formalizes the Smithian position in terms of the labor theory of value. Retail labor, like all productive labor in a competitive economy, adds to the value of a commodity. Using the example of stockings, Ricardo asserts that their value depends on "the total quantity of labour necessary to manufacture them and bring them to market." The value of stockings derives from the farm labor that produces the raw material, the transport labor moving it, the manufacturing labor making cloth and stockings, the labor of the engineer, smith, and carpenter, and the "labor of the retail dealer" (Ricardo [1817] 1971, 25).

Echoing Smith and Ricardo, John Ramsay McCulloch in his *Principles of Political Economy*, writes:

> It is frequently, indeed, alleged, that the number of retailers is, in most places, unnecessarily great, and that in order to subsist, they charge an enormous profit. But it is easy to see that there can be no real ground for these statements. A regard to their own interest will always prevent too many individuals from entering into the retail trade, as it prevents them from entering into any other employment . . . the competition to which they are exposed will effectually

hinder them from realizing more than the ordinary rate of profit. (McCulloch 1830, 139)

Sometimes retailers seem to earn higher than market profits, which is a confusion of "wages and profit." Retailers very often work in their shops and miscount wages on their own labor as profit (139).

In such a dominant classical reading, retail profits are in no way out of line with underlying values. Retail profits, like other profits, are a surplus paid on retail stock but created by retail labor. For small shops, that might include only the shop owner. For larger shops, it includes hired workers. Consumers buy most goods at their value and profits are simply proportional to labor inputs. As in other competitive-productive industries, profits of retail merchants represent not inflated prices but the contribution of those merchants' own labor and the labor of their employees. Goods sell at their labor values. If there is cause for complaint it is not from the consumer, but from store workers receiving wages close to subsistence.

Classical economists strongly defended retail profits. But there were dissenters. Even before the emergence of Rochdale, the Owenite, John Gray, addressed the questions surrounding retail.[15] Gray's *Lecture on Human Happiness* (1825) elaborates in detail on the distinction between productive and unproductive labor, including unproductive retail. With a "never-ceasing effort . . . to make their goods appear cheaper than their neighbour's" they undertake deceptive practices (43). With constant competition, indebtedness, and insecurity from price fluctuations, trade losses, and speculation, the "character becomes morose, sullen, avaricious, gloomy, and callous; though it were naturally excellence itself" (44). Employees in retail are doubly doomed as they not only absorb the grim social psychology of retail but are furthermore "the greatest slaves in existence" (44). Six years later in 1831, Gray's *The Social System* explicitly denies McCulloch's argument and the dominant classical understanding of retail activity as productive.[16] The current volume maintains Gray's earlier assertion: "Retailers are non-producers." There are many retailers, and they

---

15. "Original, independent, trenchant, and radical" in his younger days, John Gray (1799–1883) stood out as an analytical critic of competitive capitalism who "demanded that these defects should be dealt with by radical and preventive" methods (Foxwell 1899, xxvii). Foxwell summarizes the early John Gray "as the pioneer of modern militant, aggressive socialism," his noteworthy opposition to violence being a major distinguishing point from Marx (l–lv). According to Kimball (1948), the political economy of "voluntary collectivism" attracted the attention of John Gray only until 1850, his success in business apparently absorbing his energies thereafter.

16. *The Social System* extensively quotes the McCulloch passage discussed above (252).

extract much in profits. Gray argues that if retail profits are "regulated upon equitable principles, instead of by competition between each other, two-thirds of them, at least, might be dispensed with, and their work be infinitely better done" (252). Exactly why the competition among retailers fails to force their prices to the level of labor values is obscure in Gray's argument.

More cautious than Gray, the classical luminary John Stuart Mill also questioned whether retail activity is always productive. In his *Principles* ([1848] 1965), Mill worries "that of the price paid by the consumer, so large a proportion is absorbed by the gains of retailers." Contrary to Ricardo and McCulloch, Mill suggests that retail prices "seem to feel very slowly and imperfectly the effect of competition." He observes that "when competition does exist, it often instead of lowering prices, merely divides the gains of the high price among a greater number of dealers." Retail ends with a large share of the final price and the actual payments to producers are often surprisingly small. Mill acknowledges that in large cities competition works in its more normal mode, reducing prices and bringing them in line with costs of production. And he notes that improvements in transportation tend "to assimilate the whole country to a large town." But whatever the likely developments of the future, at mid-century outside major cities, custom regulates many prices (243).[17] Clearly, Mill anticipates the eventual incorporation of retail into the general competitive system. Presumably at that point retail corresponds to the Ricardian model. But in the 19th century, for most middling cities and smaller towns, retail profits were excessive, given the actual labor expended on trade.[18]

The Federalist movement was far from indifferent to these early debates over the nature of retail profits. The Federalists generated two important if somewhat informal theorists, William Nuttall and John Watts. The accountant Nuttall served as secretary of several cooperative organizations. He was a force in establishing the movement's publication, the *Cooperative*

17. Mill adds to this thought that such custom is "modified from time to time by notions existing in the minds of purchasers and sellers of some kind of equity or justice."

18. We add a footnote here on the position of Marx on these questions even though his system could not in any full sense be known or available to mid-century British cooperators. These thoughts appear in his third volume of *Capital*. Following Ricardo, Marx generally insists on the equalization of profits through competition including retail profits. However, Marx does not think these competitive and necessary activities generate value. Rather they share proportionally to the capital advanced in the value created in production, thus lowering the overall profit rate. The key point here is that for Marx, like Ricardo, retail does not raise prices over values (Marx [1885] 1967, Vol. 2, Ch. 6, "The Costs of Circulation").

News (Cole 1944, 198; Jones 1894, 599). Watts, the more scholarly, started as an Owenite lecturer, obtained a Ph.D. from the University of Giessen in Germany, and became a major participant in Manchester reform activities (Henderson 1976, 285–286; Lee 1899, Vol. 60, 71–72).[19]

Not surprisingly, the Federalists rejected the classical mainstream and instead took the position of dissenters like Gray and Mill. Retail labor is unproductive, its competition at best imperfect, at worst perverse. And "custom" causes retail profits to swell out of line with classical value theory. Federalists argue: There are far too many retailers. To survive, they inflate their markups. Such large markups mean that retailers and customers engage in a fundamentally unfair (and in modern terminology, unequal) exchange. In response to the classical position, Watts writes,

> Some of us have been taught to believe that the utmost economy in the distribution of commodities must be accomplished by the freest possible competition amongst shopkeepers; but practically we know that the very multiplication of shopkeepers tends to increase the capital which lies useless upon their shelves, and which yet demands profit, if its owners are to live. (Watts 1872, 589)

Retail profits are monopoly returns to unproductive capital and unscrupulous middlemen.

Retail customers buy at prices much higher than underlying values. Fair prices are close to costs of production. Hence if retail cooperatives sell at going prices, their buyers deserve a substantial dividend. As Nuttall puts it, the "true co-operative principle" is "consumers ought only to be charged cost prices; but if profit be charged, it should be returned to them as dividends on purchase" (Nuttall 1872, 268).

The Cooperative Wholesale Society and Federalism

Ultimately any plans for the retail cooperative movement can only come to fruition if the stores themselves prosper. And the Rochdale enterprises did prosper. Membership went from the group of founders in 1844 to about 6,000 twenty-five years later. By then, its sales were close to £300,000. And most remarkably its profits were about £30,000. The very prosperity

19. Engels, living in Manchester, was aware of Watts and attended some of his public lectures. At first impressed, he and Marx later disparaged Watts, in part for his Proudhonian view of property (Henderson 1976, 286). Stedman Jones (2020) also traces intellectual linkages from Owen to Watts to Engels and Marx.

of the expanding collection of retail stores generated larger and larger dividends for its base of customers. Holyoake, the historian of the cooperative movement and a friend of producer cooperatives, later claimed that had the Rochdale pioneers fully anticipated the magnitude of the profits their stores would command, the founders might have argued more deeply the pros and cons of distributing such large sums to their customers. They might have reasoned thus:

> What right had the customer to the gains of our trade? What does he do towards creating them? He receives value for his money. He gives no thought, he has no cares, he performs no duties, he takes no trouble, he incurs no risks. If we lose he pays no loss. Why should we enrich him by what we win? (Holyoake 1906, 280)

Over the years, the increasingly professional managers of the Rochdale movement balked at fully distributing the profits as dividends. Potentially profitable investment opportunities abounded in many directions. Like managers and directors in most all successful enterprises—including corporations run for profit—they commited to organizational growth. Their own careers and influence expanded with the size of the cooperatives. Growth of course requires investment. And cooperative retained earnings provided a ready source of investment funds. Rather than using cooperative store surpluses to finance self-managed Owenite internal colonies, the managers convinced the cooperative membership to integrate backward from retail into wholesale.[20]

In 1856 the Rochdale Society launched a "wholesale department" under the leadership of Abraham Greenwood. Within three years, the effort failed (Redfern 1913, 14). The department and other cooperative wholesaling activities of the 1850s suffered because they did not fall under the limited liability provisions of existing cooperative legislation. Only individuals could hold shares in a cooperative venture. But wholesale organizing is easier with shares held by the cooperative stores themselves. E. V. Neale, the wealthy Christian Socialist and lawyer, drafted new national legislation. It passed in 1862, and in 1863 the Cooperative Wholesale Society (CWS) began (25–29). The CWS was a major success, becoming the "great Gargantua" of the cooperative movement.

---

20. The idea of cooperative wholesaling emerged early in the movement. The minutes of "The Co-operative and Economical Society" provide details of a plan for consumer cooperatives: capital raised by the sale of shares; purchasing at wholesale with 5% markup to cover costs; stocking the goods in a Society-run warehouse; and ultimately employing producers (as reported in George Mudie's *The Economist*, Issue #15 5/5/ 1821, 235–237).

At first glance such developments might seem in line with the broad early statements of the Rochdale plans. Neale rationalized and restated those plans at the second Christian Socialist Conference in 1853. In opposition to his Christian Socialist colleagues, Neale advocated the Rochdale-type cooperative stores as the starting point of a much broader wholesale society movement. The next logical step was the workers' associations. Finally echoing Owen, Neale intended to build "among these productive institutions a system of exchange of labour, founded upon principles of strict justice."[21]

Neale portrayed the consumer cooperatives as great practical steppingstones to a broad Owenite movement. But many in the Christian Socialist base feared the pace and character of the new developments. From the start the Christian Socialists' theorist, John Ludlow, doubted the role of consumer cooperatives. He worried that the stores and their management, whatever their rhetoric, lacked commitment to broad cooperative reform of the economy as a whole. In their own way, Ludlow and most of the Christian Socialists committed to a reading of value that finds its source in human labor—and thus the importance of production over consumption. And of course, their theological leader, F. D. Maurice, fundamentally questioned all efforts to build a hierarchically ordered system.[22] For a time, Neale put aside such doubts. He eagerly engaged with the consumer cooperative leadership. That leadership was nothing if not dynamic. Chief in the group was J. T. W. Mitchell.

Mitchell certainly held a cooperator's pedigree. His grandfather was a major supporter of a cooperative store in Rochdale in the 1830s. Its failure provided important lessons to the Rochdale Pioneers. Born in 1828, John Thomas Whitehead Mitchell experienced a difficult childhood, raised by his single mother. He and his mother struggled to make ends meet. He grew up in a "Rochdale beerhouse and workman's lodging-house" (Redfern 1913, 201). In later years, he was a strong temperance advocate and dedicated Congregationalist Sunday school teacher. Although engaged once, he never married.

Mitchell began to work at ten and showed considerable promise. By 1848 he was the manager of a flannel warehouse. In 1853 he joined the Rochdale cooperative, becoming an active member. He had a strong personality coupled with a broad and open sense of fellowship. His cooperative

---

21. Prefatory Address of the Executive Committee Appointed by the Conference *Report of the [2nd] Co-operative Conference Held at Manchester . . . 1853*, 3–7, quoted in (Backstrom 1974, 46).
22. On the Christian Socialist positions see Chapter 5.

colleagues recognized him for managerial skill and financial acuity.[23] He was one of the strongest supporters of expanding the Rochdale organization into the wholesaling business (Redfern 1913, *passim*).

In 1867 Mitchell left his long-term job. He began on his own financial account to market cotton cloth produced at the mill of the Rochdale Cooperative Manufacturing Society. As Redfern describes, that mill effectively sold "in competition with others in the open market" (1924, 27). Mitchell essentially worked two jobs, one for the CWS and the other on his own. Through the early 1870s Mitchell worked more and more for the cooperative movement and less and less on his own account. In 1874, the CWS elected him president. At some point in this period, Mitchell's London agent went bankrupt. Redfern quotes Mitchell's close friend Sir William Maxwell that Mitchell "allowed his business to quietly slip away from him" (45). Despite his brilliant successes, his salary in the CWS remained modest. His total annual remuneration from the CWS, including travel funds, was less than £150.

Mitchell's mixing of private and cooperative business might strike a modern reader as a bit suspicious, and yet it is difficult to judge how serious Mitchell was to establish his own enterprise. Redfern is probably right in speculating, had Mitchell possessed

> a little more self-regard, a little less pride in and care for the working classes . . . [he] probably would have gone to reinforce the middle class; for a natural selection of this kind is always operating, to intensify the poverty of those who remain behind. But he gave himself to his fellows, and died a poor man. (Redfern 1913, 203)[24]

The interests that Mitchell promoted are in no sense those of his own material welfare. Rather they were the interests of the working classes as he read them.

Mitchell's Federalist understanding of the cooperative movement is fundamentally as a collective of working-class consumer-investors seeking their own financial and cultural improvement. At first the collective aims only at excluding middlemen from retail and wholesale. The vision evolves with the collective becoming the effective owner of a range of manufacturing

---

23. William Maxwell, the Scottish Wholesale Society president, eulogizes after Mitchell's death that "'it may not be too much to claim that he [Mitchell] was largely instrumental in placing the Wholesale Society in the secure financial positions it occupies to-day'" (as quoted in Webb 1921, 123).

24. At his death the director of the multi-million pound CWS held assets amounting to only £350 (Redfern 1924, 89).

and service activities including cornmills, textiles, shoes, and printing, and banking and insurance. Mitchell strove to define "consumer ownership" in a way quite parallel to the modern understanding of corporate ownership. Keep in mind that at the time the corporation was only just coming into a central role in industrialized economies.

Four key characteristics define the emerging nature of corporate ownership: first, limited liability[25]; second, corporate stockholders as "residual claimants"[26]; third, stockholder control; and fourth, a corporate right to buy stock in other corporations. Such corporate ownership emerged in mid19th-century Britain as the most appropriate organizational structure to manage the economies of scale from the new technologies of the Industrial Revolution. It is clearly a major innovation, an innovation as revolutionary as the technological discoveries themselves. But the matter is complex. While the new bourgeois manufacturing class committed to the corporate form, the traditional landed classes, with their considerable political power, remained suspicious. And their suspicion extended to the diligent cooperators, men like Mitchell, eager to use a corporate-like form for their own revolution.

This is not to say that the old ruling class, the new bourgeoisie, or even Mitchell himself viewed the expansion of the CWS as anything more than an effort to achieve low prices for cooperative stores, while encouraging thrift among the membership. Still, Mitchell's model for cooperation offered a parallel structure to the economic system arising around the modern corporation. At the heart of the Federalist alternative is the more or less full replacement of the corporate shareholder with the cooperative member/customer.

However, the Federalist vision involves a cooperative ownership structure that point for point matches the corporate ownership structure. First, like the corporation, there is the emphasis on a framework of limited liability. Only limited liability effectively allows the participation of thousands of members financing cooperative expansion. And throughout the system the residual claimants remain the ground level consumer cooperative

25. A broad right to use limited liability in British corporations only dates from the mid-19th century, the same period in which the issue became central to the expansion of the cooperative movement. In fact, John Stuart Mill bases his own somewhat reluctant support for limited liability on the grounds that such a legal framework is necessary for cooperative and profit sharing enterprises (Mill [1848] 1965, 895–896). It is also worth noting that it was the United States, not Britain, that pioneered limited liability laws. In fact, in discussing these laws Mill quotes the American economist Henry Carey.

26. As residual claimants, stockholders hold a property right in all the firm's net revenues after costs.

members. They receive the surplus either directly in dividends or through retained earnings devoted to investment expansion. Through their cooperative stores, consumer members maintain indirect control of the larger institution. In addition, the CWS can create wholly owned subsidiaries (Cole 1944, 118–121).

Dr. John Watts, Mitchell's ally, first named the scheme "Federalism." An old Owenite, Watts took the surprisingly un-Owenite position that the CWS, as a truly federal body, should own production units for the benefit of the cooperative stores (Backstrom 1974, 106). The stores are subject to democratic control and they in turn subscribe to the CWS and through that body to all the enterprises it develops. The cooperator fully substitutes for the shareholder.

The Federalist view anchors the efficiency claims for the new system in the shared scale economies it makes possible.[27] As Nuttall put it, the CWS

> enables the smallest retail stores to buy the best quality of goods, and at as cheap a rate as the largest . . . . [I]t is the means of preventing failure, and facilitating success. No society need keep large stocks . . . interest on capital is saved, less warehouse room is required, and fewer losses by goods becoming unsaleable incurred. Instead of societies sending their managers to market, as formerly, the greater part of the business is conducted by letter. (Nuttall 1869, 42, quoted in Butler 1986, 266)

Just as the cooperative store allows its members to pool their purchasing power, so the Wholesale allows the stores to pool theirs.

The federalist structure represents the path to the cooperative commonwealth. The div returns much of the surplus to members. At the same time,

> We also co-operate with other societies in owning and controlling the greatest concern in this country, viz., the Co-Operative Wholesale Society . . . we both own and control the means of production and distribution, which is of tremendous importance to the workers . . . (who) by loyally supporting their own shop . . . can claim all the advantages that associated efforts can give. (H.

27. Alfred Marshall receives credit for theoretical insights into internal economies of scale. It seems reasonable to give the consumer cooperators credit for anticipating the benefits of internal economies of scale, beginning in retail and through backward integration into wholesaling and manufacturing. Marshall, himself, points to the economies of scale in "organized buying and selling," specifically identifying the example of "centralized co-operative associations." See Book 4, Chapter 11, Section 2, added in the 6th edition of 1910 (Marshall [1890] 1961, Vols. I and II, annotations by C. W. Guillebaud, Vol. II, 333).

Whalley, President Denholme Industrial Co-operative Society, Ltd. 1930, 77, quoted in Yeo 2017, 100)

The expansion of the Federalist model reopens deep questions concerning the nature of profit and the surplus. Early cooperative theory assumes exorbitant profits of the overexpanded retailing sector. But that theory makes no such argument with respect to wholesaling and manufacturing. So why necessitate backward linkages? Federalists identify the expansion back into wholesaling as at least in part due to wholesaler prejudices against cooperative retailers (Redfern 1913, 41). They make almost no justification for integrating back into manufacturing. It is simply something they can do. Early Owenites see wholesaling and manufacturing profits as ultimately generated by the workers in those establishments. Hence, it seems natural for the Federalist movement to reconsider its almost exclusive emphasis on consumer rebates and consumer democracy. It seems natural for Federalists to consider sharing profits and decision-making power with workers. But the Federalists did not move in that direction.

At root, the Federalists deeply distrusted the social psychology of workers qua workers. The historian Stephen Yeo summarizes the point neatly: "Employees as [consumer] Co-operators should control the Movement, they should not as workers, control the works, or even (as employees) the shop" (Yeo 1995, 60). In this broad fear of a monopoly spirit among workers, the Federalist vision questions the ease of transition.

C. Fair Wages for a Fair Day's Work

Mitchell and other Federalists fell back on the concept of "fair wages for a fair day's work." Because workers tend to shirk work responsibilities, "fair" wages can be relatively low. Here the Federalists seem to have in mind wages largely set by custom. But the exact level of wages is not central to the expanded Federalist argument. If workers concentrate most of their purchases in cooperative stores and if after-div prices in those stores are close to costs, then workers as a group receive goods of value approximately equal to the labor value they expend. Consider this the Fundamental Federalist Theorem.

In practice, the CWS paid market wages or a bit better, similar to the growing corporations. Keep in mind that from 1820 to the end of the 19th century, British wages rose above subsistence (Clark 2005, 1319). The Federalists identified the general labor market as the effective arbiter of skill differentials during the transition to a cooperative economy. Similarly,

the managers and foremen of cooperative enterprises must be paid competitive wages.

At the same time, the Federalists accepted a generous interest rate as an appropriate reward for the "contribution" of capital. They were sure that capital contributes, for they had ample experience with the difficulties and ruin that follow undercapitalized productive enterprises. Why exactly this implies the old Owenite 5% rate of interest is never clear from the Federalists. But they seemed to think in a market context that is what they must pay, at least in the period of transition.

Like the emerging private corporations of the same era, the consumer cooperatives ran a risk of a separation of ownership and control. The accumulation of retained earnings increases organizational size and enhances managers' power. Understandably, managers committed to continuing institutional growth. Growth encourages a greater complexity of organizational structure and a greater need for administrative oversight. Without doubting the sincerity of the emerging cooperative executives, their plans and aspirations materialized as a claim on the surplus at least partially independent of the cooperative membership and certainly hostile to any sharing with their workforce. In many ways our Federalist writers, Nuttall, Watts, and Mitchell, identified with such a managerial class and projected that class' vision as the appropriate program of the retail cooperative movement.[28]

A man like Mitchell might easily claim that his own business acumen generated much of the profits of the CWS. Surely that is what leaders in the private sector did in similar circumstances. But true to the other-serving social psychology of cooperation, Mitchell acted as an agent for the broad class of cooperative members. It is that class, disciplining itself and exercising its common intelligence, that promises broader change. Led by a committed, and self-denying leadership, that class moves the entire structure toward a new cooperative economic system.

Federalism focuses on workers not as producers, but as consumers. Of course, such ideas do not go unchallenged in the cooperative movement. The Christian socialist theorist Ludlow consistently argued against a consumer-oriented cooperation. But the chief antagonist to Mitchell and Watts became E. V. Neale, who loaned his name and energy to making the CWS a reality. He was greatly concerned that the CWS and the cooperative

---

28. The success of these managers did not go without comment in the movement itself. The *Co-operative News* observes that Rochdale "produced a 'vast number' of comfortably situated people who had started life as 'the poorest of the poor'" (Kirk 1985, 138) quoting *Co-operative News* (March 23, 1895, 289–290).

store system were moving too far from their Owenite roots. As noted in Chapter 5, in 1851 Neale debated Ludlow defending the cooperative stores. But now he worried that cooperative production was getting short shrift from the movement. Through his continuing service and labor, Neale established creditability as a supporter of cooperation.

Neale and Ludlow played key roles in creating an umbrella organization for the cooperative movement, the Cooperative Union. Riding a broad popularity, Neale somewhat surprisingly maneuvered into the position of General Secretary of the Union in 1873. Although it lacked the heft of Mitchell's role in the CWS, the position gave Neale ample opportunity to question the centralizing tendencies of Federalism, labeling it "Caesarism" (Backstrom 1974, 113).

The immediate issue was whether totally owned subsidiaries of the CWS share profits with their employees. The early 1870s marked an extremely difficult period for producer cooperatives, the majority of which failed in a widespread business downturn (Cole 1944, 170). In 1875 the CWS under Mitchell's leadership completely repudiated profit sharing with its workers.[29] Decision-making in the shop must maintain a strict hierarchical format. The supporters of Mitchell's position argued in effect for the sacking of workers dissatisfied with their jobs in cooperative ventures (Redfern 1924, 71).

In sharp contrast, Neale put forth the central tenet of producer cooperative thinking: "[A]ll division of profit must be abandoned." Beyond the "wages of capital," profits are to accrue, not to the capitalist or the consumer, but to the worker (Neale 1877, *Co-operative News*, Vol. VIII, 394, quoted in Backstrom 1974, 123).[30] Echoing Owen, Neale was clear. The "wholesale system" of Mitchell and his colleagues is nothing more than a version of the "joint-stock system." Neale, now disillusioned with the Federalist position, put forth the traditional system of producer cooperation, the system endorsed by most Owenites, J. S. Mill, and the Christian socialists.

The Federalists rejected Neale's position, while pursuing their own goal: a world in which the CWS effectively employs the entire labor force at "fair wages" and workers participate as consumers in the management and

29. Interestingly, for several years the Scottish Wholesale Society maintained the practice of sharing a portion of profits with their workers. According to Holyoake "Though not enough to be much of an inspiration to workers, it recognizes the principle of participation which is creditable to the sense of honour and equity, associated with the Scottish character" (Holyoake 1906, 618).

30. Some of the Women's Cooperative Guild members, such as Mary Ann Lawrenson, supported the same line of argument (see Chapter 7).

benefits of cooperation. They claimed that the alternative of worker control amounts to nothing more than a "new system of competition" setting up one worker-managed shop against all others (Redfern 1924, 53). And if not competition, what could stop a section of workers from seeking out monopoly advantage?

The Federalists, following the path of classical political economists like David Ricardo and William Greg, raised the specter of monopoly against the advocates of producer cooperatives. Yes, the CWS also aims at monopoly, but it must necessarily take the form of a monopoly owned and controlled by those for whom production is directed. If the CWS creates monopoly profits, it must return them to the consumers who pay those monopoly prices. Such a clear statement stands in contrast to the somewhat vague claims about monopoly put forward by the Christian socialists and other advocates of producer cooperatives. Ludlow, for example, hoped that the various worker-controlled firms might bargain amicably about prices. He argued that those prices would gravitate toward costs of production with no section of the working class attempting to extract profits based on their monopoly position (see Chapter 5). The Federalists doubted the premise. Inevitably, they feared that workers left largely to their own devices would push for a sectional advantage. Only a firm, Federalist organization can hope to control such tendencies.

In 1891 at age 63, Mitchell put forth one of his most analytical statements, a variation on the monopoly argument against producer cooperatives. He observed the wide differences in capital per worker across industries. A CWS firm in one industry had a capital labor ratio of £50 per worker. Others had ratios of £87 and £312. And one, a new flour mill with 200 workers, had a ratio of £1500 per worker. The last establishment was earning a profit of £40,000. Is it fair or right for those 200 to claim that large profit for themselves? No, the profit simply reflects the going cost of capital and by rights should return to all workers—that is consumers as a group (Redfern 1924, 80).

This example parallels the complex "transformation problem" of Marxian economics. Under competition, the differences across industries in capital labor ratios suggest that prices reflect the scarcity of capital and thus generate more profit in those industries with high ratios.[31] In cooperation, only a large institution like the CWS can command the capital for massive capital-intensive investment. If CWS invests in a capital-intensive industry, the small portion of workers in that industry have no claim to

---

31. For Marx, these are the organic ratios of the composition of capital.

disproportionate income. Mitchell offers a simple and practical means of handling the implications of this recognition of the scarcity value of capital. The example he uses presumes competition among capitals in the background of the larger economy in which the CWS actively competes. Let the corresponding profit return broadly to the mass of all workers as consumers.[32]

Mitchell clearly looked forward to a day when large private fortunes no longer exist. But it remains unclear what future Mitchell envisioned for the intra-class differences among the members of the working class, differences painfully obvious in the cooperative movement. The practical effect of Mitchell's approach to the CWS is to favor the upper tiers of the working class who can afford to pay cash on multiple purchases and to accumulate modest savings through the cooperative stores. Indeed, that approach substitutes the upper working-class stratum for the private shareholders. However, on more than one occasion, Mitchell anticipated the cooperative movement resulting in far more equality. He told the 1887 Cooperative Congress, "What we wanted to accomplish by co-operation was absolute equality in the distribution of wealth, though that hardly seemed possible" (quoted in Yeo 1995, 48). And he never made clear how such a convergence would come about.

To the frequent claim that worker motivation improves if they possess a share of the profits in the firms in which they work, Mitchell and the Federalists responded that employees fairly hired by the cooperative movement should eventually appreciate their responsibility to the larger collective. Using profit sharing as an incentive sends the wrong message to the workers.[33] In the fully cooperative economy, the appropriate role for the modern worker is the "servant"—in service to the cooperative interest. In the meantime, the Federalist approach intends to treat workers more fairly and more equally than under the rule of capitalism, but work is work and requires hierarchy. Workers as consumers recapture the surplus extracted from them in production through the div and other democratic forms of participation. Such is the deal as Mitchell saw it.

32. It is not clear how the Federalist vision anticipates price determination in a fully cooperative economy and whether capital scarcity plays a role. Nor is it clear how Marx would respond to Mitchell's insightful argument.

33. Statement at the 1892 Royal Commission on Labour, quoted in Redfern (1924, 71).

A NEW PATH TO A COOPERATIVE COMMONWEALTH

The cooperative stores provide their customers with healthy products at reasonable prices. The div incentivizes thrift among households. During the transitional stage, high markups common in for-profit retailing assure success. The cooperative is also a source of positive community feeling. Over time, the strong financial performance of the consumer cooperatives contributes to the broadening of the movement. The Federalists abandoned the original Owenite vision of cooperative villages in favor of a corporate-like alternative.

Mitchell supported the div throughout his career in the consumer cooperative movement. He offered his own understanding of the cooperative transition. The spread of working-class education is key to the movement as is a frugal and independent working class provisioned by cooperative stores at cost. The CWS in turn supplies those stores with its expanding web of production units. Working people effectively own these enterprises and claim the div as a return. More and more of the economy comes under the direction of their democratic cooperatives. A cooperative commonwealth ultimately replaces the economy of competition. Here is a new world where "none will have too much and none will have too little" (Redfern 1924, 43).

Under Mitchell's acute and energetic leadership, the CWS grew to be one of the major business entities in Great Britain. From 1874 when Mitchell took the chairmanship until 1895 when he died, the affiliated membership of the Society grew from about 200,000 to over 900,000, while net sales grew from under £2 million to £10 million. The Society expanded into international trade, acquiring a merchant fleet by the end of the 19th century. In 1882, CWS boats opened direct trade with the Far East as part of its tea department.[34] The Society also expanded production activities. Although Mitchell dealt with the wave of manufacturing bankruptcies from the 1870s business crisis, he cautiously advanced into boots and shoes, cloth making, cocoa and chocolates, cabinet-making, soap, and others. While the list is impressive, the producing enterprises accounted for only a modest share of CWS business in the period (Cole 1944, 210–211).

Mitchell likely agreed with his Federalist colleague, Dr. John Watts, as to the future of consumer cooperation. Watts summarized his view of

---

34. One of the troubling global distributional implications of the federalist theorem is its extension of productive reach to colonial plantations. If the cooperative stores do not follow, the colonized population is left out of the cooperative and productive benefits.

transition with a calculation, oft repeated in the cooperative movement. Workers earned about £350 million a year. If they spent most all of it at cooperative stores capable of saving 7.5% of sales, they could generate an investment fund of £26.25 million a year. This capital could then employ 262,500 workers at £100 per worker. In less than 15 years the movement would then employ "all the working men in the nation" (Watts 1872, 589).

Along with such calculations, the proponents of consumer cooperation offered a fledgling theory. For Watts, cooperation is "[a] system of self- and fellow-help, by which every prudent young man may become his own land-lord, his own capitalist, and his own employer."[35] Building on their under-standing of social psychology and institutional structures it is possible to clarify three major social welfare implications. The Federalist consumer cooperatives return superabundance in material production. Consumer cooperatives generate high levels of equity in the distribution of real in-come. And they effectively diffuse economic decision-making power.

First, consider superabundance. Cooperative institutions reinforce the cooperative side of social psychology. In particular, the interaction produces intelligent, self-denying managers who promote the cooperative cause. Though vested with power, there should be little in the way of ineffi-cient rent seeking. Superabundance also results from the intentional direc-tion of retained earnings into physical investment as the CWS holds wage costs low. And relatively novel from the historical view, there are returns from economies of scale as an incorporated CWS expands across retail shops and integrates backwards.

Second, consider equity. There are multiple pathways bringing about rel-atively high equity in the consumer cooperative system. Because consumer interests are consistent with community interests, the system directs the surplus into consumer dividends. The Fundamental Federalist Theorem explains the equity of consumer cooperation: the div allows workers-as-consumers to ultimately claim the full value their labor creates. The div resolves potential distributional inequities across industries with different capital labor ratios. Further, such a system directs some of the surplus into retained earnings for the stores and the CWS. In addition to invest-ment, these retained earnings finance social services such as cooperative education.

Finally, not every person works, not every person can lay claim to pro-perty; but every person and every household consumes daily. In light of this common economic activity, the consumer cooperative theorists justify

---

35. (Watts 1871, 1; 12), quoted in (Benjamin Jones [1894] 1968, 739).

intentionally structuring institutions to diffuse decision-making responsibility across consumers. Diffusion of decision-making also derives from
assumptions about social psychology. Given that workers and retailers tend
to self-serving behavior, and whereas the consumers have a common bond,
the system vests economic decision-making power with the consumers.
There is a strong claim that managers brought up in the movement tend
to exhibit a cooperative, other-serving mindset. But with a combination of
hierarchical workplaces and the ever-expanding CWS, consumer control is
necessary to balance management power.

By Mitchell's death in 1895, the CWS was the dominant force in the
English cooperative movement. The large institutional structure was clearly
Federalist with consumers, or more accurately their leaders, at the helm.[36]

DISCUSSION

While building substantial opportunities for democratic participation by
consumers into the institutions, the leadership of the consumer cooperative movement took considerable criticism for its refusal to share profits
and decision-making power with workers in the cooperatives. For 50 years,
it remained the most divisive conflict in British cooperation. Given the
three broad implications for social welfare—superabundance, equity, and
diffused decision-making—the consumer cooperative thinkers maintained
there is no need for self-managed production. Worker-owned cooperatives
manage poorly and ultimately take monopoly profits for themselves.
Neale and others put forward compromise proposals. Some supported an
arbitrary 50/50 division of profits between workers and consumers. But
Mitchell and the CWS did not waver.[37] And, perhaps surprisingly, Mitchell

---

36. See Chapter 11 for a summary of Beatrice and Sidney Webb's thoughtful criticisms
concerning the small numbers of cooperative consumers participating politically in
their cooperative organizations.

37. At times such back and forth is described as a conflict between the working-class
supporters of consumer cooperation, like Mitchell, and the middle- and upper-class
supporters of producer cooperatives, like Ludlow, Neale, and Hughes. But as G. D.
H. Cole convincingly argues, the two sides do not break down so neatly:

In the working class camp the old Owenites and idealistic Socialists . . . regarded
Co-operative store keeping not as an end in itself but as a step towards the Cooperative or Socialist Commonwealth, which they envisaged partly in terms of
producers' self-government. At the same time among the higher classes, are men
such as Cobden and Gladstone who "regarded the Co-operative Movement mainly
as an agency for encouraging the virtues of thrift and independence among the
working classes. (Cole 1944, 170)

expanded the support for his vision of consumer cooperatives among the intellectuals of the left.[38]

The Guild socialist economist, G. D. H. Cole, cautiously defends the cooperatives' labor policies as, "employees themselves set much more store by good wage rates than by the bonus." Employees do not strongly dispute the discontinuance of bonus payments (Cole 1944, 171). Frightened by the poor performance of producer cooperatives and wage cuts occurring elsewhere in the serious recession of the late 1870s, stable pay pacified the employees of cooperative-owned businesses.[39] It is wrong, though, to claim worker satisfaction in the stores and CWS. Especially in the producing units, organization and occasional strikes tempted workers. After a failed strike in 1886, a group of CWS shoe factory workers launched their own worker-controlled establishment, The Leicester Manufacturing Boot and Shoe Society (Gurney 1996, 174). Socialists of various stripes often attacked the cooperative movement for its poor treatment of labor. And according to Peter Gurney, "What made matters more difficult was that there was more than a grain of truth in these accusations; the language of 'community' tended to conceal difference within as well as outside the movement and many co-operators were thoroughly insensitive to the status of 'labour'" (173).

Mitchell's position leaves the CWS open to serious questions. How effectively can a sub-group of consumers and their representatives redress worker grievances? Is such limited and indirect form of worker representation likely to fracture the common bond among consumers? Mitchell and his colleagues explicitly told dissatisfied workers that they could leave.[40] The policy seems less than fully cooperative.

There remains the underlying problem of shifting outlook from selfishness to an enlarged self-interest among economic constituencies. How will this be achieved among workers whether in manufacturing, retail, or wholesale? The consumer cooperative writers seemed optimistic but did not wrestle sufficiently with this concern. Hence, we speculate on the possible mechanisms to complete their argument. The goal is to convincingly

38. Consider, for example, Beatrice Potter (Webb). Her 1891 survey of the cooperative movement, in part influenced by Mitchell, strongly supports consumer cooperatives while berating the producer cooperatives. Of course, as a Fabian, she did anticipate the nationalization of major industries.

39. This interpretation stretches back at least to Margaret Llewelyn Davies (1891, 1011).

40. Conceivably, worker mobility could even change the terms of trade across commodities which consumer boards might be sensitive to. But this relies upon a competitive mechanism for solving differences among cooperators.

describe how the consumer cooperative system tends to enlarge the narrow self-interest among workers. The obvious starting point is to draw on Owen's rational-ethical education system. And as we know, the cooperative shops intentionally committed funds in this direction. Moreover, there is the fellow feeling that the cooperative store nurtures.[41] Finally, superabundance coupled with more equitable purchasing power provide individuals a secure economic base for broader community concern. It is an endogenous mechanism which the consumer cooperative theorists did not fully explicate. Federalism can provide an elaborate outlet for workers to express concerns through their consumer voices. And as Anna Doyle Wheeler suggests, social interaction can build alliances, increase sympathy, and enlarge the personal understanding of self-interest (Wheeler 1833, 280).

A related criticism of the consumer cooperators is that their movement, while anchored in the working class, did little in the short run to address tensions among strata of workers. Critics accuse consumer cooperators of representing an aristocracy of labor (Kirk 1985, 5). The system accepts two major income differentials: (i) wage inequalities deriving from differences in skill; and (ii) varying dividends, with more returns to those who consume more. However, it is important to remember that these income inequalities are much smaller than those which derive from private property rights and rent seeking through elite capture of decision-making.

Finally, it seems reasonable to suggest some skepticism about the depths of democracy in the retail shops and the CWS. There is potential for corruption, particularly with paternalistic power vested in managers and as the system grows in scale. In her history of industrial cooperation, Catherine Webb identifies the contemporary question of "whether there is not some danger of the free democratic constitution of the societies being overborne by the weight of autocratic officialism." The solutions Webb suggests are "the exercise, on the part of the movement, of its full responsibility and control over the policy and practice of the societies; and by electing as directors men of high character and ability" (1921, 127).

While advancing cooperation within the British economy, the consumer cooperative model clearly leaves unresolved several pressing issues. It is paternalistic, accepting of hierarchy, and potentially corrupt. Beginning in 1883 a new proto-feminist institution, the Women's Cooperative Guild, constructively critiqued and reformed the thinking within the consumer cooperative movement. They are more closely linked to the spirit of the

---

41. Insights from the Women's Cooperative Guild provides more depth about the relevance of the store in shaping a cooperative social psychology. See Chapter 7.

early Owenites while constructing a central platform concerning women's experiences. The Women's Cooperative Guild generated a distinct methodology for engaging participation, building equality, and elevating character in line with Owenite principles. Where Mitchell, Nuttall, and Watts constructed a worldly approach to social science that was, in places, at odds with the social psychology and institutional structure of their Owenite roots, the Women's Guild reignited the conscience of consumer cooperation.

CHAPTER 7

⌀⌀

The Women's Cooperative Guild

INTRODUCTION

The British consumer cooperative movement amassed much capital
by the late 19th century. There was solid growth in the distribution
networks and production facilities of the Cooperative Wholesale Society.
The CWS leadership developed entrepreneurial energy and sound business acumen. Despite these major gains, a spirited group of women
cooperators found that the movement was not living up to its principles,
particularly those of equality and human development. The movement
left behind the working poor generally, and housewives and working
women in particular.

Recall that in the 1820s the radical cooperators, William Thompson
and Anna Doyle Wheeler, linked full cooperation to gender equality.
J. S. Mill and Harriet Taylor Mill also intensely advocated gender equality
through the middle of the 19th century. In contrast, the practical cooperative experience of Great Britain in the last half of the 19th century
unfolded with rampant patriarchy, constraining women's full participation. Perhaps reinforcing this tendency is what G. D. H. Cole describes as
the growing participation of a "large new element attached to church or
chapel" (1944, 95).

By the early 1880s, some active cooperative women explicitly recognized
the dissonance between these patriarchal constraints and the ideals of

Building a Social Science. Kirsten Madden and Joseph Persky, Oxford University Press. © Oxford University Press 2024.
DOI: 10.1093/oso/9780197693735.003.0007

cooperation. They started up a mass transitional institution: a "'self-governing organization of women, who work through Co-operation for the welfare of the people, seeking freedom for their own progress, and the Equal Fellowship of men and women in the home, the store, the factory, and the state'" (as quoted in Webb 1927, 40). Over time, they came to challenge the underlying socialized gender oppression.

From its start the Women's Cooperative Guild (WCG) worked in close association with the Cooperative Union and the Association of Cooperative Societies, as well as the English CWS. But uniquely at this point in time, the WCG committed to a full-fledged cooperative commonwealth in order to realize the movement's "radical moral conscience" (Gurney 2020, 259). The leadership within the WCG embraced the concept of an enlarged self-interest, as reflected in a much repeated cooperative motto, "Each for All, and All for Each."[1] Given the many constraints to the realization of the co-operative conscience, the organization engaged in intervention strategies to generate reforms. Situating the base of the organization with its rank-and-file, the WCG sought to empower that base to full participation at all levels within the Guild.

In comparison to other major thinkers about cooperatives, the guildswomen's contributions bring to economics a far deeper understanding of working-class women and the everyday problems they face in production, in consumption, and in the household. Wheeler and Thompson's contributions offer sensitive insight into the dynamics of gender oppression and provide the theoretical case for cooperation as the ultimate remedy. Mill and Taylor stand out for their feminist insights; but their writing on women tends to the abstract. By contrast the guildswomen grapple with the practical problems hindering the realization of the cooperative promise for working-class women. Hence their writings on women and cooperatives have a more realistic ring and their empirical work adds to the methodology of the social science. The WCG offers direct insight into the practical economics of reform associated with later stage industrialism. Centering on participatory human development, the WCG mounted several major campaigns for institutional reform. While not phrased as a critique, the theory of the WCG emphasizes a continuing reassessment of cooperative institutions. This group narrowed in on the problematic gendered relations of British 19th-century cooperation, but their concerns and insights expand to the whole institutional structure.

---

1. See for example, Davies 1904, 72; also Webb 1921, 212.

CENTRAL CONTRIBUTORS TO WCG THOUGHT

Beginning in 1883 to well beyond the First World War, the Guild's energy derived from a group of talented women. The group included Catherine Webb, Rosalind Nash and, most notably, Margaret Llewelyn Davies.[2] Their mission, "to give to women co-operators a sense of corporate responsibility and an opportunity of sharing in the full life of the movement" (Webb 1921, 212). Primarily doers, these women devoted themselves to community development and to activism, eager to bring reforms in political, social, and economic spheres. Through a regular column, the "Women's Corner" in the widely read *Co-operative News*, and through numerous pamphlets and books, Guild writers also made significant empirical contributions to the cooperative economics of their day. They generated key theoretical insights that are still relevant to our understanding of cooperation and the socioeconomics of gender.[3]

Margaret Llewelyn Davies (1861–1944) was the central figure in the WCG for much of its early history. Her mother was an independent-minded Unitarian. Her father was a Christian Socialist minister and friend of F. D. Maurice. Maurice was her godfather (Blaszak 2000, 122). Davies attended both Queen's College in London and Girton College. Financially independent, she never married. After college, Davies unsuccessfully attempted to establish profit sharing workshops (Gurney 2020, 259). Influenced by William Thornton's *On Labour*, in 1886 Davies joined the consumer cooperative in Marylebone where she lived with her parents (Scott 1998, 37–40). She quickly discovered the WCG and committed her seemingly limitless energy to the organization. Her leadership skills were obvious, and by 1889 she was the General Secretary of the Women's Cooperative Guild. She remained in that position continuously until her retirement in 1921. During the bulk of her career and after, she maintained a close friendship with Lillian Harris. Harris also from a wealthy family became the assistant secretary of the WCG in 1901 (Blaszak 2000, 119–122).

Perhaps the most accomplished cooperative writer in the group was Catherine Webb (1859–1947). She was born into a working-class family which achieved middle-class status through participation in the cooperative movement. Her father rose to a managerial role in the Battersea

---

2. For one early history of the Guild as told by a central participant, see Margaret Llewelyn Davies (1904).

3. The historians Gillian Scott (1998) and Barbara Blaszak (2000) provide impressive coverage of the Guild. Our work builds on theirs, emphasizing the coherence of guildswomen's economic insights and how that coherence fits into the broader cooperative literature of 19th-century Great Britain.

and Wandsworth Cooperative Society of south London. Not surprisingly, Catherine strongly committed to the cooperative project. She served as vice president of the Guild Central Committee in the 1880s and again in the early 1890s (Blaszak 2000, Chs. 3–4). From 1895–1902, Webb was a central board member for the Cooperative Union (Gurney 2020, 236).

Rosalind Nash (1862–1952) was born to the landowning family of William Shore Smith. She was a cousin once removed of the renowned Florence Nightingale. Nash and Davies were close friends from their days at Girton College in the early 1880s. She married Vaughan Nash, a progressive economist. Rosalind Nash's primary field was journalism, where she covered suffrage and labor issues as well as assisting in a biography of Nightingale (Lee 2008).

Davies, Webb, and Nash were only the most visible of the WCG leadership.[4] In practice the organization drew heavily on its membership to participate. Although Davies played a central and motivating role, she led by example, encouraging members to take initiative across a broad spectrum of projects. WCG branches were active in their own right and as part of the national organization. The WCG membership over time grew in its confidence and energy.

A GENDERED SOCIAL PSYCHOLOGY

Over four decades to 1920, the central WCG activists Davies, Catherine Webb, and Nash, along with many other women of the working and middle classes, committed to realizing the vision of the cooperative commonwealth. Throughout is an emphasis on an enlarged self-interest.[5] Like Owen, and most who followed, these women built their social science on a

---

4. Davies' friendship with Virginia and Leonard Woolf led both to take on minor roles in the WCG. The Woolfs both attended the 1913 Guild Annual Congress. Leonard Woolf became involved by lecturing, visiting cooperative branches, and writing a book about cooperation, published in 1919 (see Chapter 10). Beginning in 1916, Virginia Woolf became involved with the Richmond Branch of the WCG. Her primary role was to supply speakers. She was also involved in a push to set up a grassroots bread shop in Richmond in response to flour shortages. Finally, Virginia Woolf wrote an introductory letter to the 1931 WCG publication, *Life as We Have Known It*. Virginia Woolf's views about middle-class women in social reform and about working-class women are complicated. Clara Jones presents a literary analysis that questions other literary interpretations of Woolf's introductory letter, suggesting that it "is not merely reproducing class prejudice but performing and probing it" (Jones 2015, 144).

5. Davies offers a gendered view of enlarged self-interest as follows: "At the back of women's minds is the mother's standpoint . . . to make the world a more civilized place for their children to live in. The earnest women . . . are not so much concerned about their children individually rising in the world. What they most want is to make the world a place where all children may grow up better and wiser" (Davies 1913, 3).

broad social psychology interacting with varied institutions. As apparent in the thought of Wheeler and Thompson, the WCG understanding of social psychology acknowledges substantial gendered differences.

Like Owen, these women recognize the pursuit of wellbeing and fellow feeling as original human inclinations. In the typical working-class household, women, like men, reasonably develop desires for sensation, excitement, and social connection (Nash 1907, 8). Likewise, women prefer to avoid drudgery, monotony, melancholia, anxiety, and overwork. Also aligning with Owen, the central WCG women take the assumption of plasticity and the character formation hypothesis as givens. Institutions shape—and often misshape—human character. Problematically, gender-specific socialization encourages women to repress desires toward that which is naturally attractive and to absorb much that is naturally repulsive.

Like their predecessors Wheeler and Thompson, there is cognizance that such socialization often reinforces false perceptions of women's inferiority. Rosalind Nash claims generally: "In the early days of Co-operation a married woman was no better than a slave, if we judge of her position by the law" (Nash 1907, 3). Flippantly, Nash identifies the "advanced" position of the Rochdale society: "They recognised the slave's right to her own investments and dividends" by frequently refusing a drunken husband's withdrawal of his wife's money (4). Promoted "from slaves to servants" by 1907, Nash alludes somewhat cynically to advances for married women cooperators (5). But even at the turn of the 20th century, Nash qualifies her analogy—that servants for hire receive pay and have more rights and freedoms than the British housewife (5). Even in the most advanced of 19th-century cooperative institutions, the system continues to reinforce gendered oppression.

Such systematic oppression wreaks havoc on the psyche. Davies identifies some of the intergenerationally institutionalized forces eliciting internalized oppression:

> Mistakes have been made from the beginning—boys have been given more chances than girls, and allowed to nourish a sense of superiority; and wives have been taught to be obedient to their husbands; while the fact that no money value is attached to the services of a woman in her home is also responsible for the position of so many women. (Davies 1913, 4)

These forces indoctrinate women into perceiving themselves as inferior.

For many women, gender-specific socialization results in internalized oppression, repression of healthy desires, the inability to resist that which is repulsive, and to behave in generally self-effacing ways. The WCG set out to counteract these outcomes. The underlying focus: to reestablish the

fellowship mindset inherent across humankind, particularly emphasizing the gendered twist—to undo the oppression of girls and women, and more broadly of the impoverished, so that all may fully participate in and benefit from the making of the cooperative commonwealth. While Anna Doyle Wheeler offered an earlier 19th-century theoretical expression about how misshaped character generates harmful gendered oppression and how to undo it, the WCG actually built a cooperative institutional structure to turn the tide on gendered oppression.

WCG INSTITUTION

The formation of the WCG began in 1883 with the simple desire among a handful of women cooperators to create the space and opportunity for women to meet and engage more widely and meaningfully in life (Davies 1904, 156).[6] From such humble desire, the WCG attracted the interests and dynamic energy of numerous women cooperators. The WCG achieved much even though it was a tremendously diverse organization. It brought together radical, moderate, and conservative women across the class spectrum to work toward the goals of cooperation and improving women's lives. Radicals accepted conservatives' emphasis on discipline, morality, and self-improvement, while conservatives accepted a broader sense of community outlook.

The WCG leaders organized it so that the oppressed and their advocates could work together with each other and for each other. With both the trade union and the CWS as models, the WCG adopted a federalist structure.[7] The WCG created a central committee with hierarchical leadership, including the top posts of General Secretary and Vice President. Branches formed with local working-class women driving local agendas.

Though structurally hierarchical, members came to experience the WCG as a "'splendid Democracy.'"[8] Meeting "without the aid of a leader of more exalted station," women came to recognize that each "has the power to contribute something" (Davies 1913, 6). In reflecting on more than 40 years of WCG activism, Catherine Webb puts forth a similar view from another

---

6. The "majority of women need their interests stirred from without, opportunities of taking part in a wider life and contact with others" (Davies 1904, 156). Nash writes similarly: women "long for even new walls round them, for people to work with, for something continuous to think of, something not connected with housework or family life" (1907, 6).

7. Nash describes the Guild as "a kind of trade union" for housewives (1907, 9).

8. (Davies 1931, 140–141), quoting a working-class member of the organization.

guildswoman: there is "'no patronage, but all to take their share in government'" (quoted in Webb 1927, 36). Over time, guildswomen took on their share of governance far beyond their own organization, including in municipal councils and committees as well as representation on royal commissions (Webb & Webb 1921, 172–173).

Though there were obvious differences in education and skill sets across guildswomen, and at the center there was hierarchy, the WCG structure reinforced the principle of equality through its participatory democracy. In highlighting the benefits of the WCG democracy, a guildswoman declares: "'The humblest member can feel that she stands on an absolute equality with the most lofty'" (quoted in Davies 1931, 140–141). Such a structure offers tremendous institutional potential to motivate change.

The WCG melded its activist vision into social and political campaigns aimed at achieving specific reform goals both within and beyond the cooperative movement. The WCG campaign methodology involved participant-observation, popular empiricism, and theorizing. Participant-observation provides firsthand insights into the experiences of British working-class cooperators. The guildswomen shaped and applied a popular empirical approach via fact gathering. Resistance to their reform goals sometimes led the women to elaborate original theoretical constructs.

WCG campaigns typically followed a basic strategy. The motivation behind speech-giving and pamphlet distribution was to convince Guild members of the presence of a problem and the need for action. Once motivated, the WCG enlisted membership to commit to a course of fact finding and petitioning. Their statistical work was in the first generation of sociological empiricism. The WCG then incorporated the resulting new knowledge into tracts with this explicitly empirical view. In the best of circumstances these new writings played a role in a larger political campaign on the issue in question.[9] Of course, the scenario laid out here is something of an ideal type. Often the various stages became jumbled. The empirical contributions were sometimes substantial and other times largely incidental.

The target population to benefit from reform was cooperative working-class housewives. The WCG focus was on encouraging independence and time for personal development, as well as eliciting women's abilities to form personal opinions and express them with the expectation of respectful consideration. All such efforts faced major challenges: engrained

---

9. See the description of methods in the Women's Cooperative Guild (1908a, 144).

sexism, socially imposed isolation, overwork, livelihood constraints, and the internalized oppression that characterizes many.

The WCG paralleled its campaign-driven reform activities with a program embracing cooperative education. The intention was to develop "severely practical" educational offerings proceeding "from what is concrete and affecting . . . every-day life." Abstract principles were only relevant inasmuch as they facilitate the development of critical thinking skills to address working-class issues (Davies 1922, as quoted in Webb 1927, 65).

On the ideological side of the education program, the WCG intended to raise women's consciousness concerning social issues by connecting those broad issues directly to the cooperative housewives' lives. An underlying ideological rhetoric elaborated on the problematic sides of capitalism and the benefits of socialism.[10] On the practical side, the WCG education system intended to build women's skills and self-confidence. Subject matter was diverse, ranging from sick nursing to the financial system underlying wholesale cooperation; from dressmaking to the duties of citizenship; from food, money, ironing, and the broader issue of domestic economy to the French language, women's suffrage, sick benefit societies, the Industrial Revolution, and political economy (Webb 1927, 54–56).

To bring educational offerings to working-class women in the various branches, the WCG trained "guides" who attended two-day schools as well as courses at WCG conferences. Some of this training connected to WCG campaigns and to cooperative ideology. The training also covered more practical problems women faced. After training, the guides served as conduits, transferring knowledge back to the working-class women who attended branch meetings (Davies 1913, 7–9). Guide training also emphasized the development of communication and leadership skills.

There was a participatory nature to the WCG education program. Women constructed knowledge themselves by writing papers for delivery within their branches or at WCG conferences. Early on, the WCG used the articles in the Women's Corner of the *Cooperative News* as base material. And there were the "Rank-and-File Papers" consisting of the best papers written each year by WCG non-officers (11).[11] One intention behind

10. There was noteworthy tension between the more socially liberal and more conservative women guild members. Controversial topics included suffrage, divorce, and the white slave traffic. While encouraging branches to establish their own topics, Davies also asked that each Branch commit to reading at least one address on any topic suggested by the Central Committee (Davies 1913, 5).

11. Consider, for example, Sarah Reddish (1849–1928) who worked in textiles from age 11 until her early 40s, joining the Bolton Society in 1879 and serving as president of the Bolton WCG from 1886–1901 (Gurney 2020, 279). Reddish presented a paper at the first Guild conference in the North. In her speech, she advocated that the "first

participatory education was to enhance self-confidence as women made and disseminated insights. The ultimate intention was to stimulate broad social and political participation (Davies 1904, 156). Through all their educational offerings, the WCG prompted the development of leadership skills among women. Women could then stand for election in unions and in the CWS and take on store management positions.

COMMITMENT TO UNDOING GENDER OPPRESSION

Certainly, many women within the working-class cooperative movement survived relatively intact through patriarchy with relatively healthy senses of self-worth, self-worth being necessary to speak up for personal self-interests and to effectively serve the interests of others. But many of these working-class women succumbed to the oppressive relationships in their home and work environments. It being nearly impossible "for each woman separately to assert herself against the unjust claims of home," a transformation in consciousness requires assistance from others (Nash 1907, 9). As an institution within the cooperative movement, the WCG committed itself to the process of women's reorientation.

The WCG took on no small task: to establish a self-governing institution of working-class women that undoes internalized oppression and stimulates healthy self-worth, translating over time into an enlarged self-interest and "engaged activism" (Davies 1913, 2).[12] Supportive interactions at the WCG drew the women out. In branch meeting participation, women saw "how much bigger and more interesting the married woman's life is than she had thought, and how strong and far-reaching her power should be" (4–5).

Branch participation both tapped personal strength and power and inspired a feeling of "power which they have in combination." The experience of the benefits of solidarity emotionally and intellectually fueled the

---

and highest duty . . . in schools is the sacred duty of each to labour for and promote the highest good of society, and that of society to promote the highest good of each individual comprising it" (as quoted in Davies 1904, 31). Reddish takes a position on the WCG central committee in 1889 and ultimately makes noteworthy contributions in Britain's suffrage movement (Gurney 2020, 279).

12. In her WCG address as vice president in 1885, Miss Greenwood reflected, "the weakest amongst us has a gift, however seemingly trivial, which is peculiar to her, and which, worthily used, will be a gift also to the race for ever" (Greenwood [1885] 2020, 255). Similarly but at a much later date, Davies reflected the same attitude, conveying that "everyone has the power to contribute something" (Davies 1913, 6).

desires for knowledge and for meaningful work and civic opportunities (Davies 1913, 6; see also Davies 1904, Ch. 11). Davies, for example, describes women sitting through a series of WCG classes on the issues faced by an urban district council—about "washing, infection, fire, schooling, health." Because of the personal relevance, the guild members connected deeply to these topics. That personal relevance stimulated the realization among the women that they must participate in local governance "if the interests of men, women, and children are all to be adequately cared for" (1913, 3–4).

From Davies' perspective, the "truest satisfaction" lies in the sacrifice of "individual material gains, or a part of them, for the sake of the community" ([1890] 2020, 262). Transformation out of a mindset of oppression into a sense of personal self-worth ultimately nurtures enlarged self-interest. As women connect to social issues from a personal standpoint, they come to see the need to have meaningful input "to the control of policy." In the WCG, there was an increased sense of responsibility and initiative among "rank-and-file" members, reinforcing "growing self-reliance" (Webb 1927, 36–37).

The undoing of internalized oppression and the awakening of power from combination generated personal benefits for the guildswomen at an emotional and intellectual level. These changes also stimulated energetic vitality: the women came into possession of "a most youthful spirit, taking up new ideas, attending lectures, writing papers, and throwing themselves into a wider life with enthusiasm" (Davies 1904, 156).

The WCG intended a positive gendered feedback effect reverberating across sectors. Their work is unique within British cooperation in specifically highlighting the relevance of the household sector. Outside interests and social contributions made the guildswomen "more respected and considered in their homes" (Nash 1907, 9).[13] For the wife, the expanded sense of purpose, capabilities, and self-confidence challenges culturally indoctrinated perceptions of inferiority. And her increased value and recognition beyond the home affects the perceptions of her husband. With this intellectual and social growth, there can be more effective role modeling and decision-making in the home. Multi-generational implications follow as children benefit from their mothers' WCG-stimulated human development.

---

13. Nash also advocates suffrage and motherhood allowances paid by the state to mothers of young children (1907).

THE COOPERATIVE HOUSEHOLD

The implementation of a theory of gender-specific reform across economic sectors begins with the household. While the WCG goal is one of gender equality and mutual respect, their campaign methodology uncovered distressing realities.

The Reality

Nineteenth-century Britain exhibited a complicated development of women's labor force participation, varying by region and industry.[14] Overall, however, it is clear that a majority of women depended on men's earnings through the market—dependence which occurred despite the participation of many women in the new manufactories. Horrell and Humphries (1995) document a "transition to the male-breadwinner family" in the period 1790 to 1865. By the early 20th century, British households also trended toward smaller family units.[15] For at least some of the prosperous cooperative households, the smaller male-dominated family became an important springboard for maintaining patriarchy. Consider, for example William Marcroft, a leader of the Oldham Industrial Cooperative Society, who declared after marriage the woman is "to become a sedate wife . . . ever anxious for the comfort of her husband" (Marcroft [1888] 2020, 257). As Marcroft saw it, the home "is the heaven gained in female life. There she makes a world as she wills it; order, cleanliness, regularity, and comfort are the four points of her compass. The husband is the altar of her worship . . ." (258).

Marcroft's comments suggest an obliviousness to the problematic realities his husband-adoring archetype imposed on many working-class housewives and their daughters. As part of a maternity benefits campaign, the WCG undertook formal fact gathering from cooperative working-class housewives, collecting 386 letters documenting women's qualitative experiences within the household. This sample of women cooperators had, on average, four children with each woman also typically reporting either a miscarriage or stillbirth. "These figures speak for themselves: the mere physical strain of pregnancy and childbirth succeeding each other with

14. See, for example, Atkinson (2012) on differences in labor force participation and family size in three British towns in the late 19th century.

15. For example, the average "ultimate family size" in 1881 was 5.27 children. In contrast, between 1900–1909 the average family size was 3.3 children (Gente 2001).

scarcely an interval for ten . . . years renders a healthy bodily and intellectual life impossible" (WCG 1915, 9).

The Guild printed 160 of these letters in its widely acclaimed publication, *Maternity: Letters from Working Women*. Many of these letters document experiences of isolation, over-work, underconsumption, illness, and neglect as the common reality for women in these proto-nuclear units. The reasons for the unnecessary suffering among housewives include the limited work and low wages of their husbands. But more substantially, the WCG attributes housewives' positions to their economic dependence: "both in law and in popular morality, the wife is still the inferior." She lacks independence, giving "the man, whether he be good or bad, a terrible power over her." Her "duty" is "regarded by many as the care of the household, the satisfaction of man's desires, and the bearing of children." While there are exceptions among working-class "husbands who take a higher view of married life and practice it," many "are neither good men nor good husbands." And "even where there is no deliberate evil or viciousness, these views are responsible for the overwork and physical suffering among women and for that excessive child-bearing" (1915, 8).

Most of the *Maternity* letters relay extremely confined options for isolated housewives. A dominant coping strategy was to succumb to the limits society and marriage impose by tightly managing household resources. This parsimony often involved the housewife abstaining from consumption, denying herself food, rest, and medical care in order to nourish the husband and children. A housewife might have "a cup of tea for her dinner, while she prepares her husband a beefsteak." A woman "can rarely take a holiday—she will stay indoors for weeks together; she consents to a dependence which is humiliating" (WCG 1908b, 15–16). Often economic pressures required women to increase their workload by taking in homework.

Davies repeatedly elicits the metaphor of the curtain in her attempts to convey the hidden domestic problems faced by working-class housewives:

> In the past, a heavy curtain had, on marriage, fallen on the woman's life, and the nation felt no responsibility for her personal welfare or for the conditions under which she performed her great tasks. Without money of her own, with no right even to her housekeeping savings, without adequate protection against a husband's possible cruelty, with no legal position as a mother, with the conditions of maternity totally neglected, married women in the home had existed apart, voiceless and unseen. (Davies in Webb 1927, 11)

The isolated working-class households are like "the workshops of many trades, where overtime abounds, and where an eight hours' day would be a very welcome reform." There is little social understanding of the "drudgery and lonely effort" in housework (Davies 1904, 151). Nash attributes women's inability to negotiate to widespread self-effacing mechanisms. Reinforced by state law establishing wives as property of their husbands (1907, 5). From a somewhat different perspective, Davies also relates housewives' dire life experiences to the lack of a monetary valuation on their efforts (1913, 4).

The Vision

The earliest 19th-century British cooperative thought from Robert Owen and William Thompson envisions communal living. Given the insights on gender inequality from Anna Doyle Wheeler, it seems reasonable to speculate that the early cooperators' advocacy of communal spaces and activities is meant at least in part as an attempt to guarantee personal security for women who have no legal recourse from the cruelty of their husbands.

Early in the cooperative literature, there is also recognition of overwork in the household. In the pages of the cooperative periodical, *The Economist* in 1821, there is an advocacy of technological innovations to reduce the sheer volume of domestic labor. For example, editor George Mudie recommends the steam-driven laundering machine for an Owenite village, estimating savings of the labor of 15–20 women per day (Mudie 1821 Vol. I, 116). Wanting to redress the heavy domestic workload in pre-cooperative tenements, Philadelphus recommends that working-class families housed in row homes cooperate to complete domestic work. Neighbors could reduce total workload by associating, specializing, and undertaking domestic labor for one another in activities such as laundry, house cleaning, and food preparation (Mudie 1821 Vol. I, 202).

These first British cooperative visions regarding domestic life faded away as the energy behind cooperative villages dissipated by mid-century. Moving into the late 19th century, the women in the WCG mostly assumed that families live in physically distinct household units.[16] One goal of the WCG was to expose cooperators to new ideas about household relations. What would the ideal cooperative household look like?

---

16. Sharp (n.d.) is at least one exception, providing a brief description of communal living and its benefits (15–16).

Though we find no single treatise in which the WCG sketches the institution of the cooperative nuclear household unit, there are clues scattered throughout which allow a restatement of their vision.[17] The cooperative household is one of absolute egalitarianism. Partners in marriage serve as "joint heads of family with absolute equality" (Nash 1907, 11). Both men and women study "problems of marriage and divorce, of economic independence, of the moral training of their boys and girls." Such joint consideration of household issues normalizes expectations of mutual responsibility and reinforces "true companionship in the home." The cooperative household is thus one of "equal comradeship of husband and wife" based on mutual responsibility, support, and respect (Davies 1913, 4). It seems reasonable to infer the realization of Wheeler's insight: this level playing field restructures the relations between men and women. Each comes to know that they "must learn the art of pleasing, of benevolence, of deserving love" (Thompson & Wheeler 1825, 200–201). Thus, cooperative household members encourage and reinforce the formation of respect-worthy character.

In the cooperative household, both men and women participate as equals in the completion of domestic work. Technology and collectivized housework—such as cooperative bakeries and laundries, cooperative playgrounds, and multi-housing access to labor-saving capital investments like hot water generating furnaces—reduce domestic workloads (Nash 1907, 10). Shared workloads with improved technologies reduce each person's domestic work hours and intensity. With less for each individual to do at home, wives as well as husbands have sufficient time and energy for employment beyond the four walls, and for civic, social, educational, and leisure pursuits.

COOPERATIVE PRODUCTION

The Reality

Women's real emancipation requires options for participating in work beyond the four walls of the home. Such participation helps to undermine gender inequality of the household. What better workplace than one committed to cooperation? But the WCG found that cooperation was not living up to high standards. Cooperative workplaces often exhibited problematic

---

17. This restatement draws from the following sources: Davies (1904); Davies (1913); Nash (1907); Scott (1998); Scott (2004); and Sharp (n.d.).

work conditions, low pay, and little worker voice. These problems were particularly noticeable for women workers.

Mid-century investigations across Great Britain uncovered abysmal working conditions for men, women, and children, including extreme workday hours in crowded, unventilated, and filthy workspaces.[18] Such conditions are antithetical to the ideals of the cooperative movement. And while the relative work conditions in cooperative enterprises were typically an improvement over the worst of capitalist workplaces, in the 19th century the British cooperatives did not attain the lofty workplace goals envisioned by Robert Owen. Women's employment opportunities remained limited and often substandard in the cooperative movement. Reflecting the norms of the more prosperous working class, most women from cooperative households simply did not work for pay.

For the women who did work for pay in the cooperative movement, WCG inquiries uncovered troubling realities. Working girls as young as 13 years old worked 14–15 hour shifts (WCG 1896, 14). Their work processes over long hours tended toward tedium and monotony. The WCG investigators recognized that industrial work dulls girls' "higher faculties" and serves ultimately to be "destructive of character" (WCG 1910, 15). Thirty years after the examples of horrific work conditions filled the pages of "The Working Day" in *Capital*, WCG investigations into women's working conditions uncovered similar facts: some working girls taking meals in a basement crawling with beetles (WCG 1896, 6), others regularly fainting from gas fumes (7), and yet others working in rain and snow under a leaking roof, hands so cold they cut themselves with work knives (9).

Girls and women working in cooperatives faced severe constraints on occupations. Women did work in some cooperative stores as shop assistants but not as managers. Women also provided services within the stores such as millinery, tailoring, and laundering. Girls worked in smaller scale cooperative production establishments and factories, including dressmaking, laundries, millinery, pill-box making, floristry, or factory production of sweets (WCG 1896).

One of the WCG's most intense campaigns aimed to establish a minimum wage for women employed in cooperatives. In the fact gathering stage, Lillian Harris (1897) reports data on work conditions and pay for 1,662 women employees working across 104 cooperative stores. "A Cooperative Standard for Women Workers" (WCG 1908b) reports on women's

---

18. For a compilation of some of the anecdotal evidence about "The Working Day" from the early 1860s, see Marx *Capital*, Volume I, Chapter 10, Section 3 ([1867] 1967).

wages in 809 cooperatives from evidence compiled by the CWS in 1903. In advocating a cooperative wage standard, the 1908 report relays the following anecdote. In a hosiery business, a woman manager with multiple work tasks including bookkeeping earned 24s. per week. When the business expanded, it hired a man to perform the single task of bookkeeping at a wage of 30s. per week. Beyond the anecdote, these inquiries uniformly document that the wages of women in cooperatives were lower than the wages of their male counterparts. And more generally, while wages among cooperatives were higher than the wages of noncooperative enterprises, cooperative wages nonetheless fell below the non-legislated minimum wage targets of the period.

The myth of women's inferiority negatively affects women's ability to negotiate their wages. "Women, as well as men, are responsible for this view, for they have accepted it and passed it on generation after generation" (WCG 1908b, 15). Socialization trains girls and women to make fewer demands on life. The journalist Rosalind Nash reflects on economic implications of internalized oppression among girls, that "[u]nselfishness, weakness, and custom all combine against their [girls] setting a value on themselves" (1907, 5). The imbalance of power is telling:

> Practically children, little educated, with no organisation at their back, often timid and afraid of losing their places, these young girls—who are to become the future mothers of the race—are peculiarly at the mercy of managers, who are always liable to put profit before the lives of the workers. (WCG 1910, 15)

WCG writing outlines a "self-effacement" hypothesis. When "we take a large view we shall see that self-effacement may be as . . . disastrous to the lives of her sisters, as selfishness" (WCG 1908b, 15–16). If a culturally engrained attitude of self-effacement exists in girls, they may actually negotiate their own wages down. In a competitive environment, girls who internalize a belief of inferiority and exhibit self-effacing behaviors may well lower not only their wages but also those of others. Such downward pressure on wages perversely affects women's employability in gender-stratified labor markets. If women's wages are lower than men's, men may justify policies that exclude women from the labor force in order to prevent competition-induced job losses (WCG 1908b, 10).

The WCG inquiries also document that women workers lacked appropriate opportunities for voicing their concerns. Women's participation in the Amalgamated Union of Cooperative Employees (AUCE) lagged men's. After a campaign to increase AUCE membership among girls working in the stores, the WCG publication of 1910 lauds the fact that women's

participation in the AUCE rose from 500 to roughly 3000. But by 1910, there were only seven women on AUCE branch committees across four districts along with five officers in other districts (WCG 1910, 7). Within the cooperative organization itself, as late as 1907, no woman served on the CWS Wholesale Board and there was a ban "in some parts of the country" on women running for the Central Board (Nash 1907, 4).

The Vision

The disconnect between the cooperative conscience and the realities in cooperative production—low pay, troubling work conditions, and women's lack of access to leadership positions—drove many in the WCG to push for reform within cooperative enterprises. The push for reform requires due consideration of the institutional vision for future production. The vision is one of fair wages, good quality working conditions, equal participation in higher skilled and leadership positions, and women's full participation in unions. The WCG tended to support CWS-owned and managed production, with workers expressing their voice both through unions and through their roles as consumers in cooperative stores. In places, the WCG offers detailed arguments for the institutions they advocate. There are vociferous arguments for a minimum wage standard, particularly for women. There are justifications for women claiming leadership roles. And there are debates about CWS-owned production versus worker-owned and managed workshops.

A Minimum Wage Standard for Women

The guildswomen's writing challenges economic doctrine by stating "wages and salaries are not really regulated by 'worth'" (Webb 1927, 118). This assertion opens intellectual space for considering women's wages in cooperative enterprises. In place of equilibrium wage rationalizations of the time, the WCG emphasis on social justice generates advocacy for a living wage. Most broadly, from the perspective of the cooperative conscience, are issues "of humanity and justice" (WCG 1910, 13). Low wages are "demoralizing to our movement, by accustoming Co-operators to a wrong standard" (WCG 1908b, 7). Higher wages reinforce the "pride we should feel in our movement" (11).

The WCG makes three general arguments concerning women's wages. First, they debunk stereotypes concerning women's expenditures and begin to build a picture of the serious financial responsibilities of many

working-class women. Second, they address psychological and sociological needs. And third, the WCG makes an interesting argument for higher wages to motivate more effective management.[19]

The first set of arguments for higher wages reflects upon necessary financial outlays incurred by cooperative girls and women at the turn of the century. Girls and women require sufficient pay to cover more than a "mere pocket-money wage" (WCG 1908b, 13). Flipping the gender coin to advantage, the WCG holds that working girls require higher wages in order to maintain adequate diets in developing healthy reproductive systems (WCG 1910, 18). Beyond personal living expenses, many women require higher wages to support dependents (their own children, parents, or siblings); and single women require higher wages to allow for savings buffers to secure themselves from calamity and old age (1908b, 2; also see 1910, 16). In their quest to enlist all workers in the AUCE, wages also need to be high enough to allow payment of union dues (1910, 18–19).

Beyond the "question of food," higher wages are necessary so that young women can "secure the stimulus, self-respect, and independence given by adequate earnings" (WCG 1910, 17). Higher pay can serve as one of many mechanisms to enhance self-esteem and undo internalized oppression. Independence is also relevant here. Mrs. Wimhurst Lewes argues "that co-operators 'ought not make it compulsory for girls to marry if they did not want to. . . . Girls were very often compelled to marry because the wages they received were so low that they felt compelled to accept the first offer from a decent man'" (as quoted in Scott 1998, 101). As Anna Doyle Wheeler identified decades earlier, women's independence often also creates incentives for better behavior by their male partners.

The argument extends to efficiency in production. The WCG advocates fixing a "bottom price for labour . . . because in the long run it pays to keep workers efficient" (WCG 1910, 12).[20] A common objection to a minimum wage is that it generates higher prices or business losses. The WCG deflects this view by arguing that higher profits result from "better organizing, more efficient business methods, and greater enterprise" when employers cannot offer substandard wages (WCG 1908b, 7). "Co-operative Standards" develops the management angle of efficiency in more detail. "A bad Manager may try to make profits by means of low wages." But higher

19. The point here presents a twist on the efficiency wage theory advanced by Alfred Marshall in his *Principles* ([1890] 1961, Ch. 6) who argues that maximizing firms will pay wage premiums when the increase in worker efficiency covers the extra expense.

20. For the WCG, that "bottom price" is the pay that "will maintain a man or woman in such a state of efficiency as will get a certain amount of work out of them" based on "physical needs of a hard working life" (1910, 12).

wages cause the cooperative "to insist on first-rate management, and so improve the prosperity of our business. It is really helping to make management more efficient if we prevent bad management being hidden under low wages" (8). This is an interesting positive sum proposition that higher wages can set into motion forces generating improved management.

Support for a CWS Federalist System

While working for a range of reforms in cooperative workplaces, the WCG remained divided on producer cooperatives. Key concerns were self-management and wage bonuses in these establishments. The division echoes debates that raged throughout the cooperative movement. As discussed in the last chapter, the CWS took a strong position against self-management and worker bonuses. The Society stood in favor of more traditional hierarchy in production. While there are deep roots for producer cooperatives in radical cooperative ideology, the WCG had difficulty deciding the extent to which such cooperatives serve the interests of women workers.

Robert Owen, the Christian Socialists, and J. S. Mill strongly endorsed producer cooperatives. But, at the practical level, experience in Great Britain in the last half of the 19th century (including Davies own brief attempts), suggests these cooperatives were far more difficult to establish and manage than retail cooperatives. Writing in 1891 in the "Women's Corner," Davies discusses the deep split in the cooperative movement: should production be managed by the consumer-led CWS or by the direct control of the workers in the productive facilities? Davies observes that on one side are those older idealists, such as George Holyoake, who held that worker-managed production is central to the cooperative vision. On the other hand, Davies cites the work of Beatrice Potter [Webb], arguing that producer cooperatives are hopelessly utopian.[21]

Potter's take on producers' cooperatives became the accepted position of the Fabian Society in which she and her husband, Sidney Webb, played major roles. Indeed, the view became central to the broader socialist argument in favor of national ownership of industry. Davies, however, does not argue for nationalization. While sympathetic to Potter's arguments against worker management, Davies' line of thinking rejects nationalization and supports the approach of J. T. W. Mitchell. Thus, she advocates ownership

---

21. See discussion of Potter's position as put forward in *The Co-operative Movement in Great Britain* (1891) in Chapter 10.

and management of production units by the CWS under the direction of the cooperative movement.

According to Davies, workshops owned by the CWS can avoid many of the problems Potter foresees. CWS wealth makes it relatively easy to "secure competent managers" (Davies 1891, 1010). Most importantly, the "capital supplied by the (cooperative) stores is almost exhaustless," so their workshops are well financed. Of course that assumes a moderate div: "Co-operators should discourage the payment of a rate of dividend higher than is consistent with a just regard to reasonable charges for goods, liberal treatment of employees, efficient safeguarding of the stability of the Society, and ample provision for the intellectual and social need of its members" (Davies 1904, 82). While Davies doesn't directly refer to J. T. W. Mitchell in this discussion, her view of the cooperative commonwealth is largely consistent with his. It builds from the CWS expanding backward linkages through most all production. It is here that she endorses Mitchell's fundamental position that once the system grows large enough the div guarantees workers' full share of the value they create.

Davies goes on to consider the alternative institutional structures from the point of view of the workers themselves. Admittedly in workshops owned and managed by wholesale societies, workers have no role in governance and take no direct share of profit. By the same token, and perhaps more importantly, they do not risk their wages or savings on the vagaries of the trade cycle. With the wholesale societies acting as employers, "bad times and losses can be stood much more easily; while bad effects are not felt directly by the workers, but are distributed over the whole body of consumers, so that each individual suffers as little as possible" (Davies 1891, 1011). In a later tract on the issue of worker security in a consumer-controlled cooperative, Davies et al. envision relatively stable supply and demand in cooperative economies. To maintain stable demand, cooperatives replace a variable wage system with a living wage standard for all. In such a system, supply decisions focus on production for use and yield a "much more exact adjustment between supply and demand" than competitive markets. A major result then is employment security (Davies et al. 1919, 4). Moreover, a system which produces for use also cuts out costs of the middleman, advertising, and excessive retailing. Workers can work less and claim substantial hours for leisure-time pursuits. They can also anticipate relatively constant real wages since cooperative output prices only change if production costs change. And finally, much of the surplus ultimately diffuses to workers in their roles as consumers and hence "owners" of the CWS (3).

Davies acknowledges that bonuses to workers might carry with them some incentive effects on productivity. But echoing the sentiments of J. T. W. Mitchell, she argues, "There is nothing very exalting in the idea that a man will work harder for himself than for other people." From a moral perspective that includes impacts on character development, the upshot might well be worse, not better. The fear is that workers themselves might become "profit grubbing capitalists." Moreover, workers with greater tenure might end up exploiting new hires, emphasizing exclusivity rather than openness (Davies 1891, 1011).

All said, Davies is quite aware that in the short run the CWS may not generally identify the interests of the cooperative store movement with those of the workers. Some legitimate workers' interests are likely to be disregarded. But under such circumstances, worker ownership is not a solid alternative. Rather than risking ownership, the workers do better to build trade unions (1891, 1011).

In contrast to Davies, Mary Lawrenson holds to the more traditional cooperator position of Mill and Taylor and the Christian socialists.[22] Lawrenson starts by pointing out that many women first come to the Guild motivated by the hope that workshops enable "girls to work for their own profit" (Lawrenson 1891a, 1179). At the time, women's occupational choices were largely limited to positions of subordination and low wages. In most establishments, internally oppressed women faced the disempowering realities of competing on allegedly equal grounds with men. Lawrenson's vision of women-owned and operated workshops offers a radical alternative to these common gender-stratified options.

Lawrenson goes on to make an argument that the accumulated capital of the cooperative stores could just as easily extend to worker-managed firms as to those managed by the wholesale societies. In a subsequent letter, she gives examples of several successful worker-managed firms that deserve cooperative society support (Lawrenson 1891b, 1251).

Finally, Mary Lawrenson proposes that, in traditional WCG fashion, the question of producer cooperatives become a subject of collective study, at "meetings, lectures and magic lantern views" (Lawrenson 1891a, 1251). She also encourages women to visit producer cooperatives so that they might gain firsthand experience of the differences between such workshops and those conducted on more traditional lines.

---

22. Mary Lawrenson (1850–1943), the daughter of a printer and cooperator was a founder of the Guild. She was more working-class than Davies and most of the group's leadership. Lawrenson served as General Secretary from 1885 to 1889, but the WCG inner circle viewed her as a "maverick" (Purvis 2010, 876–877; Blaszak 2000, 16).

Lawrenson's call for a campaign is very much in line with the customary WCG approach to subjects of interest. But, to the best of our knowledge the WCG did not pick up on the suggestion. Producer cooperatives did not become the center of a WCG reform campaign. The WCG did not add to the data on the subject nor formulate policy proposals. Despite interesting initial points made by both Davies and Lawrenson, the deep disagreements on the issues remain unresolved. And as the General Secretary for 30 years, Davies' views tended to prevail.[23]

Women Serving in High Positions

Through the turn of the 19th century, the WCG leadership continually nudged cooperators toward gender equality in leadership positions in the stores, in the AUCE, and in the CWS. Early on, Catherine Webb advocated that women take on management positions in the stores. Recognizing their educational disadvantages, she recommends that the WCG provide education courses in topics about running a store and balance sheet accounting so that "really suitable candidate[s] may be forthcoming" ([1892] 2020, 268).

A decade later, given the WCG successes in supporting women's education, Davies revisited the issue of women in leadership. She highlights the cooperative conscience and may in part be relying on the "mother's standpoint" in her assessment of why women must serve as leaders. Women are necessary in leadership positions "of justice in employment, of truth in business dealings, and of fellowship in a common Co-operative life" (1904, 277).

More detailed arguments appear in a 1910 WCG publication concerning women's employment in stores and factories. Beyond the issue of fairness—since women hold positions of employment, they should also manage and make decisions—this publication highlights the positive effects of women leaders in the AUCE. Given gender-based stratification, women union leaders can more effectively reach women workers and generate more women to officially register for the union. Women are then more likely to take on union duties and to provide input on events. And finally,

---

23. The historian, Barbara Blaszak suggests that Davies and the group around her tended to emphasize the role of women as home-based consumers, and this might explain their lack of interest in producer cooperatives (Blaszak 2000, 108–109). Yet it is hard to find this argument convincing in light of Davies' and Catherine Webb's strong support of the campaign for minimum wages for working women. More likely they see those women's interests as better addressed through reform legislation than through producer cooperatives that are unlikely to empower women workers.

a role-modeling effect is likely: as women observe women in positions of honor, this increases women's ambitions for themselves (1910, 25–27). More generally, since the WCG advocates unions as the institutional expression of worker voice and the mechanism for worker effect on outcomes, women's participation in all levels of worker unions matter. Women's active participation in union leadership would have major implications for the issues negotiated on compensation, hours, and work conditions.

THE STORE

The Reality

Over the course of approximately a half-century in Great Britain, a gap grew between cooperative retail ideals and practice. While the cooperative movement did prosper with cooperative propaganda promoting those successes to the British public, the underlying frictions received less press. In their critical scrutiny of cooperation by the end of the 19th century, WCG writings about the stores offer telltale signs of a disconnect from cooperative ideals.

The obvious concerns relate to the overarching goals of cooperative stores. In a transitional economic setting still much influenced by profit calculation, no business entity can avoid financial interests and financial pressures. Davies must remind cooperators that the stores are not fundamentally about profit (1920, 27–28). Catherine Webb must remind cooperators that neither the balance sheet nor the div are the center points in cooperative retail ([1892] 2020, 267).[24] And in response to a growing WCG concern about the availability of consumer credit to facilitate purchases, Mrs. Deans must remind cooperators that beyond deducting interest payments from already impoverished budgets, debt encourages meanness and deceitfulness among low-income households. Both debt and its effects on character formation entangle family members into a web of difficulties with negative intergenerational impacts (1898, 3).

Another central concern is that the social relations among stakeholders in the stores do not always reflect the spirit of fellowship. Catherine Webb writes that the cooperative stores exhibited in full measure "prejudices, jealousies, misunderstandings, back bitings, apathy, and distrust" ([1892]

---

24. In writing about the Women's Cooperative Guild, Naomi Black also identifies that the WCG argues "against using commercial viability as a criterion for movement policy" contrary to the rising business interests among the CWS (1989, 126).

2020, 272). It is also not unusual to observe that cooperators treated their store workers with contempt (270). And while there were "go-a-head committees" diligently and energetically managing some stores to fully realize the cooperative dream, Webb points to "sleepy committees" and "muddling committees" which reduced the effectiveness in promoting the cooperative agenda (268).

And finally, inequality remains the norm in the cooperative store movement. Shops tended to open in more prosperous communities, denying the reach of cooperation into impoverished neighborhoods (Davies 1913, 6). And even though the British gendered division of labor of this timeframe relegated consumer tasks to housewives, nonetheless there was noteworthy gender inequality across all angles of store life. From its earliest days, the space of the cooperative store served as meeting space but as late as the early 1880s, that meeting space was the territory of men (Webb 1927, 19).[25] When women worked in the stores, they tended to hold the lowest level positions. Through the 19th century, women remained mostly unrepresented on store committees, and when they did offer opinions, men tended to be dismissive (Webb [1892] 2020, 269). Such sexist dismissiveness is a subtle constraint on women's full participation. In a fictional dialogue about the benefits of the cooperative system, a housewife advocate of cooperation qualifies that women must be "careful not to be disagreeable and interfering" if they wish men to be receptive to their ideas about cooperative store operations (Sharp n.d., 12). Catherine Webb reinforces the reality behind this fictional depiction of store life: the cooperative store committee members have "to be taught, that women do possess sufficient common sense and intelligence to be listened to with consideration at least, when they make well-thought-out proposals or suggestions as to the management of store life" (Webb [1892] 2020, 269).

The Vision

As Davies sees it, the purpose of cooperative retail trade is the satisfaction of human need (1920, 27–28). While there are obvious material needs the store fulfills—food, clothing, household goods, etc.—there are also fundamental social needs which the store can fulfill. In "What is meant by store life," Catherine Webb identifies the life of the store as "made up of

---

25. The exception: wives of the store managers sometimes assisted in preparing the room for the men's meetings (Webb [1892] 2020, 271).

the persons whose sympathies, interests, and destinies even, centre round the success or failure of the store," where the cooperators are "so closely knit together that the good or ill of each should be the good or ill of all, as in one huge family" ([1892] 2020, 267). This cooperative family consists of the cooperative store member-consumers, store committee members, store employees, and the spouses and children of these constituent groups (Webb 1892).

Human needs also include meaningful participation in social decisions. Thus, Davies pitches the women's role on the consumer side of cooperation to extend far beyond loyal buying to taking seats on management and to promoting justice, truth, and fellowship in common cooperative life (1904, 277). The infusion of a cooperative spirit—a welcoming inclusiveness, mutual respect, and mutual service—as the norm in interactions is fundamental to human needs satisfaction. The store is not only devoted to trade, but provides meeting space for a variety of educational and other community interests.

In the WCG vision, the work of the store continues with occupation-specific roles: shop assistants, check clerks and cashiers, managers, dressmakers, milliners, tailors, bootworkers, etc.[26] But those roles would now be equally open across men and women, subject to interest and skill.[27] The stores would embody model industrial conditions with compensation, hours, and work conditions aligning with the high standards established across cooperative enterprises.[28] Women and men would be registered and active in unions, including in union leadership, to allow store employees full representation in cooperative decision-making.

There remains open the question of consumer credit and debt. The argument for ready-cash purchases among the WCG aligns with the conservative emphasis on discipline and the reduction of succumbing to temptation (Deans 1898, 3). But Davies herself offers an alternative: to create "Loan Departments" which could take security "to lend without taking advantage of necessity." These departments would directly challenge the widespread practice of "weekly pawning" in the early stages of transition to fuller-fledged cooperation (Davies 1904, 77). Davies does raise the potential

---

26. See the (WCG 1908b) appendix for the standard occupations of women working in the stores.

27. Both girls and boys would have access to educational training across the spectrum of skills so that skill differentials do not become the justification for unequal gender ratios in higher-skill roles. In the early stages of transition, the WCG offers training for girls specifically to catch up with their male counterparts.

28. Interestingly, our research has yet to turn up a source among WCG writings that advocates alternative schemes for wage-based compensation.

problem that cooperative stores might create a debt trap that could expose the stores to instability.

Finally, at least in the earlier stages of transition, the cooperative store is a force for poverty alleviation. Davies recommends opening stores in low-income areas, lowering prices, and abolishing entrance fees (Davies 1913, 6). If the stores opt for cash only payments, the payment system would certainly offer installment options before obtaining goods to facilitate consumer purchases of necessities and of high expenditure consumer capital items. And reflecting its social mission, the cooperative store of a low-income community could also serve as "a foundation and centre for constructive social work" (Davies 1904, 92).

A FEMINIST THEORY
OF COOPERATIVE TRANSFORMATION

The political economy of the WCG considers carefully how to undo forces of oppression to elicit independence, self-help, and genuine empowerment while reestablishing the fellowship mindset within cooperation. Such a line of thinking offers basic economic logic to justify association. When workers (in this case, women) have voice, working conditions are likely to improve. In turn labor productivity is likely to rise (Davies [1890] 2020, 261).

But WCG thought goes far beyond simple economic analysis of the gains to productivity from association. The insights extend through the entire system and consider how cooperation can live up to its ideals and be a strong movement. This question implies an emphasis on gender, which requires the reintroduction of domestic arrangements (first considered by the feminist cooperative theorists William Thompson and Anna Doyle Wheeler) as a central focus point.

The logic underlying a feminist theory of cooperative transition runs along these lines. Like Thompson and Wheeler, the WCG challenged internalized oppression. The WCG provided educational offerings to expand women's skill sets and advocated for equality and the cooperative conscience, all of which reinvigorated a spirit of fellowship into the movement. Going far beyond the first British cooperative feminists, WCG also agitated through campaign strategies.

More generally, numerous campaigns advocated for women's rights. On behalf of workers, other campaigns served to increase compensation and improve work conditions. The intention of such activism was to reinvigorate the spirit of Owenite fellowship, improve legal rights, and increase the standard of living, all of which then positively influence women's

self-respect and capacity for self-help. In the household, WCG women come to expect and receive respectful treatment; partners become equals in workload and decision-making. There are noteworthy positive implications for the quality of childrearing. Moreover, as women become involved in the community, they shape decisions, take on leadership positions, and generally work to improve civic institutions and civic services. The WCG worked toward women's participation as equals in the household, the workplace, and the community.

☙

CHAPTER 8

Profit Sharing

INTRODUCTION

The Rochdale Pioneers, the Cooperative Wholesale Society (CWS), and the Women's Cooperative Guild (WCG) all wrestled with deep questions of transition. The Rochdale pioneers addressed transition by centering on the institution of the cooperative store. The CWS extended the reach of cooperation back into wholesaling networks, promising the realization of the cooperative commonwealth when consumers control all of industry. Addressing the costs to women and the poor arising alongside the practical successes of the cooperative movement, the WCG developed a formidable advocacy organization with the purpose of reestablishing an all-inclusive cooperative vision. Despite all these efforts to reimagine Owen's initial insights, many middle-class reformers remained unconvinced by the effectiveness of a consumer orientation. The transition of production warranted more attention. Advocates of profit sharing offered what at first appears a pragmatic and evolutionary path to full cooperation. Such arguments in particular suggest that without disrupting the core of the economy, profit sharing can immediately confront the major economic problem, the conflict between capital and labor. At the same time, profit sharing directly addresses labor-centered inefficiencies and low levels of human development for the working poor.

While exploring new theoretical constructs, several of these advocates grappled with the contradiction between J. S. Mill's endorsement of cooperation and the reality of failed cooperative experiments, particularly

Building a Social Science. Kirsten Madden and Joseph Persky, Oxford University Press. © Oxford University Press 2024.
DOI: 10.1093/oso/9780197693735.003.0008

in production.[1] Reflecting on those failures, some echoed Mill's primary qualification: that the British "people are not yet sufficiently advanced" both in intelligence and morality (Fawcett 1871, 205). The gradualist case for profit sharing appealed to several political economists: Mill, Henry Fawcett, Sedley Taylor, William Stanley Jevons, and even Alfred Marshall all advocated profit sharing. And at least some of these political economists foresaw that, as the workforce evolves, profit sharing enterprises might transform into worker-owned and -operated cooperatives, the base of a new economy.

EARLY INSIGHTS ON THE PRODUCTIVITY OF PROFIT SHARING

Charles Babbage, the creator of the "Calculating-Engine," was among the first to analyze the advantages of profit sharing.[2] He began serious study of industrial machinery and organization in the 1820s (Babbage 1846, iii). Babbage's visits to productive establishments over a ten year period led him to lecture at Cambridge and write a book titled, *On the Economy of Machinery and Manufactures*. The study of real-world technology also exposed Babbage to political economy. Divided in two sections, his book covers technological issues in the first and political economy of manufacturing in the second.

The section on the political economy of manufacturing covers a wide variety of topics, including money, prices, and advantages from the division of labor; large scale manufacturing, "over-manufacturing," and the deleterious effects of both labor combinations and capitalists' combinations. The inter-combination conflicts lead to the neglect and sometimes even the destruction of physical capital, as well as unrealized gains when disgruntled workers refuse to apply innovations or improve skills (Babbage 1846, 250).

---

1. The Ralahine society in Ireland was one such failure. See Fawcett (1871) and Taylor (1884, 100–108) for details.

2. About the same time that Babbage began his investigation, the pages of George Mudie's *Economist* drew attention to a scheme identified as the Motherwell proposal. The plan involved turning over a farm in Lanark "on perpetual lease" to volunteer applicants (screened by a committee). The idea attracted interest across classes, but a petition for the new arrangement stalled in parliament in 1821 (Mudie, Vol. I, 387–388). *The Economist* reports an estimated £96,000 for start-up capital, to be raised through subscription. Curiously, there is a profit sharing element in these plans. The intention was to divide the surplus: 5% to subscribers, one-half of the remaining surplus to capital, and the other half for "the disposal of the working proprietors" (Mudie, Vol. 2, 27–28). It is doubtful that Babbage or any of the political economists in this chapter read Mudie's *Economist*.

As an early technocrat, Babbage was against all types of combinations.[3] For Babbage, when capitalists prosper, there is a diffusion of benefits accruing to all classes over the longer run. But uneven distribution of immediate returns and delays in the accrual of workforce benefits effectively mask the common interests between capital and labor (251). Conflict tends to result.

In his explorations of industry, Babbage discovered impressive exceptions to the growing capital–labor conflicts of the 1820s. Profit sharing created a common interest in industries as diverse as the Cornwall mines, whaling, and South England net fishing (1846, 259).[4] When profit sharing aligns the personal self-interest of workers with business decision-makers, mutual respect and mutual confidence arise between the formerly combatant parties and productivity improves.[5]

A full account of profit sharing appears in Babbage's Chapter 26, "On a New System of Manufacturing" (1846). He highlights this chapter in the preface to the second edition: "I am inclined to attach some importance to the new system of manufacturing" as it "would greatly increase the productive powers" of countries that adopt the system (viii).[6] In contrast to problematic capital–labor conflicts at the time, Babbage portrays profit sharing as improving labor relations and therefore productivity: workers take more care with the physical capital, and they seek to adopt innovations and improve their skills. Because of his interest in technological innovations, Babbage particularly advocates a profit sharing rule that offers larger shares of new profits deriving from innovation to the innovator (254).

John Stuart Mill and Harriet Taylor commented approvingly on Babbage's proposals. Mill and Taylor were not the least surprised by

3. Babbage's book also argues against patent laws, asking: "What constitutes an invention?—Few simple mechanical contrivances are new" (1846, ix). The diffusion of technology is a secret to economic success: "The only real secrets of trade are industry, integrity, and knowledge: to the possessors of these no exposure can be injurious; and they never fail to produce respect and wealth" (viii).

4. According to William Thornton, Babbage also identified forms of profit sharing in the Flintshire lead mines, the Skipton mines in Yorkshire, and the Cumberland copper mines (1869, 345).

5. Writing on the subject over three decades later, William Thornton also theorized profit sharing within the context of self-interest. Thornton assumes that workers only willingly work harder for employers "for the sake of proportionately better pay" (1869, 367). And employers "cannot be expected to continue a system whose only result is the unfruitful transfer of money from his pocket to the pockets of his workpeople" (366).

6. Curiously distinct from many educated British commentators on the working classes during the early 19th century, Babbage communicates that the "greater intelligence and superior education of the working classes" make Great Britain particularly fertile ground for profit sharing (1846, viii). This refreshing perspective concerning working-class intelligence may well be due to his extensive firsthand interactions with workers about technology.

developments of profit sharing in capitalism. By the early 19th century, the growth in workforce literacy and widespread access to a variety of different types of publications translated into important effects on social psychology. Previously subjected to systems of protection and dependence, the Mill and Taylor hypothesis is that as new generations of workers adapt to higher education, they are less willing to be led. Education fuels the working-class drive for independence and self-governance ([1848] 1965, 763–766).

While the social psychology transformation is in its early stages, full-fledged cooperation remains out of reach. But "association of the labourers with the capitalist," or profit sharing, appears in parallel to the fledgling partial experiments in full cooperation (Mill [1848] 1965, 769). Profit sharing effectively offers an additional training ground to shape future generations of cooperators. That training ground introduces and reinforces the "excellencies" of public spiritedness, generosity, justice, and equality. "[A]ssociation, not isolation, of interests, is the school in which these excellences are nurtured . . . to enable them to work with or for one another in relations not involving dependence" (768). The profit sharing innovator in the painting trade of Paris, Maison Leclaire is a case in point. Leclaire's initial motivation to reform his business lay in the desire to align the self-interest of his workers with himself, to create "some bond of mutual security" through "a yearly division of profits" (772).

Building off Charles Babbage's initial analysis of tremendous productivity gains through profit sharing, Mill and Taylor's coverage of the early French and British experiences highlight additional reasons for rising productivity. A claim on variable profits stimulates sober, respectful responsiveness toward employer suggestions. There is increased worker "zeal" for industrious activity. And paralleling Babbage, Mill and Taylor's account also identifies innovation within the workforce. Further and distinct from cooperation, profit sharing allows "unity of authority" under a private capitalist. With an eye firmly fixed on productivity gains, and "exempt from the control of a body, if he is a person of capacity" the private capitalist "is considerably more likely than almost any association to run judicious risks, and originate costly improvements" (Mill & Taylor [1848] 1965, 793). The views of Babbage and Mill and Taylor concur: the creation of a common interest through profit sharing opens multifaceted pathways to higher productivity.[7]

---

7. Later work reinforces and expands the productivity arguments, highlighting cost reductions. Rather than carelessness with inputs, workers economize on input use. Workers cease wasting worktime. And they take more care toward the physical capital

WHY PROFIT SHARING? BROADER GOALS

Like Babbage and Mill and Taylor, the other mid 19th-century political economists contemplating profit sharing highlight its productivity enhancing and conflict diminishing implications. Henry Fawcett, of the Mill school, provides rich insights regarding how profit sharing reduces capital–labor conflict. Part of the appeal of profit sharing is its seamless alignment with the social psychology predominant in competitive capitalism.

> The fact has long been almost universally recognized that the most effectual way to secure the active energy and the best exertions of any particular person engaged in a business, is to stimulate in him a personal interest in the success of the undertaking, by conferring upon him a certain share of the profits. (Fawcett 1871, 177; similarly see 1860, 10).

When business enterprises offer the workforce a stake in the profits, that serves as a "powerful inducement of self-interest," and workers labor "with far greater energy and effect" (Fawcett 1871, 173). Careful to make profit sharing appealing to a capitalist audience, Fawcett highlights that the "share of the profits allotted to labour does not represent any loss to the capitalist." Capitalists lose nothing if they establish a minimum profit target at the average rate in the industry. If profits fall below the minimum profit standard, labor only claims normal wages (174).

In "Strikes: Their Tendencies and Remedies," Fawcett (1860) explains how "copartnership," or profit sharing, redresses capital–labor conflict. Problematic labor strikes affect future business decision-making. Some employers turn to profit sharing as a voluntary mechanism to avoid potential strikes and their associated losses (9–10). Ineffective strikes also teach workers lessons. Workers learn that striking for higher returns is only effective when businesses are profitable. Workers begin to stay informed on the profit situation of their employers, pressing for claims when profits are high. In effect, profit sharing becomes a conciliatory mechanism, transforming opposing interests into "an identity of interests" (9; similarly, see 1871, 169).

As profit sharing inspires solidarity across the classes, frictions diminish between labor and capital. In Fawcett's view, "'two agents assisting each

---

at hand, knowing "that wanton destruction of tools or materials is merely one way of throwing their own money into the sea" (Taylor 1884, 21). Oversight costs drop, as there is less need to superintend such workers. Managers can more productively apply their efforts and time toward business planning.

other to secure a common object'" end up with "'more harmonious relations'" where "'employers and employed are both made to feel that they
have an immediate and direct interest in the success of the work in which
they are engaged'" (Fawcett 1871, 164–165, cited in Taylor 1884, 75). The
primary qualification is trust (Taylor 1884, 74; 99; Thornton 1869, 364).

These improved labor relations can carry over in crises. Consider, for example, when a profit sharing enterprise experiences business gluts. Rather
than lay workers off, the workforce shifts to cost reduction activities and
to repair and improvement of the physical capital. Assuming sound business planning during periods of prosperity, there are sufficient reserves to
cover the fixed portion of wage payments. This shift in labor activity directly addresses the glut by cutting immediate supply while also enhancing
efficiency for future production (Babbage 1846, 257).

The claims among political economists about the results of profit sharing
extend beyond productivity and mitigating conflict. As an institutional
structure with tremendous flexibility, profit sharing can also ameliorate
social ills and stimulate whole human development.

Mill and Taylor offer details underlying the profit sharing system of
painter Leclaire. Out of profits, he both established a Provident Society
and financed a library and lecture series for workers ([1848] 1965, 773–
774). Mill and Taylor also credit a manager of a Parisian printing press for
dedicating a portion of profits to cover workers' medical expenses (773).

Sedley Taylor best epitomizes the extension of profit sharing outcomes
to social reform and human development. Perhaps better known for
contributions on the science of music, in his political economy Sedley Taylor
is a major proponent of profit sharing. A professor at Trinity College in
Cambridge, Taylor prepared six pamphlets on the topic between 1880 and
1883 and published these as a single volume in 1884 dedicated to Henry
Fawcett. Taylor's primary intent was to reintroduce French successes in
profit sharing to an English audience. In that spirit, his volume describes
various profit sharing ventures and highlights their benefits.

In Sedley Taylor's view, and contrary to Fawcett, central to any version
of profit sharing is a social psychology of "mutual confidence," paralleling
what commonly appears in the cooperative literature:

> The workman of a house must feel assured that its chief, when introducing these
> altered industrial relations, is not merely or mainly led by self-interest, but has
> their material and moral elevation at heart, and intends to be personally at hand
> with counsel, suggestion and active co-operation, in order to secure from the
> participatory system the full benefits which it has elsewhere been the means of
> conferring on the working classes. (1884, 73)

Sedley Taylor's case studies on profit sharing repeat numerous reasons for enhanced workplace efficiency, productivity, and thus profits. As profit sharing incentivizes worker "zeal," physical effort increases. But the greater effects lay in stimulating the worker's intelligence, alertness, orderliness, and attention (1884, 94–95).

Because workers share in the productivity gains, their immediate income and material conditions improve. In typifying approaches to profit sharing, Sedley Taylor further elaborates on effects from the "system of deferred possession." This system places a portion of net profits into an interest-earning fund which effectively serves as insurance. A deferred possession component of profit sharing is a means of enhancing the social security of workers.

Beyond the pure material outcomes, profit sharing offers gains in overall human development. The worker experiences improvement in intelligence, morality, and self-respect.[8] The worker's social status rises as he becomes "in a real though restricted sense, a co-partner with his employer" (Taylor 1884, 65). Profit sharing is more than "a means of improving the pecuniary situation." Profit sharing serves as "a powerful lever for raising their moral condition, and with it of course their whole social status" (17).[9]

Profit sharing has the capacity to generate non-material benefits for the employers as well. As foreseen by Fawcett, when employees become more trustworthy, there is less supervisory effort and anxiety, which frees time and energy for higher order and more creative management and planning tasks (Fawcett 1871, 177–178; see similarly Taylor 1884, 95). Unique to Taylor's account is the assumption that the employer looks to set an example, growing in virtue and in competence (95). William Thompson's vision of enlarging self-interest comes into play. The employer positively experiences feelings associated with the enhanced welfare of workers and growing workplace solidarity. Further, the employer is the recipient of social respect from customers and the general community in response to the higher quality products and services created by the business.

---

8. Babbage also highlights that "the moral effect . . . would be useful in the highest degree, since it would render character of far greater value to the workman than it is at present" (1846, viii).

9. Likewise, Fawcett identifies profit sharing as a stimulus to improved social relationships across the classes and increased self-respect among workers (1860, 10–11). Even earlier, Mill and Taylor quote a Dr. Barham: " 'each man feels, as a partner in his little firm, that he meets his employers on nearly equal terms' " ([1848] 1965, 770).

INSTITUTIONAL DETAILS AND PROFIT SHARING GOALS

Profit sharing mixes seamlessly into capitalist production, while also serving as a way station between capitalism and cooperation. Different goals for profit sharing require different institutional structures. Precisely because this is an institutional compromise in the middle ground between two distinct economic systems, there are details to consider. Political economists grapple with questions about how much profit to share, how to share that profit, who to share it with, what industries are appropriate, and who makes decisions.

In initiating the formal discussion of how much profit to share, Babbage's general proposal is to arrange payments so "that every person employed should derive advantage from the success of the whole; and that the profits of each individual should advance, as the factory itself produced profit, without . . . making any change in the wages" (1846, 251). Profit sharing is a conditional promise of additional returns to workers, over and above wages. Conditionality is key, the important condition being that workers only share in profits when an enterprise rises above the average rate of profit in the industry (Thornton 1869, 365–366).[10] Workers reap gains when their productivity rises. This minimum profit condition also protects the interests of the capitalists (see for example, Fawcett 1871, 174).

The specific numerical example Babbage offers includes ten workers and two capitalists, and in his example, the workers and the capitalists each front one-half of the initial financial capital. Recognizing the reality of workers' material insecurity, as their "daily labour procures for them their daily food," Babbage recommends fixing a portion of returns as wages (1846, 251). Concerning profit sharing, he offers two general principles:

1. "That a considerable part of the wages received by each person employed should depend on the profits made by the establishment" (253–254); and
2. "That every person connected with it should derive more advantage from applying any improvement he might discover, to the factory in which he is employed, than he could by any other course" (254).

Babbage's rule of thumb for wage setting is that, for every one that works (whether skilled labor, bookkeepers, clerks, etc.), each "receive one-half of

---

10. There is a wide divergence among anecdotal cases, stipulating anywhere from a 5% to 15% minimum before the workers' share of profit kicks in. Workers did not participate in the extreme case requiring profits to rise above 15% (Thornton 1869, 356).

what his service is worth in fixed salary, the other part varying with the success of the undertaking" (256).

Technological innovations especially fascinate Babbage. His second general principle stimulates innovation and adoption of better work processes across the enterprise.

> For the promotion of such discoveries, it would be desirable that those who make them should either receive some reward, to be determined after a sufficient trial by a committee assembling periodically; or if they be of high importance, that the discoverer should receive one-half, or two-thirds of the profit resulting from [the discovery] (Babbage 1846, 256).

While recognizing the necessity of structuring pay for base level material security, Babbage also recommends incentivizing innovation through this pecuniary appeal to self-interest.

Babbage's specific recommendations did not gain widespread acceptance. Many involved in profit sharing continued to grapple with the question: what is the workers' fair share of profits?[11] No uniform answer materialized out of the experiments of formal profit sharing. Some of the producer cooperatives divided profit across capital, labor and the consumer in relatively equal amounts.[12] Others provided a larger absolute share to capital with roughly equal smaller shares to the workers and the

11. The question of what share is fair presumes that workers can claim a share of profits. Alfred Marshall offers two arguments for why workers can claim a share of profits. The context of Marshall's first argument is one of rational business deliberation. Profit sharing occurs as a result of prudent reflection about incentives. Beyond diminishing friction, a share of profits increases the "willingness of . . . employees to go out of their way to do little things that may be of great benefit comparatively to the firm." Likewise, in his address to the Cooperative Congress, Marshall declares profit sharing as "the most efficient means" to induce a worker "to take a pleasure in advancing its [the firm's] prosperity by all means, whether they fall within the technical limits of his ordinary work or not" (1889, 253). Further, profit sharing attracts "workers of more than average ability and industry" ([1890] 1961, 178). Marshall's second argument is unique and concerns quasi-rents. That argument appears at the end of the current chapter.

12. Alfred Marshall identifies that J. C. Gray writes a series of "excellent papers" about cooperative production (1889, 250). J. C. Gray attracted the attention of E. V. Neale as Gray participated in the establishment of a co-partnership at Hebden Bridge Fustian Manufacturing Cooperative Society. In 1883 Gray became assistant secretary to Neale at the Cooperative Union. When Neale retired in 1891, Gray took over as General Secretary. Gray's "forte is business organization," while also exhibiting "capacity for friendship and for winning goodwill" (Greening 1902, 270). The question of fair share appears clearly in Gray (1887, 5). J. C. Gray's coverage of profit sharing includes a share to consumers. His work does not describe how the consumers receive their shares of profit. Perhaps these transfers occur as rebates on purchases.

consumers. In most cases, the formula for dividing the workers' aggregate share centers on proportionality to wages.

The precise division of profits is likely to reflect the primary profit sharing goal. If productivity is the major focus, most likely the business offers the smallest possible share to workers that incentivizes effort. Where the goal is resolution of capital–labor conflict, somewhat higher shares to laborers are likely: to win the workers' trust, the employer must not secure himself too large a claim of profit nor the workers "too low a rate of bonus" (Taylor 1884, 99). Social-centered goals and human development likely recommend substantially larger worker shares.[13]

There is also substantial variety in the concrete methods of profit sharing. The "system of immediate distribution" provides cash payments out of net profits in fixed proportions to select employees each year (Taylor 1884, 31). In contrast, the "system of deferred possession" places a proportion of net profits into an interest-earning fund. Effectively serving as retirement insurance, a worker only lays claim to shares after meeting specific criteria concerning age and/or years employed at the establishment. If the worker experiences a disabling accident or death, the accumulated deferred share, or a portion of it, typically goes to family members (33). There are also numerous examples of combinations across these two systems. A third profit sharing method credits a worker's portion of profits as shares in the business until the worker claims a minimum stake in ownership.[14]

---

13. In contrast to the political economists, the historian and jurist Frederic Harrison represents a more cynical view on the question of how much to share. To Harrison, such discussions always end "in absurdity," devolving into one of many crude "metaphysical puzzles." Equal shares make no sense, as Harrison doubts the ideal of equality is just. Resorting to market price conventions are equally problematic, as these are simply measures from the

> very industrial system which is declared to be *so radically unjust* . . .. Generals win battles in spite of bad soldiers, and soldiers win battles in spite of bad generals: what is the share of each in the result? A capitalist of consummate skill makes a business thrive in spite of every opposition; a reckless capitalist ruins the most promising business. And if labour and capital share equally, what becomes of talent, so justly considered in Fourierism? Who is to estimate the share which mechanical genius, instinctive sagacity, and personal ascendency, *ought* to secure for a masterly trader? All sorts of ingenious rules have been suggested to determine this just share mathematically, and each is a fresh absurdity. (Harrison, 1866, 494)

Likewise, Harrison critiques the idea of profit as a return for abstinence, asking where is the sacrifice when a rich man saves out of a large fortune (493–495).

14. £20 is the norm for the minimum ownership stake in (Gray 1887). Frederic Harrison critiques the practicality of labor holdings of shares on numerous grounds. Problematically, given property laws of the time, neither women nor working children could own shares. More generally, as enterprises succeed there is a tendency for shares to concentrate in fewer hands and reinforce growing inequality rather than diffusion of ownership (Harrison 1866, 489–491). See Blasi, et al. (2013) on employee stock ownership plans as contemporary variations on these 19th-century approaches to profit sharing.

Other, more elaborate profit sharing schemes include dedicating portions of profits to education and social funds (Gray 1887; see also Mill & Taylor [1848] 1965, 773–774). Businesses emphasizing goals of productivity and capital–labor conflict resolution are likely to rely upon the system of immediate distribution and perhaps on investments in company stock. Businesses emphasizing social and human development goals are likely to apply variations and combinations of all four methods.

There tends to be agreement that the overall viability of profit sharing depends on the quality of character within its workforce. Babbage, for example, highlights worker characteristics of intelligence and skill, sobriety, and "steadiness" (1846, 254). But there is debate regarding which workers should receive offers to share profits. In some practical applications, profit sharing only applied to managers of the workforce. If the goal is productivity, then the narrow application might make some sense, as might the slightly wider extension of profit sharing to the highly skilled segment of the workforce. In contrast, to be effective in improving labor relations and the conditions of labor generally, profit sharing must reach workers at all levels. In his early search for remedies to social problems among the working class, Fawcett advocates profit sharing with the less as well as the most educated workers in a business (1860, 10).

The political economists question which industries are most appropriate for profit sharing. Where the goal is enhancing productivity and profitability, labor-intensive industries are the target (Taylor 1884, 41; see also Thornton 1869, 371). It is only when labor is the dominant input that its incentivized effort realizes substantial pecuniary returns (Thornton 1869, 371). Profit sharing is also relevant to industries with difficult or costly superintendence (Taylor 1884, 41). While the "master's eye cannot be everywhere . . . when capital takes labour into partnership, every labourer in becoming a partner becomes also a partaker in a master's motives for vigilance." The superintending implication: "[E]veryone is watched by everyone else. Everyone has upon him not one, but hundreds perhaps of pairs of eyes, and every eye the eye of a master" (Thornton 1869, 368). In contrast, where the goals are either social or for purposes of human development, profit sharing might apply to any industry with sufficient margins to maintain business viability.

Finally, there is a major divergence of opinion around worker participation in decision-making. Babbage provides little guidance.[15] His

---

15. Advocating specialization and the division of labor, Babbage's piece only provides one minor example concerning workers in decision-making. He asks what to do when a worker who finances the organization exhibits incompetence or other enterprise-harming behaviors. Babbage suggests "such cases might be determined . . . by meetings of the whole establishment" (1846, 259).

silence might in part be due to his emphasis on the goals of productivity and mitigating conflict. To meet both these goals, the norm of capitalist decision-making need not necessarily be challenged. Similarly, political economists who advocate profit sharing to ameliorate social ills may well endorse capitalist decision-making. But when the goals extend to human development and to profit sharing as a steppingstone to full cooperation, laborers' involvement in decision-making is paramount.

The thought of marginalist economic theorist William Stanley Jevons is the most dogmatic in advocating capitalist control. Jevons takes pains to make explicit the limits he considers appropriate for "industrial partnerships." He emphasizes, "the sharing of profits does not entail the right to control in any degree, the affairs of the firm . . ." Like small stockholders, workers must rest their trust in the decisions of the directors and managers of companies. In these industrial partnerships, Jevons is confident that workers have an incentive to maintain the quality of their work and that of their fellow workers, even though they have no role in management. This deal is one in which the employer "buys" the workers' marginal "exertions and goodwill with a share of profits." Jevons makes the comparison to the military, where the "successful leader must be perfectly unfettered in judgment and supreme in executive power; and yet he must manage to earn the confidence and devotion of his men." Jevons looks forward to the day when "our works and factories will become so many united and well-organized regiments of labourers" (1883, 142).[16] This vision is one of vertical employer–employee relations rather than horizontal combinations of workers: "The workman's interests should be bound up with those of his employer and should be pitted in fair competition against those of other workmen and employers" (Jevons as quoted in Taylor 1884, 74).

In contrast, Sedley Taylor is the voice for more elaborate worker participation, shading into broader cooperation. Taylor gives more detail on the case of the French painter turned successful businessman. Leclaire's Provident Society involved twelve workers annually rotating into its administration to care for fellow employees in need, to participate in

---

16. Jevons expressed similar views on labor force hierarchy nearly a quarter century earlier. Beatrice Potter quotes from Jevons' 1859 report on the Padiham weavers' strike. In the report, he brings up two pre-strike cooperatives and writes:

No such concerns can possibly succeed unless the functions of managers and operatives are kept distinct, and shareholders working as operatives are prepared to submit to a manager who is their servant. This difficulty the Rochdale men have overcome; but in Padiham it led, combined with other causes, to the total failure of both Co-operative mills. (Jevons as quoted in Potter 1891, 127–128)

committees, to make and receive reports, to provide decision-making input, and "perhaps even to have been entrusted . . . with weighty disciplinary powers and attendant responsibilities" (1884, 20). Thus, the worker "'is called upon to weight interests not his own; . . . and he usually finds associated with him in the same work minds'" that can "'supply reason to his understanding and stimulation to his feeling for the general good'" (Taylor 1884, 20).[17] Leclaire's system is one of "moral renovation . . . the principle of participation by workmen in the profits of enterprise" (27). For Taylor, while profit sharing initially puts workplace control in the hands of the business owners and managers, as workers evolve wholistically, it is only reasonable that workers encroach on management and directing functions (67).

THE EVOLUTION OF THE ECONOMIC SYSTEM

Early on Babbage forecasts the general expansion of profit sharing. Profit sharing begins with "some of the most prudent and active workmen" in an industry (1846, viii). If successful, Babbage expresses confidence that others will follow.

> The small capitalist would next join them, and such factories would go on increasing until competition compelled the large capitalist to adopt the same system; and ultimately the whole faculties of every man engaged in manufacture would be concentrated upon one object—the art of producing a good article at the lowest possible cost:—whilst the moral effect . . . would be useful in the highest degree. (Babbage 1846, viii)[18]

While profit sharing is to become an economy-wide institution, Babbage makes no explicit prediction of a shift to full cooperation. He does leave an opening, though. Beyond positive productivity and innovation effects,

---

17. Here Taylor quotes J. S. Mill from *Representative Government*.
18. Like Babbage, J. S. Mill's colleague and friend William Thornton considers that profit sharing establishes a common interest across workers and employer. And where it works as a win-win for employees and employers, "there may be no reason why an employer who has once adopted the system should afterwards abandon it." As others in the industry take note of the augmented surplus, "there will be excellent reason why their master's example should be followed by other masters, and eventually by all so circumstanced as to be able to apply the same principles with prospect of similar effect" (Thornton 1869, 367).

Babbage portrays profit sharing as an institution which enlarges self-interest, particularly eliminating discord among workers and capitalists:

> The workmen and the capitalist would so shade into each other, —would so *evidently* have a common interest, and their difficulties and distresses would be mutually so well understood, that instead of combining to oppress one another, the only combination which could exist would be a most powerful union *between* both parties to overcome their common difficulties. (italics original, Babbage 1846, 258).

J. S. Mill and Harriet Taylor pick up on Babbage's ideas and offer a wider vision. In the early stages of the education of the workforce, both cooperation and more limited profit sharing arise ([1848] 1965, 792). Both institutions provide additional training grounds for workers. Workers learn to be industrious and innovative. They have higher material returns and more social security. Interpersonal relations between profit sharing workers and employers improve (773–774). Under these changing conditions, more and more workers refuse work for mere wages: "both private capitalists and associations will gradually find it necessary to make the entire body of labourers participants in profits" (793). The economy thus evolves over a longer run toward cooperative competition, as discussed in Chapter 4.[19]

Contrary to Mill and Taylor, some political economists conclude that "the partnership or bonus system can never affect more than a portion of the labouring population" (Thornton 1869, 371–372). Critics point out that most examples of profit sharing are simply "wise and spontaneous act[s] of munificence from the capitalists." They hold more generally, "[n]o effort of the labourers can advance its introduction" (Harrison 1866, 498n; see also Thornton 1869, 371–372).[20] This constraint to the initiation of profit sharing, if binding, is an important qualification to its general application.

---

19. J. E. Cairnes of the Mill School describes the "bargain" in the North Wales slate quarries. The bargain might be one type of transitional institutional arrangement that Mill and Taylor envision. Land and major physical capital in the slate quarries remained in the hands of capitalists. They contracted and recontracted jobs to "bargains" of organized groups of slate workers. Generally the only quality a worker needed to participate in a bargain is "the moral capital of good character" (Cairnes 1864, 187). Though typically one worker served as lead, the workers in the bargain were partners, making all decisions on the work process. Cairnes claims that this institution stimulates intelligence, "reflective powers," and widened sympathies. The main drawback is that the capitalist and the laborer still "do not coalesce in the same man" (189).

20. Thornton's supply and demand analysis underscores the lack of market power among laborers. On the supply side, there is a perfectly perishable commodity— today's labor cannot be bottled and sold tomorrow—and poverty also reduces bargaining power among potential laborers (1869, 70–71). On the demand side, capital provides flexibility for employers to withhold jobs in the labor market if wages rise, and the ease of employer combinations also facilitates their abilities to set wages (72; 76). Thus, in the case of physical labor, market power tends to rest on the side of employers.

Chief among those suggesting only a limited role for profit sharing is William Stanley Jevons. Nowhere does Jevons' writing consider cooperation as a replacement for the system of private ownership. His support for "industrial partnerships" is not meant as a bridge to full cooperatives but only as a reform of the dominant system. In particular, as suggested above, Jevons explicitly rejects any form of worker control.

Jevons' soft version of the profit sharing theme appears in his 1870 lecture entitled "On Industrial Partnerships." He first offered this lecture "under the auspices of the National Association for the Promotion of Social Science." Shortly after Jevons' death the lecture was published in *Methods of Social Reform* (1883). In the piece, Jevons cites Mill (and Taylor's) discussion of profit sharing and cooperatives. Jevons uses several examples from Mill and Taylor and like them gives considerable credit to Babbage. But as his title suggests, Jevons limits his support to various forms of profit sharing and avoids completely the question of full cooperatives. Like Mill and Taylor, Jevons suggests the current system of employer/employee relations is untenable; but in contrast, he does not suggest the capitalist can (or should?) be fully done away with.

Jevons' approach to profit sharing draws heavily on the then ongoing expansion of the joint-stock companies. He observes that the move toward joint-stock companies makes the performance of a company more transparent and undermines owners' reluctance to be open about the level of profits. Jevons considers joint-stock companies as excellent candidates for profit sharing since these companies necessarily depend less on "vigilant superintendence of their business when managers are not the actual capitalists." Under the circumstances, "[I]t is all the more necessary that they should give each man an interest in the result" (1883, 138).

Jevons' piece ends with a broad attack on unions. Their efforts are ultimately fruitless and divisive. By contrast, industrial partnerships represent a natural evolution of the firm as it moves toward the joint-stock form of organization. Like Mill and Taylor, Jevons emphasizes the evolution of capitalist institutions, but Jevons balks at an endorsement of worker self-management. Just the contrary, as discussed earlier, Jevons advocates the continuing role of "leadership" and the "healing of the discords of capital and labour" (1883, 148).

Alfred Marshall's writing certainly does not quibble with Jevons about the important role of managers in modern industry. Even so, and following Mill and Taylor, Marshall identifies profit sharing "as but a step towards the still higher but much more difficult level of true co-operation" ([1890] 1961, 627; see also 1889, 252). Beyond suitably delaying thorny practical questions about (in)effective management as well as insufficiency of capital

in producer cooperatives, profit sharing appeals to Marshall because it resonates with his appreciation for forethought, self-reliance, and freedom in industry.[21]

Of course, Marshall was a theoretician of the first rank. In that capacity, Marshall's *Principles* explores why and how labor claims profit. This understanding of profit sharing includes two original analytical points: composite quasi-rents and implicit benefits of prosperous enterprises.

The first, composite quasi-rents, anticipates elements of Gary Becker's (1964) theory of specialized human capital. Marshall identifies a situation where a worker has non-transferrable skills of value to the firm. In this case, the firm and the worker both experience major losses if the worker leaves for employment elsewhere. The firm enjoys what Marshall calls a composite "quasi-rent." Since the worker with non-transferrable skills is in part responsible for the composite quasi-rent, it seems reasonable that a portion goes to the worker. Marshall does not elaborate further, suggesting that "bargaining, supplemented by custom and notions of fairness" determine the distribution of the composite quasi-rent ([1890] 1961, 626).[22] As discussed earlier, there is a broad range of methods that 19th-century businesses applied to share such composite quasi-rents.

The second more general argument relates to Marshall's understanding that workers in prosperous firms enjoy a range of benefits that serve as implicit profit sharing. These benefits include better prospects of advancement, "continuous employment when trade is slack and much coveted overtime when trade is good" ([1890] 1961, 627). Marshall argues, "there is *de facto* some sort of profit-and-loss sharing between almost every business and its employees" (627).

Overall, even with his conservative view on authority in the workplace, Marshall's thought stands for broad reform of the employment relationship. In part addressing his longstanding advocacy for conditions that stimulate full human development, profit sharing can serve to educate and to create "opportunity and scope for a worthy ambition to act, not merely as a hand, but as a thinking and thoughtful human being"

---

21. Chapter 11 in the current volume covers Marshall's critiques of cooperation.

22. Marshall's address to the Cooperative Congress also expresses ambiguity regarding how much profit to share in noncooperative production and trade. Concerning an "abstract or 'metaphysical' principle . . . to settle rigidly what share of the profits should go to labour and what to capital, and what to the consumer, I find myself unable to follow it; whether it is put forward in the interests of labour or of the consumer" (1889, 252).

(1889, 253).[23] He speculates that occasionally, under existing employer–employee relationships,

> the solidarity of interests between those who work together in the same business is recognized with cordial generosity as the result of true brotherly feeling. But such cases are not very common; and as a rule the relations between employers and employed are raised to a higher plane both economically and morally by the adoption of the system of profit-sharing. ([1890] 1961, 627)

Profit sharing for Marshall is a concrete step in the development of the "latent social asset" of unselfish service. He is sure people "are capable of much more unselfish service than they generally render: and the supreme aim of the economist is to discover how this latent social asset can be developed most quickly, and turned to account most wisely" ([1890] 1961, 9).

---

23. Marshall's interests in broad human development appeared at least as early as 1873, in "The Future of the Working Classes."

PART III

———— ⌀ ————

Toward System

While redressing patriarchy, the Women's Cooperative Guild insists that the theory and practice of cooperation address all sectors of the economy: production, consumption, and the household. William Morris further complicates the picture by emphasizing the interdependence of happiness and human development with creativity. Much influenced by Morris, G. D. H. Cole of the Guild Socialists makes a major effort at integrating cooperative thought. Cole draws a cooperative institutional structure for a complete industrial system. He envisions bargaining between guilds, consumer cooperatives, and civic organizations. The plan is nothing less than a full cooperative alternative to market structure. It is the closest anyone comes to achieving Owen's social science.

Photo 3. Kelmscott Manor, from the frontispiece to the 1893 Kelmscott Press edition of William Morris's *News from Nowhere*. The Manor was the Morris's family home for many years.

CHAPTER 9

⚬⌣⚬

Creativity, Craft, and Cooperation

NICHOLAS ARMSTRONG, COAUTHOR

INTRODUCTION

William Morris declared unambiguously he is "neither a professional econo-mist or a professional politician." But decades as a successful craftsman and businessman in the arts sector of a capitalist economy generated dismay in him about the state of the world. The societally generated "uglinesses" Morris perceived "are but the outward expression of the innate moral base-ness into which we are forced by our present form of society" (1903, vii).

There are numerous links between William Morris and the cooperative thinkers of the 19th century. From the start, he embraced Robert Owen's understanding that "the conditions under which man lived could affect his life and deeds infinitely, that not selfish greed and ceaseless contention, but brotherhood and co-operation were the bases of true society" (1903, vii). He echoed Thompson and Wheeler in his critique of authoritarian control. He drew on Maurice's Working Man's College (1855). And Morris influenced the next generation of cooperative thinkers. Perhaps most im-portantly, his novel, *News from Nowhere*, with its broad insistence on crafts-manship, inspired the young G. D. H. Cole. Despite Morris' much asserted devotion to Marxist socialism, he was at root committed to cooperative themes growing out of Owenite foundations. No vision of 19th-century British cooperation is complete without considering Morris' thought.

Building a Social Science. Kirsten Madden and Joseph Persky, Oxford University Press. © Oxford University Press 2024. DOI: 10.1093/oso/9780197693735.003.0009

Like many of our cooperative thinkers, Morris stresses the centrality of happiness and whole human development. Unique to Morris is his insistence on the societal goal of "popular art." Following 19th-century utilitarian trends, Morris' worldview treats people as fundamentally pleasure seeking and social, while uniquely emphasizing creative inclinations. The aim is to restructure institutions to resonate with such inclinations. The principled institutions of equality, liberty, fellowship, and social responsibility are the base for achieving the three societal goals. Throughout, his work points toward "the humanization of human life" both at home and at work (Mackail 1899, 293–294).

While Morris is not a tight theoretician, his approach to social science is rich in concepts and their interdependencies. At times, his discussion of social psychology and institutions can leave a sense that everything willy-nilly influences everything else. However, we maintain that reviewing the body of his thought is worthwhile. Underneath are the outlines of an original and complex system. In trying to formalize Morris' gestalt, the reconstruction presented in this chapter specifies what amounts to a system of equations. The methodology may appear anachronistic, but it provides a glimpse of the insights his thought offers in determining his three goals in a cooperative environment.

BACKGROUND

William Morris (1834–1896) was born into a prosperous family. His mother (nee Emma Shelton) and father (William) shared a conventional middle-class outlook. Altogether they brought nine children into the world, with the younger William growing particularly close to his two older sisters. The senior William, a discount broker, made highly profitable investments on his own account, most notably in the British copper industry. During the 1840s the family became "seriously rich" (MacCarthy 1995, 22). William senior, however, died in 1847 and through much of his youth, the younger William drew substantially on his inherited share of the copper mine investments (Mackail 1901, 14). He remained fond of his bucolic upbringing and maintained long and close relations with his mother. However, as William aged, he expressed embarrassment about his father's profession and success in the copper industry (MacCarthy 1995, 24–27; Mackail 1901, 26).

Although reading by the age of four, Morris received little formal education before age nine. He spent much of his childhood outdoors, lost in dreams of medieval adventures. By 1848, he started in the newly established

Marlborough College. He disparaged his early formal education, asserting it taught him only "rebellion" (Morris, as quoted by MacCarthy 1995, 21). Morris found escape in tales "of knights in armor, lovely ladies, slaugh- terous hand-to-hand combats, witches . . . lovelorn heroes . . . all under medieval conditions" (Bernard Shaw in May Morris 1966, xxviii–xxix). He went on to Oxford, originally intending to take religious orders. Although critical of the narrow and pedantic characters of Oxford academics (Mackail 1901, 34), at Oxford he developed a new sense of fellowship in the "Brotherhood" which includes his lifelong friend Ned Burne-Jones as well as some of the founders of his later company. John Ruskin strongly influenced the Brotherhood, with Morris regularly chanting Ruskin's verses to the group (47).[1] While developing close bonds with these men, Morris also exhibited an ill temper which on occasion exploded in violence. Throughout his life, Morris suffered from incidents that George Bernard Shaw describes as "eclampsia." The fits left him drained and vacuous (Shaw quoted in MacCarthy 1995, 78). Even so, Morris' virtually unlimited en- ergy fueled his explorations of what he found a fascinating world (Mackail 1901, 328).

During college, Morris unleashed some of that energy by writing poetry (Mackail 1901, 51; 53). After graduation, he flirted with architecture and painting and moved on to interior decoration and manufacture. He lived a Bohemian lifestyle (128). Somewhat impulsively, Morris married his model, Janey Burden in 1859. They had a long and challenging marriage.

Established in 1861, Morris was the primary founder of Morris, Marshall, Faulkner and Co. Hiring a foreman from the Working Men's College and employing twelve boys and men, the company produced highly original or- namental works in the form of murals, stained glass, metalwork, furniture, embroidery, and stamped leather (151). The business prospered and ex- panded to include famously dyed textiles, wall hangings, and chintzes. In 1875 the firm reorganized as Morris and Co.

The company placed a priority on quality and strove to educate the consumer (Harvey & Press 1995, 185; 186). In many ways the company violated rules of profit maximization. It committed to quality, limited ex- pansion, and favored manual technologies. It turned business away over moral concerns about intended product uses (188). Certainly, the com- pany made ethical compromises, but did "much to give practical effect to Ruskin's exhortations" on virtuous economic behavior (186).

---

1. John Ruskin (1819–1900) was a major influence on many in late 19th-century British society. His primary field was art criticism, but his social criticism made a much deeper impact. See Chapter 11 for a brief overview of Ruskin's cooperative vision.

The "dreamer of dreams," Morris was complex and multifaceted (Mackail 1901, 213). Throughout his adulthood, he continued writing poetry and expanded into novels and translations.[2] Morris traveled widely, mesmerized in particular by Iceland and its culture. He subscribed to a deep utilitarianism with an emphasis on pleasure, seeking to make "his whole work into a fascinating and absorbing recreation" (218).

Approaching middle age, Morris surveyed his native country and found it deeply imperfect, describing London of 1874 as "a sordid loathsome place" (Mackail 1901, 302). With customary confidence that he could achieve what he imagined, Morris plunged into political activities. He started close to home with the architectural concerns of the Society for the Preservation of Ancient Buildings, moved on to the anti-imperialism of the Eastern Question Association and, much to his family's chagrin, committed to the Marxist Socialist League.[3]

Morris increasingly intertwined lectures on art with his understanding of socialism. In 1883 he gave a talk on the topic of "Democracy and Art" to Oxford undergraduates. He unabashedly declared himself a socialist and invited undergraduates to join him, bringing down the wrath of the administration (Mackail 1899, 118; MacCarthy 1995, 477–479).[4] As Bernard Shaw saw it, though Morris was clearly of the middle class, his interest in socialism intertwined with his close affiliation with manual workers.[5]

Throughout the 1880s, Morris devoted himself wholeheartedly to socialist activity including lecturing, demonstrating, and editing *Commonweal*, the paper of the Socialist League. With Bax, he wrote a Marxist European history (1886–1888). Morris also absorbed his energy in fictional accounts echoing his socialist principles: *The Dream of John Ball* originally published in *Commonweal* in 1886–1887; and *News from Nowhere* originally published in *Commonweal* in 1890. The latter offers echoes of the Owenite village,

2. Morris' artistic activism inspired J. R. R. Tolkien (Massey 2007, 2; 28). "Morris's romance provided Tolkien with both the inspiration and the building blocks with which he could fashion a fantasy world that was truly his own" (52–53).

3. Perhaps Morris' ambivalence toward his father's participation in high finance influenced his move to political activism and then the Socialist League. Consider for example, that in part he blamed "[g]reedy gamblers on the Stock Exchange" as Britain moved toward war against Russia in the 1877–1878 conflict on the Eastern Question (Mackail 1901, 349).

4. Morris (1894) explains why he becomes a socialist.

5. In Shaw's words, Morris "would have been more out of place in our drawing rooms than in a gang of manual laborers or craftsmen" (Bernard Shaw in May Morris 1966, xviii).

but greatly embellished with Morris' artistic-utilitarian approach to work and life.[6]

ELEMENTS OF THE SOCIAL PSYCHOLOGY

William Morris was personally cognizant of troubling elements within human nature as his own personality unfolded in recurrent fits of rage.[7] As the author of a fictional piece, he wonders about a medieval fighter: "how wrath and grief within him were contending with the kindness of the man" (Morris 1888, 68). Unlikely to fully ascribe to Robert Owen's belief in inherent goodness, Morris' thought does recognize good heartedness as a common human inclination, reinforced with an inherent concern about justice that he likely drew from Ruskin. But in Morrisian thought, the central propensities of humankind are pleasure seeking, creativity, and sociality.

The deep concern that there be pleasure in work derives from Morris' utilitarian philosophy, with a primary qualification: his writing acknowledges some parts of life—and work—are not going to be pleasant. He advocates to "accept life itself as a pleasure" (Morris 1897, 202), encouraging openness to the full experience that life offers (233).

Morris considers the creative impulse central to human nature,[8] and it reflects in his recognition that everyday art combats "dull work and its wearing slavery" (Morris 1882, 5–6), his belief of the necessity for beauty in product, and in his conviction that "the material surroundings . . . should be pleasant, generous, and beautiful" (Morris 1903, 29). With respect to

6. Of his fictional writing, Morris' *News from Nowhere* is explicitly labeled as utopian. Nevertheless, according to David Leopold, "Morris is no idle dreamer here, but is rather engaged in serious reflection on difficult questions of socialist design" (Leopold 2016, 30). Leopold identifies two functions of *News from Nowhere* that have particular relevance to our argument. *News from Nowhere* is particularly insightful in constructing ideals within economics. That is, Morris' fiction provides ideas for building the economy anew and motivating readers toward the new ideals. Two such economic constructs are the notion of creative, fulfilling, and pleasurable work and the intention to make art central to economic activity. *News from Nowhere* also serves a clarifying function. The work is "a complex thought experiment seeking to think through some aspects of the desirability and feasibility of Morris's account of a communist society." For Morris, the good society commits to equality, community, meaningful work, and widely diffused art (29).

7. " 'I have a religious hatred to all war and violence' " (Morris quoted in Mackail 1901, 98). In contradiction, documentation of his periodic fits of rage appears throughout his biography (see, for example, 35, 43, and 215).

8. In Morris' words, "art or work-pleasure . . . sprung up almost spontaneously . . . from a kind of instinct amongst people, no longer driven desperately to painful and terrible over-work" (1897, 149–150).

everyday arts, Morris recognizes an innate tendency toward ornamentation present across human history (1882, 3). Beauty stimulates aesthetic and creative sensibilities and triggers mental acuity to perceive and correct faults in one's surroundings (4; 21).

People are also innately social, experiencing hell when it is "but every man for himself" (Morris 1888, 30). Each exhibits an "instinctive reciprocity of service . . . a consciousness of the existence of a society of neighbours" (Morris 1891, 261). "[C]ombination is the life of the workers" (Morris 1903, 14), as each is "worthless without the co-operation of his fellows" (192). The cooperative social psychology is one of "moral consciousness" where, free from coercion, the individual identifies with broad social interests.[9] When coupled with cooperative institutions, inherent social nature makes it "inconceivable" for the typical person to divorce individual from social interests. Morality rises "into a higher atmosphere" elevated by "conscious responsibility to one's fellows" (Morris & Bax 1893, 298). Morris perceives empathy as a natural outcome deriving from innate sociality. Empathetic distress arises when witness to antisocial activity. Writing a letter to a Mrs. Howard, Morris explains, "'Do you know, when I see a poor devil drunk and brutal I always feel, quite apart from my aesthetical perceptions, a sort of shame, as if I myself had some hand in it'" (as quoted in Mackail 1901, 305). With regard to the lack of prisons in *News from Nowhere*, Morris asks, "how could they look happy if they knew their neighbors were shut up in prison, while they bore such things quietly" (Morris 1897, 48).[10]

THE INSTITUTIONAL FRAMEWORK
OF MORRIS' COOPERATION

Across multiple sources of both fictional and social styles, Morris provides an institutional vision of a fully realized cooperative society. Some of Morris' institutional vision heralds back to the cooperative villages of Owen and of Thompson. Some anticipate Cole's quasi-guild factories.

---

9. For example, Morris writes that each "ought to feel . . . that he is working for his own interest when he is working for that of the community" (1903, 192).

10. Curiously, while there are no criminal prisons in *News from Nowhere*, in the case of psychological "madness" Morris may impose "restraints" until the "sickness or madness is cured." There are no further details into these "restraints" (Morris 1897, 91; originally noted in Waithe 2006, 297).

Living Arrangements

Morris presents a healthy variety of living arrangements: rural towns and villages (Morris 1897, *passim*), scattered homes in the country (29; 81), and transient tent living (164). Environmental health appears particularly in the thought about social settlements.[11] As rural areas benefit by introducing social amenities that are more common in towns, larger population centers require significant infusions of "countryside" for pleasant inhabitability.

Cities are distribution hubs. Morris and Bax offer three models for larger population centers. If the industrial and political cities of capitalism remain, they require lower population densities to be both ecologically sensitive as well as aesthetically pleasing. Such cities incorporate cleanliness, airiness, and gardens throughout, and the "erecting of noble public buildings" of education including "theatres, libraries, workshops, taverns, kitchens, etc." (Morris 1897, 314). The second population settlement is the model of the English university town (Morris & Bax 1893, 315). The third type of larger population settlement is something akin to the 21st-century suburb. Dense settlements surround a central open space. The dense settlements give way to more sparsely populated areas bordering natural and publicly accessible countryside (316).

In addition to more private, personal, or family living arrangements, there are examples of communal living throughout *News from Nowhere.* Such abodes include remote houses reminiscent of monasteries, where the "most studious" of single young men choose to reside (Morris 1897, 81). There are many guest houses for travelers (11, 13) which may include food halls for the surrounding community (109–112; 157). Perhaps, most striking is Morris' archetype of a true communal living hall:

> visions of the noble communal hall of the future, unsparing of materials, generous in worthy ornament, alive with the noblest thoughts of our time, and the past, embodied in the best art which a free and manly people could produce; such an abode of man as no private enterprise could come anywhere near for beauty and fitness, because only collective thought and collective life could cherish the aspirations which would give birth to its beauty, or have the skill and leisure to carry out. (Morris 1903, 31)[12]

11. Morris' system normalizes ecological conscientiousness. Social priorities include beautifying the earth through labor and habitation (Morris & Bax 1893, 319).

12. In our reading, Morris uses the term "manly" as a synonym for chivalrous, communicating one who is not necessarily tamed by fear of death. More on the gender bias present in some of Morris' writing is in the conclusion.

Principled Institutions

Living arrangements presuppose the infusion of a core set of principled institutions across the cooperative: equality, liberty, fellowship, and social responsibility. Equality is central to interpersonal relations, whether these are familial, economic, or sociopolitical. The system requires an equal responsibility to work and equal access to natural resources and capital. Equality is necessary in the access of provisions.

Inspired by J. S. Mill's *On Liberty* (Waithe 2006, 223), Morris' social psychology requires freedom from all forms of individual and social tyranny (Morris 1903, 154). Such liberty extends to accessibility of the means of production and freedom of movement. Morris believes that when individual liberty is the norm, in association with innate sociality, people tend to make voluntary sacrifices in service to others' needs (168).

For Morris, fellowship involves self-governing "societies of equals" which establish their own rules and abide by them (Morris & Bax 1893, 87–88). The ethic is one of friendly affiliation in community where, in a state of perfect liberty, the individual identifies with broad social interests (298).

Equality and liberty are the foundations for the societal norm of fellowship. Coercion is inconsistent with genuine fellowship; people must experience the freedom to participate socially with others and the freedom to exit social situations. Such liberty in fellowship extends to the household with people freely choosing to reside where there is "mutual inclination and affection" (Morris & Bax 1893, 299–300).

" 'I don't want people to do just as they please; I want them to consider and act for the good of their fellows—for the commonweal in fact' " (quoted in Waithe 2006, 217; 226). The institutionalization of the value of social responsibility is necessary as a balance to individual liberty. The fictional society of *News from Nowhere* replaces punitive legal justice with liberty-centered mechanisms to align individual behavior with the society's values of tolerance, hospitality, and work. Such liberty-centered mechanisms rely both on individual conscience and on "informal laws and customs" to moderate a range of difficult behaviors from simple self-absorption to blatant interpersonal transgressions (229).[13] In part due to inherent sociality, "when transgressions occur, everybody, transgressors and all, know them for what they are; the errors of friends, not the habitual actions of

---

13. Morris writes, for example that with the end of employment-based tyranny, people are no longer "bidden to be any man's servant, everyone scorning to be any man's master." The condemnation of mastership is instrumental in maintaining an end to mastership (Morris 1882, 36).

persons driven into enmity against society" (Morris 1897, 88). People tend to internalize social expectations, knowing the difference between socially supporting and socially alienating behaviors. In most cases, the individual self-censures. They modify their own behavior when awareness arises of a social faux pas.[14] Self-censure extends to voluntary self-ostracism (leaving a community) in rare cases of violence.[15] When the individual does not self-censure, social censuring norms may kick in, from the simpler form of humor,[16] to discreet reminders of crossing a social boundary when someone lacks self-awareness,[17] to the more complex form of shunning[18] in the rare cases of extreme or unrelenting antisocial behavior.[19]

The norm of social responsibility is central for high functioning in an equal, liberty-centered society. Though people naturally censure antisocial behavior because they are social by nature, in Morris' system social *responsibility* per se is not an innate human characteristic; there must be intentionality to build it. Morris builds social responsibility into equality: all are to equally contribute to work. Morris builds social responsibility into pleasure: when workers derive pleasure from socially useful work, workers seek socially useful work. Morris builds social responsibility into the definition of art: all genuine art is useful. And Morris builds social responsibility into his emphasis on fellowship and the utility derived therefrom.

Education

Like Robert Owen (1813–1816) and William Thompson (1830), William Morris puts some thought into the educational requirements for

---

14. For example, see examples concerning fictional characters of News from Nowhere pp. 9–10; 37.

15. For example, in relaying the story of a man who, acting on a passion of the heart commits murder in *News from Nowhere*, the reader learns: "It was quite clear that the slayer took the whole consequences of the act upon himself, and did not expect society to whitewash him by punishing him" (Morris 1897, 187–188).

16. For example, see *News from Nowhere* pp. 17–18; 22–23.

17. For example, see *News from Nowhere* p. 16.

18. For example, see *News from Nowhere* pp. 60; 186.

19. Waithe is the originating source of these ideas on censuring in the *News from Nowhere* fictional society. Waithe does not question the soundness of such policies to constrain selfishness in a liberty-centered society even though the censuring norms do effectively constrain freedom. More problematic to Waithe is whether the fictional society requires "prior exclusion of unwanted elements." Waithe explores Morris' hypothesis in detail and concludes that if taking his *News from Nowhere* seriously as a social blueprint, "those excluded from his world—'lepers,' ugly people, the victims of idleness or 'Mulleygrubs' . . . become . . . uncomfortably resonant of a darker vision" (2006, 229).

cooperation. At the core of Morris' thought on education is his belief that it is inappropriate to force people to learn that which they do not need or want to learn (Morris 1897, 32; 71). Consistent with his negative experiences in his own formal education, Morris proposes no mandatory, systematized educational structures. Rather, necessity and genuine personal interest are the motivations for learning. Individuals realize education through a combination of cultural osmosis, independent study, and work.[20]

The realization of an educated public requires universally available educational opportunities (Morris 1882, 35) while also respecting diversity (Morris 1897, 29–33; 42). All should have the opportunity for a "share of whatever knowledge there is in the world according to" their "capacity or bent of mind" (Morris 1903, 24). Such education requires "abundant leisure," access to materials for the development of craft or art skills, access to instruction from knowledgeable individuals, as well as written materials and freedom of travel (24–26).[21] From a practical and social perspective, and like the early 19th-century cooperators, Morris advocates learning "more than one craft to exercise for the benefit of" the community (24).

Independent voluntary education does not necessitate the absence of places of learning. Beyond craft schools and repurposed colleges, factories serve as centers of education (William Morris as quoted in May Morris 1966, 137).[22] "Children who seem likely to develop gifts towards its special industry" go to the relevant factory which supplements "their book learning" at the factory library with "technical instruction" through apprenticeship. Since apprenticeship aligns with natural talents and interests of children, they enjoy this education and "look forward eagerly to the time when they will be allowed to work at turning out real useful wares" (136). These opportunities for education are lifelong (136–137).[23]

20. For Morris, in an ideal society "most children, seeing books lying about, manage to read by the time they are four years old" (Morris 1897, 31). Once able to read, it seems natural to Morris that individuals will seek out material independently or with the help of knowledgeable individuals, with new material aiding in further developing knowledge or skills (32). While strongly supporting a link between education and individual preferences, Morris advocates universal exposure to the core subjects of art, history, and nature to inform all on quality workmanship and beauty (1882, 21–25).

21. The responsibilities of established craftspeople include "the duty and honour of educating the public" regarding production and quality, as well as the use of the product (Morris 1882, 30).

22. More on Morris' factories in the case study below.

23. The factory is also generally accessible to the public to stimulate interest and knowledge about the production process and product quality (William Morris as quoted in May Morris 1966, 137).

Provisioning

Like the cooperators of the early 19th century, the social institutions in Morris' vision require communal property. Be it land or capital, the basic idea is property accessibility for all who might make effective use of it.[24] All members in a given community may claim access; when there are multiple claimants, community discussion and decision-making ensues along the lines of the mote described below. The community holds responsibility for maintaining communal resources. If an individual has active claim and use, as the resource deteriorates, the worker claiming use would likely begin repairs. In a society where fellowship predominates, where work is pleasurable and people desire the application of their skills, there is an inclination for community members to assist one another.

Morris adopts Ruskin's sentiment of justice in exchange—trading at fair prices and producing quality products under pleasurable work conditions (Morris 1882, 30). Exchange involves doing right by one's neighbors, "giving his due to everyman, the determination not to gain by any man's loss" (66). A social system based on communal access to property requires social responsibility, in particular, the expectation that all work. Without personal claim to capital and all working, "the price of an article would be just the cost of its production; and what we now call profit would no longer exist" (Morris 1903, 195–196).

In his more visionary thinking about markets, Morris goes beyond justice. He uses the term "market" to mean "the market of neighbours, the interchange of mutual good services" (1891, 261). Morris abandons the activities of buying, selling, and pricing, and even abandons anticipated future reciprocity between two specific people. Production takes place to fulfill neighbors' needs generally, in a spirit of fellowship (Morris 1897, 107).

There is the question of how producers learn about user's needs. Morris is particularly "attracted by . . . a direct relationship between producer and consumer, and the local nature of craftmanship" (Harvey & Press 1995, 189). At a small scale, shopkeepers are fully knowledgeable of the product, inquisitive of and attentive to the needs of shoppers.[25] Presumably the fully informed distributors communicate user information to producers.

---

24. For a full discussion on property, see Morris 1903, 193–196.

25. When a visitor called "Guest" needs a pipe in the fictional *News from Nowhere*, for example, the young shopkeep identifies that Guest will also need a bag to carry tobacco. When Guest responds that he can simply use a kerchief to carry the tobacco, the shopkeeper gently chides Guest and directs him to the higher quality, aesthetically pleasing, and useful bags in the store that more effectively serve the need. Guest leaves with the pipe and bag of his liking, without payment or expected future reciprocity.

There arises the question of aligning supply and demand. Morris adopts Ruskin's norm of "simplicity of taste" (Morris 1882, 32) which in part moderates demand.[26] The inclination toward fellowship fixes the principle of "giving every man his due" and thus also moderates what individuals demand for themselves (67). There is the presumption that socially responsible people do not make excessive claims, as excessive claims would only generate waste.[27] Distribution services then align genuine need with best quality product (Morris 1903, 21). Further, as workers evolve into their social nature and as equals, they then also "regulate their labour in accordance with their own needs" (16). In such a society, "the supply and demand shall be genuine, not gambling; the two will then be commensurate, for it is the same society which demands that also supplies" (17). Distribution emphasizes getting the right thing to the right person at the right time.[28] Overproduction and artificial scarcities are unlikely.

In Morris' system, manufacturing is the work of handicrafts people who hone "the spirit of handicraftsman" and apply "instinct" about their wares' "essential use" while working to generate the highest quality output in the craftsperson capability set (Morris 1891, 261). Across the community is an engrained expectation that "neighbours must make goods in the same spirit . . . and each, being a good workman after his kind, will be ready to recognize excellence in others" (261). In this process, producers contemplate "conscious usefulness" for the user (Morris 1903, 165).

Task variety is the norm across producers in such an economic system. Each person typically takes on three distinct types of jobs, one being predominantly physical, the second predominantly intellectual, and the third predominantly aesthetic. People have the liberty to determine how long they concentrate on a given task on a given day.[29] Social networks facilitate job switching. When someone wishes to shift to a different task, that person uses their social network to find another to take over

Thus, there is information exchange about need and product availability, with those needs filled (Morris 1897, 38–40).

26. From Ruskin's *Unto This Last*: "We need examples of people who, leaving Heaven to decide whether they are to rise in the world, decide for them selves that they will be happy in it, and have resolved to seek-not greater wealth, but simpler pleasure; not higher fortune, but deeper felicity; making the first of possessions, self-possession" (in *Complete Works*, Vol. 17, 112).

27. Like Ruskin, because Morris considers life itself as wealth, any "waste of labour, skill, cunning . . . [is] waste of life in short" (Morris 1903, 9).

28. Again, Ruskin is the source of the idea of virtuous distribution, see his *Complete Works*, Vol. 17, 88–89.

29. Spontaneous breaks and flexible work arrangements reflect how Morris approached his own workday in his business (Mackail 1899, 65).

the task and uses that network to shift into someone else's task (Morris 1897, 11).

In the market of neighbors, Morris qualifies that people understand the need to balance freely satisfying one's own desires in pursuit of happiness with social responsibility. This society embodies an

> instinctive reciprocity of service . . . a consciousness of the existence of a society of neighbours, that is of equals; of men who do indeed expect to be made use of by others, but only so far as the services they give are pleasing to themselves; so far as they are services the performance of which is necessary to their own well-being and happiness. (Morris 1891, 261)

Morris intends his system to rest in a "soil . . . of freedom and mutual respect" (261).

Social Relations

Morris' ideal society has no formal government (Morris 1897, 83). In the absence of the complicating influences of property, class, and government "differences of opinion about real solid things" do not radically divide communities (95) and are often easily settled through simple observation.[30] At the most local of levels, "direct expression of opinion would suffice for carrying on the administration" (Morris & Bax 1893, 292). However, when decisions impact the entire group, independent communities of freely acting individuals do require structures for negotiation.

Norms of liberty and fellowship infuse interpersonal decision-making structures. In "political" processes, liberty requires dramatically decentralized and non-coercive administrative systems. The infusion of meaningful fellowship in larger groups requires participatory democratic decision-making.

While relying largely on consensus generated via custom, social responsibility, and general goodwill, Morris is adamant about the commitment to settle disagreements by majority (Morris 1897, 97). For personal decisions (what to eat, drink, write, read, wear, etc.) the majority is one, therefore "there can be no difference of opinion, and everybody does as he pleases" (97). In a small-scale community, Morris proposes that non-personal

---

30. Morris provides an example by asking how a community decides when to harvest produce. Should there be a disagreement, he presumes easy settlement by simply going and looking at the crops (1897, 96).

matters come up at the "mote," a community meeting in which to raise and discuss propositions and then evaluate them through rounds of voting (26; 97–98). Once there is a clear majority, the "minority is asked if they will yield to the more general opinion, which they often, nay most commonly do." If the minority does not yield, the neighbors hold another discussion and "if the minority has not perceptibly grown, they always give way." If the mote reaches no clear majority, the norm is that the slight majority yield to status quo, but "the minority very seldom enforces this rule" (98).

Now Morris notes a serious qualification: the majority cannot force the minority to work out the majority will. The minority can refuse to participate in the decision and its accompanying work (1897, 99). Here the minority either comes to realize the rightness of the decision and its community benefits or the minority receives the pleasure of saying "I told you so" (100). Also remember the emphasis Morris places on freedom of movement and association. Should individuals feel strongly in their disagreement (or experience significant harm from the general will) they always have the option to migrate, either forming a new community, or joining a more agreeable one.

In more complex social systems, Morris and Bax, while somewhat vague, suggest federations based on occupation and industry units (1893, 283). The highest unit across the federal system is a "great council." Throughout the federalist system, there can be "no coercion" (289). While responsibility for the administration of production rests with the great council, the intention is to leave the bulk of details to subordinate bodies (291–292; see also Morris 1903, 198). Morris particularly argues against "'huge national centralization'" as a way to organize economic life. Wherever possible, decision-making should remain at the local level. He writes in a June 1889 *Commonweal* article:

> [I]ndividual men cannot shuffle off the business of life on to the shoulders of an abstraction called the State, but must deal with it in conscious association with each other: that variety of life is as much an aim of true Communism as equality of condition, and that nothing but a union of these two will bring about real freedom. (as quoted in Mackail 1899, 244–245)

Generally, Morris and Bax believe that with an end to private property and the promotion of liberty, administration is simpler, about things rather than people; and that most criminal law "would tend to become obsolete" (1893, 290).[31] One qualification is that criminal law would have a "necessary duty to safeguard the then recognized principles of society . . . [from]

31. Morris and Bax might at first appearance seem a bit naïve here in repeating Marxian socialist ideology, ignoring in particular the tragedy of the commons. But there

reverting to methods or practices which would be destructive or harmful to the socialist order, such as any form of the exploitation of labour" (291–292).[32] Such hints into the administration of social decision-making anticipate the more elaborate guild institutions that G. D. H. Cole devises early in the 20th century.

THEORY—A RECONSTRUCTION

Devoting innumerable hours to envisioning the decent life, Morris was also quite cognizant of tremendous deprivation the majority experiences under 19th-century capitalism. While working intensively as an artistic craftsman and entrepreneur, Morris contemplated social arrangements that can harness people's pleasure seeking, creative, and social impulses in attainment of three goals: the greatest happiness for all, popular art, and whole human development. "Let us be fellows working in the harmony of association for the common good . . . for the greatest happiness and completest development of every human being in the community" (Morris 1903, 177). While happiness and human development played center stage in cooperation throughout the century, Morris was unique in contributing the idea of popular art to the cooperative vision.

In consideration of these goals, while Morris' thought is complex, it is also informal. It is easy to miss his system in his casual style. But we claim there is system here. What follows is an attempt to formalize that system with the purpose of clarifying the major causal hypotheses implicit in Morris' thought.

The Major Influences on Happiness

The social psychology discussion describes happiness as a pleasure-seeking drive inherent to human nature. A state of happiness is also an outcome. What influences the level of happiness people actually experience from a Morrisian standpoint?

---

is consistency and depth in their thought. Key is that individuals take due account of community welfare and act in socially responsible ways when making decisions about resource use. As equals, there is also the norm of respect about the choices others make and the needs others have in claiming resources.

32. Morris and Bax do not clarify what safeguards appropriately meet the principled institutions of liberty, equality, and social responsibility.

One obvious answer: people can't be happy without fulfilling basic needs through the provisioning institutions of society. Key to Morris' provisioning institutions is that the market of neighbors responds directly to human need and produces quality output to satisfy those needs.

Happiness also requires satisfaction of the social and creative inclinations. "[F]ellowship is heaven, and lack of fellowship is hell: fellowship is life, and lack of fellowship is death" (Morris 1888, 29). By directly satisfying the social inclination, fellowship expands the general state of happiness. As an artist and craftsman, Morris argues that art is also key to happiness: "'that art, using that word in its widest and due signification, is not a mere adjunct of life which free and happy men can do without, but the necessary expression and indispensable instrument of human happiness'" (quoted in Mackail 1899, 244–245).[33]

Beyond highlighting the relevance of provisioning, fellowship, and art to happiness, Morris concentrates on work. Morris challenges classical beliefs about the inherent disutility of labor. He replaces the idea of "the curse of labour" with a deep exploration of the potential for pleasure in labor (Morris 1882, 5–6). It is work that absorbs a large chunk of time each day, and thus work that can directly contribute to happiness by satisfying pleasure-seeking, social, and creative inclinations. While work necessarily generates some pain, it also generates much pleasure. Happiness is strongly influenced by the labor pleasure-to-pain ratio.

To summarize, in Morris' system, happiness depends on provisioning, fellowship, popular art, and the labor pleasure-to-pain ratio (LPPR).[34]

The Labor Pleasure-to-Pain Ratio

People typically dedicate many hours each day to work. Most seek happiness. Thus, it seems worthwhile to figure out how to transform work into pleasure returning activity.[35] Morris and Bax suggest maximizing the labor pleasure-to-pain ratio (LPPR), defined as:

$$\frac{pleasure\ from\ successful\ exercise\ of\ energy\ in\ work}{pain\ from\ work\ required\ out\ of\ necessity}$$

33. "These arts . . . all people and times have used them . . . joy of free nations, and the solace of oppressed nations . . ." (Morris 1882, 9).

34. Or put formally in terms of a function:

Happiness = f(Provisioning, Fellowship, Popular Art, LPPR).

35. The thought of cooperator Charles Fourier is a precursor to Morris' thinking on "attractive labor" (see, for example, Morris & Bax 1893, 305).

Maximization of the LPPR requires the "successful" exercise of energy in a work process—resulting in useful, high-quality product (1893, 301–302). Useful is that which "minister to the body when well under command of the mind" and which "amuse, soothe, or elevate the mind in a healthy state" (Morris 1882, 31). Writing at a time when the economic system tended to disregard human degeneration resulting from work, Morris reflects, "how can we enjoy something which has been a pain and a grief for the maker to make?" (68). Thus, in a justice-centered society, the reduction of pain while working matters directly for the worker and indirectly for the consumer.

Minimization of pain in work requires nondegenerative work processes and conditions. Nondegenerative work is of reasonable duration and allows sufficient rest to regenerate.[36] Nondegenerative work includes task variety and may involve "miracles of ingenuity," that is, labor complementing machinery to reduce pain from monotonous or grueling tasks (Morris 1903, 170). Nondegenerative work also includes security of livelihood (Morris & Bax 1893, 305).

While the direct effect of nondegenerative work conditions is the reduction of pain from labor, fulfillment of these conditions opens richer possibilities for work to stimulate pleasure. Labor realizes positive net utility when labor aligns with innate tendencies to seek pleasure, fulfills social inclinations, and satisfies creative impulses.

For Morris, the satisfaction of developing and exercising physical and intellectual capacities returns pleasure from labor: "the main pleasure of life is the exercise of energy in the development of our special capacities" (Morris 1903, 198). In effect, Morris recognizes that human development, as defined in more detail below, enhances pleasure resulting from labor.

Pleasure in labor requires an appropriate match of tasks to individual capacities (Mackail 1899, 64). "[C]onscious sensuous pleasure" results during the work process itself when the worker skillset is appropriate for the task—and this is particularly relevant in the unleashing of artistic spirit (Morris 1897, 102). Pleasure results when a well-trained worker excels in activity for which the worker is well-suited.[37] Such pleasure is, in part, also due to comfort stimulated by habitual activity (102).

Morris holds that liberty is central to derive pleasure from labor. Most degenerative work occurs when workers lack liberty, whether in slavery or hierarchical employment systems of direction. Liberty is important to

---

36. Morris (1903, 142) specifically raises the "hope of rest" for workers.

37. Recall that in the proposed education system of this society, pleasure seeking students select training in activities that align with their interests and abilities. Thus it seems reasonable that the overwhelming majority of students-turned-workers receive pleasure when they excel at that work.

eliminate pain associated with degenerative work processes dictated by overseers. A liberty-centered outlook for work also opens space so that people may explore their interests and align work activities with personal inclinations and capacities (1897, 102). Liberty opens space for worker spontaneity in the time devoted to various tasks (Mackail 1899, 64). At his most radical, Morris suggests that the "new order of things says . . . why have masters at all? Let us be fellows working in the harmony of association for the common good" (1903, 177).

As social beings, people experience pleasure in fellowship, working with others toward a common goal in nondegenerative work processes. Morris writes, for instance, that "to do handwork in which working together is necessary or convenient; such work is often very pleasant" (1897, 50). More broadly, even factory-based labor " 'of a group of people working in harmonious co-operation towards a useful end' " holds pleasure potential (Morris, as quoted in May Morris 1966, 136).

> In such factories labour might be made, not only no burden, but even most at-tractive; young men and women at the time of life when pleasure is most sought after would go to their work as to a pleasure party; it is most certain that la-bour may be so arranged that no social relations could be more delightful than communion in hopeful work; love, friendship, family affection, might all be quickened by it; joy increased and grief lightened by it. (Morris 1897, 129–130)

When workers produce useful things well, there is product-generated es-teem. Through the "market of neighbours," those items fall into the hands of others who benefit from their use, and the associated social esteem returns pleasure to the maker (Morris 1897, 102).

Innately creative, labor returns pleasure to workers from the sheer act of creation—willing and working something into being (101; Morris 1903, 144). Creation exercises "the energies of his mind and soul as well as of his body" (144). Morris highlights the pleasure that derives from creating aes-thetically pleasing products: "to give people pleasure in the things they must perforce use, that is one great office of decoration; to give people pleasure in the things they must perforce make, that is the other use of [decora-tion]" (Morris 1882, 4).[38] Further, "[t]hese arts . . . they are the sweeteners of human labour . . . . They make our toil happy, our rest fruitful" (9).

---

38. Morris interchanges "decoration" with "ornamentation," and both are non-trivial in all art, most importantly, popular art. Related, recall that William Thompson also advocates "embelishments or elegancies" so long as these adornments return net utility (see Chapter 3).

The pleasurable returns from aesthetics extend to the performance of work in "pleasant surroundings" (Kinna, 504). The workplace returns pleasure when beautifully adorned, whether it be in the home, the craftshop, the field, or the factory. And Morris extends this to the beauty of natural surroundings (see, for example, Morris 1897, *passim*).

Thus, Morris argues that labor increases utility, assuming labor is nondegenerative, e.g. reasonable hours with task variety, labor-complementing machinery, and security of livelihood. Labor returns pleasure when completed by a worker whose aptitude matches the tasks and when that work generates high-quality, useful products. Labor returns pleasure when it taps innate social and creative inclinations. Morris assumes liberty and equality are underlying social institutions for labor to return pleasure. People must have the freedom to identify their natural proclivities. People must have the freedom to engage in and withdraw from specific work processes and workplaces. And there must be equality in social relationships, in the responsibility to work, and in access to materials and mentors to develop appropriate skills.

Generally, Morris posits that pleasant labor "matters for the carrying on of a dignified daily life, that life of mutual trust, forbearance, and help, which is the only real life of thinking men" (Morris 1882, 61).

Taking his observations together, Morris in effect suggests the LPPR depends positively on nondegenerative work, human development, job-aptitude match, liberty, fellowship, popular art, and equality.[39]

Popular Art

For Morris, art is visionary and revolutionary. Art derives from "freedom of fancy and imagination" (Morris 1897, 202). Art informs "'the true ideal of a full and reasonable life'" (Morris 1894 quoted in Jay & Jay 1986, 196). As such, "it is not possible to dissociate art from morality, politics, and religion"—or from labor (Morris 1882, 66). Popular art adds a unique dimension to Morris' cooperative vision.

Popular art is "art made by the people, and for the people" (Morris 1882, 64). It involves the creation of widespread intelligent ornamentation in "familiar matters of everyday life" (3). Popular art manifests in useful

39. Writing this relation as an equation gives:

LPPR = f(Nondegenerative Work, Human Development, Job–Aptitude Match, Liberty, Fellowship, Popular Art, Equality).

product—e.g. shelter, furniture, dishes—as well as beautiful surroundings, whether these be the workplace, social meeting places, the home, or the natural environment. Morris' aesthetic attributes beauty to that which "is in accord with Nature, and helps her" (4).[40]

Popular art is the "spontaneous expression of the pleasure of life innate in the whole people" (Mackail 1899, 296). And, more specifically, pleasure in labor generates popular art: "That thing which I understand by real art is the expression by man of his pleasure in labour. I do not believe he can be happy in his labour without expressing that happiness . . ." (Morris 1882, 58).[41]

The art of Morris' vision is art for all, of perfectly equitable availability. Writing in a newspaper venue regarding an ill-received lecture by some in his audience, Morris asks: "'What business have we with art at all unless all can share it?'" (quoted in Mackail 1899, 100). All participate in its creation and in its appreciation. He clarifies, "'I specially wished to point out that the question of popular art was a social question involving the happiness or misery of the greater part of the community'" (100). A fair distribution of happiness across society matters for popular art to manifest across the population.

Fellowship is also relevant to the creation of beauty. The dramatic beauty of the community hall derives in particular from "collective thought and collective life" (Morris 1903, 31). The satisfaction of social inclinations through fellowship combines with the "hope of the pleasure of creation" to "produce those ornaments of life for the service of all" (168).

And finally, popular art depends upon the "general well-being of the people" (Mackail 1899, 296). Morris' liberty-centered education promotes human development and thus popular art. In Morris' view, the "general cultivation of the powers of the mind, general cultivation of the powers of the eye and hand" are the "*direct* means" of the "Decorative Arts" (Morris 1882, 28). Developed human capacity and artistic sensibilities motivate the ornamentation and beautification of one's surroundings (4; 21).

To summarize, Morris' ideas on popular art are as follows. Popular art depends on happiness, LPPR, equality, fellowship, and human development.[42]

---

40. Some of the living arrangements as described in the social relations section importantly center around nature. Transient tent living allows individuals to commune with nature, thus informing artistic sensibilities. The design of larger population centers also includes ample greenspace with which to inform this sensibility.

41. Among the numerous variables influencing LPPR, here it is important to reiterate the necessity of liberty for pleasure in labor, and thus popular art.

42. In a formal statement this gives:

Popular Art = f(Happiness, LPPR, Fellowship, Human Development).

Human Development

Morris' thought on human development reflects Ruskin's influence: "THERE IS NO WEALTH BUT LIFE" (*The Complete Works of John Ruskin*, Vol. 17, 105, caps original).[43] In contemplating wealth, Morris centers on what a reasonable person can actually make use of for "well-being, well-doing, bodily and mental" (1903, 194; similarly, see 33–34). Whole human development extends beyond the physical and intellectual, involving healthy social relationships (Morris, as quoted in Mackail 1899, 63) and engagement in "a beautiful world" (Morris 1903, 33–34).[44] In Mackail's words, Morris consistently focuses on the "humanized life, in which comfort and happiness should be alike within the reach of all" (Mackail 1899, 293–294). It seems fair to capture this under the term "human development."

The cooperative society provides occupation fit for a healthy body and an active mind (Morris 1903, 33–34). Work processes that have high LPPR also offer substantial outlets for innate social and creative impulses. It seems unreasonable that a system returning high LPPR could generate low human development. Conversely, if labor is pleasurable, it exercises all facets of being human—physical, intellectual, and social—and results in a healthy body and active mind, etc.

Coupled with the provisioning institutions, part of a component of pleasurable labor is that workers produce quality output—healthy food, pleasant and comfortable clothing, shelter, etc.—that others can and do use. This consumption of high-quality product aids in health and can be used to develop and exercise the "special capabilities" by individuals.

The liberty-centered education that facilitates the expression of pleasure-seeking, social, and creative inclinations brings about growth in "real capacities" (Morris 1903, 35). This education requires leisure, as when "we are no longer hurried, and the information lies ready to each one's hand when his own inclinations impel him to seek it. In this as in other matters we have become wealthy: we can afford to give ourselves time to grow" (Morris 1897, 70–71).[45]

Fellowship is also a stimulus to human development. As Morris sees it, each "is but a part of a harmonious whole . . . worthless without the

43. See (Morris 1903, 149) for an explicit definition of wealth.
44. To Morris, "a beautiful world" is not simply aesthetically charming. One of a small number of 19th-century British voices expressing concern about the ecological toxicity of industrialism, Morris highlights a healthy ecosystem as a prerequisite for health (1903, 22).
45. On sufficient leisure, see also (Morris as quoted in Mackail 1899, 63).

co-operation of his fellows, who help him according to his capacities" (Morris 1903, 192). Fellowship both builds off and builds proclivities for generosity, hospitality, and goodwill (192). When people care about others, they become inclined toward mutual aid which assists in human development.[46]

Recall the social relations institutions of the mote and, for societies on a grander scale, federations of local organizational units and the "great council." All these institutions stress local scale and local needs, liberty, equality, and social responsibility. They require political voice by everyday people, providing many opportunities for the exercise and expansion of individual cooperative capabilities, thus stimulating the social angle of human development.

Finally, consider popular art. As with LPPR, it seems unreasonable to argue that it is possible to have high levels of human development with low levels of popular art. In Morris' words "I say without these arts, our rest would be vacant and uninteresting, our labour mere endurance, mere wearing away of body and mind" (Morris 1882, 4). Popular art effects human development in at least two ways. First, people cannot be whole without building off innate inclinations; popular art is an important outlet for creative inclinations. Second, popular art informs "'the true ideal of a full and reasonable life,'" a key component to all "morality, politics, and religion" (Morris 1894; Morris 1882, 66). Popular art enhances the understanding of what a full human life is all about and what to strive for.

Working from Morris' logic, the determinants of human development are LPPR, provisioning, education, fellowship, social relations, and popular art.[47]

Notice the interdependence in this reconstruction of Morris' vision: each goal appears as an explanatory variable in the function of the others. There are substantial feedback effects between popular art, human development, and overall happiness. For popular art to thrive, people need to be whole as well as happy. And popular art itself feeds into the overall level of happiness and human development.

---

46. Petr Kropotkin authored the book *Mutual Aid*. Kropotkin's ideas originally published as essays in *Nineteenth Century* between 1890–1896. Morris and Kropotkin "met often." Both Morris and Kropotkin "believed that the impulse to form communities for mutual benefit was natural" (Boos & Boos 1986, 500).

47. As a formal equation, this gives:

Human Development = f(LPPR, Provisioning, Education, Fellowship, Social Relations, Popular Art).

CASE STUDY: MORRISIAN FACTORIES AND
THE THREE GOALS

As a case study, consider the cooperative factory in light of the reconstruction of Morris' system. While Morris typically focuses on production at the individual level (i.e. the craftsperson or artist) he is also vocal about "places where people collect who want to work together" (Morris 1897, 50). Morris identifies a factory as "a group of people working in harmonious co-operation towards a useful end" (136).[48] These factories tend to focus on the production of quality products intended to satisfy bodily necessities (May Morris 1966, 138).[49] Such factory styled production is pleasurable, creative, and a stimulant to social relations and thus reinforces pleasure in labor, popular art, and human development (129–131).

The Morrisian factory resides "in a pleasant place" surrounded by green spaces in the countryside or in villages with "ample room . . ., abundant air, a minimum noise" (William Morris, quoted in May Morris 1966, 129). For Morris, "our factory must make no sordid litter, befoul no water, nor poison the air with smoke" (132). Rather, the factory increases "the beauty of the world" (133). Thus it is likely that the factory is relatively small-scale, though certainly this depends on the technological requirements of the manufactured product and the interests of the workforce. Morris portrays the factory "amidst gardens" with those workers, who have interest, gardening the spaces in return for "open air relaxation." This is "co-operative gardening for beauty's sake" which can also return useful product (131).

Morris' factory is more than a workshop (May Morris 1966, 132). Reminiscent of Owenite villages and college campuses, Morris' multifaceted factory includes a "dining hall, library, school, places for study of various kinds, and other such structures" all healthfully ornamented (132). Given its community orientation, there are spaces for social gatherings and entertainment (137). And the factory serves as an educational center for "citizens outside" as well as workers within (137).

Factory production processes meet Morris' criteria for nondegenerative work (133). The factory minimizes the use of superfluous machinery, but where necessary, the machinery is the best of its kind, labor-complementing, and particularly reductive of degrading toil (134). Where necessary, workers share responsibilities of "mere machine-tending"

---

48. "Banded-workshops" are relevant as well, where craftspeople gather together for "handwork" (Morris 1897, 50).
49. Workers may also participate in collective factory work to derive the pleasure from fellowship (Morris 1897, 50).

(135). Morris estimates a four-hour factory workday (134–135). Reduced work hours are due in part to equity, all working "their due quota of necessary work for the common good" and in part to labor-complementing machinery (William Morris, as quoted in May Morris 1966, 138). By educating the public, the factory increases interest in its workers, product, and production processes which then elevate the status of labor, returning pleasure through social esteem (William Morris as quoted in May Morris 1966, 137).

The short factory work hours provide ample time for leisure, rest, education, and skill development.[50] Such intelligent, skilled, properly provisioned and well rested workers "develop a love for art . . . a sense of beauty and an interest in life," stimulating "the desire for artistic creation" (William Morris as quoted in May Morris 1966, 137).

Curiously, Morris does not fully address the question of factory management and worker participation in decision-making. People may fill administrative or managerial roles who "delight . . . in administration and organisation . . . people who like keeping things together, avoiding waste" (Morris 1897, 93). Past having an affinity for such work, the "director of labour" must be "fit for it," meaning, "he does it easier than he would do other work, needs no more compensation . . . his special reward for his special labour is . . . that he can do it easily, and so does not feel it a burden . . . since he can do it *well* he likes doing it" (Morris 1903, 197–198). Importantly, one charge for the director of labor lies is lightening the labor of others and making it more pleasant (198). Given the centrality of liberty it seems reasonable that, through consensus, workers might select the group member most fit for this position. While social responsibility is central to intrafactory relations, managerial coercion would be discouraged, and workers always have the freedom to leave.

Further, it seems reasonable to infer that the decision-making processes of social relations institutions might apply in the factory. The mote allows full participation of an educated workforce in factory decision-making. Federations of factories and the great council might serve in some ways to coordinate production decisions across factories. Federations also aid in "finding out what work such and such people are fittest for and leaving them free to do that" (Morris 1903, 198). Some of these ideas are precursors to G. D. H. Cole's ideas on industrial cooperatives.

---

50. This self-education includes the additional benefit of adding variation to labor (Morris as quoted in May Morris 1966, 137).

FINAL THOUGHTS

William Morris is an inspiration for any cooperative movement to rekindle humanity in economy through social and pleasurable work and through art. Like Thompson and Wheeler, Morris' system makes a laudable commitment to liberty while maintaining equality. In a system of liberty, public inputs, and the equal requirement that all work, this analysis provides a deeper explanation of why people might rise to their work responsibilities. The core characteristics of human social psychology—pleasure seeking, sociality, and creativity—if institutionally reinforced, make such a society quite robust when shocks arise. It is not difficult to imagine socially minded cooperators sharing losses and brainstorming creative solutions to shocks.

Some of the strengths of Morris' contribution noted, there are certainly questions and qualifications. Begin with the principled institution of liberty so central to Morris' thought. In the context of social relations, institutions—whether the mote or a federalist system with a great council—he does not adequately address the question of whether such a system protects the minority from the tyranny of a majority. Fellowship offsets this concern to a degree if people do genuinely look out for the interests of their neighbors when conflicts arise. In the case of irreconcilable conflict within the mote structure, the option for the minority to take the liberty to leave—"voting with your feet"—ignores the high costs that moving may impose, particularly if deep roots exist within the community.

While we applaud the centrality of daily variety in the worker's tasks and the personal liberty to shift tasks, there are questions of viability in a large, integrated, interdependent economic system. Recall that she who wishes to follow through on the impulse to shift tasks is to recruit a volunteer within her social network to take on her shedded task. If the system has a relatively tight match between workers and tasks, it seems shifting might generate problematic domino effects throughout the worker chain whenever anyone initiates a task shift. Small changes might reverberate and amplify through the system, with destabilizing results. And it seems there could also be abandoned tasks. The task shifting social networking system would require buffers to provide slack in the system. Perhaps there are clues to potential system-wide stability in Morris' emphasis on popular art. When work is art, the inexhaustibility of artistic potential as well as the implications of increasing standards of excellence mean there is always work to be done (Morris 1897, 108).

Other questions arise regarding the principled institutions of fellowship and social responsibility. Regarding fellowship, the question raised concerning Robert Owen's thought in Chapter 2 continues to

haunt: might maliciousness prevail in particular contexts? In Morris' case, the provisioning institution presumes that fellowship is sufficiently strong to motivate worker effort toward the satisfaction of neighbor's needs—but is it? Regarding social responsibility, innate sociality is a key prerequisite. But since responsibility per se is not innate, social responsibility seems to require conditions that are not fully identified in the reconstruction of Morris' thought. Does a liberty-based education system generally nurture social responsibility? If not, how does social responsibility replicate itself? Related, are self-censuring norms along with relatively innocuous social-censuring norms sufficient to right problematic social behavior?

Morris does recognize that social transgressions arise. An attitude of treating transgressions as "errors of friends" is truly commendable. But if there is substantial or repeat betrayal and mistrust, how many violations can an "errors of friends" attitude survive? Morris only offers social ostracism as an answer. He does not explicitly anticipate ideas like restorative justice which might serve the society well.

Morris' decentralized, liberty-based system of self-governing "societies of equals" might potentially develop unresolvable conflicts across communities if group affinities arise and prevail over general fellowship, sowing division and discord. Could such group affinities lead to instability? Morris' solutions to grievances across groups rely on an openness to learning from others, travel, and emigration. Are these solutions sufficient?

Another set of critical challenges concern the biases Morris brings into his social thought. The obvious one is gender bias. Though he pitches equality of the sexes in personal relationships, this paper identifies incongruities. He limits at least one of his education institutions to studious young men and he attributes as "manly" at least one virtue; we leave it to the reader to find other examples across his writing.

More generally, Morris perceives the world through his own lens and assumes as universal his own experiences and preferences. For example, drawing from his own life, he infers that all children can read by age four, and that artistic, historical, and natural education are subjects absolutely central to education. He also extrapolates his own hedonism to all others, suggesting for example, that artistic output depends positively on the artist's level of happiness. The general point here is that Morris takes his own worldview as the norm. As a knowledge creator, his work sometimes seems to lack awareness about a tendency to project personal preferences and experiences.

Returning to Morris' biases, while he clearly positively values diversity in many contexts, he does not always remain with that ideal. For example, he considers sociality to be innate. While this does not seem unreasonable, he

ignores the variability in sociality across people: those who are social, but prefer small groups; those who are naturally introverted; and those who are antisocial.[51] When writing about artisanal work involving the application of "instinct" about their wares' "essential use": is there an essential use? Perhaps he unknowingly reflects here the Enlightenment view which builds off similarity, but by the end of the 19th century there is a recognizable shift to the Darwinian view that highlights difference.[52]

51. Although to Morris' credit, he does juxtapose liberty with sociality—the liberty to come and go offers leeway for those with less than fully social personas. And perhaps this critique arises from our own lack of imagination about socialization—maybe these less than fully social personas primarily arise in a socioeconomic system that reinforces competitive, antisocial behavior.
52. Peart and Levy (2005).

CHAPTER 10

⌒⌣⌒

Guild Socialism

The Integration of Cooperative Themes

INTRODUCTION

At the end of the long 19th century, as Britain came out of World War I against the backdrop of the Russian Revolution, a radical reorganization of the economy seemed a real possibility. In such a heady environment, G. D. H. Cole (1889–1959) of the Guild Socialists elaborated a sweeping blueprint of a new cooperative world. In contrast to the decades-long squabbling among advocates of producer cooperatives and consumer cooperatives, Cole put forward a rich theoretical synthesis of the two major strands of the 19th-century cooperative movement. Such a new vision is not one of simplified, semi-autarchic Owenite village economies. It accepts and builds upon the full urban complexity of the modern industrial economy. The synthesis aims at replacing labor markets, consumer markets, and investment markets with a broad new approach to bargaining between self-managed, service-oriented, and artisanal cooperative producers and democratically controlled, community-oriented cooperative consumers, with voice for civic representatives. Although the theory is thin in places, the vision is nothing short of breathtaking. As a path to the new economy, the Guild Socialists lay out an ambitious strategy of transition. Cole's Guild Socialism points toward a radical realization of the promise of the Industrial Revolution. It is effectively an apotheosis of the British cooperative movement; yet, by the mid-1920s it was little more than a memory, lost in a pre-Soviet fog.

Building a Social Science. Kirsten Madden and Joseph Persky, Oxford University Press. © Oxford University Press 2024.
DOI: 10.1093/oso/9780197693735.003.0010

Cole's background was distinctly middle class. His father, although starting as a pawnbroker, became a partner in a successful estate management business. Cole's personal interest in socialism began early, when he read Morris' *News from Nowhere*, while still at St. Paul's day school (M. Cole 1971, 33).[1] Once in university at Oxford, he joined the Fabians, then very much the province of Sidney and Beatrice Webb. He became an active member and rose quickly in the organization. Cole built extensive experience with the British labor movement as the head of the Fabian Research Department through the late 1910s.[2] He left the Fabians in a dramatic split with the Webbs in 1915 when he could not bring the group over to Guild Socialist ideas. After the demise of the guild idea, Cole returned to be a major leader of the Fabians (1928). While following an academic career, he remained deeply engaged in left politics, worker education, and the labor movement. Throughout his life he was a prolific writer (L. Carpenter, 1973; M. Cole 1971).

Cole's early writings on Guild Socialism, like those of his colleagues, focus on the expansion of producer cooperatives. But as his guild writings mature, the vision becomes a full alternative economics: an analytical economics of worker *and* consumer cooperatives. Thinking seriously about institutional context, Cole's work offers a synthesis of cooperative thought. This system certainly draws on ideas from earlier writers in the cooperative movement. But different from Owen and Thompson, there is no retreat to a village economy. Instead, the cooperative system design intends to absorb and transform the urban-industrial economy in all its complexity. It is a serious and comprehensive effort to envision the structure of an integrated economy built on cooperation across all sectors.

Cole is the first to craft anything near a complete institutional structure for a national cooperative economy. Most fundamental to his vision is the design of democratic institutions capable of replacing capitalist firms and capitalist markets. Admittedly, Cole's efforts have a speculative air. But he does identify more clearly than any previous writer the positive and normative issues of the fully cooperative economy. Given the breadth of the task and the relatively short period Cole devotes to it, his writings sometimes are vague and aspirational.[3] The acute economic observer Lionel

1. Cole found Morris' vision attractive in large part because there work is "not a daily drudgery to be indefinitely repeated, nor a mere means to an external, money-making end, but in itself satisfying and in harmony with the satisfactions of their leisure days and hours" (from "*Revaluations*, by G. D. H. Cole; a lecture published in 1931 by the City Literary Institute" quoted in (M. Cole 1971, 34)). Cole remained a Morris enthusiast, eventually editing a volume of his selected works.
2. The Fabian Research Department later became the Labour Research Department.
3. Cole writes actively on Guild Socialism from 1913 to 1921.

Robbins, who early on found attraction in guild ideas, gave up on guild economics as hopelessly murky (Robbins 1971, 56–58; 64–67). Robbins depicts the Guild Socialist discussion of 1920 as a "Sahara of constitutional controversy . . . . The fundamental assumption throughout was that the economic problem did not really exist" (65). The counterclaim advanced here is that faults notwithstanding, Cole's guild writings starting from ground zero persuasively tackle the full range of economic problems. Cole builds up a social psychology with an emphasis on worker motivation. He constructs a set of institutional structures focused on worker-controlled guilds, cooperative consumption, and civic organizations. He then offers a coherent, non-trivial, and normatively attractive theory of how the cooperative economy can achieve both a major expansion of production and a broad improvement in the welfare of working people.

The current chapter draws most heavily on Cole's treatment in *Guild Socialism Restated* (Cole 1920d), which fully lays out a vision of an integrated cooperative economy of producers and consumers. For context, we also make use of several of his other writings, including his extensive contributions to Alfred Orage's magazine, *The New Age*,[4] which hosts a number of Guild Socialist writers in addition to Cole. At times they disagree on major economic points, disagreements that also air in other publications or within the Guild Socialist organization. We do not attempt a full history of Guild Socialism or even Cole's role in that movement.[5] Rather our focus is on Cole's integrative contribution to the social science of cooperation.

CONTEXT AND EARLY ENUNCIATION
OF GUILD SOCIALISM

The roots of Guild Socialist ideas are the very substance of the present book. They include Robert Owen in the early 19th century, the writings of William Thompson and Anna Doyle Wheeler, the efforts of the Christian Socialists, the advocates of producer cooperatives, like George Holyoake

---

4. George Bernard Shaw of the Fabians provided original financing for *The New Age* (Scholes n.d.).

5. In an article in the *Economic Journal*, Helen Reynard (1920) covers fundamental disagreements among leading contributors to Guild Socialism. In the *American Economic Review*, Amy Hewes (1922) provides detailed coverage of the Guild Socialist Literature, the formation of the National Guild League, and the practical experiment of the Building Guild in Britain. Niles Carpenter (1922) is an early but still serviceable history of Guild Socialism. L. Carpenter (1973) does an excellent job of putting Cole into his Guild Socialist milieu.

and William Morris. Guild Socialism represents a direct challenge to the centralizing tendencies prominent in the socialism of the Fabians, not to mention the early 20th-century German and Russian socialists.

John Ruskin proposes the reintroduction of something like medieval guilds as a solution to modern industrial problems, but like much of Ruskin's economics, the idea falls into the "reign of impractical dreams" (Penty 1906, Preface). William Morris' writing too, finds medievalism attractive, particularly its focus on quality craftsmanship. The first to offer serious proposals for practical operationalization of Ruskin's idea was the architect Arthur J. Penty, who in 1906 began the "medievalist school" of guild thought (Hewes 1922, 216).[6] Following Ruskin and Morris, Penty emphasizes justice, honing in on the medieval concept of "just price."[7] This concept lacks precise definition, but in Penty's discussion of quality craftsmanship, he raises three pertinent issues: that the worker can perform the work "leisurely," receive a "fair" price (e.g. covering all costs), and maintain "security of employment" (1906, 29). Like Ruskin and also Morris, to some extent, Penty's early writing laments the use of machinery in production but later modifies his position, accepting small-scale machinery to reduce drudgery in the work process (Penty 1913, 423–424).

In 1919 the medievalist school picked up a second leading advocate, G. R. Stirling Taylor, whose *Restoration of the Gild* (sic) *System* follows Penty in providing "reverential allusions to the middle ages" (Hewes 1922, 216). Highlighting the local control that predominated in Middle Ages governance, Taylor dismisses other contemporary Guild Socialists who promote centralized national guild schemes as missing "'the whole essence of the creed.'"[8] Guild socialism is a system of democratic distribution of power and wealth, though Taylor entertains the possibility of unequal rewards (217). Taylor also leaves open a limited role for the state. In particular, the state may serve as the charter granting agency for guilds which pay a fee in return for a charter. Taylor's scheme includes the possibility of a minimum

---

6. See Thistlewood (1987) for background on Penty.

7. "Just price" has a complicated history. In his review of the concept across the history of economic thought from Aristotle to the early 20th century, Boyd (2018) distills one common element: a range of prices that prevents "coercion or compulsion in economic" transactions for either the buyer or the seller (2; 6). Most interpretations of justice also concern equity, to "'restore to another as much as one is enriched by what belongs to the other'" (13n). Some understand the "'common estimation'" (14) of the just price as full costs of production; others perceive market negotiation under perfect conditions providing that estimation. In Cole's formulation, the consumer cooperative fills the role of the "intelligent, uncoerced buyer" (31) with the Guild receiving compensation for full costs of production.

8. (Taylor 1919, *The Guild State*, 25), as quoted in (Hewes, 1922, 217).

pay standard established by the State, with each Guild distributing its surplus among members based on majority vote (Reynard 1920, 323–325).

Both Taylor and Penty advocate a peaceful, nonrevolutionary transition to Guild Socialism. Because capitalist workers lack the skill to manage
business, Taylor advises gradual transition through "co-partnership and
co-management."[9] After worker takeover, Penty anticipates worker mag-
nanimity toward their former capitalist oppressors (Reynard 1920, 326).
And for both Taylor and Penty, some competition in the guild system is
desirable.

In 1912 S. G. Hobson wrote his first in a series of articles on guilds
in A. R. Orage's *New Age*, publishing the collection as *National Guilds* in
1914. The "Hobson-Orage school" attacks both the wage system and the
reformist nature of British socialism. In this early work, Hobson advocates
the replacement of the capitalist class and the state with the guild. By
1920, Hobson's ideas shift, elevating the state "as supreme," though the
state does delegate control of production to producer guilds (Hewes 1922,
216). Cole aggressively disputes this central role for the state.

Reckitt and Bechhofer's *Meaning of National Guilds* (1918, revised
in 1920) endorses national, as opposed to local, control but otherwise
the "nature of the state" is not their interest. Rather, they focus on the
contemporary labor movement and its ability to take over the direction of production. As to the payment of workers in the guilds, Reckitt
and Bechhofer "reject absolutely any idea of remuneration in relation to
output."[10] Central to Reckitt and Bechhofer is "that each National Guild
must have a complete monopoly" over the labor in its industry (Reynard
1920, 324–325).[11]

Somewhat strangely, none of the guild writing considers at all the question of distribution. It ignores consumption and provides no channel for
consumers to influence the composition (or pricing) of the national product.
At the time, the only major socialist writer to take consumption seriously is

---

9. Such reformism is problematic for Cole.

10. More on pay and economic content in the section "Adjustments to Changes in
Demand" below.

11. Perceiving finance as the real threat to worker-based industrial control, Major
C. H. Douglas makes his credit proposal in 1919. He emphasizes democratic, community control of credit through labor banks. A major theoretical schism among
Guild Socialists appears in response. Reckitt appears to offer support to Douglas. The
medievalists, as represented by Penty, oppose the shift in emphasis to finance, "'a mere
reflection of reality'" and "a 'mere reshuffling of the cards'" (Penty 1921) as quoted in
Hewes (1922, 219, 220).

Leonard Woolf.[12] Woolf was something of a protégé of Margaret Llewelyn Davies of the Women's Cooperative Guild. His wife, the well-known writer Virginia Woolf, participated in the work of that group (Woolf [1967] 1989, 27).[13] Leonard Woolf remained a Fabian throughout and never joined the Guild Socialists, although obviously sympathetic to guild ideas.[14] In 1919 he published *Co-operation and the Future of Industry* which argues that labor unions and consumer cooperatives are natural allies.[15] This publication outlines a transitional period in which the consumer cooperative societies expand their control of industry. Workers through their unions achieve "a share in regulating the conditions under which work is carried out." Moreover, conflicts between the consumer cooperatives acting as "employers" and the workers are to be decided by "some process of a judicial nature or by compromise in which the consumer's interest shall be represented by his society and the worker's by his trade union" (Woolf 1919, 81). Woolf goes on to suggest that over time "District and National Boards" made up equally of consumer and labor representatives could take on full responsibility for "fixing formal rates of wages, hours, and conditions of employment" (85).[16] Woolf briefly reasserts his perspective in Cole's publication, *The Guildsman*, in a 1920 article entitled "Co-operation and Guild Socialism" (Woolf 1920).

As insights and controversies emerged from the theoretical conversations among the various tendencies within Guild Socialism, the formation of the Shop Stewards' and Workers' Committee movement among radical workers during World War I provided a serious working-class audience for guild proposals (L. Carpenter 1973, 76). Against such a background, and in the midst of the post-war radical optimism, Cole took on the challenge of

---

12. Woolf, a member of the Apostles at Cambridge and close friend of Thoby Stephen, married Stephen's sister Virginia in 1912. Together they famously became central actors in the Bloomsbury Group.

13. Leonard Woolf's biographer, Victoria Glendinning, suggests that Virginia Woolf engaged with the Women's Guild "[t]o please him [Leonard], but not only to please him." She goes on to assert "the Guild's earnestness was not her [Virginia's] cup of tea" (Glendinning 2006, 187).

14. In fact, Woolf thought that Cole and his wife, Margaret, in their efforts to take over the Fabians treated the Webbs rather shabbily (Woolf [1967] 1989, 220).

15. Recall that as early as 1891, Margaret Llewellyn Davies of the Women's Cooperative Guild advocated consumer cooperative control of industry with workers organizing in unions (see Chapter 7).

16. While Woolf emphasizes the need for workers to feel in control over their work, he argues, "the labour necessary for industrial production is an unpleasant necessity." He envisions in a fully developed cooperative commonwealth that labor would be "conscripted" for four months a year, thus earning a "fixed wage of, say, 4 pounds a week for the year." The other eight months, workers would be free to pursue any activity they wished (1919, 126–127).

theorizing a full Guild Socialist system, one that functionally integrates the productive cooperation of guilds with the consumer cooperatives.

BACKGROUND ASSUMPTIONS

G. D. H. Cole's Guild Socialist proposals draw on a set of evaluative norms and a broad socialist critique of capitalism.

Evaluative Norms

Cole assumes a basic evaluative norm that is welfarist (Cole 1920d, 11–12). While Cole doesn't aggressively argue the point in his guild writings, he implicitly holds a strong assumption of the interpersonal comparability of something like cardinal utility. Hence the normative standard is presumably an aggregate welfare function, perhaps a simple sum of individual utilities. Cole's position is essentially the same as that of Owen and echoes the values of the Christian Socialists. Such a standard is also close to the welfarism of late classical (Mill) and even early neoclassical (Marshall) economics.[17]

Cole goes on to assert fundamental political and economic rights to participation (Cole 1920d, 12). "Co-ordination is inevitably coercive unless it is self co-ordination" (124). Notice that such rights derive (somewhat loosely) from a utilitarian argument. They are not absolute or natural, but are necessary for "societal health." This emphasis on democracy picks up on themes important to Thompson and Wheeler but are largely missing in Owen and the Christian Socialists.

The Critique of Capitalism

It is hardly surprising that Cole's framework shares the broad socialist critique of capitalism. It includes fundamental doubts about profits,

---

17. In "Utlitarianism," J. S. Mill (1863, Ch. 2), establishes the utilitarian objective as the pursuit of pleasure and reduction of pain. Intellectual pleasure, as well as pleasures of emotion, creativity, and morality matter more in Mill's view than physical sense stimuli. Furthermore, Mill posits that utilitarianism promotes noble behavior even when the noble person's actions reduce personal utility if the increase in societal happiness exceeds the personal loss. This emphasis on nobility also resonates with Morris' views. It seems reasonable to infer that a noble-centered utilitarian philosophy underlies Cole's Guild Socialist worldview.

competition, and markets. While doubts might be logically derivable from first principles, for the most part, they function in Cole's thought as a set of givens.

Start with profits. For Cole, as for Owen and Maurice, profits are equivalent to "greed." As such, the drive for profit is essentially "immoral" and "antisocial" (Cole 1920a, 19–20). Moreover, in Cole's vision, as workers become more self-conscious and confident, they necessarily become less docile and more prone to questioning capitalist authority through strikes and other disruptions (20). Under such circumstances, the profit seeking capitalist is not only immoral, but increasingly inefficient. Here Cole echoes themes in John Stuart Mill's understanding of the evolution of working-class social psychology.[18]

Unlike Mill, but consistent with most all of the 19th-century cooperators, Cole is highly critical of competition. Competition encourages price cutting and pits one group of workers against another. It amounts to the "crushing-out of the weak by the strong." As such it is another evidence of the immorality of capitalism. And it is far from clear that competition is in any sense fundamentally "necessary." With the expansion of large-scale trusts, Cole sees even "the capitalists themselves rapidly abandoning the original central and essential 'necessary evil' of the whole system—competition" (1920a, 7).[19]

SOCIAL PSYCHOLOGY

Although Cole does not address the question at length, he is sympathetic to Owen's emphasis on the plasticity of human character: Cole writes, "If environment does not, as Robert Owen thought, make character in an absolute

---

18. See Chapter 4 of this volume; also Persky 2016, 129–131.

19. By way of contrast, as emphasized in Chapter 4, John Stuart Mill (Mill [1848] 1965, 794–795) anticipates that worker control and competition are quite compatible. And it is interesting that at least one Guild school, the medievalists, presents benefits to specific types of competition. Penty advocates "the rivalry of producers" (1906, 2) to promote "general excellence of . . . craftsmanship" (26): he is clear this is not price competition by financiers, which degrades quality (1). G. R. Stirling Taylor envisions multiple guilds engaging in a competition on a "very limited field" (1920, 94). He suggests the "gentle prick of competition develops an energy in a man." Taylor proposes a soft more regulated competition between parallel guilds. In this controlled form, competition might be productive, not destructive. In Taylor's words "There is a vital distinction between playing the piano and dancing on it" (93). The other schools of Guild Socialist thought do not pick up on this theme of encouraging even mild competition.

sense, it does direct and divert character into divergent forms of expression" (1920d, 25). Like Owen, he expects public education to do much. Cole offers a rich theory of the social psychology of the workplace. At the center of his theory are the incentives that motivate workers.

Workers obviously need food and shelter. Lacking wealth, they work to satisfy such pressing needs. The fear of hunger acts as a powerful, almost coercive, incentive. But in addition to basic needs, workers have higher desires, too. Here Cole elaborates on themes from William Morris, citing Morris' call "for a nobler conception of human nature" (Cole 1920b, 419).

According to Cole some work processes such as artistry, skilled crafts, and skilled brainwork innately incentivize work effort. Joy in labor arises in such cases due to the "sense of successful self-expression" (1920b, 419). Workers in these occupations are not only working for instrumental reasons, but also for the pleasure of creating. They work not only to eat, but to enjoy the work itself.

Cole goes on to assert there are noble incentives available even to more ordinary and mundane labor, including industrial processes. He never goes quite as far as Morris who argues that virtually all work can become art. But like Morris, Cole emphasizes social responsibility, particularly the pleasures of exercising responsibility and personal initiative, as well as the enjoyment generated from a sense of community service.

Human nature responds to a range of incentives from the mundane to the noble. But Cole argues that the structure of the employment relation under capitalism leaves only the most basic incentives in play for the vast majority of workers. To realize the nobler incentives, the worker must be free both from enslavement to other human beings and to machines, for, "the sense of being owned is deadening" (1920b, 420). Workers struggling to achieve subsistence have no energy left for their nobler aspirations.

The challenge then is to design an economic system, a set of economic institutions, that can tap into such nobler aspects of human nature. For the Guild Socialist Cole, such a system certainly involves doing away with the private ownership of the means of production.[20] But, as we will see in

---

20. Cole writes:

The effectiveness of this motivating factor requires eliminating private ownership. Workers do not respond to an appeal to work based on free service if gains accrue to a master. If we abandon coercion by the fear of hunger and unemployment as the motive to industry for the many, it is of no use to dream of replacing it by other forms of coercion. We must abandon the idea of external coercion to labour, and rely upon the willingness of men to work as soon as they can see that their work is worthwhile. (Cole 1920a, 23)

the next section, much more is required. At the very least, workers must be secure in their employment and receive pay they consider just. Security makes irrelevant low-level incentives such as hunger and fear of dismissal. And it vitiates the effectiveness of hierarchical systems of authority. Under such circumstances, worker motivation and productivity depend on the deeper, nobler incentives—incentives presuming freedom, not coercion. Cole wants to argue that these higher drives do not just match, but far outpace the productivity achieved under the ancient incentives of coercion. If Cole is right, harnessing the higher elements of human nature greatly increases the level of social welfare both through the new direct enjoyment of work and the much-enhanced superabundance it makes possible (1920a, 21).

INSTITUTIONS OF GUILD SOCIALISM

Working from his assumptions, G. D. H. Cole aspires in his Guild Socialism to construct a blueprint of an alternative economic system. He aims to describe an economy that meaningfully integrates the creative institutions of the guilds and the democratic institutions of the consumer cooperative movement. Guild Socialism "appears largely as a theory of institutions" (Cole 1920d, 25). Individual wellbeing presupposes effective institutional structure and organization:

> To get the [social] mechanism right, and to adjust it as far as possible to the expression of men's social wills, is . . . the surest way, not only to the well-being of the body politic, but to the happiness and sense of well-directed achievement which chiefly constitute individual well-being. It is not because they idealize industrialism or social institutions that Guildsmen spend so much time in theorizing and planning about them: it is because they see the best chance of human well-being in getting these aspects of life put firmly and properly into their right place. (Cole 1920d, 26)

At root, the challenge in designing the social machinery or institutional structure is one of achieving harmony with human desires and instincts (25).

Cole's search for design begins with a study of the medieval guild, "an association of independent producers or merchants for the regulation of production or sale" as well as "the common form of popular association" in medieval towns for social, charitable, and educational purposes (1920d, 42). Medieval guilds are religious and local, their production handicraft and

small-scale.[21] Cole emphasizes other specific characteristics: security to the members, just pricing, craftsmanship, and quality service to the community. With the medieval guild as background, Cole's economics starts with production and consumption. The system builds on institutions that foster an engaging work experience for the worker and a quality product for the consumer. But along with work and consumption, civic society affects wellbeing. Thus, Cole (1920d) demarcates Guild Socialist institutions into three realms: the realm of production, the realm of consumption, and the civic realm (see Figure 10.1).

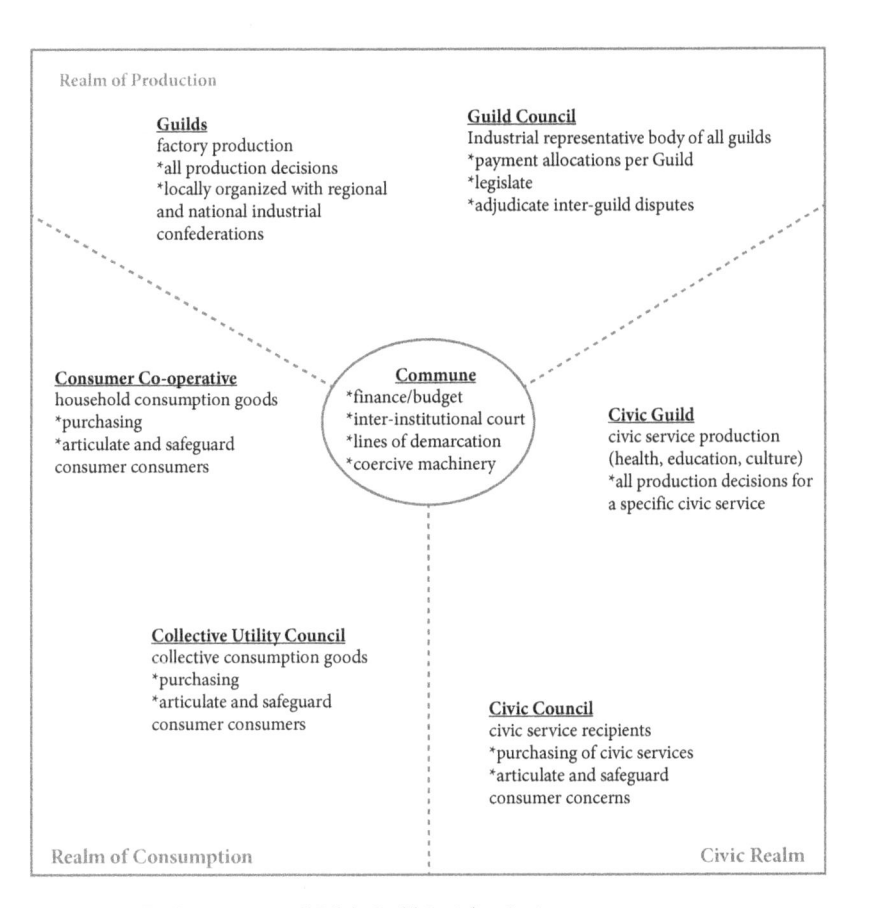

Figure 10.1 The Institutions of Cole's Guild Socialist Society

21. Historically, guilds broke up with the extension of markets. A classic account of the rise and fall of medieval guilds is Renard ([1918] 2000).

Production

Cole is not attempting to turn the industrial clock back in time to medieval guild society. The factory is the basic unit in the realm of production under Guild Socialism. The intention in revisiting the guild form of organization is to identify its constructive spirit and how to infuse that spirit into large-scale production.

Fundamental to industrial guild organization is that control over the production process rests with the workers themselves. Bottom-up democracy in the workplace is a prerequisite for freedom from tyranny in production (Cole & Mellor 1919, 40). The system replaces the self-appointed owner, boss, and corporate board with worker self-management.

Cole's guild system entrusts responsibility for decisions in the realm of production to "workers by hand and brain" (Cole 1920c, 9)—amalgamating workers and managers. Like many Owenites and Christian Socialists, Cole perceives the necessity of management within the modern workplace. But management selection occurs through democratic process, with workers electing their own foreman and other managerial staff. Discipline rests "upon a basis of confidence, and not upon external force. Obedience to the foreman will mean . . . harmony with the Guild fellowship and mutual trust" (27). Together all the "workers by hand and brain" come to understand and control the industry, becoming "the accredited agents of the community in the economic sphere" (Cole & Mellor 1919, 22).

A national guild confederates all the local guilds (or production units) within an industry (Transportation Guild, Structural Materials Guild, Agricultural Guild, etc.) Responsibility for all production decisions rests with the guild. To handle issues of inter-industry trade, members of relevant guilds meet to inform one another's decisions.

There is direct representation of each guild in the Guild Council, the industrial representative body in production.[22] The Guild Council makes decisions on the total payments per guild and serves as legislator and as court for inter-guild disputes.

Cole strongly emphasizes the local level guilds to promote participatory democracy and to prevent bureaucratic ossification. Realities of large-scale production require regional and national institutions as well. As appropriate per industry, local guilds select representatives to form regional and national guilds and councils (Cole 1920d, 70).

---

22. The "Industrial Guilds Congress" is the name of the national level Guild Council.

Consumption

As guilds represent worker interests, the cooperative retail organizations represent consumer interests in private consumption.[23] Circa 1920, the cooperative consumer movement was especially strong in Great Britain, providing a widespread network of retail outlets and acquiring considerable expertise on the quality and cost of a range of consumer goods. As discussed in Chapter 6, British consumer cooperatives expanded into wholesaling and manufacturing activities via the Cooperative Wholesale Society (CWS) and were completely dominated by consumer interest.

Cole's emphasis on consumption represents a major innovation in the guild model. L. Carpenter suggests that Cole here follows the lead of Leonard Woolf (L. Carpenter 1973, 65). But there is a deep distinction between the two. Where Woolf treats the consumer cooperatives as employers, for Cole it is crucial that workers not be "servile" to consumers (1920d, 88). The guild must control the workplace. That is its function.[24] Workers meet consumers not as employee members of joint boards but as producers with full responsibility for the organization and maintenance of their work effort. While the system clearly relies on bargaining, it is bargaining between two well-defined functional bodies, the guilds representing production and the consumer cooperatives representing consumption. Consumption motivates production, but if production is to be a true act of free service, it must in a real sense leave to the workers the responsibility for carrying out the effort akin to what Morris might call the craft or art. Workers must control the immediate space of production.

Cole's vision denies consumers the role of employers while asserting the necessity of consumer cooperatives taking up one side of the new bargaining mechanism that is meant to replace the market. In a highly decentralized structure, this bargaining brings the guilds face-to-face with the consumer cooperative. The resulting system aims at a full integration of producer and consumer cooperation, without the suppression of either function.

23. This formulation of consumer cooperatives as parallel structures to the guilds represents Cole's final approach to consumer representation. Earlier Cole (1917a, 86) identifies the state as the representative of consumers, but later he explicitly limits the power of the state (1920d). Hewes (1922, 216) suggests that the role of the state constitutes the chief disagreement between Hobson and Cole. Hobson considers the state as supreme with power delegated to the guilds; where in his early formulations, Cole considers the state and guilds as co-equal. In *Guild Socialism Restated*, Cole reduces the state to a secondary role.

24. The term "function" plays a central role in R. H. Tawney's approach to Guild Socialism. Cole draws freely on Tawney's ideas. See Tawney (1920).

Taking functional perspectives does not mean that either side to bargaining holds a narrow maximizing view in formulating positions. The guilds' commitment to free service implies that their efforts ultimately must produce for social needs and wants. While taking pleasure in producing quality, such pleasure must balance with the emphasis on community service. Although not fully developed by Cole, the consumer cooperatives, with their memberships made up of producing families, are sympathetic to the logic of worker control of production. Functionalism does not rule out sensitivity for either side to bargaining. Rather, it establishes legitimacy for each.

In this spirit, Cole proposes two institutions in the realm of consumption. The consumer cooperative holds responsibility for wholesale purchasing of household consumption goods and articulating and safeguarding consumer concerns. The Collective Utilities Council performs the same functions but for collective consumption goods such as electricity, water, public transportation, etc. As in the realm of production, the local organizations are the important ones, but the institutions may also have regional and national levels with local decision-makers sending representatives to the broader levels.

The Civic Realm

Cole (1920d) devotes a chapter to "The Civic Services." The Civic Realm consists of two primary institutions (see Figure 10.1). The workers by hand and brain in a specific, civic service form relevant civic guilds: the Education Guild, the Health Guild, the Culture Guild, etc. The civic councils represent the interests of civic service recipients. General elections among the local population determine the members of the civic councils (108). The structure here is familiar, echoing the relation of guilds and consumer cooperatives.

The Commune

As apparent in Figure 10.1, Cole's guild institutions include the Commune, or communal body. As with the other institutions, Communes are local, regional, and national, with the important level being local.[25]

___

25. The one exception to the emphasis on local control is the military, which is under the national Commune. Cole does not raise the question of whether a national level military might usurp local decision-makers.

Members of the institutions across the three realms each democratically elect representatives to the Commune. The basic functions of the Commune are: finance and allocating resources across area guilds; an appeals court for interinstitutional disputes; establishing lines of demarcation between functional bodies with overlapping interests and making decisions on town-specific issues (such as town boundaries); and responsibility for the "coercive machinery" such as police (Cole 1920d, 127–128).

The financial role of Communes is primarily one of coordination. Communes receive budgets detailed by specific guilds and bring them into alignment given available resources (Cole 1920d, 144–147).[26] Communes balance saving and spending to avoid inflation and deflation (147–148). The Commune is the controller of currency, "and the general banking system would also be communal" (148).[27]

The Commune is responsible for financial resource allocation. Local, regional, and national Communes allocate financial resources across consumption goods, capital, and civic services. The Commune holds responsibility for these decisions because, for example, financing capital for the Building Guild reduces what is available for civic needs such as education (Cole 1920d, 144).

Cole advocates community ownership of industrial property. Unchecked, worker ownership of property can lead to profiteering at the expense of other community interests (1920c, 7).[28] Public or community ownership of the means of production and its surpluses is necessary "to secure the working of economic and industrial democracy in the common interest."[29] Cole originally sees guild control of production as consistent with a form

---

26. Guilds make budgets. The guilds' budgets pass to the consumer institutions, and with amendment go to the Commune (or to its Finance Committee with expert statistical staff). The Commune brings the individual budgets "into harmony with the estimated national production," and the whole budget goes to the Commune for ratification (Cole 1920d, 145). Civic organizations have input as well. Because the budget process occurs under self-governing institutions, all interests and views have opportunity for expression in communal decision-making. Again, to avoid centralization wherever possible, Cole emphasizes the local and regional process over the national level (146). The stress on local and regional levels applies not only to budgeting, but also to financial operations.

27. Note that earlier, in the same volume, Cole identifies bank control as resting with the guilds themselves. It is not clear which structure he is advocating here.

28. Cole here is criticizing what is essentially the position of the Syndicalists. Also in that camp is Hilaire Belloc, usually categorized as a Distributist, who advocates a guild system in which workers might own shares in their own and also in other guilds (Belloc 1913, 9–10).

29. (Cole 1920c, 10); on public ownership, see also (Cole 1920a, 59).

of nationalized ownership (1914, 470–471). Later writings suggest that ownership should be vested in the Commune, which also holds ultimate responsibility for approving capital expansions proposed in factory and national guild budgets (1920d).

Interinstitutional Relations

Cole's guild system institutionalizes democratic participation in decision-making, while assuming the motive of free service in the interest of the community. Even under such an assumption, the existence of information asymmetries across the stakeholders and scarcity of resources means that people must meet to inform, coordinate, and bargain. Relevant representatives from guilds, cooperatives, and/or civic institutions meet on regular, intermittent, or ad hoc bases, as circumstances necessitate. Cole reflects, for example, on the situation of bargaining between the consumer cooperatives and the guilds. In meetings, representatives of the consumer institutions communicate their needs and interests and bargain with guilds without exercising direct control over production (1920d, 88; 90–91; 94). Similarly, civic representatives on the civic council meet with civic guilds to inform and shape decisions when relevant to their concerns (109). In effect, frequent bargaining sessions replace wholesale markets.

Guilds provide one another with primary and intermediate goods. Provisioning parallels relations between final goods-producing guilds and consumer cooperatives. Just as the consumer cooperatives meet, inform, and bargain with the final goods-producing guilds, guilds meet, inform, and bargain about intermediate goods. Bargaining among these bodies becomes the guild alternative to a range of intermediate markets. In cases of substantial production interdependencies across guilds, each would "require on its staff experts who understood the technique of the others, and there would have to be special joint committees, and probably . . . mutual exchange of seats on the governing bodies of the Guilds" (Cole 1920d, 68).

Such voluntary and fluid interinstitutional relations allow the full integration of the cooperative system and the emergence of what Cole calls "just prices." If these bargaining structures are somewhat bulky, their design provides more options for sharing information. Where bargaining does not settle matters across two guilds, the matter moves to the Guild Council, where issues under dispute are of broad significance and discussion and settlement takes place at the level of the Commune.

COLE'S ANALYSIS OF PRODUCTION

The Employment Relationship and Social Welfare

Cole theorizes the economy of Guild Socialism, with a focus on the interactions between social psychology and the institutions of the workplace. In the capitalist firm, workers have interests at odds with those of their employers and little awareness or concern for broader social purposes. Of course, socialist writers of many stripes emphasize the tension between worker and employer under capitalism. Most notable are insights from Marx's discussion of worker alienation (1988 [1844]). But Cole, more clearly than those before looks not only at the past, but also at the future. He analyses in detail the interaction of social psychology and the institutions of the guild system. In effect, he offers a rigorous argument that Guild Socialism will generate large gains in social welfare broadly conceived.[30]

Workers under industrial capitalism have virtually no interest in their product. The employment relation encourages slacking. Employers attempt to monitor, reducing morale even further. Productivity is low (Cole 1920d, 23). The worker in the capitalist workplace is without motivation to do more than the absolute minimum.

Cole, drawing on his assumptions about the hierarchy of worker motivations, considers the situation where the guild separates work from pay, institutionalizes democracy in workplace decision-making, and makes an honest appeal to free service. The principal now is not capitalist financial returns, but society. Guild workers are keenly aware that their labor provisions consumption and makes possible the enjoyment of life for all. Guild workers are conscious that they serve a central social function. In this new institutional setting, with economic security and democratic control, workers respond to the noble incentives. They find pleasure in the work itself and its social purpose. Rather than doing the minimum to get by, shirking or using asymmetric information to undermine the project, workers respond to the common effort. Workers take responsibility, seek out opportunities to show initiative, and where possible, demonstrate their creativity.

---

30. In carrying out his analysis, Cole clearly anticipates much of the message of the modern theory of the employment relationship. While he does not use the modern vocabulary, he captures the central concerns of that theory. For a more recent argument on the connection between the employment relationship and self-management, see Bowles and Gintis (1993).

The new institutional structure erases the dependence on the meanest incentives used by the capitalist workplace. The new institutional structure brings to fruition the ideals of earlier cooperative thinkers like Morris: workers now find pleasure in unleashing their nobler natures. The new institutions take work from a disutility worth avoiding to a sought-after utility, at least given reasonable working hours and some variety.

We reconstruct Cole's argument here as follows: in moving from a coercive employment relation to a fully democratic and secure cooperative one, work generates positive utility, and material production increases impressively in quantity, in quality, and in meeting social needs. Taken together such changes greatly enhance social welfare. The higher motivations lead to greater output than the older motivations of coercion. By definition, they also generate utility directly, where the old system generates disutility in work. Hence the "new" total must be greater than the old total.[31]

Of course, Cole's "theorem" rests heavily on his key assumptions about human behavior and social psychology. The motivating capacity of free service is the deep social-psychological claim of Cole's system. Cole admits the strength of such motivation is not a known but an assumption. Conceivably, from the perspective of productivity, the new incentives are inadequate to replace the older coercive ones. He recognizes that some regard the "appeal to free service as a 'leap in the dark.'" But Cole, himself, prefers to consider it "as a 'tremendously big,' but splendid 'adventure'" (1920a, 23). Of course, to unleash the power of free service requires a complete rebuilding of economic institutions along guild lines.

The key is to align—in a free environment—worker interests in craftsmanship and service with the guild's social function. Cole is cautiously optimistic that the guild structure can achieve this end:

> If men do not give such ungrudging devotion to industry, is not that because in industry the right appeal—the appeal to free service—has never been made? I believe that men will work for an ideal as they can no longer be made to work for fear. And, if I am wrong, then who is in the right, and what hope is there for society at all? For, if men cannot be forced to work and will not work for an ideal, it is plain that they will not work at all. If that is so, the sooner some straying planet crashes into the earth, the better will it be for the human race. (Cole 1920a, 25)

---

31. At the risk of over-formalizing: the higher motivations lead to greater output (Q') than the older motivations of coercion (Q). They also generate utility directly (+C'), where the old system generates disutility in work (−C). Hence the "new" total (Q' + C') must be greater than the old total (Q − C).

Technology, Quality, and Creativity

Cole argues that worker-managed production units and free service re-orient production away from the endemic slacking under capitalism. He also argues these same forces fundamentally change the evolution of technology.

The capitalist system develops machines to cut production costs, re-ducing the skill needed to work and lowering labor status (Cole & Mellor 1919, 36). Anticipating future left arguments concerning "deskilling," Cole holds that capitalist technological change reduces differences be-tween skilled and unskilled labor, undermining the demand for skilled craftsmen (1920b, 321).[32] Capitalism also uses technology to speed up the unskilled workforce. Cole intuitively demonstrates the "externality" concept in assessing the application of technology in capitalist sys-tems. To Cole, "the 'speeding-up' system is only profitable because the employer reaps the fruits without paying for the damage." Cole draws a simile between the speeding-up system's profitability to the large profits of motor-bus companies that do "not have to pay for the wear and tear of the roads" (323). Self-governed worker organizations internalize the costs, providing the incentive to avoid technologies that aim at exces-sive speed.

Early on, Cole suggests that worker-centered organization makes allies of machinery and workers. The thought echoes Robert Owen and William Thompson and reinforces Mill's hopes for the future of the laboring classes in a cooperative economy.[33] The result is technology that does the dirty work: "It should be the main business of inventors to eliminate dirty work without reference to the will of sweating profiteers. The cheapness of human labour is no reason for its employment in unworthy callings" (Cole & Mellor 1919, 36–37). When inventors emphasize machines doing the dirty work in labor processes,

> [A]ll those trades in which the cheap and nasty has ousted the good and serviceable could then be restored to the artist, who . . . could resume his true function in a democracy—the making of everyday things for everyday folk. The artists and the men of imagination have turned against machinery

---

32. Cole's position on deskilling is close to that of Braverman (1974).

33. Mill asserts that through most of modern history technological improvements served "no other purpose but the increase of wealth" where they might in the cooper-ative future of the stationary state "produce their legitimate effect, that of abridging labour" ([1948] 1965, 756).

because it has destroyed craftsmanship; but it has done this, not because it is machinery, but because it has been the bond-slave of capitalism. (Cole & Mellor 1919, 37)

Indeed, Cole envisions the very process of innovation as integrated into the structure of the guilds: "Each Guild would have its inventive departments, as increasingly great factories are now coming to have them" (1914a, 710). But in worker-controlled guilds, machines evolve to serve workers, ending "the tyranny of machinery" (Cole & Mellor 1919, 37). Work, including machine-based labor, can be joyous if the worker "is its master instead of its servant" (Cole 1920b, 420). The technological transformation of the activities of the worker gives "a fair prospect for the development of all his faculties, industrial, social, and individual" (Cole & Mellor 1919, 38).

Motivated by the appeal of craftsmanship and service, guild workers also develop technologies that enhance the quality of products. The result is a range of useful and aesthetically appealing products. The Guild Socialists, in the spirit of William Morris, anticipate a great improvement in consumer-good quality. Evidence from the experience of the post-World War I British Housing Guild suggests that a guild spirit can translate into substantial quality enhancements (Joslyn 1922, 121–123).

Recall that in Cole's guild institutional structure, guilds establish relations with consumer-centered cooperatives. The same cooperatives articulate the consumer view on quality of product, as well as quantity, price, etc. (Cole 1920d, 88). Sympathetic to the principle of service to the community, the workers are "eager to elicit and respond to" the thoughts of consumer representatives (89). Where J. T. W. Mitchell argues that consumers must control labor to achieve good work at reasonable cost, Cole understands the new service-oriented workers of the guilds as free of the monopolistic selfishness so feared by Mitchell and others.

Beyond the provisioning of high-quality consumer products, the guild civic institutions produce public goods and fulfil "spiritual, mental, and other non-economic needs and desires" (Cole 1920d, 96). The proposed guild education system offers a more concrete institutional structure while retaining Morris' spirit. The goal is to elicit "the fullest possible capacity for initiative and self-expression" (98). An Education Guild allows educators to be self-governing. As with other guilds, the Education Guild's emphasis on the local level is likely to encourage "multiform experiment[ation], for freedom to develop individual ideas and peculiar notions . . ." (101). Self-governing student organizations serve to clarify the impact of teaching methods on those being taught (102–103).

Workers' Pay and Job Assignments

Early Guild Socialist observers, such as Reynard, note the lack of consensus across guild writers on the matter of pay (1920, 325–326).[34] Yet to operationalize the nobler incentives, workers must consider their pay fundamentally just. How does Cole's Guild Socialism determine worker's pay in the absence of a wage system? Cole argues that, in the long run, the good society distributes products and services based on need. But he suggests it is achievable only through "the actual experience of free and democratic industrial and social conditions" (Cole 1920d, 72). Until that new "consciousness" arises, some inequalities in pay are necessary.[35] Cole observes that early guild writers suggest that each guild receive a salary fund proportional to its number of members and then divide the sum as the guild sees fit. Here he is most likely referring to Reckitt and Bechhofer (1918). While cautious as to the character of the best system for determining pay, they hold,

> First the amount apportioned to each national Guild for the remuneration of its members should be in exact proportion to its membership . . . . Secondly, the manner of distributing pay to its members should be at the discretion of each National Guild, as a democratic and self-governing body. (Reckitt & Bechhofer 1918, 314–315)

Reckitt and Bechhofer raise, as an explicit possibility to be determined by the guild, whether all guild members should receive equal amounts. Cole clearly leans in this direction since he expects that over time members realize the "impossibility of attempting to measure in economic rewards the respective values of different kinds of service" (Cole 1920d, 73).[36] That

---

34. Guild writers insist on the term "pay" reserving the term "wages" for capitalism. As Cole puts it: "In demanding the abolition of wagery, they (guildsmen) are repudiating utterly the idea that labour is a commodity . . . . By 'wage,' they mean the price paid for labour as a commodity, and for this method of payment they wish to substitute another and better method" (1917b, 462). Similarly, Reckitt and Bechhofer (1918, 39) write: "for between 'wages' and 'pay' there is all the difference that there is between slavery and freedom. 'Wages' represent the cost of hire . . . the upkeep of the worker as for that of any other machine. 'Pay' represents the reward for service, something due to one who is contributing to the common good." They also make the comparison to the soldier who receives pay.

35. In effect, such development of worker consciousness is the long tail of the transition process discussed below.

36. Cole recognizes that equal per-capita payments to all guilds may not be "practicable" in the earlier stages of the guild transformation.

said, Cole adjusts for the greater disutility associated with some jobs within the guild. Guilds mechanize or completely do without work which is both "unpleasant" and "degrading." "No human being ought to be either allowed or compelled to do work that degrades." For the "dull or unpleasant" work that remains, Cole proposes not differential pay, but differential hours. Cole anticipates that reduced-hour jobs appeal to specific individuals who are "full of desires to do unpaid work in their own individual way." He offers as a simile the willingness of "many an original writer" to earn their support by engaging in "part-time hack journalism" (76–77).[37]

The converse of such a situation raises a broader issue. How does a guild allocate workers across skill/education training programs leading to more engaging jobs? Following Cole's logic for handling disagreeable work by mixing activities, Guilds might pair these better jobs with intrinsically less attractive employments. Then a workday that combines some limited time in a disagreeable job and a good deal of time in an attractive activity would be a rough equivalent of a workday devoted to an intermediate job. Cole does not develop the point.[38]

COLE'S ANALYSIS OF DISTRIBUTION
Full Costs and Just Prices

Cole attempts to integrate the economics of the guild with the economics of the consumers. Here he directly addresses the broader question of structure suggested by the Christian Socialists and the consumer cooperators, even as he rejects the notion of competition maintained by J. S. Mill. Central to this integration is the question of distribution and particularly the wholesale prices charged by guilds. The guilds and the consumer cooperatives are

37. Somewhat at odds with Cole on this point, Reckitt and Bechhofer quote the *Syllabus* drawn up by "a group of National Guildsmen" to the effect that "labour in 'dirty industries'—scavenging, etc.—will probably be in the main of a temporary character, and will be undertaken by those who are for the time unable to obtain entry elsewhere" (Reckitt & Bechhofer 1918, 183).

38. Cole here may be drawing on Charles Fourier who emphasizes job sharing (Taft 1972, 48). And Morris' emphasis on task variety likely is of influence. Such an approach requires the training of more workers in skills than necessary under a system that leaves a skilled worker putting in full time at a single skilled activity. This is clearly an efficiency loss in production narrowly conceived. But it generates a more skilled and diversified worker with positive implications for adaptability, innovation, and creativity—results supportive of Guild Socialist values and welfare-enhancing in its own right.

to work with a system of "just prices." More specifically, for most goods, Cole identifies just prices with full production cost.

Cole outlines in some detail how to arrive at just prices. For example, in the case of milk, the Distributive Guild buys milk from the Agricultural Guild and sells it to the Cooperative Society which markets to the public. Presumably, in quoting a price to the Cooperative Society, the Distributive Guild adds its own costs to the price it pays the Agricultural Guild (1920d, 142). The largest share of all such costs are labor costs.[39] Labor costs include payment for direct and indirect labor. The latter arises from both intermediate goods and the depreciation of capital goods.[40] Presumably, just pricing involves full costs which include pay for work at a "leisurely" pace to ensure commitment to guild standards of quality, employment security to reflect guild commitment to its workforce, and no unaccounted negative externalities.

How different is such an outcome from the traditional one of supply and demand? Indeed, on its surface, the traditional story comes to a similar conclusion. For industries with constant returns to scale, supply and demand theory predicts that long-run prices in a competitive economy converge on long-run average costs. From a normative point of view, both systems focus on cost as the controlling factor in prices.

The important difference between the two stories lies in the mechanism that achieves prices at cost. In the almost fictional world of perfect competition, all producers act as price takers, the actions of many competitors disciplining offering prices in line with underlying costs. But Cole rejects competition as the pricing-at-cost mechanism because it incentivizes negative externalities that burden workers and civic society and because competition generates agency problems that undermine craftsmanship and quality product. Furthermore, from Cole's perspective, capitalist economies do not actually generate competition; a large portion of capitalist production goes on under conditions in which producers enjoy considerable market power and claim positive profit. But where monopolies and oligopolies face disorganized consumers, guilds face organized consumers and organized representatives from civic society. Cole puts forward a system of bilateral, and often multilateral, bargaining. To continue with the milk case, the Distributive Guild communicates full

---

39. Cole remains vague on the question of land rent.

40. Cole does not discuss whether a premium or an interest charge should be added to labor costs embodied in capital goods. We suspect he would oppose such an addition. Presumably, the Commune, when making investment decisions, would arrive at a sense of social priorities.

costs of production to the cooperative and any other civic stakeholders. Presumably in doing so, the Distributive Guild offers supporting data on long-run costs. If now the cooperative or civic representatives disagree over the cost calculations, either can take its case to the "Commune (local, regional, or national as the case may be) for discussion and final decision" (1920d, 142).

The Distributive Guild and for that matter any other guild may violate the principle of "free service," taking advantage of an essentially monopolistic power and either pad expenses or shed costs by imposing negative externalities on the community. Such problems closely resemble those of modern, regulated public utilities. Interestingly, for such regulated utilities, market economies also fall back on bargaining and judicial-like hearings. The outcomes are generally not disastrous.

Presumably, the advantage of Cole's system over such modern public hearings is the access consumer and civic representatives have to information in meetings with the guilds. Recall, in the case of interactions between guilds, the related guilds likely have "mutual exchange of seats on the governing bodies of the Guilds" (1920d, 68). Correspondingly, "a consumers' body could claim representation and facilities for consultation and common action in relation to any guild with whose working it was concerned" (93) and Cole also leaves room for "close and constant" relations with civic institutions concerning areas of mutual concern (109). As a result, participation of civic organizations may internalize negative externalities. If guild activity causes environmental degradation that affects health, for example, then the Health Council or Health Guild might devote a part of its budget to protect natural resources or might finance research on alternative production techniques. Finally, though Guild Socialism vests all production decision-making power with workers, it is not unreasonable to assume that a Commune might provide consumer or civic representation on the governing body of guilds that misappropriate power to their own pecuniary advantage. The result of this institutional structure, under appropriate assumptions: just pricing at full cost.

A prime guild purpose is to achieve meaningful democracy in production and distribution. But putting that to one side, the larger institutional structure of the guild economy, the balancing of producer guilds with consumer cooperatives and civic groups, promises a strong check on monopoly and oligopoly power. Here is a thoughtful answer to those who fear monopoly, for example, Mill who embraces competition and Greg the critic of Christian Socialism. The guild asserts production is for the wellbeing of the community. If one guild goes rogue, trying to produce for monopoly profit, the other guilds, the consumer cooperatives, the civic guilds, and

ultimately the Commune could counterpoise (Cole & Mellor 1919, 27). Similarly, for the quality of goods.

Cole aspires to "build a community in which tyranny will be difficult, the chances of conflict small, and the settlements that result for the good of all" (Cole & Mellor 1919, 32). Of course, resolving questions in the guild context involves a considerable amount of meeting and bargaining, since interinstitutional consultations replace what in traditional economic theory is the role of markets. Critics of Guild Socialism, like Hartley Withers, the editor of the longstanding magazine *Economist* from 1916–1921, argue that the plans of the guild advocates must involve great inefficiencies from all the interinstitutional consultation (Withers 1920, Chs. 9–10). To such concern, Reckitt and Bechhofer make a telling counterargument: even in the capitalist economy, conferences and meetings are omnipresent. The capitalist who owns his own firm must confer "with his banker, his partners, his managers, and even his foremen and workers. Presumably he confers also with his customers and with the agents of the chief sources from which he obtains materials." They go on to suggest that even under capitalism "Joint Conferences" are the way to advance "a common purpose—to exchange goods, enlarge the business, alter its scope, arrange new rates of pay" (1918, 208). In practice, formal markets mediate relatively few transactions under capitalism. It is not obvious whether a Guild Socialist system requires more or fewer meetings than a capitalist system dominated by large corporations. Indeed, such corporations, according to modern economic theory, are themselves in the business of suppressing the market in the interest of profit.[41]

One other point deserves mention. Cole argues for subsidies to those guilds producing merit goods and taxes when they generate negative externalities (1920d, 143). The Commune sets such taxes and subsidies. Subsidies and taxes presumably pass to consumers through full cost pricing.

Adjustments to Changes in Demand

In a profit-based system, profits and losses arise from the ability to sell over average price or the need to sell below average price. Presumably such outcomes send signals to producers concerning the state of demand. While

---

41. The core idea here is due to Coase (1937). For a review of Coase's original work and more recent contributions, see Williamson and Winter (1993). We do not know of any serious attempt to demonstrate the optimality of the present division of labor between markets and market-suppressing institutions, such as firms.

traditional economic content provides little detail as to whether such signals are in any sense optimal, the profit system does channel key information to the residual claimants thus guiding their production and investment plans. In a rather similar vein, proponents of market socialism advocate using the price system to send information to central decision-makers for planning purposes.

Cole's guild system has no such "automatic" guidance mechanism. Cole does not advocate market socialism. Rather he struggles to envision a system capable of superseding market relations in much the same way that the capitalist firm in its own internal dealings attempts to suppress market relations.[42] Allowing prices to vary with market conditions is not appealing to guild writers. But, without a market system, how does quantity adjust?

Here are a few hints from Cole's *Guild Socialism Restated*. First, keep in mind that production in the guild system is for use. Presumably, before production the relevant parties communicate. Most notably, Cole's guild structure requires direct quantity bargaining between many guild factories producing final goods and their local consumer cooperatives.[43] For Cole, the factory remains the basic unit of production in the guild democracy. Generally local bargaining between local guilds and local consumer cooperatives is sufficient to guarantee a match between supply and demand. However, Cole suggests that if "finished products were not disposed of directly from the factory," that responsibility falls to the district or national guild (1920d, 60). Thus, "where necessary," the higher-level guilds "co-ordinate the production of various factories, so as to make supply coincide with demand" (60). Presumably such efforts involve transferring goods between regions, in consultation with consumer representatives as necessary. Still, Cole proposes to keep the district and national guilds as small as possible to prevent the development of "a new form of bureaucracy resulting in the ossification of the Guild." Short-term interventions by these higher-level institutions are the exception, not the rule (61).

Yet, in a dynamic society, more permanent longer run imbalances are likely, on occasion. From Cole's Guild Socialist perspective, appropriate responses depend greatly on whether the imbalance is one of oversupply or undersupply. Consider first oversupply. In a system predisposed toward multiparty meetings, it seems straightforward enough to unload surplus

42. Recall Christian Socialist John Ludlow's response to critic Greg highlighting the overlooked applications of "concert" within many presumably capitalist enterprises (see Chapter 5).

43. As previously noted, Civic Guilds and Civic Councils have parallel bargaining arrangements.

product toward alternative uses that other guilds, consumer cooperatives, or civic institutions identify.[44] The labor adjustment is more challenging. Guilds facing systematic decline in demand undoubtedly move only slowly to rectify the situation. Maintaining excess labor capacity through a period of adjustment is the kinder course. And every guild commits to income security for all its members. Presumably, over time, the oversupplying guild reduces output and searches for repostings for its labor force, hopefully within the guild, but if necessary, in related guilds.[45] But presumably, in such periods of adjustment the guild slows or halts recruitment of new guild members. If there is a widespread slowdown, it is easy to imagine that the situation might generate serious underemployment problems among young workers. Guild writers including Cole are quiet on this point.

On the other hand, the guild immediately faces a potentially serious rationing problem in a situation of undersupply. Such challenges offer stimulus to the broader sense of community service. While expansion is possible in the future, in the short run people are likely to reason toward proportional rationing of consumer goods. In the case of intermediate goods, there might be some preference toward industries producing more socially significant final products.[46] Notice that this may leave other industries in a position of curtailing production. Presumably, guilds negotiate rationing plans with their partners, including the consumer cooperatives. Where no agreement is reached, the problem is referred to the Guild Council or even to the Commune.

TRANSITION AND THE THEORY OF ENCROACHMENT

Cole's elaborate blueprint, built on a cooperative understanding of social science, provides an elaborate description of a guild economy integrating worker and consumer cooperatives along with civic organizations. It refers not to the here and now, but to the future, a future achievable only after a

---

44. And there might be efficiency gains here relative to the capitalist system which incentivizes firms to destroy surplus product in pursuit of desired price and profit targets.

45. Notice, in the short run, the budget includes funds for any surplus labor associated with a guild in its product cost calculations. The maintained workforce income should temper multiplier effects of a slowdown. Further if some workers have multiple occupations, a decline in demand for labor in their first occupation may be more easily offset by shifting hours to their second. For such reasons, business cycles in a guild economy might be less severe than in capitalist economies.

46. Guild Socialists do well here to keep in mind William Thompson's distinction between the production of necessaries, comforts, and superfluities (see Chapter 3).

period of extensive social transition. Like earlier cooperative thinkers, Cole attempts to draw out the necessary features of that transition.

Owen's early understanding of transition emphasizes the fundamental importance of developing a cooperative character. But after initial successes in New Lanark, he never was able to launch a society-wide program of educational reform. The several experiments with cooperative Owenite villages raise serious doubts about the ability of that institution to survive in the broader capitalist economy. Mill and Taylor trace the outline in the evolution to full cooperation, with additional hints from the Mill school advocates of profit sharing. Mitchell and the CWS also present a clearly enunciated practical plan for a cooperative transition. Cole, too, makes a serious attempt to lay out a clear path that moves the economy toward cooperative goals. For Cole, a theory of transition acts as a guide to political and economic action by the working classes. Without such a theory, the blueprint of a fully formed guild economy is academic.

During World War I, Cole worked intensively with members of the radical Stewards' Movement. From the Glasgow shop steward, J. M. Paton, Cole, and other Guild Socialists take the idea of encroaching control and make it the centerpiece of an extended transition from capitalism to Guild Socialism (N. Carpenter 1922, 99–100). The starting point was the ongoing struggle of trade unions for power in the workplace. Nineteenth-century unions largely framed their demands in terms of opposition. Looking forward, they had to push into the very operation of the shops. Unions, increasingly organized on broad industrial (as opposed to craft) lines, framed their demands to include elements of control over production. Mounting these demands over time left more and more of workplace decision-making in the hands of the workers themselves, while capital retreated to the role of a mere rentier. Thus, encroaching control in effect turned the unions into guilds.

Encroaching control of the workplace proceeds in three key steps. The first is the expansion of the power of shop committees and their shop stewards. The second is the election of foremen. The third is the implementation of "collective contracts" which bargain for a lump sum to be divided by the workers themselves (N. Carpenter 1922, 206–207).

But the shop floor is not the only arena for encroaching control. It also stretches into central management. Increasingly, higher management—rather than answering to the capitalist owners—work in concert with the productive workers, the meaning of a rapprochement between hand and brain. Ultimately, then, transition moves to a stage of expropriation. The final stage consists of "(1) encroachment over rent, interest, and profits;

(2) nationalization; (3) catastrophic action; and (4) 'rough and ready justice' to the present owners of industry" (210).

Clearly at odds with William Thompson's aversion to all forms of force,
Cole more or less "dismisses the question of compensation" to capitalists.
As transition proceeds, the emerging guild society handles the capitalists
as it deems fit. For Cole, transition includes no contact between labor and
"capitalist methods" such as temporary partnerships which "might en-
danger its independence." However, Cole suspects that "a transition period of divided control is almost inevitable" (Reynard 1920, 327). For Cole,
transition culminates with a general strike and a revolution which entails
(hopefully minimal) violence (Cole 1920d, Ch. X; Reynard 1920, 328).

AFTERTHOUGHTS

The Guild Socialist movement with its plans for encroachment leading
to a fully cooperative economy came to a sudden end in the early 1920s.
Margaret Cole asserts that the demise of the organization was essentially
"political and Lenin was in fact its executioner" (1971, 121). Additionally,
there can be no doubt that the aggressive rule-or-ruin policies of the new
British Communist Party wreaked havoc among the guild leadership.

Still, it would be disingenuous to ignore the fact that G. D. H. Cole himself
came to seriously doubt the broad assumption of the power of democratic
participation so central to the guild vision. Indeed, after the dissolution of
the movement, he explicitly denied the eagerness of much of the workforce
to achieve democratic control. In something of a repentant mood he wrote:

> The idea of work under an externally imposed discipline was repellent to me in
> my own crafts of writing and teaching; and I therefore assumed that it ought be
> repellent to everybody, whatever the character of his job and whatever the cast
> of his own mind might be . . . I ignored the fact that most men's daily work is
> dull, and that provided it is not positively irksome, they do not even want to find
> in it the overmastering interest which I find in my own job. They have other fish
> to fry . . . . Self-government—the conscious and continuous exercise of the art
> of citizenship—seemed to me not merely a good in itself—which it is—but *the*
> good—which it is not. (Cole 1929, 161)

Cole continues, damningly:

> In fact of course this Utopia could not exist at all. The machinery devised for
> it might conceivably be called into existence; but it would not work. Asked to

elect masses of committees to perform all manner of representative functions on their behalf, and to keep their delegates constantly up to scratch by persistent attention to their doings, the mass of factory workers would speedily settle the question for themselves by not bothering to vote, and the committees would die of inanition. (1929, 161)

Perhaps Cole's later thoughts and not his early optimism on guild assumptions concerning the eagerness of workers to participate in the democratic control of their workplace are closer to the truth. Still, we find it difficult to believe that the bulk of workers are dead to the meaning of their work and the institutional structures that surround their productive contributions to society. To accept Cole's later reflections is to deny the very heart of the rich social psychology which Guild Socialist institutions are meant to draw out. Perhaps in his damning critique Cole simply misidentifies the deadening character effects of the capitalist workplace for underlying psychological proclivities.

PART IV

Reflections and a Reconstruction

From Robert Owen to G. D. H. Cole, the dedicated adherents of cooperation make serious analytical efforts to understand its economic system. A substantial body of economic thought results. That thought, as well as the practical experiments in cooperation, do not go unnoticed by the leading voices in British political economy. Thomas Robert Malthus, David Ricardo, Alfred Marshall, Karl Marx, and Beatrice Potter Webb are among those offering serious reflections on cooperation. Some reflections are supportive. For example, a social psychology built around an enlarged self-interest has some appeal to Alfred Marshall. And consumer cooperation seems a valuable ally in the Fabian approach to socialism. The political economists are also critical. The voices on the right specifically doubt the claims of economic productivity. The voices on the left challenge cooperation where it simply reproduces capitalist shortcomings. In most cases, the considerations of the leading political economists provide valuable insights into cooperative thought. Chapter 11 provides a synopsis of those reflections. The book then concludes with our own attempt to draw out the theoretical underpinnings of the first social science. This reconstruction builds from a distinct understanding of social psychology and a core set of institutions. This social science hypothesizes three normatively attractive outcomes and a self-reinforcing mechanism bringing stability. Unresolved is the question of transition to a fully functioning cooperative economic system.

CHAPTER 11

✧

Reflections from Left, Right, and Center

INTRODUCTION

Through the long 19th century, cooperation interacted with a wide range of ideologies in political economy. Much in that interaction involves critical input from thoughtful contemporaries. The earliest classical critics, for example, insist that cooperation is wholly utopian. It does not help that, as an outspoken proselytizer, Robert Owen becomes an obvious target. Already by 1821 the criticism was so widespread that the editor of the original *Economist*—the periodical dedicated to promoting cooperation— makes it a point to list and then respond to seven common objections.[1] It seems fair to summarize the early classical political economy view: the appealing world described in cooperative thought is a chimera. But these early critiques fail to seriously engage the cooperative theories of social psychology and institutions.

As the 19th century wears on, the British cooperative theorists continued to attract critical attention from the left, right, and center.[2] Most of

---

1. Based on editor George Mudie's reading, those objections to cooperation are: (1) the inability of people to cordially unite; (2) the likelihood of free riders; (3) ambition and jealousy stimulated by overseer positions; (4) the prevalence of "a dull uniformity of character" arising from moral education (275); (5) abundance-stimulated overpopulation; (6) the overthrow(!) of Christianity; and the list is incomplete without acknowledging the fear of (7) violent and/or covert political overthrow of contemporary society (Vol. I, 1821, 275).

2. Some of the first principles of economics textbooks dedicate an entire chapter to cooperation. See, for example, all eight editions of Fawcett's *Manual of Political Economy*, 1863–1907. In his version of *The Principles of Political Economy*, McCulloch includes a chapter on cooperation in the fifth edition printed in 1864 (Chapter 3 of Part III).

Building a Social Science. Kirsten Madden and Joseph Persky, Oxford University Press. © Oxford University Press 2024.
DOI: 10.1093/oso/9780197693735.003.0011

the criticism acknowledges attractive angles to the cooperative economy. As socialism splinters, cooperation receives particularly constructive criticism from the left and the center. Both highlight what works in cooperation and why. And most of the late century criticism offers insights, specifying conditions under which transitional institutions of cooperation might flourish. But almost always there is a struggle with the belief that the original sin of selfishness is not so easily overcome.

THE CLASSICAL RESPONSE
Thomas Robert Malthus

Thomas Robert Malthus (1766–1834) had a compelling need to take on cooperative thinkers. Quite simply if they are right, he is wrong. The fight was predestined. In 1798, before Owen even began to assemble his arguments for cooperation, Malthus in the first edition of his famous *Essay on Population* (1798) attacks the Enlightenment philosopher William Godwin. Godwin's thought, we know, profoundly impacted the young Owen. Malthus' father, Daniel Malthus, also embraced Godwin's thought. Malthus' *Essay* identifies that the deep motivation for the population theory is to offer an explicit answer to the optimism of William Godwin. Malthus asserts, "The substitution of benevolence as the masterspring, and moving principle of society, instead of self-love, is a consummation devoutly to be wished." Malthus was after all a clergyman. But this cannot be. According to Malthus, Godwin makes a fundamental mistake. Where Godwin traces the misery of the world to the institution of private property (Malthus 1798, Ch. 10), for Malthus human misery begins in nature and most specifically with the growth of population. Even if all other conditions of Godwin's fantasy can be established with benevolence reigning in all hearts, within fifty years Malthus predicts the direst misery and vice generated "by laws inherent in the nature of man, and absolutely independent of all human regulations" (Ch. 10). Under the circumstances, a system of private property and the institution of marriage very similar to those of Malthus' day would necessarily emerge under the pressure of scarcity. The result is inevitably the inequality so common in Europe of the early 19th century.

Cooperation also receives a chapter of coverage in textbooks produced by economists in the United States. See, for example, Richard Ely's *An Introduction to Political Economy* (1889) and F. W. Taussig's *Principles of Economics* (1911).

Given the early history of Malthus' essay, it is no wonder that as Robert Owen's ideas gained an audience, Malthus (in his third edition of 1817) expanded his range of criticism from Godwin's philosophical anarchy to Owen's system of cooperation. Now Malthus acknowledges that Owen is "a man of real benevolence, who has done much good" (1817, 274). And he appropriately credits Owen (unlike Godwin) with a deep understanding of manufacturing and management at a large scale (275).

Nonetheless, Malthus attacks. The first argument is one of incentives under the assumption of aversion to labor. The state of equality "both according to experience and theory" is unable to motivate the "exertion which can alone overcome the natural indolence of man and prompt him to the proper cultivation of the earth . . ." (1817, 276). It is here in his essay that Malthus offers his famous defense of inequality:

> A state in which an inequality of conditions offers the natural rewards of good conduct, and inspires widely and generally the hopes of rising and the fears of falling in society, is unquestionably the best calculated to develop the energies and faculties of man and the best suited to the exercise of improvement of human virtue. (277)

Malthus offers as evidence the "depressing and deadening effects" observed in every historical attempt to establish systems of equality. But somewhat curiously, here, Malthus reverses gears and allows there may be exceptions. It may be that the stimulus of inequality is needed to raise man from barbarism, but in modern times the continuation of that institution may no longer be necessary (1817, 278–279).

After this somewhat surprising speculation, Malthus returns to an echo of his attack on Godwin. He offers his second and (he thinks) conclusive argument: any system of equality necessarily generates poverty and misery because of the principle of population. Again, Malthus argues that a system of equality must evolve toward the necessary institutions of private property and marriage. Here is the old standby, without further elaboration. And surely at the time (1817) with his reputation at its height, Malthus' population argument might strike many as fundamental. But economists over time became less and less sure of the population principle. By the 1830s support for it was thin, leaving an up-to-date reader of Malthus with only the first argument, the argument Malthus himself acknowledges as doubtful. Perhaps, then the early attack by Malthus is not all that damning.[3]

---

3. The argument of this paragraph draws on Dean (1995).

David Ricardo

David Ricardo (1772–1823) was the central figure of classical political economy in the early 19th century. Where Malthus as a churchman regularly participated in discourses on benevolence, Ricardo with his background in the financial markets of the day largely dismissed such talk. Where Malthus might fondly wish for a human psychology matching the cooperative ideal, Ricardo hardly took that psychology seriously. At times Ricardo's thoughts are simply playful barbs toward Owen. For instance, in response to a letter in which James Mill explains he could not visit due to his heavy workload for the East India Company, Ricardo writes:

> The Directors must reason as Robert Owen does—he finds it his interest not to exact too much from those he employs; he finds that he gets more work done by employing them a less number of hours; by so doing, he keeps them in good heart with their energies both of body and mind undiminished. (10 August 1819, in Sraffa 2005, Vol. 8, 48)

Ricardo effectively diminishes the seriousness of Owen's labor practices in a half-joking attempt to lure his friend away from work for a visit.

And then there is a letter to Hutches Trower highlighting the common bond between the two men of growing numbers of grandchildren. Ricardo playfully juxtaposes Malthusian arithmetic against the men's common experiences with increased family sizes, and then writes: "I have some notion of consulting with Mr. Owen on the best plan of establishing one of his villages for me and my descendants, admitting only in addition a sufficient number of families to prevent the necessity of celibacy" (23 August 1817, in Sraffa 2005, Vol. 7, 177).

In other contexts, Ricardo's challenges go to the heart of early cooperative theory. In his pamphlet "On Protection to Agriculture," Ricardo discusses the implications of superabundant production in corn on total revenues. Assuming inelastic demand, an increase in supply drives revenues down in a competitive system. In his only public recognition of Owen's villages, Ricardo then completely dismisses the serious analysis underlying cooperative superabundance with the following quip:

> If we lived in one of Mr. Owen's parallelograms, and enjoyed all our productions in common, then no one could suffer in consequence of abundance, but as long as society is constituted as it now is, abundance will often be injurious to producers, and scarcity beneficial to them. (1822, 223)

More substantially, when in Parliament he was nominated to sit on a committee evaluating Owen's plans for the poor, Ricardo writes to Hutches Trower:

—Can any reasonable person believe, with Owen, that a society, such as he projects, will flourish and produce more than has ever yet been produced by an equal number of men, if they are to be stimulated to exertion by a regard to the community, instead of by a regard to their private interest? Is not the experience of ages against him? He can bring nothing to oppose to this experience but one or two ill-authenticated cases of societies which prospered on a principle of a community of goods, but where the people were under the powerful influence of religious fanaticism. (8 July 1819, in Sraffa 2005, Vol. 8, 45)

Here Ricardo takes a standard classical tack, dismissing Owen's argument that character can be formed to motivate toward the commonweal. For the commercially minded Ricardo, it is not rational-ethical education, but only fanatical religion, which generates any such empirical—but "ill-authenticated"—evidence.

What most rattles the laissez-faire theorists is the cooperative claim of superabundance. Certainly Owenite communities, rather than raising productivity, in fact greatly reduce productivity. The trope becomes the core of the classical argument against cooperation. For example, as early as October 1819 Robert Torrens writes a review of Owen's early works for the *Edinburgh Review* which takes issue with the claims of abundance.[4]

Robert Torrens

The adult life of Robert Torrens (1780–1864) unfolded in an eclectic career that includes military service, publishing, and a central role in administering Australian colonization. Amid these activities, he emerged as a classical economist of the first rank, credited as one of the four classicists to rediscover the law of diminishing returns.[5] Torrens' thought also demonstrates an early understanding of the theory of comparative

4. There is some controversy regarding who is actually the author of the article, McCulloch or Torrens. A short piece by de Vivo (1985) provides additional evidence to suggest Torrens is the author.

5. The other three are Ricardo, Malthus, and West, all around 1815. Turgot usually receives credit with the first clear statement of the law in 1765. (See, for example, Landreth & Colander 1989, 91).

advantage and contributes to the development of the theory of the terms of trade.[6] Torrens' critique of Owen was strongly endorsed by David Ricardo (1821, 163–164).

Starting with the usual acknowledgement of Owen's sincerity as a reformer, Torrens finds Owen's approach to political economy totally misdirected. For Torrens, Owen's cooperative solution of creating largely self-supporting villages simply cannot work. Torrens predicts that productivity in these villages will be much lower, not higher than in Britain at large. For example, any effort to expand agricultural output must accept the diminishing returns to land so central to the classical understanding of political economy. Mr. Owen does not demonstrate that the villages' instruction and moral training alters "this essential property of the soil" (Torrens 1819, 465). Whether at the extensive margin or intensive margin, additional farming effort can only result in reduced average productivity. Even more devastating, there is a very rudimentary division of labor in a largely self-sufficient village. In a Smithian thematic, Torrens emphasizes that productivity growth fundamentally rests on the division of labor and the size of the market. Autarchy throws out "the great principle which multiplies the effective powers of industry" (468). It is equivalent to destroying all the means of commerce.

> What should we think of the person who should propose to increase wealth of the country, and to give uninterrupted employment to the plough and the loom, by breaking up our roads and destroying our canals, by obstructing our rivers and closing our ports, by everywhere intersecting the country with impassible mountains? But Mr. Owen's project for penning up the population in quadrangular villages, and causing each village to consume its own productions, is in effect the same. (467)

Torrens admits his predisposal "to approve his [Owen's] experiments in education and moral training" (469). But Torrens nowhere discusses any possible connection between Owen's insights about the underlying social psychology and the enhancement of productivity. Indeed, without argument he asserts an inability "to discover any conceivable relation or connexion between his [Owen's] premises and his conclusions" (463). In his assertion, Torrens pays no attention to Owen's substantial success at raising productivity in the New Lanark Mill precisely on the basis of "education and moral training." For Torrens the great discovery of classical

6. But see Ruffin (2005) on "Debunking a Myth: Torrens on Comparative Advantage."

political economy is the Smithian understanding of the relation between the division of labor and productivity. As for policy, Torrens shrugs aside the cooperative idea in favor of expanding the market and plays out the classical tropes: free trade and reduced taxation.

John R. McCulloch

By mid-century the mainstream of laissez-faire economists continued their intense consideration of the cooperative project. The tone now is more pragmatic, the message is much the same. Take for example, *Principles of Political Economy* by John R. McCulloch (1789–1864). In the first edition (1825), McCulloch makes no mention of Owen or the cooperative movement. In the fifth edition (1864), he interestingly pairs cooperatives in a chapter that also discusses the emergence of the joint-stock companies. McCulloch remarks that the critical shortcoming of producer cooperatives is their low quality of management. In the cooperative, the power of the workers always restrains management and compromises its hiring and supervising activities. The result: the ruin of many establishments. In sum,

> work-people have neither time nor opportunities for making themselves acquainted with the knowledge required in the conduct of great joint stock associations; and it is idle to expect that establishments over which they have a control should be able to maintain a successful competition with establishments managed by individuals wholly devoted to the business, and having their fortune and position in society dependent on the skill and economy with which they carry it on. (1864, 367)

Workers are better off if they avoid such risks and place any small savings they accumulate in "safe, convenient, and profitable places of deposit" (367).

As to consumer cooperatives, they surely must learn that competition reduces retail profits to the same normal level achieved in all industries, and there is little to be gained by the cooperatives. The consumer cooperatives work on ready cash, and McCulloch argues any consumer dealing with "respectable retail tradesmen" on the same basis obtains efficient service and competitive prices with no risk. It is perhaps worth noting that McCulloch's own political economy says little about the structure of "unrespectable" tradespeople. In any case, McCulloch's treatment of consumer cooperatives suggests a grudging respect.

REFLECTIONS FROM THE LEFT

For much of the 19th century, the political economy of the British working class was the political economy of cooperation. But over time British socialists replaced such cooperative visions with plans of nationalization and centralized socialism. In the process Marx, Engels, and the Fabians offer significant commentary on the cooperative positions.

Karl Marx and Frederick Engels

Key to this shift is the new socialism of Karl Marx. Marx's attitude toward worker cooperatives is complex. His conflicts with various anarchist and syndicalist elements in the First International hinged on their hostility to central planning and nationalization of the means of production. Similarly, his 1847 critique of Proudhon, *The Poverty of Philosophy*, attacks the French anarchist's utopian outlook in endorsing freestanding cooperatives (1847). Proudhon, as much as Mill, anticipates that cooperatives could grow up within the capitalist market structure. Marx of course insists that for workers to achieve their class goals they must intensify the struggle with the bourgeoisie and eventually institute some form of central planning, a program many supporters of cooperatives strongly oppose.

The *Communist Manifesto* expresses noteworthy ambivalence toward cooperatives, where Marx and his coauthor Frederick Engels devote one short section to the "Critical-Utopian Socialism and Communism" of Owen, Saint-Simon, and Fourier. Marx and Engels comment favorably on elements of the early socialist programs. In particular, the socialists foresee the antagonism building between the working and capitalist classes at an early stage in its social expression. They appropriately take the side of the working classes. And their critiques of capitalist institutions—the property system, the wage system, the family structure—"are full of the most valuable material for the enlightenment of the working class" (Marx & Engels [1848] 1969, 33).

But ultimately, Marx and Engels derisively criticize the early cooperative thinkers and their disciples due to "their fanatical and superstitious belief in the miraculous effects of their social science" ([1848] 1969, 33). The works of the early cooperative visionaries are rife with problems from the standpoint of Marx and Engels. Critical Utopians like Owen cognize the starting point of a historical dialectic process yet to unfold, but ultimately serve as a reactionary force. They inappropriately objectify the suffering of the working classes, effectively infantilizing that population. Considering

"themselves far superior to all class antagonisms," they falsely presume the fantastical "new social science" of their imaginations is more powerfully adept at sweeping away the problematic conditions than historical forces (32). While initially revolutionary in understanding, the cooperative movements devolve into mere reaction, effectively anesthetizing the transformative class struggle. In order "to realize all these castles in the air, they are compelled to appeal to the feelings and purses of the bourgeois" and problematically oppose political action of the working classes (33).[7]

Whatever Marx's early criticisms, his later thought suggests a softening in his attitude toward the cooperative form of organization. As argued by Bruno Jossa, there are a "number of passages in which Marx explicitly extolled the cooperative movement . . ." (2005, 4).[8] Marx's 1864 Inaugural Address of the Working Men's International Association lavishes great praise on producer cooperatives:

> there was in store a still greater victory of the political economy of labour over the political economy of property. We speak of the co-operative movement, especially of the co-operative factories raised by the unassisted efforts of a few bold hands. The value of these great social experiments cannot be over-rated. By deed, instead of by argument, they have shown that production on a large scale,

7. Modern commentators are critical of Marx and Engels' labeling Owen's thought as utopian. For example, Gregory Claeys writes, "Given Owen's adherence to a stadial conception of history derived from the Scottish writers and similar in many respects to some of Marx and Engels' later views, for example, it is manifestly an exaggeration to argue that the Owenites . . . believed that socialism . . . 'had only to be discovered to conquer the world by virtue of its own power'" (1989, 8, 320). Claeys goes on to argue the essential continuity between the Owenites and the Marxists. This position is supported by Owen's deep materialism and his emphasis on the potential of super-abundance made possible by the Industrial Revolution (See Chapter 2 of this volume). Claeys concludes that the terms "utopian" and "scientific" socialism are best replaced with the "less absolute separation into early and later socialism" (320).

8. Bruno Jossa builds the case that Marx's broader works point to a specific type of worker cooperative, the labor managed firm (LMF), as the basis for a future mode of production (2012, 822; 2012a, 402–403; 2015, 648). The LMF is a worker-centered democracy which relies on loan capital for investments (not worker-based financing). While its means of production are typically publicly owned, the LMF determines the distribution of surplus after paying interest on loans (see 2012a, 824–825 for more detailed description of the LMF). As Jossa argues, the LMF is the institution to trigger a revolutionary change in the mode of production due to its reversal of the capital–labor relation (2012a, 404–406). In capitalism, "capitalists or their representatives hire workers, pay them a fixed income (the wage rate) and appropriate the residual (the firm's profit); in the democratic, cooperative, or self-managed firm, workers (or their representatives) 'hire' capital (capitalists), remunerate it at a fixed rate of interest and appropriate the residual" (2012, 825). Through the LMF, this revolution can be peaceful (833); in Jossa's reading, Marx and Engels do not hold violence as necessary (834n).

and in accord with the behest of modern science, may be carried on without the existence of a class of masters, employing a class of hands; that to bear fruit, the means of labour need not be monopolized as a means of domination over, and of extortion against, the labouring man himself; and that, like slave labour, like serf labour, hired labour is but a transitory and inferior form, destined to disappear before associated labour plying its toil with a willing hand, a ready mind, and a joyous heart. (Marx 1864, 11, as quoted in Jossa 2012b, 402)

Cooperative productive successes establish the feasibility of worker-led production on a large scale: associated labor can effectively both own capital and take on management.

And yet, consider Marx's qualified comments in Volume 3 of *Capital*:

The co-operative factories of the labourers themselves represent within the old form the first sprouts of the new, although they naturally reproduce, and must reproduce everywhere in their actual organisation all the shortcomings of the prevailing system. But the antithesis between capital and labour is overcome within them, if at first only by way of making the associated labourers into their own capitalist, i.e., by enabling them to use the means of production for the employment of their own labour. (Marx [1894] 1967, 440; quoted in Jossa 2005, 5)

While cooperative factories are early examples of a new force of production and within their walls they are rid of the capital–labor conflict, nonetheless the factories cannot help but to continually reproduce the defects of capitalism. As we shall see in Beatrice Potter Webb's critique below, producer cooperatives could tend to succumb to the search of profits.

Whatever Marx's ultimate understanding of cooperatives, the growth of a British socialist movement in the last decade of the 19th century set up a tension between those continuing to advocate cooperative organization and those anticipating a broader system of national planning.

Beatrice Potter Webb and Sidney Webb

Beatrice Potter, later Beatrice Webb (1858–1943), and her husband Sidney Webb (1859–1947), both of the Fabian movement, most clearly demonstrate the tension just described. Interestingly, the Fabians claim to carry on the traditions of John Stuart Mill (Webb 1889, 58). They advocate a radical reformist program in favor of national ownership of industry that eschews violent revolution. It would be natural to expect them to strongly endorse Mill's program of producer cooperatives. Yet in 1891 when Beatrice

Potter published her study, *The Cooperative Movement in Great Britain*, while applauding consumer cooperation, she takes a hostile position to producer cooperatives, perhaps more hostile than that of Marx himself.

Though lacking strong formal academic credentials, Beatrice Potter was very much involved in the economics of her day. From a well-off Unitarian family, she worked closely with her cousin Charles Booth (1893) on his notable research into London poverty, publishing as *Life and Labour of the People in London*.[9] She became an authority on dock workers.[10] Around this time, Beatrice began to write her sole-authored monograph on the cooperative movement.[11]

Unlike many of the other critics, this early work by Potter recognizes the importance of social psychology, as it supports the institutions of cooperation, titling Chapter 2 "The Spirit of Association." Her take underscores social, moral, and political angles. She documents the first forms of democratic association in response to the early "dark days" of the Industrial Revolution (1891, 37–38). Exploitative labor conditions somewhat unexpectedly stimulate "a new spirit of fellowship . . . leavening the common lump of men, and initiating an intellectual and moral fermentation" (38). Potter repeats George Holyoake's claim that cooperative success depends on the moral obligations and moral conduct of its members. While she identifies differences across societies concerning what precisely defines moral conduct, she captures the general spirit from a phrase adopted by the cooperative Warrington Society: "They helped every one his brother, and every one said to his brother, 'Be of good cheer'" (46). She makes an important link between social psychology and institutions, inferring that when fellowship abounds, the atmosphere is generally ripe for the introduction of democratic self-government into cooperative industry (180).

In response to early industrialization, many forms of "democratic association" arise. Among the manifold forms that Potter highlights, the cooperative movement adds the Owenite "high ideal of communal life, a tenderness for vested rights, a conception of social service and social welfare wide enough to include honest citizens of all ranks" (1891, 39).

Potter then goes on to specify the core characteristics of a highly functioning democracy, particularly: careful selection by the majority of its representatives who are to embody "energy, enthusiasm and integrity

9. Booth's work ultimately extends over multiple volumes.
10. Potter first published her insights on dock workers in the *Nineteenth Century* magazine (1887).
11. Interestingly, she talked extensively with Alfred Marshall on her plan. Marshall discouraged her, suggesting instead that she focus on women's labor (Groenewegen 1995, 518).

for public service"; watchful, albeit trusting and generous oversight of those representatives by the general population; and, importantly, that each cooperator abides "loyally by the decisions of the majority; without this initial self-subordination no democratic society is possible" (1891, 36). Cooperatives succeed or fail to the extent that they accept or deny these essential principles of democratic self-governance (39). For all his virtues, Potter reflects on Owen's primary downfall: "He had not grasped the significance of Democracy . . ." (31).

Like other critical enthusiasts, Potter expresses the concern that the population as a whole is unready for cooperation. She carefully qualifies that this lack of readiness is due to "present social conditions" (1891, 235). "Poverty and irregular habits" constrain the worst off to remain below "the social plane upon which voluntary association becomes possible" (226). She also enumerates a detailed list of characteristics among the upper and middle income classes making them unsuitable for association, including the love of personal possessions, general indifference bred by luxury, and the expectation of silent subservience by servants (227). Given the social conditions associated with competitive capitalism, only the working "intermediate class neither too poor nor too wealthy" exhibit the social psychology required for effective cooperation (232).

Against this background, Potter expresses optimism about consumer cooperatives.[12] Importantly, she applauds the federalist Wholesale Society for staying wedded to the core characteristics of democracy. Overall, she accepts the federalist consumer cooperative system as an important partner to trade unions.[13]

---

12. Among Potter's social circles at the time, there were dissenters. Herbert Spencer, who was one of many visitors to Potter's childhood home, read Potter carefully. He concludes the consumer cooperative movement is not truly cooperative at all. "When they appointed paid servants, the members became wholly, as they were from the beginning mainly, associated consumers, adopting an economical method of supplying themselves." They "have what they purchase at cost price plus the actual cost of distribution—the cost of shop rent, wages, and interest on capital" (Spencer 1898, 565).

13. Potter is against profit sharing with employees of the CWS. In her view, profit on price arises from identifying output markets and "securing a large margin" between buying and selling prices (1891, 160). Where the federalist system extends backwards into production, it purchases inputs to produce for use by its consumer members, not for broader exchange (96). In consumer cooperation, "the market is secured" (97). Thus, there is no profit for the CWS and no profit to share with CWS labor. Writing with Sidney Webb thirty years later, the two repeat this argument (Webb & Webb 1921, 185–186). They summarize in blunt terms, there is no point in "sharing with the [CWS] employees a "profit" which it is the very object of the Co-operative society to eliminate" (187). In both books, all arguments support trade unions as the core institution to represent labor interests.

But, when it comes to producer cooperatives, Potter is highly critical of their record and damning of their prospects. The lengthy chapter on producer cooperatives is scathing. The Christian Socialists at mid-century put forward a "fair vision of a brotherhood of workers." That vision vanishes "into an indescribable industrial phantom." A third of the establishments are nothing more than profit sharing schemes. The majority of the "so-called associations of workers are constantly resolving themselves into associations of small masters—into an industrial organization, which is perilously near, if it be not actually included within the domain of the sweating system" (1891, 147–148).

In more detail than any mainstream economist, Potter identifies three reasons for "this dismal record of repeated failure." They are:

1. "Want of capital" (149). Insufficient capital forces cooperative producers to buy inputs in expensive small lots and to purchase inferior machinery. When borrowing, the cooperatives must pay high interest rates. The result must be low wages, increased effort, or bankruptcy. Producer cooperatives are anachronistic, ignoring the industrial revolution, mass capital, and scale industries (168). Marginal activities are their only domain.

2. "Want of custom" (149). The producer cooperatives are "frequently based on the old fallacy of the Labour Exchange; they form under the delusion that with industry and skill the worker must create value, whether or not the commodity he manufactures corresponds to any available demand" (151).[14] Cooperatives typically set up during depressions or in dying industries. "These associations are foredoomed to failure" (152).

3. "Absence of administrative discipline" (149–150). There is no possibility of order if the workers can constantly question the managers. As a result, in practice producer cooperatives subvert their own constitutions. Through any number of "ingenious and elaborate devices . . . the working shareholders are stripped of their ordinary rights as property-holders and are disfranchised from active participation in the government of the concern in which they work." In the end the firm faces a "reversion to the purely capitalist organization of industry" (153).

14. Earlier in her book, Potter traces the disregard of demand within cooperative thought to William Thompson. It takes the abandonment of Thompson's labor theory and adoption of "sound economics" by the cooperative stores and wholesalers to bring about economic success (1891, 49).

Potter goes on to speculate that even if producer cooperatives could grow and prosper, they would likely seek monopolistic power just as readily as more traditional firms. Cooperatives embedded within competitive capitalism tend to revert to profit seeking just as avidly as capitalists themselves, bringing about "all the lower passion of human nature" (155). Particularly problematic for the integrity of cooperation is participation in international trade. She declares that when cooperators explore that trade they "taste the forbidden fruit of industry—profit on price" (231).[15]

Ultimately Potter traces the contribution of cooperative thought not so much to its economics, but more to its creation of the conditions for democratic self-governance. She concludes:

> the nation at large must possess those moral characteristics which have enabled Cooperators to introduce democratic self-government in to a certain portion of the industry, commerce, and finance of the nation. It is, therefore as moral reformers that Co-operators pre-eminently deserve the place in the vanguard of human progress. (1891, 239–240)

Producer associations are not the way to go as they simply add "to the economic helplessness of two hundred" workers "the moral difficulty of association" (168). It is the moral reform within the consumer cooperative movement that supports true democracy.

Whereas Potter's background was that of privilege, Sidney Webb was purely middle-class, his father an accountant and his mother a shopkeeper. As a young man, Sidney Webb worked while attending evening classes. He also taught at the London Working Men's College. After Bernard Shaw introduced him to the Fabian Society in 1885, Webb began his long-term involvement with the organization. His first major Fabian contribution comes in the form of *Facts for Socialists*, published in 1887.

15. The later view of Beatrice and Sidney Webb on international trade is far more visionary: if the CWS

of one nation becomes a member of the Co-operative Wholesale Society of another nation, with representation according to its purchases, we merely extend the Co-operative movement beyond the limits of our own community and include within the circle of the open democracy all the races that are within the organisation of purchasers! To put it paradoxically, there ceases to be, within that enlarged circle, any export trade, in the sense of commodities that are sent away to be sold in another country in order to extract profit out of alien purchasers. Thus we may gain a vision of the whole of the international transmission of commodities being managed as imports by interlocked communities of consumers, without any toll of profit to the capitalist trader or banker, and without any opportunity either for loss or profit in the mercantile sense. (Webb & Webb 1921, 289)

Potter met Webb in 1890, and the two married in 1892. Her inheritance provided the material support for both to engage full-time in scholarship and politics, pushing for social reform. They are coauthors of *The History of Trade Unionism* (1894) and *Industrial Democracy* (1897). These two key institutions remain central in all their thinking about political economy, including in their joint consideration of *The Consumers' Co-operative Movement* (1921).

As in Potter's first book on cooperation, the Webbs maintain a negative stance regarding producer cooperatives, instead endorsing trade unions. An entire chapter critiques the Cooperative Union, established in 1872.[16] As the Webb's convey, in the 1870s the term cooperation applied to a broad amalgamation of organizations, including worker associations, savings clubs, profit sharing capitalist enterprises, and consumer cooperation. Thus, the Cooperative Union adopted a broad definition of cooperation as the "formula of 'conciliating the conflicting interests of the capitalist, the worker, and the purchaser, through the equitable division among them of the fund commonly known as profit.'" But 50 years on, the Webb's declare:

> this definition has passed into obsolescence. It has become more and more clear that, whatever the word Co-operative may at different times have been used to cover, the Co-operative Movement to-day is essentially one of associations of consumers, founded on the idea of production for their members' own use instead of for exchange, and consequently not sharing, but altogether eliminating, "the fund commonly known as profit." (Webb & Webb 1921, 156)

The Webbs continue to express enthusiasm for the British federalist consumer cooperative system. They particularly highlight its adherence to and extension of democratic principles among the working classes. The *Consumers' Co-operative Movement* (1921) intentionally highlights the weaknesses of consumer cooperation—but only to strengthen it (vi–vii). Chapter 5 compiles and comments on roughly 20 "remediable defects and shortcomings" of the British consumer movement (291). The economic and political shortcomings covered here are those with deeper or novel insights.

This second monograph on cooperation offers relatively scant explicit recognition of the centrality of cooperative social psychology. But the Webbs do repeatedly acknowledge the problems that arise from narrow

---

16. Recall that E. V. Neale served as General Secretary of the Cooperative Union in 1873 (see Chapter 6).

self-interest. One such example is the hunt for the highest div among consumers. As the Webbs understand it, the higher div typically derives from higher prices charged on goods. Following common thinking at the time, they recognize the stimulus to working-class savings from a high div (1921, 295). Their concern is not the high div, but rather the high output prices that are necessary to obtain that high div. Those high prices discourage lower income class membership (296–297).

In advancing individual property, the payment of a div also problematically reduces common property holdings (1921, 297). In contrast they identify "nothing but good from the growth of such a feeling of Co-operative fraternity . . . to appropriate an appreciable part of the divisible surplus not only to 'Education,' but also to other common needs" (298).

The Webbs also carefully consider the issue of "cooperative deserts." There are geographic cooperative deserts and social cooperative deserts. Consumer cooperation does not reach the poorest, the casual laborer with irregular income, or most of the young unmarried men and women of the working classes. And cooperation has little appeal for those of the upper-middle and upper income classes. The cooperative deserts are economically problematic because they reduce the potential growth from economies of scale so paramount to the success of the wholesale societies. Redistributive taxation is the primary recommendation to reduce the upper income desert. Missionary work might serve as a solution for the desert of the poorest. And the Webbs strongly encourage the cooperative movement to ferment cooperation among young adults by establishing youth-appealing hostels, restaurants, and a variety of social clubs (1921, 312–318).

Given the local and voluntary initiative driving the establishment of cooperative societies, there is also the "disease of overlapping" cooperative societies, with competition for members and sales the leading symptoms (Webb & Webb 1921, 321). While the Webbs acknowledge the valuable role competition plays among capitalist retailers as a "substitute for honesty," the "internecine warfare" across mostly honest cooperative retailers is simply "wasteful and socially injurious" (322). Overlapping cooperative societies cause unnecessary duplication in capital, management, and advertising (69). And overlapping societies tend to devolve into a "progressive pandering to the ignorance or to the economic weakness of the customers," one society going lax on credit, another succumbing to the temptations of a higher div or lower prices, "to the eventual disadvantage of all alike" (68).[17]

---

17. And at least in some cases, these overlapping small societies succumb to competitive pressures, tending toward problematic employment conditions (Webb & Webb 1921, 69n).

Competition among overlapping and precarious transitional societies can undermine the social psychology necessary to fuel the system.

None of the economic problems are damning for consumer cooperation, so long as each resolves. Turning to their political concerns, the Webbs consider apathy the "gravest remediable shortcoming" (1921, 305). The evidence indicates that a mere 2–5% of members attend meetings; typically, they are the biggest shareholders, former management, or cooperative employees attempting to shape policies toward their own interests (49). Ninety-five percent of members do not bother to vote in their societies' management committee elections (51). Beyond the lack of political participation and across rural and urban societies, the Webbs report not a single society in which more than 5% of its members actively engage in the social and intellectual life, even though such engagement is "so much clear gain to the community . . . . It is here that the Co-operators have most fallen short of the hopes and aspirations with which the Movement began" (84–85).

Given the facts, it is curious that the Webbs highlight cooperation as a mecca of democratic participation. They clarify it is the "free association of autonomous democracies in free and autonomous federations" that serves as the major contribution "to the art and science of democratic organisation" (1921, 179–180). Here the consumer cooperative system exhibits many signs of democratic health. The elected representative assembly is an effective oversight for the executive (59–65; 118–119). Quarterly meetings enhance information flows from the representatives to the directors. There is organizational transparency. And as the Webbs see it, consumer cooperatives tend to select delegates who conscientiously represent the interest of their constituents (125).

In an age of growing economies of scale, the Webbs support the consumer cooperative tendency toward professional, specialized, and salaried management positions (1921, 334). But problems of favoritism, nepotism, and bureaucracy arising in organizations of any scale with task specialization (327–328; 332–333) are endemic. There are two offsets to these problems. Voluntary cooperative membership reduces the likelihood of a tyrannical bureaucracy (334). And highly qualified members in the representative assemblies serve as vital controls on the executive (337).

Finally, the Webbs both raise and respond to the stereotype of cooperation as unimaginative. Quoting from an "ardent revolutionary of a younger generation":

> The main failure of Co-operators is psychological: they are devoid of artistic taste; they lack intellectual distinction; they are keen on a certain rough genuineness of quality, but they are blind to the supreme importance of excellence,

alike in the wares they produce, in the ways in which they pack and display these wares, in the recruiting of their staffs, and in the character of the enterprises that they undertake—in fact, where the Co-operative Movement most seriously falls short, is in its lack of imagination. (as quoted in Webb & Webb 1921, 373)

In defense of cooperation, the Webbs suggest that this ardent revolutionary exaggerates and even exhibits "a certain poverty of imagination" (377). Lower incomes for most consumer cooperators do reduce education access, keep dormant the seeds of elevated taste, and make unaffordable high quality output. But the critic misses that, out of their sense of social responsibility, cooperators creatively redress practical barriers to success, such as identifying and reducing cooperative deserts (375). The critic also appears unaware of the expanding intellectual horizons across thousands of cooperators (376).

Nonetheless, cooperation does frequently fail "in vision and in prevision" with many cooperators unaware of "higher standards and nobler values than those within their ken" (1921, 379). The obvious solution to the poverty of imagination: reinvigorated cooperative education. Here this reinvigorated education is one which de-links from cooperative propaganda, increases financing and organization of education, and reinforces cooperative principles (36–39).

The Fabian Society accepts Beatrice and Sidney Webb's endorsement of consumer cooperation and their rejection of producer cooperatives. Instead of producer cooperatives, the Fabian Society promotes national ownership and administration of industry. The alternative Fabian "road" toward radical reform, which the Webbs are so instrumental in building, includes economic and political alliance between trade unions and consumer cooperatives, pushing toward a worker class-centered socialism.

REFLECTIONS FROM THE CENTER: ALFRED MARSHALL

At the turn of the 20th century, the neoclassicist, Alfred Marshall (1842–1924), was the very embodiment of mainstream economics. Yet cooperation also attracted Marshall's interest. Marshall's work acknowledges John Stuart Mill's influence on his thinking vis-a-vis cooperatives. He also gives credit to Mill's wife Harriet Taylor in this regard (Marshall [1873] 1925, 101). In one of his first efforts, Marshall quotes from Mill and Taylor's discussion of cooperatives.[18]

---

18. Peter Groenewegen emphasizes the connection to Mill (1995, 455).

Marshall is also well aware of the chapters on cooperation written by Thornton.[19]

Throughout his academic writing, the idea of cooperatives appeals to Marshall, the reformer and moralist. Even in *Principles* Marshall idealistically dreams:

> If competition is contrasted with energetic co-operation in unselfish work for the public good, then even the best forms of competition are relatively evil; while its harsher and meaner forms are hateful. And in a world in which all men were perfectly virtuous, competition would be out of place; but so also would be private property and every form of private right. Men would think only of their duties; and no one would desire to have a larger share of the comforts and luxuries of life than his neighbours. Strong producers could easily bear a touch of hardship; so they would wish that their weaker neighbours, while producing less should consume more. Happy in this thought, they would work for the general good with all the energy, the inventiveness, and the eager initiative that belonged to them. ([1890] 1961, 8–9)

Beginning in 1873 through his last publication in 1919, Marshall repeatedly affirms two strands associated with the long 19th-century cooperative movement: cooperation as a social-centered movement based on selflessness and cooperation as a stimulus to the "spontaneous energies of the individual" (Marshall 1889, 227). For Marshall, the historical trajectory of cooperation in Great Britain—leading to centralized consumer cooperation—is one which cannot achieve its moral goals on a mass scale. Regarding and in contrast to Beatrice Potter's thoughts, Marshall argues that, beyond education, it is primarily cooperative production that facilitates ethical transformation.

The "The Future of the Working Classes" highlights work as a fundamental human character-shaping institution. Here Marshall envisions a "supposed country" with the shaping of "gentlemen" as a primary social goal. Marshall argues that thorough, long-lasting education is imperative to attain well-rounded human development and its substantial social returns (1873, 118).[20]

---

19. In response to a request early in 1875 for references on cooperation, Marshall asserts that Thornton provides "the best account of it on the whole" (Marshall 1996, 30). See Chapter 4 for a discussion of Thornton's insights.

20. Marshall goes so far as to declare education as a social duty with the failure to educate warranting punishment "as a form of treason against the State" (1873, 114).

But education alone is insufficient. "Work, in its best sense, the healthy energetic exercise of faculties, is the aim of life, is life itself" (Marshall 1873, 115). Reflecting norms obvious to Robert Owen, William Thompson, and other early cooperators, Marshall identifies the ideal work life as well compensated, moderate physical activity, stimulating the mind and creative impulses, and involving intelligent, emotionally sensitive social engagement across relatively large numbers. A roughly six-hour workday frees time for intellectual and artistic enjoyments (110). At this early juncture in his career, Marshall advocates the establishment of Taylor and Mill's labor associations, qualifying only that the success of an association depends on the education of its members (114). In the ideal work setting, "every man's energies and activities will be fully developed . . . most of their work will be a work of love; it will be a work which, whether conducted for payment or not, will exercise and nurture their faculties" (118). And thus, the community will prosper.

Decades later in 1889, Marshall gives the (largely honorary) presidential address to the 21st Annual Cooperative Congress in Ipswich. He continues to emphasize human development as the main purpose of cooperation. Among schemes for social reform, cooperation has the strongest business foundation while also the "noblest and the most aspiring" aims ([1889] 1925, 255). "Other schemes for developing the world's material resources are equally practical and equally business-like, but they have not the same direct aim to improve the quality of man himself" (227).

Given his cooperative audience, Marshall's presidential address enumerates many positive characteristics of the movement from a business standpoint. Cooperation is the only system to develop *en masse* "The Waste Product," that is, the under-capitalized skill among the working classes ([1889] 1925, 229; similarly 237). There is honesty in accounting and trade. With consumers as proprietors, products tend to high quality, and trade occurs at or near production cost. There are also "great inherent economies" of two types (232). First, cooperative retail eliminates unnecessary middlemen, does not require advertising or décor to attract customers, and there are large savings from cash only trade. Second, wholesale economies of scale exist in what is, effectively, a protected monopoly arising from voluntary customer choice for preferential dealing in a cooperative setting. Thus, by the end of the 19th century, the cooperative movement has the capacity to buy, at lowest cost, large quantities of final products for its consumers as well as of raw material inputs for its production units (235).

While much business planning for centralized consumer cooperation is sound, Marshall returns to the primary goal—human development—and

raises a red flag. Centralization does not provide sufficient opportunities for human development on a massive scale. Centralized consumer cooperation only offers broad work-centered educational opportunities for a handful of people on the central committee ([1889] 1925, 242). The overwhelming majority of consumer cooperators—hundreds of thousands of people—can only participate through occasional voting, and often on issues of relatively remote interest (241).

He asserts again that independent associations of cooperative producers are the ground source for human development. But Marshall the economist is quick to recognize their business problems.[21] He points to numerous inefficiencies arising in managing committees that are run by workers ([1889] 1925, 243). Where managers are for hire, they tend to be second-rate, particularly with respect to innovation, marketing, and responsiveness to market conditions (244–245). Where producer cooperatives experience success, it is often due "entirely to a few men, perhaps to one man, of exceptional ability, fervent and strong in the co-operative faith. And then it is constantly at the mercy of cruel Death" after which the enterprise typically converts "into a greedy joint-stock company" (246). Also, there is the constant question about capital. In an ideal setting, workers finance their own worker-owned enterprises. But in reality, most workers have little capital to contribute and scarce business savvy to effectively manage that capital (245).

Marshall ([1889] 1925) is clear that there are major problems in producer cooperatives. Nonetheless, he cheers his cooperative audience forward. Reiterating a lesson from an undergraduate math tutor, he declares that there is "'great good in trying to do those that you can't do, but that are worth doing' . . . the difficulties of non-centralised co-operative production are just those at which it is best worth while to take a long pull, and a strong pull, and a pull all together" (246). So how to move forward? Marshall provides numerous recommendations.

Producer cooperatives are flexible organizations which can learn from their management errors and adapt. Marshall advocates rethinking management by a full workforce committee; instead, bring outsiders with industry expertise onto the committees ([1889] 1925, 247). Given inherent

---

21. Elaboration on some of these business weaknesses appeared a decade earlier. Published in 1879 with his wife, Mary Paley Marshall, *The Economics of Industry* distinguishes between management skills of entrepreneurship and of superintendence. Producer cooperatives tend to be weak in both. The Marshalls advocate that producer cooperatives steer clear of industries requiring substantial entrepreneurial skill and complex management (Bankovsky 2018, 55). The Marshalls also advocate workers' access to positions which might develop managerial skills (67).

management weaknesses, he advocates that producer cooperatives focus on industries which are low risk and stable, requiring minimal entrepreneurial adaptability (247–248). He argues for industry–worker characteristics matching. In Marshall's view, this means producer cooperatives should operate in industries which require "punctuality, and order, and neatness, and careful economy in matters of detail, and a steady resolute tread along a well-beaten path" (248). Given the constraints on capital, he recommends that cooperative production be set up in low capital industries; if capital intensive, the cooperative is likely to be more successful if the industry is relatively low risk (248). He also advocates differential pay. Cooperation must pay high enough to those of truly exceptional ability, so they are not siphoned away by competitors (255). Marshall also prods cooperators to balance their inclinations to mutual aid with common sense: "they must not be merciful either to wrong-doing or to incompetency" (254).

Marshall's general critique of cooperation emphasizes the problems arising from centralization and ineffective management. He recommends an interesting resolution to both. Rather than centralization, there might be a cooperative business clearinghouse to support independent cooperative production, possibly under the aegis of the Cooperative Union. Such a clearinghouse would first and foremost respect autonomy in decision-making by cooperative producers ([1889] 1925, 250).[22] The clearinghouse would be "a common centre for help and advice; serving as a channel by which any member that is in special need may receive the aid of others" (249). The clearinghouse might offer both guidance and funds. In terms of guidance, the clearinghouse acts

> as a common centre of information as to their special wants, and to warn them against pressing into a field that was already full; to take part in acquainting distributive societies with what they are doing; in acquainting them with the needs of distributive societies; in organising arrangements for depots, exhibitions, commission agents, and travellers; and, lastly, might it not act as a kind of board of arbitration and conciliation for troubles that may arise either within a society, or between it and others? (250)

In return for its financial support, the clearinghouse would nominate members onto the committees of those cooperatives which request financial aid. Comparing his proposal for board diversification to university boards,

---

22. The one qualifying requirement to independence is that the producers adhere "closely to high co-operative principle" (Marshall [1889] 1925, 250).

such nominations might include representatives from outside the enter-prise. He also advocates that such nominations draw a wide circle of rep-resentatives from within the cooperative, "and so to give to many men the opportunity of showing what they are worth as administrators . . . finding for a man who had done one task well something more responsible to go on with" (251).

In his *Principles of Economics*, Marshall develops some of these themes, but now with a stronger note of caution.[23] Cooperation does make sense in a society with "growing earnestness . . . growing intelligence" and growing means of mass communication ([1890] 1961, 25). But problematically, the historical evidence suggests people are incapable of "pure ideal altruism for any considerable time" and that "it is worse than folly to ignore the imperfections which still cling to human nature" (9). While cooperation can obviously stimulate social sympathy, in *Principles*, Marshall echoes Mill in conveying his longstanding support for competition as a stimulus to in-dependence and self-reliance (Bankovsky, 59).

Nonetheless, in *Principles*, Marshall does still highlight some benefits of producer cooperatives. Cooperatives are attractive to people who are both socially and ethically inclined, who exhibit mutual trust and confidence, and who find themselves "under the influence of various motives besides that of pecuniary gain" ([1890] 1961, 25). As workers with industry know-ledge and as "employers and masters of their own managers and foremen," cooperators can serve as a check on the honesty, efficiency, and compe-tence of its administration. There are also reduced business costs of super-intendence, for the workers' "own pecuniary interest and the pride they take in the success of their own business make each of them averse to any shirking of the work" (177).

Meanwhile, Marshall continues to stress inefficiency-generating tensions between workers and managers, noting that cooperative workers are likely to underestimate the burdens of management. The lack of com-petitive challenge might also undermine the development of coopera-tive managers' skills of alertness, versatility, and inventiveness ([1890] 1961, 177).

23. Marshall's early approval of cooperation links to his focus on community-centered ethics and human character formation (Bankovsky 2018, 52). But even here his views are complex because he appreciates the somewhat contradictory values of self-reliance and independence along with social values to promote the common weal (54). Considering the trajectory of Great Britain's cooperative movement, Marshall also questions whether consumer cooperation offers much educational opportunity to shape human character toward mutual aid (57).

As noted by Peter Groenewegen, Marshall's endorsement of cooperatives weakens through subsequent editions of his text. In a speculative mode, Groenewegen offers as one possibility that Marshall's shift in attitude might have been prompted by "taunts from some of the reviewers of the *Principles*—that he was a 'socialist of the chair'" (Groenewegen 1995, 457).[24] Whatever the truth of Groenewegen's speculation, it is clear that by the early 20th century, the major orthodox descendant of Mill still wrestles with the broader cooperative vision.

END-OF-PERIOD REFLECTIONS FROM THE RIGHT

John Ruskin

The cooperative idea also wins attention from the right. Rather than dismiss cooperation, a few writers attempt to find a reactionary compromise with the morality emphasized in cooperative literature. In the mid-19th

---

24. Groenewegen is here quoting the *Observer*, 24 August 1890. In a sweeping critique of the moralism in Marshall's 1889 presidential address to the "Congregational [sic] Congress at Ipswich," *The Economist* (1889, 759) might also hold some responsibility for stimulating Marshall's shift in attitude. While agreeing wholeheartedly with Marshall that cooperative distribution is one of resounding business success due to sound business-making principles, *The Economist* (not to be confused with George Mudie's 1821–1822 *The Economist* cooperative periodical) bristles at Marshall's "sentimental tone" for obscuring his valuable economic insights. True to their individualist faith, *The Economist* declares unambiguously, "we do not see where the self-sacrifice comes in." Cooperation "is based on intelligent self-interest" as expressed in governance, in the sharing of profits, in the div, and even in the penchant for honesty in trade. Cooperation is simply thousands of people with the common sense to understand that combined purchases of wholesale leather for the making of boots will get them good cheap boots. In other words, cooperation has no special claim as a force for social regeneration. Applying economic principles to their logical conclusion, *The Economist* foresees:

> Some co-operators dream a dream of co-operative society growing so large as to monopolise business, but supposing that dream realized, business would be badly done. Everybody would grow lazy, the goods would deteriorate in quality, as they do under Protection, prices would become larger, and by-and-by some philanthropic co-operators, purely in the public interest, would be compelled to revolt and set up competition again. (June 15, 1889, 759–760)

What *The Economist* misses here is that cooperation lacks the true characteristic of monopoly. Based in pure voluntarism, its customer base can never be monopolized. Continuing with their argument: assuming the disutility of work, *the Economist* concludes that human nature "never can conquer the disposition to take its ease, and if it is to strain itself and always do its best in business or anything else, it needs a heavy whip. No whip has ever been discovered so effective as competition" (759–760). Here *The Economist* seems to miss Marshall's emphasis on the role of competition among cooperatives and between cooperatives and private businesses.

century, elements of such an effort appear in the economics of John Ruskin (1819–1900). Ruskin had longstanding ties with Maurice and the Working Men's College. Three different tracts of Ruskin's writing also contribute to the cooperative vision.[25]

Publishing initially in 1860 as four essays in *Cornhill Magazine*, Ruskin's *Unto This Last* is a scathing critique of the ethics underlying mainstream economics, with J. S. Mill's *Principles* being the primary whipping post. In his essays, Ruskin offers an alternative economy based squarely on the virtues of justice, affection, integrity, and "sense and firmness" (3). Ruskin's *Time and Tide* (1867) provides some of the additional framework for social reform based on a Platonic ideal that is directly contradictory to self-governance. Ruskin's vision relies upon explicit social stratification: wise leaders are to fulfill prescribed roles for the commonweal; workers are to earnestly fulfill the duties their leaders impose (Cook & Wedderburn, Vol. XXVII, lviii–lx). Beginning in the early 1870s, Ruskin made public appeals for leaders to step up and organize model agrarian communities based on his proposals. When no one did step up, he began a fund and called for donations to start the Guild of St. George.[26] While there is only ever partial realization toward Ruskin's Guild, his voluminous writing provides detailed guideposts for a right-leaning vision of a cooperative. Interestingly, Ruskin also inspired some on the left with the craftsman, William Morris, and Arthur Penty, a founder of Guild Socialism, as two such examples (see Chapters 9 and 10 of this volume).

Ludwig von Mises

At a theoretical level, laissez-faire economists tend to be certain that cooperation cannot work. The Austrian Ludwig von Mises is particularly hard on the Guild Socialists.[27] At root, he asserts that the decentralized guilds have no chance to stand up to the central authority. Guild Socialism leads to the same liberty-denying, centralizing tendencies as all socialism. Writing in 1922, just as the Guild Socialists entered their rapid decline, von Mises

---

25. Ruskin's complete works consist of 39 volumes, all freely available online (see Cook & Wedderburn, eds.).

26. Ruskin's appeals for leaders and for funding appear in his *Letters to the Workmen and Labourers of Great Britain*. Cook and Wedderburn provide an overview of the practical application of the Guild of St. George in the introduction to Volume XXX.

27. von Mises of course was not a British economist, but his thoughts on Socialism spread widely in Britain by Hayek and others. Moreover, his writing explicitly considers the British Guild Socialists including, in particular, G. D. H. Cole.

faults them for avoiding the reality that state taxation and planning will ultimately control guilds. Making no distinction between Cole's Commune and the State, von Mises asserts that this centralized entity will emerge with full control of the productive units.[28] The State will not

> refrain from occupying itself with the internal affairs of the guild. If it is not allowed to exercise direct control by appointing managers, and works directors, then in some other way—perhaps by the means which lie at hand in the right of taxation, or the influence it has over the distribution of consumption goods— it must endeavour to reduce the independence of the guilds to a meaningless façade. (von Mises 1922, 231)

Without such state intervention, production inefficiencies prevail. von Mises gives no credence to the social psychology underlying the thought of Cole and other Guild Socialists. He makes no attempt to address the possibility that workers might develop a more sophisticated understanding of the needs of themselves and their fellows. Quite the contrary, as suggested by Trincado, von Mises relies on "Cantillon's and Bentham's elitism in questions of entrepreneurship" (Trincado 2018, 86). Cooperatives cannot match entrepreneurs in reading the signs of the market.

von Mises focuses on the period of transition when cooperative producers and stores are in direct competition with their capitalist counterparts. He quickly dismisses producer cooperatives as a failed movement, because the number of associations was so small ([1947] 1990, 239). Cooperative store numbers are better; but in most countries, their share of retail markets was far from impressive. This despite considerable tax advantages. They simply cannot compete with private businesses. Hiding behind a rhetoric of social concern, they are not fundamentally different from the private distributors they castigate. And at their most successful, they are large and impersonal. Even there, however, they lack entrepreneurial skills and fail to attract sophisticated management. They are a drag on the economy (249–250). While cooperative thinkers muse on a transition to a "monopolistic control of the retail markets," they struggle with the "inherent inferiority of the cooperative way of business" (262).

von Mises has no interest in addressing the internal logic of a cooperative economy. That noted, he makes a telling criticism of cooperation's efforts to win market share in competition with capitalist business. He

---

28. In fairness to von Mises, earlier versions of Cole's writings give many of the later functions of the Commune to the state. But Cole insists that the state must be denied sovereignty over production (Cole 1920c, 4–8).

raises serious doubt about a transition to a cooperative commonwealth based on superior productivity.

CONCLUSION

Some of the best minds in British 19th-century economics reflected on the writing of the cooperative theorists. While many tended in the end to write off cooperation, there are critical insights worthy of serious consideration. On the right, mostly there are obligatory nods to the value of benevolence and then its compartmentalization by way of economic argument. There are more valuable challenges concerning industrial organization and questions about efficiency. But notice that in raising these concerns, there tends to be a complete disregard to any implications for human development. On the left, Marx and Engels challenge whether cooperation might ultimately serve to ameliorate rather than to transform the system in the interests of the majority. For the rest, their reflections recognize what works and why. Their recommendations often derive from careful consideration of transitional cooperative institutions. Particularly insightful is the recognition by both Potter and by Marshall of reinforcing links between cooperative institutional structure and its social psychology.

CHAPTER 12

⌒◡⌒

Reconstructions

PURPOSE

The main purpose of this chapter is to provide a reconstruction of 19th-century British cooperative theory. Before turning to that task, however, it seems useful to review the highlights in the cooperative critique of classical liberal political economy. Notice such a critique is not the same thing as an evaluation of the individual competitive (or capitalist) economy itself.[1] The cooperative theorists do both, and in both cases their critiques are damning. Their critique of capitalism provides the stimulus for developing a new economic system. Here the question is not why capitalism itself is a failure but why classical liberal political economy cannot serve as a theoretical base for building an alternative economic system.

THE COOPERATIVE CRITIQUE OF CLASSICAL LIBERAL POLITICAL ECONOMY

Cooperative theorists fault classical thought for a narrow treatment of incentives, an unacceptable disregard for workers' welfare, a failure to recognize the waste in the capitalist system, a superficial analysis of social

---

1. Note over the 19th century cooperative thinkers shift their target from "individual competition" to "capitalism." For simplicity in this chapter we use the latter term.

Building a Social Science. Kirsten Madden and Joseph Persky, Oxford University Press. © Oxford University Press 2024.
DOI: 10.1093/oso/9780197693735.003.0012

problems, and a general resistance to a historical view of capitalism. We turn to a brief consideration of each.

Incentives

The cooperative theorists consider the classical creation and acceptance of "homo economicus" a central shortcoming. This theoretical treatment of human social psychology focuses on narrow selfishness, more or less forcing an endorsement of incentives that work at that level. Too much of human nature and human behavior remains unexplored.[2] The classical approach to incentives leaves private property as virtually the only feasible institution for accumulating and managing capital. Apart from its destructive reinforcement of inequality (including gender inequality), privatization of capital constrains the diffusion of innovations. With its narrow psychology of selfishness, classical thought provides little insight into solutions for shirking. More generally, the classical focus rules out incentives based on a desire for creativity or natural social pleasures (including benevolence).

Labor

Cooperative writers are highly critical of the broad classical approval, even glorification, of the division of labor. Particularly concerning is the tendency of new machinery to reduce human labor to mindless drudgery.[3] Closely related is the classical failure to take seriously the alienation of

2. Given the emphasis on narrow self-interest, many classical sympathizers applaud that science for explicating the mechanism of the invisible hand which, they assert, is counterintuitively responsible for generating abundance from selfishness. But even under capitalism, each person also exhibits other-regarding behavior. From a cooperative standpoint, the seemingly selfish version of economic science may only work because of unacknowledged underlying currents of concert, mutual aid, and cooperation. If true, this is a radical challenge to classical liberal political economy. A challenge that was quietly pushed under the rug over the decades. Some serious 20th-century economists recognize the problem. Again, see the work of Coase (1937), Simon (1993), and Williamson (1993).

3. Ironically, a major exception is Adam Smith, the classicist credited with the discovery of the power of the division of labor. Late in the *Wealth of Nations*, Smith warns of the likely negative consequences of the division of labor for human development (see Chapter 1 of this volume).

much of the labor force. Deskilling and denial of creative opportunities for most workers intensifies that alienation. And there is insufficient attention to problems arising from gender-based occupational segregation common in the new factories. Classical economists venerate the patriarchal division of labor that relegates most women to the household. The gender-based self-effacement that can result negatively influences wage negotiations on behalf of workers. Finally, the cooperative theorists are most disparaging of the classicists' insistence that the subsistence wage represents a "natural" equilibrium for the vast majority of workers.

Efficiency

Many cooperative writers criticize classical thought for its claim that the competitive pricing mechanism is efficient in balancing production and consumption. Competitive markets do occasion general gluts. In promoting specialization among workers, classical thought ignores the difficulties of adapting from one type of work to another. Such specialization-induced labor rigidity tends to prolong business gluts. Competitive pricing also undermines quality and craftsmanship, while incentivizing negative externalities. And from the cooperative perspective, classical economists are too forgiving of many unproductive occupations including most retailers, military men, lawyers, and clergymen.[4]

Social Problems

The cooperative theorists find egregious the classical treatment of poverty and the broad acceptance of Malthusian population theory. Classical justifications for the Poor Laws are unnecessarily harsh. As to Bentham, he is simply wrong to insist that security demands the vast inequality that characterizes capitalism. Similarly problematic is the support for patriarchy and thus, the artificial dependence of women on men. This support encourages internalized oppression for many women and leaves no room for mitigation of the not uncommon abuse of women in the household.

---

4. But note the cooperative writers fully endorse classical political economy's frontal assault on the class of unproductive and parasitic landlords.

The Future

The cooperative writers perceive classical theorists as unimaginative, unable to envision the possibility of a better world. The classical endorsement of Christian principles and, in particular the Golden Rule, seems a deep hypocrisy. The cooperative thinkers also point to a noteworthy lack of historical perspective in classical thought. In that theory, it seems the selfish character of humans is writ in stone and can never change. The classical imagination is one of stasis, defining possibilities now and forever. For them, capitalism is an end-state, never to be superseded.

Such are the important critiques by the cooperative theorists. For the most part, there is no direct classical response. Our purpose here is not to outline a hypothetical dialogue or evaluate the critiques. Seldom is it enough to critique an old theory. As we hope the book shows, cooperative thought extends far beyond a critique of classical liberal political economy. The bulk of cooperative effort consists in designing a new theory to serve as a blueprint for successful cooperative economies.

INTRODUCTION TO A RECONSTRUCTION OF COOPERATIVE ECONOMIC THOUGHT

The cooperative theorists ask a radical and ambitious question: How to design an economic system that taps into benevolent motivations? Their answers anchor in their understanding of social psychology and cooperative institutions in the context of the technological dynamism generated by the Industrial Revolution.

Classical economists from Smith to Malthus have a sense of people's better nature. They do not deny that there is a benevolent side to common psychology. But they assume it is limited in practice to close relationships. It seems that margin is inactive, in effect, frozen. Owen's new social science does not begin with perfect people but people for whom there is potential at the margin of benevolence. Is it so implausible that individuals capable of extending personal concern to a few can expand that concern to the many? In theorizing this potential, the cooperative theorists make a serious contribution. At the same time, the foundations of their new social science connect to the long history of ethical thought.

To realize such a connection, the cooperative theorists are among the first in Britain to intentionally design an entire economic system. They describe institutions they think capable of eliciting, channeling, and reinforcing benevolence across the community. The cooperative theorists

attempt to demonstrate that their new system brings unparalleled material abundance, happiness, and human development. An enlarged self-interest supports these results, and these results in turn reinforce an enlarged self-interest. Their deepest and most original theorem is that the cooperative system is self-reinforcing and stable.

By the beginning of the 20th century, elements of the social science—elements meant to substantiate its major claims—remained inconsistent. Thus, here we also explore the inconsistencies in cooperative social psychology, institutional structures, and economic theorems. We identify what we consider the strongest features of the new cooperative social science. Our analytical survey becomes an exercise in clarification. It necessarily points toward some of the outstanding theoretical challenges.

SOCIAL PSYCHOLOGY

The cooperative understanding of human nature starts by postulating a set of inclinations. Like the classical theorists, they assume that human nature includes an inherent inclination to seek wellbeing. But for the cooperative theorists a desire for wellbeing is only one of a group of basic inclinations. The most important other inclinations are a love of truth and an inclination toward fellow feeling.[5]

Cooperative theorists emphasize the plasticity of human character. Plasticity means that people can be socialized in any number of ways, including contrary to basic inclinations. Even the deepest inclinations can be unwittingly suppressed, creating a type of false consciousness. None of the cooperative theorists attempt anything like a quantitative summing up of the losses associated with such false consciousness. But for all of them, living a life out of line with our inherent inclinations is deeply problematic at both the individual and social levels.

Inclinations

We turn to a brief review of the three basic inclinations and reflect on the possible suppression of each.

---

5. In addition to inclinations toward wellbeing, truth, and fellow feeling, some later cooperative theorists posit an inclination toward creativity (see Chapters 9 and 10).

Wellbeing

An inclination toward wellbeing is common to all persons. Almost all societies recognize and encourage a desire for physical wellbeing. It is difficult to imagine an educational system or a set of social institutions that could fully suppress this inclination. Cooperative theorists consider such disposition as healthy and deserving of respect. To be successful, the institutions of an economy must recognize the fundamental inclination toward wellbeing, harness it in a constructive fashion, and then actually deliver wellbeing for all the individuals in the society.

Love of Truth

Our cooperative writers claim that human nature includes an inherent love of truth. This inclination holds promise for educational systems that encourage rationality and the development of an ability to weigh honestly the consequences of actions, both one's own and others'. Experiments in progressive education, like those at New Lanark, offer empirical support for the claims. However, the love of truth can be suppressed by inauthentic institutions. Most dangerous here may be systems of factitious rewards and factitious punishments.[6] By design these are most often meant to control individuals and shape their character to the interests of one or another dominating class. Seeking such rewards and avoiding such punishments ultimately involves losing sight of the inclination toward truth.

Fellow Feeling

Like much of the moral philosophy written in the 18th century, cooperative writing often postulates an innate inclination toward fellow feeling.[7] For the cooperative theorists, this inclination can be quite broad, potentially including all people. Again, the plasticity of character development may result in a sharp curtailing of this inclination. Educational and social institutions can emphasize selfish pursuits without concern for others. Factitious systems of rewards and punishment can loom large here and undermine fellow feeling.

---

6. See Chapter 2 for William Thompson's insights on factitious returns.

7. Recall that some of our cooperative thinkers link the inclination toward fellow feeling to an underlying desire for union with God (see the coverage of the Christian Socialists in Chapter 5).

The Development of an Enlarged Self-Interest

Cooperative thought posits more than the mere existence of fellow feeling as an underlying inclination common to all. It is also possible for every human being to develop a behavior pattern of enlarged self-interest. Such a behavior pattern is central to the prospects of any voluntarily arising collective economy. How might enlarged self-interest commonly develop among people?

The first approach to the development of enlarged self-interest assumes the existence of the underlying inclinations, particularly that of fellow feeling. The assumption appears in the thought of most cooperative theorists. Given the assumption, the drawing out of that fellow feeling requires institutional structures to elicit it. For example, when an educational system builds on the love of truth and nourishes the inclination for fellow feeling, children begin to exhibit behavior patterns consistent with an enlarged self-interest. They come to regularly consider not only themselves but others as well. Other institutions across society are equally important to reinforce such behaviors over the human lifespan. In effect, this approach considers enlarged self-interest as simply a reflection of the inclination of fellow feeling in everyday activity. Remember that while all of our cooperative theorists draw on fellow feeling, they also understand that even a strong inclination can be suppressed by negative experience.

Alternatively, it is possible to sketch a different understanding about the formation of enlarged self-interest. The alternative combines the ideas of our cooperative theorists with ideas from some of their contemporaries. Instead of positing a preexisting inclination toward fellow feeling, here an associationist mechanism plays the central role.[8]

In this understanding, behavior patterns emerge from the coupling of sensory experience with their naturally arising pain–pleasure responses. Through the mind, ideas form around sensory experiences as interlinked with pleasure or pain. Stronger associations occur where pleasure (or pain) is more intense and where experiences are more frequent. Social experiences, as they tap into a more primitive awareness of pleasure and pain, are central to the drawing out of a behavior pattern of enlarged self-interest. For example, hearing another cry, a baby associates that cry with their own experiences of distress and is likely to cry. Thus, the baby begins to experience pain in sympathy with another. If education and other socialization

---

8. The approach here draws heavily on Godwin's notions of sympathy and the Hawtrey-Mill insights into associationism. See Chapters 1, 2, and 4 of this volume.

thoughtfully encourages the development of sympathy, the child rationally comes to realize that others are very much like itself. Over time, social experiences associated with pleasurable feelings (or with reductions in
pain) can stimulate and reinforce an enlarged self-interest. Of course, if
experiences fail to build on early positive associations of socialization, the
result may be a common selfishness.

In our reading of the cooperative theorists, the tendency to develop an
enlarged self-interest is overdetermined. For most of them, both approaches
stated above are implicitly invoked and sometimes confused.[9] The first approach is easily open to criticism that it virtually assumes the point to be
demonstrated. That of course does not mean it is wrong. However, we find
the second approach to be intellectually sophisticated and appealing. It
derives from the psychological understanding of that time. And we think it
continues to have relevance today.

AN INSTITUTIONAL FRAMEWORK

The cooperative economic system structures institutions to engage and
reinforce an enlarged self-interest. Recall that principled institutions are
broad social guidelines establishing presumptive expectations within a
community. Concrete institutions are specific procedures, conventions,
and arrangements, often required by principled institutions.

A variety of concrete institutions can grow out of each principled institution. Reflecting the philosophical norms arising through a century of
political tumult in Europe, the cooperative thinkers actively engage the general principled institutions of liberty and equality. Voluntarism and self-
governance are two cooperative reflections of liberty. The idea that each
person counts as one and only as one among equals is a cooperative reflection of equality. The realization of equality requires concrete specifications
in many forms including, for example, equal effort, equal access, equal proprietorship, and gender equality.

9. A third possible theoretical derivation of an enlarged self-interest draws upon
Adam Smith's *Theory of Moral Sentiments*. Assuming a basic desire for love and respect
from others, the psyche tends to develop its own impartial spectator. It is that impartial spectator which moderates self-serving behavior. Though the concept of the impartial spectator is widely available at the time among the educated, curiously, there are
no direct allusions to the impartial spectator in the cooperative writings analyzed for
this book. That written, Godwin, Owen's sometime mentor, does use the term impartial spectator, but does not explicitly link it to Smith's work (see, for example, Godwin
1793, 796).

The third clearly agreed upon principled institution is that of fellow-ship. And perhaps responding in part to the 19th-century debates with the Malthusians and the associated clamor about public assistance as the leading cause of indolence, social responsibility is importantly relevant to cooperative concerns. Since social responsibility is not innate, there is intentionality in building it. Arising through explicitly communicated expectations that each works and maintains community resources, such communication might emphasize the pleasures associated with taking in-itiative and engaging in community service. The intentional association of joy and work might also stimulate social responsibility, including where that work satisfies creative impulses toward self-expression. Highlighting the pleasures of socially useful work and stressing usefulness as a core char-acteristic of art might reinforce social responsibility. Although there is no consensus on the appropriate cooperative response to slacking, all grapple with the questions of what to do in cases of incompetence and wrongdoing.

While there is tremendous flexibility in constructing a cooperative eco-nomic system, the 19th-century British thinkers are relatively consistent in requiring all four principled institutions: liberty, equality, fellowship, and social responsibility—principles that for the most part come out of the Enlightenment. As Anna Doyle Wheeler conveys, voluntary social in-teraction as equals builds alliances, increases sympathy, and enlarges self-interest. The cooperative theorists are sure that realizing the four principled institutions in a capitalist economy is deeply problematic. The answer must be cooperation. Indeed, the entire cooperative project is to build from the ground up concrete institutions that reflect these fundamental principles.

Across the cooperative literature, education and common property stand out as the two broadest, most considered concrete institutions. Both draw heavily on all four principled institutions.

While all agree about the importance of education, there is no final word on the form of cooperative education. Robert Owen elaborates a program of rational-ethical education. The consumer cooperators lean toward an educa-tion that motivates personal discipline and social responsibility. The Women's Cooperative Guild approach is one of consciousness-raising through civic or-ganizations, particularly in support of working-class women. And William Morris stands out in his advocacy of informal, self-directed independent study, with G. D. H. Cole picking up some of those ideas. In all cases, coopera-tive education matters because it shapes human material, serving as a spring-board for the central principle of concern for others as equals to oneself.

Common property is the other key concrete institution across the co-operative theorists. Whether they are common lands, buildings, and tools of a semi-autarchic village, the consumer-owned and operated cooperative

stores with the div as the primary distribution of surplus, the worker-owned and operated production plant, or the surplus funneled into publicly available social services and amenities, the basic idea is of social security through public access. Explicitly contributing to a common stock and laying voluntary partial claims to that common stock in a socially responsible way reinforces the sense of community and its relevance to oneself.

Throughout the 19th century, there were continuous revisions of the concrete institutions designed for cooperation. And each principled institution, particularly liberty and equality, might have somewhat different weight at different times and in different contexts. This is likely in no small part due to the actual economic transformation toward full industrialization and urbanization over the course of the 19th century. The early century vision is one of semi-autarchic villages; the mid-century vision of growing scale economies with distinct economic sectors of household, workshop, and store; and by century's end, that vision shifts to fully industrialized townships. Cooperative theorists creatively architect the associated concrete institutions throughout the long century, ending with no less than a full-fledged system of bargaining among guilds, cooperatives, and councils.

Across the 19th century early and late, cooperative theorists wrestled with the extent to which the cooperative society manipulates its own members. On the path to an enlarged self-interest, the contradicting ideas of Robert Owen and F. D. Maurice are worth keeping in mind. This is the question of shaping character early on toward altruism via reasoning and experience versus encouraging mature decisions among people assumed to have free will, a central problem that continues to haunt modern efforts at socialism.

Closely related, cooperation throughout the long century failed to fully solve the problem of how to respond to those who consistently exhibit narrow selfishness. As Alfred Marshall warns, it seems unwise to expect perfection out of human material. Thompson provides the clearest explanation of false pleasures and the factitious returns that distort reasoning toward selfishness. Most cooperative theorists reflect carefully on the institutional structure to minimize selfish acts. Even so, it seems more reasonable to leave open the question of whether antipathy is innate and so to anticipate some selfishness and tension. Is a group that operates from the principle of enlarged self-interest able to maintain that stance in the face of consistently self-serving responses? Thompson anticipates that rational cooperators take into account expected negative reactive behaviors; Owen's planned cooperative villages allow excommunication; Morris also relies heavily on self-censure and light social censure. As federalized systems grow larger, as in guild socialism, this question weighs more heavily: there are many more players and thus more ephemeral social bonds.

Another major institutional debate across the century concerns the question of hierarchy. The extreme version manifests between John Ludlow and F. D. Maurice among the Christian Socialists. Ludlow anticipates the vision of guild socialism with its multiple levels of bargaining and noteworthy power at the center. Maurice insists on horizontal organization and opposes "system," seeing it as always attempting to draw good from evil.

Our understanding is that the spirit of cooperative theory, while anchored in Owen's rational-ethical education, endorses mature, well-reasoned decision-making. It takes full responsibility for consequences. It involves the ability to work with people even when they exhibit selfish behavior. It requires horizontal organization—though with full (but still voluntary) willingness to conform to temporary unfoldings of hierarchy as situations require. It is understandable that cooperative writers may see pragmatism as requiring adaptability. The question is to what extent cooperative institutions can compromise on these issues without undermining the reinforcement of enlarged self-interest.

THE THEORETICAL LOGIC OF THE COOPERATIVE COMMONWEALTH

In what follows, we attempt a reconstruction of the logic of the cooperative commonwealth, which involves a pooling of ideas across our major writers.

The Outcomes of the System

Assumptions

a. Humans have deep inclinations toward wellbeing, truth, and fellow feeling.
b. The population of the cooperative economy is characterized by enlarged self-interest.[10]
c. The cooperative economy includes the full panoply of cooperative institutions.

---

10. Notice we start with an assumption of an enlarged self-interest, but in the subsection "Feedback" below we argue that in a fully functioning cooperative enlarged self-interest will itself be continually recreated and reinforced by the outcomes of the system. Of course, such an argument doesn't address the transitional problem of achieving enlarged self-interest in the first place. On this question, see the section "Evolution of the Economic System."

Superabundance

Early on, Robert Owen argued that, under the new conditions ushered in by the Industrial Revolution, the cooperative economy can generate superabundance. Over time, many of the cooperative theorists expanded on his proposition. Multiple overlapping causes bring about superabundance. Key to the process is enlarged self-interest interacting with the major cooperative institutions. Superabundance emerges from conflict reducing fellowship in production. Superabundance reflects the readiness among self-governed workers to innovate new and labor-complementing technologies. Fellowship and equality inspire the diffusion of new knowledge and thus stimulate superabundance. Superabundance is the result of social responsibility generating rational consumption standards and allowing substantial economies of scale. Rational consumption standards also allow for large communal savings and investment. And not least of all, superabundance is possible when equality expands the labor force in productive activity. In turn, superabundance provides a material base to make possible happiness and human development.

Happiness

The second major claim across the cooperative literature is that the cooperative economic system leads to unparalleled levels of happiness for the overwhelming majority. Again, the causal pathways are multiple and overlapping. Enlarged self-interest funneled through cooperative institutions fuels happiness. Happiness is made possible by cooperative education which disentangles factitious pleasures and allows a full expression of children's love of truth. Most of the time, such education puts a check on pain-generating behavior and trains to account for the reactive behavior of others in happiness calculations. Full gender equality deeply enhances outcomes as women's happiness counts on par with men's. Interdependencies within relationships bring about multiplier effects. The institution of fellowship encourages social pleasures, pleasures which Thompson declares are reflective and contagious. Cooperative institutions also stimulate happiness in work itself. Fellowship in work serves as a school for the pleasures of sympathy and intelligence. Happiness at work results from social responsibility which normalizes industriousness; that industriousness enhances respect for work well done, thus expanding social pleasure. Happiness in work is a result of equality, as nondegenerative workplaces elicit satisfaction.

Happiness at work is a result of liberty, which elicits the pleasures of self-expression and creativity.[11]

Human Development

Cooperative theorists reason that their new economy produces tremendous gains in human development. Once again, the outcome is overdetermined. Enlarged self-interest stimulates spontaneous energy in the individual and, perhaps somewhat counterintuitively, motivates self-development. The cooperative educational system combined with an inclination toward truth fundamentally encourages human development. The cooperative workplace becomes a lively extension of the schoolroom, encouraging both rational thinking and creativity. Under such circumstances, the institution of equality plays a central role in guaranteeing a broad distribution of opportunities for human development. Equality ensures that human development cannot be limited to a small elite. And in a gender-equal system, human development is available to women as well as men. Women have equal access to all the incentives, opportunities, and outcomes. Equality generates wide investments in human capital, labor-complementing technology, and social security. Equality insists on moderation in all work processes. Such moderation frees up time and energy for leisure and self- and social development. Equality also leads to designing task variety and job switching within the economy, thus encouraging the development of a broad set of skills within each person and expanding opportunities for creativity. In addition, the institution of liberty enhances human development, as reflected in self-government and voluntarism. Self-governance facilitates the development of higher-order problem solving and social skills across the self-governed. And voluntarism stimulates reasoning.

Interplay of the Outcomes

It should be clear that the three outcomes—superabundance, happiness, and human development—are mutually reinforcing. Superabundance

---

11. In part, all these gains in happiness are purchased at the cost of disutility or pain associated in part with socially necessary work. However, the cooperative workplace is not primarily a center of disutility, given an explicit commitment to limiting such disutility. It is the goal of the cooperative economy to guarantee that on net, work itself is a positive experience for all.

of material product most obviously supports happiness from physical pleasures. Superabundance also provides a substantial surplus to apply to human development. Widely available opportunities for human development reinforce the happiness of creativity and of intellectual and social pleasures. Happiness works to incentivize producing and, hence, reinforces superabundance.

Feedback on System Stability

Assumptions

i. For most people their personal observations and experiences shape their social and economic commitments.
ii. In particular, people are likely to be more serious about and committed to a system that reverberates with their deepest aspirations for themselves and society.
iii. Rational-ethical education along 19th-century utilitarian lines attunes individuals to monitor superabundance, happiness, and human development for themselves and their community.

Outcomes Reinforce Cooperative Economy

Observing and experiencing the positive outcomes of superabundance, happiness, and human development in a cooperative setting supports the psychological commitment to society. In particular, under such circumstances, members strengthen their sense of enlarged self-interest, which plays such an important role in producing the three major outcomes. And at the same time, these outcomes blunt any doubts about cooperative institutions.

Cooperative theorists identify a multiplicity of experiences that reinforce confidence in the system. For example, experiencing material security for oneself and the larger community reinforces a commitment to equality and common property. Similarly, observing the results of social encouragement for self-expression, creativity, and innovation incentivizes commitment to cooperative education and liberty. And the experience of social pleasures arising in education and in work processes strengthens the commitment to an enlarged self-interest.

A Schematic of the Generalized Self-Reinforcing Mechanism

Our reconstruction is meant to capture the central theory of the cooperative economy as put forth in the thought of the 19th-century British writers analyzed in the current volume. They might shrink at the formalism, but we hope they would recognize its origins and acknowledge its usefulness. Figure 12.1 captures the essence of the argument. The circle on the left represents the cooperative economy with its strong interactions (*) between enlarged self-interest (ESI) and cooperative institutions (CI). Assume for the moment that there is solid enlarged self-interest across the community and established core institutions. This causes the system to produce superabundance (S), happiness (H), and human development (D), as represented by the top solid arrow in the figure.

Furthermore, as depicted on the right in Figure 12.1, the three outcomes of the system are mutually reinforcing. For example, superabundant material output (S) reinforces physical pleasure (H); high levels of happiness (H) from sharing innovations stimulates human development (D); and physically healthy and intellectually active people (D) tend to have high productivity (S).

But will the cooperative social psychology and institutions prove resilient over time? Under plausible psychological assumptions, the realization of the three highly desirable outcomes supports the very social psychology so critical to the system. And the realization strengthens the commitment to cooperative institutions and cooperative engagement. The bottom dotted arrow in Figure 12.1 depicts that support. The impressive success

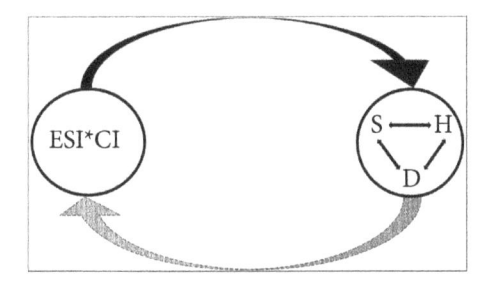

Figure 12.1 A Generalized Self-Reinforcing Mechanism in Cooperative Systems
The final state cooperative economy (circle on the left) includes enlarged self-interest (ESI) across its populace interacting (*) within cooperative institutions (CI). The top solid arrow depicts the resulting production of material superabundance (S), happiness (H), and human development (D). These three outcomes are mutually reinforcing. The bottom dotted arrow signifies that these three outcomes support the commitment to cooperative institutions and cooperative engagement.

of the system in production—in material product, happiness, and human development—leaves virtually no room for an infectious and narrow self-interest to take hold.

Criticisms and Outstanding Questions

We find the broad 19th-century argument for a cooperative economy compelling. But the common criticisms of cooperation challenge the three hypothesized outcomes of superabundance, happiness, and human development. Those criticisms predict the inevitable self-destruction of the cooperative system. The critics fail to consider the central theoretical claim that for a fully developed cooperative system, a strong self-reinforcing mechanism is at play. Nevertheless, many of the criticisms are important to reiterate with the hope of encouraging more scrutiny.

The hypothesis of superabundance has its critics. Critics deny the validity of appeal to the commonweal as an effective incentive. Critics argue the likelihood of fractured interests in self-governing production, inferring that where liberty prevails, collective action problems are likely. Critics identify the inefficiencies of job switching undertaken to stimulate whole human development. Critics question the skill set of the cooperative manager without competitive stimulus to versatility, innovation, and speed. In the case of the semi-autarchic villages, critics highlight constraints on division of labor and connective infrastructure along with diminishing returns to land. In the case of a full-fledged guild system, critics highlight the likelihood of over-regulation and bureaucratic slowdown from excessive meetings and bargaining.

Historically, the classical political economists strongly question the ability of cooperatives to generate broad happiness. Ricardo and Malthus tend to assume people are naturally indolent. If so, a system that rests on expectations of effort and responsibility is primarily going to irritate and annoy. And though no one can reasonably claim the initial village experiments in cooperation fully captured the theoretical ideals, the record suggests substantial discontent in those villages—discontent which led in turn to their fairly rapid failures.

The cooperative theorists generate much support for the hypothesis of high human development. There are also outstanding questions. The most basic is one that generally haunts 19th-century British political economy: is there a human inclination to lethargy and laziness, nonparticipation, and thus a tendency toward free riding? The cooperative theorists assume these are outcomes specific to the competitive capitalist system, but if wrong, such

foundational cracks may well bring the system down. And then there are questions of cooperative socialization. Among the first criticisms of cooperation is whether a moral education creates dull, uniform character. A variation of this question appears in the thought of economists like Marshall, questioning whether cooperative management through workforce participation can thrive in industries that require quick-witted adaptations. More generally, there is still the outstanding question of whether friendly competition is necessary to stimulate alertness, versatility, and inventiveness. Throughout his intellectual career, J. S. Mill argued to this point, with at least one of the guild socialists in agreement. And finally, there is no final word on the questions about horizontal association versus hierarchical centralization. But as centralization takes the stage in consumer cooperation, Marshall and others raise a noteworthy concern: how much does centralization deny opportunities of participation on a massive scale, with input limited to the occasional vote?

Finally, there are at least three other broad concerns that we believe lack satisfactory resolution in the cooperative literature. These are the possible persistence of antisocial behavior; the question of a desire for variety and excitement, particularly among the young; and entrenched conflicts in self-governance. For the most part, cooperative writers anticipate voluntary or compulsory separation from the community for antisocial behavior; advocate youth-appealing attractions and allowing the young the opportunity to explore other communities; and push for resolution of deep disputes through communal mitosis. All the early solutions have the potential to generate atmospheric externalities and remain problematic.

EVOLUTION OF THE ECONOMIC SYSTEM

Virtually all of the cooperative theorists address both the final cooperative commonwealth, as described in the previous sections, and the pragmatic questions of transition. The cooperative theorists uniformly recognize the dominant economic system in 19th-century Great Britain as based in a social psychology of narrow, selfish aggrandizement. The only complete overlap in desired principled institutions across the two systems is liberty. The cooperative theorists do not recognize competitive capitalism as a system based in equality, fellowship, or social responsibility. Where formal education exists, the cooperative theorists perceive it as reinforcing individualism and the pursuit of personal gain. And our theorists treat private property, along with its criminal justice support, as problematically central to capitalism.

In order for the system to evolve, there must be an unravelling of all of the noncooperative characteristics. All the cooperative theorists identify the central social psychological problem of capitalism: institutionally reinforced selfishness. Given the embeddedness of that social psychology, most of our theorists declare that the people are not yet fully ready for cooperation, lacking the moral, social, and intellectual grit to participate effectively in a highly functioning cooperative system.

No single cooperative theorist identifies the full range of associated social psychological problems in competitive capitalism. The current survey brings many to light. These problems include false pleasure-seeking in a system based on factitious rewards and factitious punishments. These problems include coerced servitude and internalized oppression. These problems include a litany of embedded disincentives to work, creative boredom, and the associated unintended consequence of free riding. Effective transition must undo them all.

In transition to a cooperative-friendly social psychology, there is a noteworthy distinction to draw across this literature between simply advocating the alignment of narrow self-interest across relatively selfish people and broadly advocating an extension at the margin of enlarged self-interest. Perhaps it is helpful to conceive of transition in social psychology along a continuum. In the initial stages of transition, profit sharing and cooperative forms of insurance are two examples of institutions that assist in aligning narrow self-interest. Civics organizations that unravel internalized oppression also play an important role early on. With evolution, further along the cooperative continuum, there is a systematic shift toward cultivating a concern for the welfare of others as equals and extending the margin of that concern. There are hints about how to do this captured in the three stories of evolution below. Ultimately, concrete institutions must evolve which reinforce social responsibility and encourage a fully enlarged self-interest based in fellowship, while building out voluntarism and self-governance.

Beyond the important problems concerning social psychology, another major issue is transitioning out of private property and inequality to common property and relatively high equality. Profit sharing might serve as one promising institution to initiate these changes, although problematically, the rights to initiate profit sharing rests heavily on the concessions of the capitalist. The bigger debate concerns the question of force. Thompson clearly argues that any meaningful cooperation cannot evolve through forced expropriation of property. For Thompson, cooperation can only evolve by means of perfect security and voluntarism. He has a point here—it seems unlikely that a genuine society-wide shift toward enlarged self-interest can flourish in any system which encourages

force, even if narrowly applied to the fraudulent and the coercive. If so, cooperatives can only attain property through voluntary contributions and through economic growth. But as the economy expands in scale and complexity, some of our later thinkers—G. D. H. Cole in particular—argue contradictorily that full transition requires some expropriation and most likely involves some violent measures. Cole is silent regarding the social psychological implications.

Across the 19th-century British cooperative literature, there are three stories that frame the evolution to a full cooperative economic system. In the first half of the century, the first focuses on obtaining start-up capital, ideally through worker buy-ins, supplemented with subscriptions, loans, and perhaps philanthropy from the middle- and upper-income classes. That capital funds the construction of an entire community from the ground up. The major benefit of this approach is that it allows for immediate and system-wide institutionalization of the principles necessary to extend the margin of enlarged self-interest. The funding of sound cooperative education plays a predominant role. Given the large upfront cost, this approach almost always requires at least partial financing from non-worker sources. Assuming no problematic outcomes deriving from those financing schemes, as the initial cooperatives experience superabundance, they invest in the establishment of new cooperative communities, and the system expands.

Haunting this first transitional story is a serious question concerning access to resources and capital, in particular. Major differences exist in the literature. Some limit the raising of capital to workers only. Worker-pooled capital is necessary, they say, to stimulate motivation, discipline, and prudence. Others accept capital from non-worker sources. While such sources of capital are expedient, each introduces fissures in the foundation-building stage of cooperation. Particularly at the start, loans introduce inequality, and donations tamper with the inducement of a sense of social responsibility. Closely related to the question of capital sourcing are questions about participatory decision-making. Typically, unequal provisioning of capital links to unequal voice in community decision-making. And of course, the effectiveness of managing that capital in transition is a key concern.

Circumventing the problem of upfront financing for a full community are two other transition stories in this literature, each beginning more narrowly in specific sectors of the economy. In the middle of the 19th century, cooperative theorists, such as J. S. Mill, Harriet Taylor, and F. D. Maurice, envision workshop-initiated transition. The transition begins either with profit sharing initiated by capitalists or through independent worker-owned and operated producer cooperatives. As the initial start-ups

realize economic success, others follow suit. If economists like Mill are correct about the falling rate of profit, ultimately ownership for all productive enterprises transfers to workers. Presumably, the expansion in workers' responsibilities and rewards are sufficient to stimulate an enlarged self-interest. Cole offers a variation on the production-centered story, which centers on labor union action and encroaching control, leading to full-scale guild structures over major industries. All these production-centered stories are silent concerning the shift in social psychology beyond the workplace, particularly in the household.

The third sector-specific transition story is that of John Watts, William Nuttall, and J. T. W. Mitchell, with strong support from Margaret Llewelyn Davies. The pragmatists here center transition on consumption through the cooperative store. As the stores prosper, they adopt a strategy of backward integration. The consumer cooperative theorists deduce from their federalist theorem that as transition proceeds, working-class families-as-consumers derive more and more of the value of their labor product. Workers become more and more comfortable in their employment and more committed to fair service. Thus, what under capitalism is a conflict of interest (between producer and consumer) becomes common ground for the initiation of enlarged self-interest. Problematically of course is the historical record of consumers hunting for the highest div. The Women's Cooperative Guild elaborates on the role that civics organizations may play to rectify transition problems associated with self-centered gain.

The last two transition stories have shared problems. Beginning in certain sectors, they risk generating only a piecemeal set of reforms. Underlying the thought of the earliest 19th-century cooperative thinkers—Owen, Thompson, and Wheeler—is an understanding of the importance of a systemwide approach. In the semi-autarchic villages, all sectors of the socioeconomic system contribute to the flourishing of enlarged self-interest. In contrast, the sector-oriented stories most often fail to appreciate the larger canvas while they respond to the demands of the marketplace. The necessity for a system-wide approach, even if incremental, is also obvious in the Women's Cooperative Guild's critiques. Their efforts at transition underscore this difficult truth. Cooperation in consumption but not in production generates contradictions. Cooperation in production and distribution with patriarchy in the household generates contradictions. Cooperative education within a cutthroat competitive system generates contradictions.

And this seems to be how the long century ends. While our book is not meant to analyze the relevance of past ideas for current day efforts at social reform, our sympathies are perhaps obvious throughout. The best educational insights of Owen and other cooperative theorists are

worthy of modern attention. In addition, we find attractive the continuing possibilities for efforts at consciousness raising, profit sharing, and encroaching control. In the current environment of a reenergized union movement, all three are worthy of careful consideration. The 19th-century theories of transition, while rich and suggestive, remain inadequately developed. The building of a full and convincing theory of cooperative transition continues as the fundamental challenge, the key to completing Owen's social science.

BIBLIOGRAPHY

Atkinson, Paul. 2012. "'Isn't it time you were finishing?': Women's Labor Force Participation and Childbearing in England, 1860–1920." *Feminist Economics* 18:4, 145–164. DOI: 10.1080/13545701.2012.725942.

Babbage, Charles. 1846. *On the Economy of Machinery and Manufactures*, 4th Ed. London: John Murray. https://archive.org/details/oneconomyofmachi00babbr ich/mode/2up.

Backstrom, Philip. 1974. *Christian socialism and co-operation in Victorian England: Edward Vansittart Neale and the Co-operative Movement.* London: Croom Helm.

Bankovsky, Miriam. 2018. "Alfred Marshall on Cooperation: Restraining the Cruel Force of Competition." *History of Political Economy* 50:1, 49–81.

Baum, Bruce. 2007. "J. S. Mill and Liberal Socialism." In *J. S. Mill's Political Thought: A Bicentennial Reassessment*. Nadia Urbinati and Alex Zakaras, eds. Cambridge: Cambridge University Press, 98–123.

Becker, Gary. 1964. *Human Capital*. New York: Columbia University Press.

Belloc, Hillaire. 1913. "An Examination of the National Guild System." *The New Age* XIV:1 (November 6), 9–10.

Bernstein, Eduard. [1899] 1967. *Evolutionary Socialism*. New York: Schocken Books.

Black, Naomi. 1989. *Social Feminism*. Ithaca: Cornell University Press.

Blanc, Louis. [1840] 1911. *The Organization of Work*. (Marie Dickore, trans.) University of Cincinnati Studies Series II:7, 1–59. Cincinnati, OH: University Press.

Blasi, Joseph R., Richard B. Freeman, and Douglas L. Kruse. 2013. *The Citizen's Share: Putting Ownership Back into Democracy*. New Haven, CT: Yale University Press.

Blaszak, Barbara. 1988. *George Jacob Holyoake (1817–1906) and the Development of the British Cooperative Movement*. Lewiston, NY: Edwin Mellen Press.

Blaszak, Barbara. 2000. *The Matriarchs of England's Cooperative Movement: A Study in Gender Politics and Female Leadership, 1883–1921*. Westport, CT: Greenwood Press.

Bodkin, Ronald G. 1999. "Women's Agency in Classical Economic Thought: Adam Smith, Harriet Taylor Mill & J.S. Mill." *Feminist Economics* 5: 45–60.

Boos, Florence and William Boos. 1986. "The Utopian Communism of William Morris." *History of Political Thought* 7:3, 489–510. http://www.jstor.org/stable/26213314.

Booth, Charles, ed. 1893. *Life and Labour of the People in London*. Vol. 4, "The Trades of East London." London: MacMillan.

Bowles, Samuel and Herbert Gintis. 1993. "The Revenge of Homo Economicus: Contested Exchange and the Revival of Political Economy." *Journal of Economic Perspectives* 7:83–102.

Boyd, William. 2018. "Just Price, Public Utility, and the Long History of Economic Regulation in America." *Yale Journal on Regulation*, 35, 721–777.

Braverman, Harvey. 1974. *Labor and Monopoly Capital: The Degradation of Work in the Twentieth Century*. New York: Monthly Review Press.

Burawoy, Michael. 1985. *The Politics of Production: Factory Regimes Under Capitalism and Socialism*. London: Verso Press.

Butler, John. 1986. *The Origins and Development of the Retail Co-operative Movement in Yorkshire during the Nineteenth Century*. PhD thesis, University of York, Department of Economics and Related Studies.

Cairnes, J. E. 1864. "Co-operation in the Slate Quarries of North Wales." *Westminster Review* 11 (January), 181–190.

Cairnes, J. E. 1874. *Some Leading Principles of Political Economy, Newly Expounded*. New York: Harper and Brothers.

Carpenter, L. P. 1973. *G. D. H. Cole: An Intellectual Biography*. London: Cambridge University Press.

Carpenter, Niles. 1922. *Guild Socialism: An Historical and Critical Analysis*. New York: D. Appleton & Company.

The Christian Socialist: A Journal of Association. Conducted by Several of the Promoters of the London Working Men's Associations. 1851. Vol. I. London: Working Printers' Association. https://books.google.com/books?id=dK4RtKAcDXMC&printsec=frontcover#v=onepage&q&f=false.

Cinelli, Carlos and Rogerio Arthmar. 2018. "The Debating Tradition in Britain and the New Political Economy: William Thompson and John Stuart Mill at the London Co-operative Society in 1825." *Nova Economia* 28:2, 609–636.

Claeys, Gregory. 1986. "'Individualism,' 'Socialism,' and 'Social Science': Further Notes on a process of Conceptual Formation, 1800–1850." *Journal of the History of Ideas* 47:1, 81–93.

Claeys, Gregory. 1987. *Machinery, Money and the Millenium: From Moral Economy to Socialism, 1815–1860*. Princeton, NJ: Princeton University Press.

Claeys, Gregory. 1989. *Citizens and Saints: Politics and Anti-Politics in Early British Socialism*. Cambridge: Cambridge University Press.

Claeys, Gregory, ed. 1993. *Selected Works of Robert Owen*. London: Pickering and Chatto.

Claeys, Gregory. 2013. *Mill and Paternalism*. Cambridge: Cambridge University Press.

Clark, Gregory. 2005. "The Condition of the Working Class in England, 1209–2004." *Journal of Political Economy* 113:6, 1307–1340.

Coase, R. H. 1937. "The Nature of the Firm." *Economica* New Series 4, 386–405.

Cole, G. D. H. 1914. "Nationalisation and the Guilds—II." *The New Age* 15:20 (September 17), 470–471. https://repository.library.brown.edu/studio/item/bdr:443636/PDF/.

Cole, G. D. H. 1920a. *Chaos and Order in Industry*. London: Methuen. https://archive.org/details/chaosorderinindu00coleiala.

Cole, G. D. H. 1920b. *The World of Labour*, 4th Ed. London: G. Bell & Sons. https://archive.org/stream/worldoflabourdis00coleuoft#page/xi/mode/1up.

Cole, G. D. H. 1920c. *Workers' Control of Industry*. Sydney, Australia: Australasian Coal and Shale Employees' Federation.

Cole, G. D. H. 1920d. *Guild Socialism Restated*. London: Leonard Parsons. https://archive.org/stream/guildsocialismre00coleuoft#page/n7/mode/2up.

Cole, G. D. H. [1925] 2019. *The Life of Robert Owen in Routledge Library Editions: The Labour Movement*. London: Routledge.

Cole, G. D. H. 1929. *The Next Ten Years in British Social and Economic Policy*. London: Macmillan.

Cole, G. D. H. 1944. *A Century of Co-operation*. George Allen & Unwin, for the Co-operative Union.

Cole, G. D. H. and W. Mellor. 1919. *The Meaning of Industrial Freedom*. London: George Allen & Unwin. https://babel.hathitrust.org/cgi/pt?id=mdp.39015065646 922;view=1up;seq=5.

Cole, Margaret. 1953. *Robert Owen of New Lanark*. London: Batchworth Press.

Cole, Margaret. 1971. *The Life of G. D. H. Cole*. London: MacMillan.

Cook E. T. and A. Wedderburn, eds. 1903–12. *The Works of John Ruskin*. 39 volumes, Library Edition. London: George Allen. https://www.lancaster.ac.uk/the-ruskin/the-complete-works-of-ruskin/.

Cory, Abbie L. 2004. "Wheeler and Thompson's 'Appeal': The Rhetorical Re-Visioning of Gender." *New Hibernia Review/Iris Eireannach Nua* 8:2 (Summer), 106–120.

Davidson, Carol. 2016. *The Original Rochdale Pioneers*. Lulu.com.

Davies, Margaret Llewelyn. [1890] 2020. "The Relations Between Co-operation and Socialistic Aspirations." Manchester: Co-op Union, 12–13. In *Contemporary Thought on Nineteenth Century Socialism. Vol. 2. Socialism and Co-operation in Britain, 1850–1918*. Peter Gurney, ed. London: Routledge, 259–265.

Davies, Margaret Llewelyn. 1891. "Co-operative Workshops." In the "Women's Corner" *of The Co-operative News and Journal of Associated Industries* (October 3), 1010–1012.

Davies, Margaret Llewelyn. 1904. *The Women's Co-operative Guild 1883–1904*. Kirkby-Lonsdale, Westmoreland, England: Published by the Women's Co-operative Guild.

Davies, Margaret Llewelyn. 1913. *The Education of Guildswomen*. London: Co-operative Women's Guild (1913 Annual Congress).

Davies, Margaret Llewelyn, A. Honora Enfield, and Lilian Harris. 1919. *Co-operation and Labour Unrest*. Manchester: The Co-operative Printing Society, Ltd.

Davies, Margaret Llewelyn. 1931. *Life as We Have Known It by Co-operative Working Women*. London: Hogarth Press.

Davis, Robert, 2011. "Robert Owen and Religion." In *Robert Owen and His Legacy*. Noel Thompson and Chris Williams, eds. Cardiff: University of Wales.

Dean, Russell. 1995. "Owenism and the Malthusian Population Question, 1815–1835." *History of Political Economy* 27:3, 579–597.

Deans, Mrs. 1898. *Credit and High Prices*. Manchester: Women's Co-operative Guild.

Dempsey, Bernard W. [1850] 1960. *The Frontier Wage. The Economic Organisation of Free Agents. With the Text of the Second Part of the Isolated State by Johann Heinrich von Thünen*. Chicago: Loyola University Press.

de Vivo, Giancarlo. 1985. "The Author of the Article on Owen in the October 1819 Edinburgh Review: some Neglected Evidence. With a reply by William O Thweatt." *History of Political Economy* 17:2, 199–202.

Donnachie, Ian. 2000. *Robert Owen: Owen of New Lanark and New Harmony*. East Lothian, Scotland: Tuckwell Press.

Donnachie, Ian. 2011. "Robert Owen: Reputations and Burning Issues." In *Robert Owen and His Legacy*. Noel Thompson and Chris Williams, eds. Cardiff: University of Wales Press, 13–31.

Donner, Wendy. 1991. *The Liberal Self: John Stuart Mill's Moral and Political Philosophy*. Ithaca: Cornell University Press.

Dooley, Dolores. 1995. "Anna Doyle Wheeler (1785–1850)." In *Women, Power, and Consciousness in 19th Century Ireland, Eight Biographical Studies*. Mary Cullen and Maria Luddy, eds. Dublin: Attic Press, 19–53.

Dooley, Dolores. 1996. *Equality in Community: Sexual Equality in the Writings of William Thompson and Anna Doyle Wheeler*. Cork: Cork University Press.

Dooley, Dolores, ed. 1997. *William Thompson Appeal (1825)*. Cork: Cork University Press.

Dos Passos, Katherine and Edith Shay. 1940. "New Harmony, Indiana." *The Atlantic* (November).   https://www.theatlantic.com/magazine/archive/1940/11/new-harmony-indiana/654827/.

Dunn, Alastair. 2004. *The Peasants' Revolt: England's Failed Revolution of 1381*. United Kingdom: Tempus.

[No Author Given]. 1889. "Professor Marshall on Co-operation." *The Economist* (June 15), 759–760.

Ely, Richard T. 1889. *An Introduction to Political Economy*. New York: Chautauqua Press. https://archive.org/details/introductiontopo02elyr/page/n5/mode/2up.

Fawcett, Henry. 1860. "Strikes: Their Tendencies and Remedies." *Westminster Review* 74 (July), 1–13.

Fawcett, Henry. 1863. *Manual of Political Economy*. London: Macmillan. https://arch ive.org/details/manualofpolitica02fawc/page/n7/mode/2up.

Fawcett, Henry. 1871. *Pauperism: Its Causes and Remedies*. London: MacMillan. https://archive.org/details/pauperismitscau01fawcgoog/page/n8/mode/2up.

Fawcett, Henry. 1876. *Manual of Political Economy*, 5th Ed. London: Macmillan. https://archive.org/details/manualofpolitica00fawcuoft/page/n7/mode/2up.

Fawcett, Henry. 1888. *Manual of Political Economy*, 7th Ed. London: Macmillan. https://archive.org/details/manualpolitical00fawcgoog/page/n7/mode/1up?ref=ol&view=theater.

Fawcett, Millicent Garrett. 1870. *Political Economy for Beginners*. London: Macmillan. https://www.google.com/books/edition/Political_Economy_for_Beginners/VERVAAAAcAAJ?hl=en&gbpv=1.

Fawcett, Millicent Garrett. 1917. "The Position of Women in Economic Life." In *After-War Problems, by the Earl of Cromer, Viscount Haldane, the Bishop of Exeter, Professor Alfred Marshall, and Others*. W. H. Dawson, ed. New York: Macmillan, 191–215.

Fawcett, Millicent Garrett. 1918. "Equal Pay for Equal Work." *Economic Journal* 28 (March), 1–6.

Ferguson, Susan. 2020. *Women and Work: Feminism, Labour and Social Reproduction*. London: Pluto Press.

Feugueray, Henri Robert. 1851. *L'Association Ouvriere Industrielle et Agricole*. Paris: Harvard.

Folbre, Nancy. 1998. "The Sphere of Women in Early Twentieth-Century Economics." In *Gender and American Social Science*. Helene Silverberg, ed. Princeton, NJ: Princeton University Press, 35–60.

Foxwell, H. S. 1899. "Introduction." In *The Right to the Whole Produce of Labour: The Origin and Development of the Theory of Labour's Claim to the Whole Product of Industry*. Anton Menger, ed. London: MacMillan, v–cx.

Garnett, R. C. 1972. *Co-operation and the Owenite Socialist Communities In Britain, 1825–45*. Manchester: Manchester University Press.

Gente, Magali. 2001. "The Expansion of the Nuclear Family Unit in Great Britain between 1910 and 1920." *History of the Family* 6:1, 125–142. DOI: 10.1016/S1081-602X(01)00063-X.

Glendinning, Victoria. 2006. *Leonard Woolf: A Biography*. Berkeley: Counterpoint.

Godwin, William. 1793. *An Enquiry Concerning Political Justice, and its Influence on General Virtue and Happiness*. London: G. G. J. & J. Robinson. http://files.libe rtyfund.org/files/90/0164-01_Bk.pdf.

Godwin, William. [1798] 1976. *Enquiry Concerning Political Justice and Its Influence on Modern Morals and Happiness*. 3rd Ed. Isaak Kramnick, ed. Harmondsworth: Pelican Books.

Gray, J. C. 1887. *Co-operative Production in Great Britain*. Manchester: Central Co-operative Board. https://books.google.com/books?id=u5tBAQAAMAAJ&print sec=frontcover&source=gbs_ge_summary_r&cad=0#v=onepage&q&f=false.

Gray, John. 1825. *A Lecture on Human Happiness; Being the first of a Series of Lectures on that Subject in which will be Comprehended a General Review of the Causes of the Existing Evils of Society, and a Development of Means by which they may be Permanently and Effectually removed. To which are added the Articles of Agreement drawn up and Recommended by the London Co-operative Society for the Formation of a Community on Principles of Mutual Co-Operation within Fifty Miles of London*. London: Sherwood, Jones. https://archive.org/details/in.ernet.dli.2015.234 148/page/n5.

Gray, John. 1831. *The Social System: A Treatise on the Principle of Exchange*. Edinburgh: William Tait.

G[reening]., E[dward]. O[wen]. 1902. "Notable Personalities: Mr. J. C. Gray, J. P." *Agricultural Economist* xxxv (August 1), 270. https://www.google.com/books/ edition/The_Agricultural_Economist_and_Horticult/AORMAQAAMAAJ?hl= en&gbpv=1&dq=J.C.+Gray+economist&pg=PA270&printsec=frontcover.

Greenwood, Miss. [1885] 2020. "Vice President's Address." In *Contemporary Thought on Nineteenth Century Socialism*. Vol. 2. *Socialism and Co-operation in Britain, 1850–1918*. Peter Gurney, ed. London: Routledge, 253–255.

Greg, William Rathbone. 1851. "English Socialism and Communistic Association." *Edinburgh Review* 93 (January), 1–33. https://www.google.com/books/edition/ The_Edinburgh_Review_Or_Critical_Journal/b7RKAAAAcAAJ?hl=en&gbpv= 1&printsec=frontcover.

Greg, William Rathbone. 1852. "Investments for the Working Classes." *Edinburgh Review* (April), 405–453.

Groenewegen, Peter. 1995. *A Soaring Eagle: Alfred Marshall 1842–1924*. 1st Ed. Aldershot: Edward Elgar.

Gurney, Peter. 1996. *Co-Operative Culture and the Politics of Consumption in England, 1870–1930*. Manchester: Manchester University Press.

Gurney, Peter, ed. 2020. *Contemporary Thought on Nineteenth Century Socialism*. Vol. 2. *Socialism and Co-operation in Britain, 1850–1918*. London: Routledge.

Hamilton, Walton. 1932. "Institution." *Encyclopaedia of the Social Sciences* 8, 84.

Harris, Lilian. 1897. *The Treatment of Women Employees in the Co-operative Movement, Being a Report of an Enquiry into the Wages, Hours, and Conditions of Women Working in Co-operative Stores in 1895*. Manchester: Co-operative Newspaper Society.

Harrison, Frederic. 1866. "Industrial Cooperation." *Fortnightly Review* (January), 479–503.

Hartley, David. 1749. *Observations on Man, his Frame, his Duty, and his Expectations*. London: S. Richardson. https://archive.org/details/b30529049_0002/page/n7/ mode/2up.

Harvey, Charles and Jon Press. 1995. "John Ruskin and the Ethical Foundations of Morris & Company, 1861–96." *Journal of Business Ethics* 14 (March), 181.

Hayek. Frederick A. 2015. *Hayek on Mill: The Mill-Taylor Friendship and Related Writings The Collected Works of F. A. Hayek.* Vol. 16. Sandra Peart, ed. London: Routledge.

Henderson, W. O. 1976. *The Life of Friedrich Engels.* Vol. 1. London: Routledge.

Hewes, Amy. 1922. "Guild Socialism: A Two Years' Test." *American Economic Review* 12, 209–37.

Hill, Christopher. 1972. *The World Turned Upside Down: Radical Ideas During the English Revolution, 1642–1660.* London: Temple Smith.

Hobson, S. G. 1914. *National Guilds: An Inquiry into the Wage System and the Way Out.* London: G. Bell & Sons.

Holyoake, George Jacob. 1893. *Self-Help by the People: The History of the Rochdale Pioneers*, 10th Ed. London: Swan Sonnenschein.

Holyoake, George Jacob. 1900. *The History of the Rochdale Pioneers*, 3rd Ed. London: Swan Sonnenschein.

Holyoake, George Jacob. 1906. *The History of Co-operation.* London: T. Fisher Unwin.

Horrell, Sara and Jane Humphries. 1995. "Women's Labour Force Participation and the Transition to the Male-Breadwinner Family, 1790–1865." *Economic History Review,* New Series 48:1, 89–117.

Jacobs, Jo Ellen ed. 1998. *The Complete Works of Harriet Taylor Mill.* Bloomington, IN: Indiana University Press.

Jakalski, David Frank. 2017. *Secret Springs of Action: Necessity and Anglo-American Literature in the Age of Revolution.* Thesis. University of Illinois at Chicago. https://hdl.handle.net/10027/21859.

Jay, Elisabeth and Richard Jay, eds. 1986. *Critics of Capitalism: Victorian Reactions to "Political Economy."* Cambridge: Cambridge University Press.

Jevons, William Stanley. 1883. *Methods of Social Reform and Other Papers.* London: MacMillan. https://www.google.com/books/edition/Methods_of_Social_Reform/wBUiAAAAMAAJ?hl=en&gbpv=1&pg=PP9&printsec=frontcover.

Jones, Benjamin. [1894] 1968. *Co-operative Production.* Oxford: Oxford University Press. Reprinted in New York: Augustus M. Kelley.

Jones, Clara. 2015. "Virginia Woolf and the Women's Cooperative Guild 1913–1931." In *Virginia Woolf Ambivalent Activist.* Cambridge: Cambridge University Press, 108–153.

Joslyn, Carl. 1922. "The British Building Guilds: A Critical Survey of Two Years' Work." *Quarterly Journal of Economics* 37, 75–133.

Jossa, Bruno. 2005. "Marx, Marxism and the Cooperative Movement." *Cambridge Journal of Economics* 29, 3–18.

Jossa, Bruno. 2012a. "A System of Self-Managed Firms as a New Perspective on Marxism." *Cambridge Journal of Economics* 36, 821–41.

Jossa, Bruno. 2012b. "Cooperative Firms as New Mode of Production." *Review of Political Economy* 24: 3 (July), 399–416.

Jossa, Bruno. 2015. "Historical Materialism and Democratic Firm Management." *Review of Political Economy* 27: 4, 645–665.

Kaswan, Mark. 2014. *Happiness, Democracy, and the Cooperative Movement: The Radical Utilitarianism of William Thompson.* Albany: State University of New York Press.

Kimball, Janet. 1948. *The Economic Doctrines of John Gray—1799–1883.* Washington DC: Catholic University of America Press.

Kingsley, Charles. 1850. *Alton Locke.* London: Chapman and Hall. https://babel.hathitrust.org/cgi/pt?id=hvd.hwkqe6&view=1up&seq=5.

Kingsley, Charles. 1894. *Charles Kingsley: His Letters and Memories of his Life* ("Edited by his wife.") Abridged Edition. New York: Scribner & Sons.

Kinna, Ruth. 2000. "William Morris: Art, Work, and Leisure." *Journal of the History of Ideas* 61:3, 493–512. DOI:10.2307/3653925.

Kirk, Neville. 1985. *The Growth of Working Class Reformism in Mid-Victorian England.* London: Croom Helm.

Kolmerten, Carol A. 1981. "Egalitarian Promises and Inegalitarian Practices: Women's Roles in the American Owenite Communities, 1824–1828." *Journal of General Education* 33:1 (Spring), 31–44.

Kuiper, Edith. 2022. *A Herstory of Economics.* Cambridge: Polity Press.

Kurer, Oscar. 1998. "Mill's Recantation of the Wage-Fund Doctrine: Was Mill Right after All?" *History of Political Economy* 30:3, 515–536.

Landreth, Harry and David Colander. 1989. *History of Economic Theory*, 2nd Ed. Boston: Houghton Mifflin.

Lawrenson, Mary. 1891a. "Comments on Davies." In the "Women's Corner" of *The Co-operative News and Journal of Associated Industries* (November 21), 1179.

Lawrenson, Mary. 1891b. "Comments on Davies." In the "Women's Corner" of *The Co-operative News and Journal of Associated Industries* (December, 12), 1251.

Lebowitz, Michael. 2012. *The Contradictions of "Real Socialism": The Conductor and the Conducted.* New York: Monthly Review Press.

Lee, J. M. 2008. "Nash, Vaughan Robinson (1861–1932)." *Oxford Dictionary of National Biography Online.* https://doi.org/10.1093/ref:odnb/40819.

Lee, Sidney. 1899. *Dictionary of National Biography.* London: Smith Elder.

Leopold, David. 2015. "Scientific Socialism: The Case of Robert Owen." In *Scientific Statesmanship, Governance, and the History of Political Philosophy.* Kyriakos N. Demetrious and Antis Loizides, eds. New York: Routledge, 193–209.

Leopold, David. 2016. "William Morris, News from Nowhere and the Function of Utopia." *Journal of William Morris Studies* XXII:1, 18–41.

Leopold, David. 2019. "Beyond the 'Grand Designs' Owenism, Architecture, and Utopia." In *Socialist Imaginations: Utopias, Myths, and the Masses.* Stefan Arvidsson, Jakub Beneš, and Anja Kirsch, eds. London: Routledge, 63–90.

Lowenthal, Esther. [1911] 1972. *The Ricardian Socialists.* Clifton, NJ: Augustus M. Kelly Reprints. https://archive.org/details/ricardiansociali00lowerich/page/n7/mode/2up.

Lucas, Edward. 2019. "Religious Dreams of a Socialist Future: The Case of Owenism." In *Socialist Imaginations: Utopias, Myths, and the Masses.* Stefan Arvidsson, Jakub Beneš, and Anja Kirsch, eds. London: Routledge, 41–61.

Ludlow, John, ed. 1850–1851. *The Christian Socialist: A Journal of Association. Conducted by Several of the Promoters of the London Work Men's Associations.* Vol. I. London: Working Printers' Association. https://books.google.com/books?id=dK4RtKAcDXMC&printsec=frontcover#v=onepage&q&f=false.

Ludlow, John. 1851. *Christian Socialism and Its Opponents.* London: John W. Parker. https://books.google.com/books/about/Christian_Socialism_and_Its_Oppone nts.html?id=8tQuxgEACAAJ&hl=en&output=html_text.

Ludlow, John. 1981. *John Ludlow: The Autobiography of a Christian Socialist.* A. D. Murray, ed. London: Frank Cass.

MacCarthy, Fiona. 1995. *William Morris: A Life for Our Time.* New York: Knopf.

Mackail, John William. 1899. *The Life of William Morris.* Vol. II. Internet Archive. London: Longmans Green. https://archive.org/details/in.ernet.dli.2015.211 035/mode/2up.

Mackail, John William. 1901. *The Life of William Morris*. Vol. I. London: Longmans Green. https://archive.org/details/lifeofwilliammor01mack/page/n9/mode/2up.

Madden, Kirsten and Nicholas Armstrong. 2021. "Designing a Virtuous Political Economy: An Adaptation of *Unto This Last* Emphasizing Individual Conscience and Self Determination." *Review of Social Economy*, DOI: 10.1080/00346764.2021.1878260.

Madden, Kirsten and Joseph Persky. 2018. "The Economic Thought of the Women's Co-operative Guild." In *Routledge Handbook of the History of Women's Economic Thought*. Kirsten Madden and Robert Dimand, eds. New York: Routledge, 150–168.

Madden, Kirsten and Joseph Persky. "Anna Doyle Wheeler: Gender Equality and the Need for a Cooperative Economic System." *Feminist Economics*, forthcoming.

Malthus, Thomas. 1798. *An Essay on the Principle of Population*. London: J. Johnson. https://www.gutenberg.org/cache/epub/4239/pg4239-images.html.

Malthus, Thomas Robert. 1817. *An Essay on the Principle of Population*, 5th Ed. Vol. 3. London: John Murray. https://archive.org/details/essayonprinciple02maltu oft/page/n3/mode/1up?ref=ol&view=theater.

Marcroft, William. [1888] 2020. "The Marcroft Family and the Inner Circle of Human Life." In *Contemporary Thought on Nineteenth Century Socialism*. Vol. 2. *Socialism and Co-operation in Britain, 1850–1918*. Peter Gurney, ed. London: Routledge, 256–258.

Marshall, Alfred. [1873] 1925. "The Future of the Working Classes." In *Memorials of Alfred Marshall*. A. C. Pigou, ed. London: MacMillan; 101–118.

Marshall, Alfred. [1889] 1925. "Co-operation." In *Memorials of Alfred Marshall*. A. C. Pigou, ed. London: MacMillan, 227–255. https://archive.org/details/in.ernet. dli.2015.275351/page/n3/mode/2up.

Marshall, Alfred. [1890] 1961. *Principles of Economics*. 9th (Variorum) Ed. (Annotations by C. W. Guillebaud). London: MacMillan.

Marshall, Alfred. 1996. *The Correspondence of Alfred Marshall: Economist*. John Whitaker, ed. Cambridge: Cambridge University Press.

Marshall, Peter. [1984] 2017. *William Godwin: Philosopher, Novelist, Revolutionary*. Oakland: PM Press.

Marx, Karl. 1847. *The Poverty of Philosophy*. Paris: A Frank. https://www.marxists.org/archive/marx/works/1847/poverty-philosophy/#:~:text=In%201880%20M arx%20attempted%20to,the%20original%201847%20French%20edition.

Marx, Karl. [1867] 1967. *Capital*. Vol. 1. New York: International Publishers.

Marx, Karl. [1885] 1967. *Capital*. Vol. 2. New York: International Publishers.

Marx, Karl. [1894] 1967. *Capital*. Vol. 3. New York: International Publishers.

Marx, Karl. 1988. *Economic and Philosophic Manuscripts of 1844*. (Martin Milligan, trans.) Amherst, NY: Prometheus Books.

Marx, Karl and Frederick Engels. [1848] 1969. "Manifesto of the Communist Party." In *Marx/Engels Selected Works*. Vol. 1. Samuel Moore, trans. Moscow: Progress Publishers, 98–137. https://www.marxists.org/archive/marx/works/1848/communist-manifesto/index.htm.

Massey, Kelvin Lee. 2007. *The Roots of Middle-Earth: William Morris's Influence upon J. R. R. Tolkien*. PhD thesis. University of Tennessee. https://trace.tennessee.edu/utk_graddiss/238.

Masterman, N. C. 1963. *John Malcolm Ludlow: The Builder of Christian Socialism*. Cambridge: Cambridge University Press.

Maurice, F. D. [1850] 1995. "Tracts on Christian Socialism, Tract 1." In *Reconstructing Christian Ethics: Selected Writings.* Ellen Wondra, ed. Louisville: Westminster John Knox Press, 196–206.

Maurice, F. D. 1854. *The Doctrine of Sacrifice Deduced from the Scriptures, A Series of Sermons.* Cambridge: Macmillan. https://babel.hathitrust.org/cgi/pt?id=uc2. ark:/13960/t02z1cj81&view=1up&seq=29&skin=2021.

Maurice, F. D. 1855. "Administrative Reform, and its Connexion with Working Men's Colleges." An Address delivered by the Principal of the Working Men's College, at a Meeting of the Members, held May 31, 1855. Cambridge: Macmillan; London: Bell and Daldy. https://babel.hathitrust.org/cgi/pt?id=nnc1.cu56766 181&view=1up&seq=13&skin=2021.

Maurice, F. D. 1869. *Social Morality.* Twenty-One Lectures Delivered in the University of Cambridge. London: MacMillan. https://babel.hathitrust.org/cgi/pt?id=hvd. ah5c46&view=1up&seq=158&skin=2021.

Maurice, F. D. 2007. *To Build Christ's Kingdom: An F. D. Maurice Reader.* Jeremy Morris, ed. Norwich: Canterbury Press.

Maurice, F. D. and John Ludlow, eds. 1848. *Politics for the People.* London: John W. Parker, West Strand. https://catalog.hathitrust.org/Record/000635788.

Maurice, Frederick. 1884a. *The Life of Frederick Denison Maurice.* Vol. 1. London: MacMillan. https://archive.org/details/lifeoffrederickd0001maur/ page/n7/mode/2up.

Maurice, Frederick. 1884b. *The Life of Frederick Denison Maurice.* Vol. 2. London: MacMillan. https://archive.org/details/a592475702mauruoft/page/n59/mode/2up.

McCabe, Helen. 2019. "Navigating by the North Star: The Role of the 'Ideal' in John Stuart Mill's View of 'Utopian Schemes and the Possibilities of Social Transformation." *Utilitas,* 31:3, 291–309.

McCabe, Helen. 2020. "Mill's 'Modern' Radicalism Re-Examined." *Utilitas* 32:2, 147–164.

McCabe, Helen. 2021. *John Stuart Mill, Socialist.* Montreal: McGill-Queen's University Press.

McCulloch, John Ramsay. 1830. *The Principles of Political Economy with a Sketch of the Rise and Progress of the Science,* 2nd Ed. London: J. Moyes.

McCulloch, John Ramsay. 1864. *The Principles of Political Economy with Some Inquiries Respecting Their Application,* 5th Ed. Edinburgh: Adam and Charles Black.

Mill, John Stuart. [1844] 1967. "On the Definition of Political Economy." *In Essays on Some Unsettled Questions of Political Economy* in *Collected Works of John Stuart Mill.* Vol. IV. J. M. Robson, ed. Toronto: University of Toronto Press, 309–340.

Mill, John Stuart. [1848] 1965. *The Principles of Political Economy with Some of Their Applications to Social Philosophy.* Vols. 2–3 of *The Collected Works of John Stuart Mill.* John M. Robson, ed. Toronto: University of Toronto Press. https://oll. libertyfund.org/title/mill-the-collected-works-of-john-stuart-mill-volume-ii-the-principles-of-political-economy-i. Also https://oll.libertyfund.org/title/ mill-the-collected-works-of-john-stuart-mill-volume-iii-principles-of-political-economy-part-ii.

Mill, John Stuart. [1863] 1987. *John Stuart Mill and Jeremy Bentham: Utilitarianism and Other Essays.* Alan Ryan, ed. London: Penguin Books.

Mill, John Stuart. 1869. "Thornton on Labour and its Claims." *Fortnightly Review* 11:29 (May), 505–518. https://socialsciences.mcmaster.ca/econ/ugcm/3ll3/ mill/thorn.html.

Mill, John Stuart. [1869] 1984. "The Subjection of Women." In Vol. 21 of *The Collected Works of John Stuart Mill*. John Robson, ed. Toronto: University of Toronto Press, 259–340. https://oll-resources.s3.us-east-2.amazonaws.com/oll3/store/titles/255/0223.21_Bk.pdf.

Mill, John Stuart. [1873] 1981. "Autobiography." In Vol. 1 of *The Collected Works of John Stuart Mill*. John Robson and Jack Stillinger, eds. Toronto: University of Toronto Press, 1–290. https://oll-resources.s3.us-east-2.amazonaws.com/oll3/store/titles/242/0223.01_Bk.pdf.

Mill, John Stuart, ed. 1878. *Analysis of the Phenomena of the Human Mind by James Mill*, 2nd Ed. London: Longmans, Green, Reader, & Dyer.

Mill, John Stuart. 1963. *The Earlier Letters of John Stuart Mill, 1812–1848. Part II*. In Vol. 13 of *The Collected Works of John Stuart Mill*. Francis Mineka, ed. Toronto: University of Toronto Press. https://oll-resources.s3.us-east-2.amazonaws.com/oll3/store/titles/250/0223.13_Bk.pdf.

Mill, John Stuart. 1988. "Debating Speeches, 1823–29." In Vol. 26 of *The Collected Works of John Stuart Mill*. John Robson, ed. Toronto: University of Toronto Press, 308–325. https://oll-resources.s3.us-east-2.amazonaws.com/oll3/store/titles/260/0223.26_Bk.pdf.

Miller, Dale. 2003. "Mill's 'Socialism.'" *Politics, Philosophy, & Economics* 2, 213–238.

Mitchell, J. T. W. [1892] 2020. "J. T. W. Mitchell's Presidential Address, The 24th Annual Co-operative Congress." Manchester: Co-op Union. In *Contemporary Thought on Nineteenth Century Socialism*. Vol. 2. *Socialism and Co-operation in Britain, 1850–1918*. Peter Gurney, ed. London: Routledge, 213–221.

Montes, Leonidas. 2003. "Das Adam Smith Problem: Its Origins, the Stages of the Current Debate, and One Implication for Our Understanding of Sympathy." *Journal of the History of Economic Thought* 25, 63–90. DOI:10.1080/1042771032000058325.

Morris, Jeremy. 2007. *To Build Christ's Kingdom: F.D. Maurice and his Writings*. Jeremy Morris, ed. Norwich: Canterbury Press.

Morris, May. 1966. *William Morris: Artist Writer Socialist*. Vol. 2. New York: Russell & Russell.

Morris, William. 1882. *Hopes and Fears for Art*. London: Roberts Brothers. https://archive.org/details/hopesandfearsfo00morrgoog/page/n6/mode/2up.

Morris, William. 1888. *A Dream of John Ball and A King's Lesson*. Reprinted from *Commonweal*. London: Reeves & Turner. https://archive.org/details/adreamjohnballa01morrgoog/page/n8/mode/2up.

Morris, William. 1891. "The Socialist Ideal." In Vol. 23 of *The Collected Works of William Morris, with* introductions by May Morris. London: Longmans Green, 255–263.

Morris, William. 1894. "How I Became a Socialist." *Justice* (June 16). .

Morris, William. 1897. *News from Nowhere; or, An Epoch of Rest, Being Some Chapters from a Utopian Romance*, 5th Ed. London: Longmans Green. https://archive.org/details/newsfromnowhereo00morruoft/page/n7/mode/2up?ref=ol&view=theater.

Morris, William. 1903. *Signs of Change: Seven Lectures Delivered on Various Occasions*. London: Longmans Green. https://archive.org/details/signsofchangese v00morr.

Morris, William and E. Belford Bax. 1893. *Socialism: Its Growth and Outcome*. London: Swan Sonnenschein.

Mudie, George, ed. 1821. *The Economist*. Vol. I, https://babel.hathitrust.org/cgi/pt?id=uc1.b3332314&view=1up&seq=211&skin=2021.

Mudie, George, ed. 1821–1822. *The Economist.* Vol. II, https://babel.hathitrust.org/cgi/pt?id=uc1.b3332315&view=1up&seq=9.

Nash, Rosalind. 1907. *The Position of Married Women.* Manchester: Consumer Wholesale Society Printing Works.

Newell, J. Philip. 1981. *A. J. Scott and His Circle.* PhD thesis, University of Edinburgh.

Newell, J. Philip. 1983. "The Other Christian Socialist: Alexander John Scott." *Heythrop Journal* XXIV, 278–289.

Nuttall, William. 1872. "Productive Cooperation: How Best to Extend It." *Co-operative News* (May), 2:23, 268. https://babel.hathitrust.org/cgi/pt?id=njp.32101064160607&view=1up&seq=488.

O'Hagan, Francis. 2011. "Robert Owen and Education." In *Robert Owen and His Legacy.* Noel Thompson and Chris Williams, eds. Cardiff: University of Wales Press, 71–90.

Owen, Robert. [1813–1816] 1927. *A New View of Society and Other Writings.* London: J. M. Dent & Sons. https://archive.org/details/owennewviewsocietyandotherwritings/page/n1/mode/2up.

Owen, Robert. [1817] 1993. Concerning Benefits of Villages of Unity and Mutual Co-operation. In Claeys, Gregory, ed. *Selected Works of Robert Owen.* Vol. 1. London: Pickering & Chatto, 174–182.

Owen, Robert. [1825a] 1993. "First Discourse on a New System of Society 1825." In *Selected Works of Robert Owen.* Vol. 2. Gregory Claeys, ed. London: Pickering & Chatto, 3–17.

Owen, Robert. [1825b] 1993. "Second Discourse on a New System of Society 1825." In *Selected Works of Robert Owen.* Vol. 2. Gregory Claeys, ed. London: Pickering & Chatto, 18–30.

Owen, Robert. [1825c] 1993. "A New Society is about to be Commenced at Harmony, Indiana." In *Selected Works of Robert Owen.* Vol. 2. Gregory Claeys, ed. London: Pickering & Chatto, 30–37.

Owen, Robert. [1825d] 1993. "Constitution." In *Selected Works of Robert Owen.* Vol. 2. Gregory Claeys, ed. London: Pickering & Chatto, 42–47.

Owen, Robert. [1826] 1993. "The Social System." In *Selected Works of Robert Owen.* Vol 2. Gregory Claeys, ed. London: Pickering & Chatto, 56–104. First published in *New Harmony Gazette,* 2:8 (22 November).

Owen, Robert. [1827] 1993. "Address to the Agriculturalists, Mechanics, and Manufacturers, both Masters and Operatives, of Great Britain and Ireland." In *Selected Works of Robert Owen.* Vol. 2. Gregory Claeys, ed. London: Pickering & Chatto, 105–114.

Owen, Robert. [?1832] 1993. "Robert Owen's Reply to the Question, 'What would you do if you were Prime Minister of England'?" In *Selected Works of Robert Owen.* Vol. 2. Gregory Claeys, ed. London: Pickering & Chatto, 213–223.

Owen, Robert. [1833] 1993. "The Address of Robert Owen at the Great Public Meeting, held at the National Equitable Labour Exchange, Charlotte-Street, Fitzroy-Square [London] on the 1st of May, 1833, Denouncing the Old System of the World, and Announcing the Commencement of the New." In *Selected Works of Robert Owen.* Vol. 2. Gregory Claeys, ed. London: Pickering & Chatto, 224–231.

Owen, Robert. [1834] 1993. "Address to the Trades' Unions, and to all the Producers of Wealth and Knowledge Throughout Great Britain and Ireland." In *Selected Works of Robert Owen.* Vol. 2. Gregory Claeys, ed. London: Pickering & Chatto, 232–235. First published in *The Crisis,* 3:20 (11 January), 156–157.

Owen, Robert. 1835. *The New Moral World Magazine* 27 (May 2), 210.

Owen, Robert. 1836. *The Book of the New Moral World, Containing the Rational System of Society, Founded on Demonstrable Facts, Developing the Constitution and Laws of Human Nature and of Society*. London: Effingham Wilson, Royal Exchange.

Owen, Robert. [1841] 1993. "A Development of the Principles and Plans on Which to Establish Self-Supporting Home Colonies." In *Selected Works of Robert Owen*. Vol. 2. Gregory Claeys, ed. London: Pickering & Chatto, 337–407.

Owen, Robert. [1842a] 1993. "The New Moral World, Second Part." In *Selected Works of Robert Owen*. Vol. 3. Gregory Claeys, ed. London: Pickering & Chatto, 81–123.

Owen, Robert. [1842b] 1993. "The Book of the New Moral World, Third Part, Conditions Requisite for Human Happiness." In *Selected Works of Robert Owen*. Vol. 3. Gregory Claeys, ed. London: Pickering & Chatto, 125–191.

Owen, Robert. [1844a] 1993. "New Moral World, Fifth Part." In *Selected Works of Robert Owen*. Vol. 3. Gregory Claeys, ed. London: Pickering & Chatto, 24–298.

Owen, Robert. [1844b] 1993. "New Moral World, Seventh Part." In *Selected Works of Robert Owen*. Vol. 2. Gregory Claeys, ed. London: Pickering & Chatto, 361–409.

Owen, Robert. 1857 [1967]. *The Life of Robert Owen Written by Himself*. Vol. 1. New York: Augustus M. Kelley.

Pankhurst, Richard. [1954] 1991. *William Thompson (1775–1833): Pioneer Socialist*. London: Pluto Press.

Parssinen, T. M. 1973. "Thomas Spence and the Origins of English Land Nationalization." *Journal of the History of Ideas* 34:1, 135–141.

Peart, Sandra and David Levy. 2005. *Vanity of the Philosopher: From Equality to Hierarchy in Post-Classical Economics*. Ann Arbor: University of Michigan Press.

Pellarin, Charles. 1848. *The Life of Charles Fourier* (Francis Shaw, trans.) New York: William H. Graham.

Penty, Arthur J. 1906. *The Restoration of the Guild System*. London: Swan Sonnenschein.

Penty, Arthur J. 1913. "The Restoration of the Guild System II." *The New Age* 8:15 (August 7).

Persky, Joseph. 1990. "Retrospectives: A Dismal Romantic." *Journal of Economic Perspectives* 4:4, 165–172.

Persky, Joseph. 2016. *The Political Economy of Progress: John Stuart Mill and Modern Radicalism*. New York: Oxford University Press.

Persky, Joseph. 2017. "Producer Co-operatives in 19th Century British Economic Thought." *European Journal of the History of Economic Thought* 24:2, 319–340.

Persky, Joseph. 2018. "John Stuart Mill." In *Great Economic Thinkers*. Jonathan Conlin, ed. London: Reaktion Books, 54–72.

Persky, Joseph. 2019. "Von Thünen's Political Economy of Justice." *Review of Political Economy* 31:3, 430–444.

Persky, Joseph. 2020. "Mill's Socialism Re-Examined." *Utilitas* 32:2, 165–180.

Persky, Joseph and Kirsten Madden. 2019. "The Economic Content of G. D. H. Cole's Guild Socialism: Behavioral Assumptions, Institutional Structure, and Analytic Arguments." *European Journal of the History of Economic Thought* 26:3, 427–463.

Pitzer, Donald and Josephine Elliott. 1979. "New Harmony's First Utopians, 1814–1824." *Indiana Magazine of History* 75:3, 225–300.

Potter [Webb], Beatrice. 1887. "The Dock Life of East London." *Nineteenth Century* 22 (October), 483–499.

Potter [Webb], Beatrice. 1891. *The Cooperative Movement in Great Britain*. London: Swan Sonnenschein. https://archive.org/details/cu31924030083921/mode/2up.

Prendergast, Renee. 2021. "William Thompson and the Mills on Co-operation and the Rights of Women." Working Paper (August).

Purvis, Martin. 2010. "Lawrenson [née Molyneux], Mary Ann (1850–1943)." *Oxford Dictionary of National Biography* Online, 876–877. https://doi.org/10.1093/ref:odnb/60018.

Raven, Charles. [1920] 1968. *Christian Socialism 1848–1854*. London: MacMillan.

Reckitt, Maurice and C. E. Bechhofer. 1918. *The Meaning of National Guilds*. New York: MacMillan.

Redfern, Percy 1913. *The Story of the C. W. S.: The Jubilee History of the Co-operative Wholesale Society Limited, 1863–1913*. Manchester: Co-operative Wholesale Society Limited.

Redfern, Percy. 1924. *John T.W. Mitchell: Pioneer of Consumers' Co-operation*. London: T. Fisher Unwin.

Reeves, Richard. 2007. *John Stuart Mill: Victorian Firebrand*. London: Atlantic Books.

Renard, Georges. [1918] 2000. *Guilds in the Middle Ages*. (Dorothy Terry, trans.) Kitchener: Batoche Books. http://socserv2.socsci.mcmaster.ca/econ/ugcm/3ll3/renard/guilds.pdf.

Reynard, Helen 1920. "The Guild Socialists." *Economic Journal* 30:119, 321–330.

Ricardo, David. [1817] 1971. *On the Principles of Political Economy and Taxation*. Harmondsworth: Penguin.

Ricardo, David. 1821. "Letter to Hutches Trower, March 1820." In *The Works and Correspondence of David Ricardo*. Vol. 8 *Letters 1819–June 1821*. Indianapolis: Liberty Fund. https://oll.libertyfund.org/title/sraffa-the-works-and-correspondence-of-david-ricardo-vol-8-letters-1819-june-1821.

Ricardo David. 1822. "On Protection of Agriculture." In *The Works and Correspondence of David Ricardo, Volume 4, Pamphlets and Papers, 1815–1823*. Piero Sraffa, ed., M. H. Dobb, collaborator. Indianapolis: Liberty Fund, 209–268. https://oll.libertyfund.org/title/sraffa-the-works-and-correspondence-of-david-ricardo-vol-4-pamphlets-and-papers-1815-1823.

Robbins, Lionel. 1971. *Autobiography of an Economist*. London: Macmillan.

Rose, Mary. 1986. *The Gregs of Quarry Bank Mill: The Rise and Decline of a Family Firm, 1750–1914*. Cambridge: Cambridge University Press.

Rossi, Alice, ed. 1970. "Sentiment and Intellect: The Story of John Stuart Mill and Harriet Taylor Mill." In *John Stuart Mill and Harriet Taylor Mill, Essays on Sex Equality*. Chicago: University of Chicago Press, 1–64.

Rostek, Joanna. 2021. *Women's Economic Thought in the Romantic Age: Towards a Transdisciplinary Herstory of Economic Thought*. Routledge: Abingdon, Oxon.

Ruffin, Roy J. 2005. "Debunking a Myth: Torrens on Comparative Advantage." *History of Political Economy* 37:4, 711–722.

Ruskin, John. 1867. *Time and Tide by Weare and Tyne: Twenty-five Letters to a Working Man of Sunderland on the Laws of Work*. In *The Complete Works of John Ruskin*. New York: National Library Association. http://www.gutenberg.org/files/31196/31196-h/31196-h.htm.

Ruskin, John. 1903–1912. *The Complete Works of John Ruskin*, 39 volumes, Library Edition. E. T. Cook and A. Wedderburn, eds. London: George Allen. https://www.lancaster.ac.uk/the-ruskin/the-complete-works-of-ruskin/.

Scholes, Robert. n.d. "General Introduction to The New Age 1907–1922." The Modernist Journal Project (searchable database). https://modjourn.org/general-introduction-to-the-new-age-1907-1922-by-scholes-robert/.

Scott, Gillian. 1998. *Feminism and the Politics of Working Women: The Women's Co-Operative Guild, 1880s to the Second World War*. London: UCL Press.

Scott, Gillian. 2004. "Webb, Catherine (1859–1947)." *Oxford Dictionary of National Biography*, 829.

Seligman, Edwin R. A. 1886. "Owen and the Christian Socialists." *Political Science Quarterly* 1:2, 206–249.

Sharp, Amy. n.d. "What Has a Woman to Do with Co-operation?" Manchester: Central Co-operative Board.

Sigot, Nathalie and Christophe Beaurain. 2009. "John Stuart Mill and the Employment of Married Women: Reconciling Utility and Justice." *Journal of the History of Economic Thought* 31:3, 281–304.

Simon, Herbert. 1993. "Altruism and Economics." *American Economics Review, Papers and Proceedings of the 105th Annual Meeting* 83:2, 156–161.

Smith, Adam. [1776] 1976. *An Inquiry into the Nature and Causes of the Wealth of Nations*. R. H. Campbell and A. S. Skinner, eds. Oxford: Oxford University Press.

Smith, Adam. [1776] 1937. *An Inquiry into the Nature and Causes of the Wealth of Nations*. Edwin Cannan, ed. New York: Modern Library.

Smith, Adam [1790] 2004. *The Theory of Moral Sentiments*. Knud Haakonssen, ed. Cambridge: Cambridge University Press.

Spencer, Herbert. 1898. *The Principles of Sociology*. Vol. 3. New York: D. Appleton.

Sraffa, Piero, ed. 2005. *The Works and Correspondence of David Ricardo*, 11 volumes. M. H. Dobb, collaborator. Indianapolis: Liberty Fund. https://oll.libertyfund.org/title/ricardo-the-works-and-correspondence-of-david-ricardo-11-vols-sraffa-ed.

Stedman Jones, Gareth. 2020. "Malthus, Nineteenth-Century Socialism, and Marx." *Historical Journal* 63:1, 91–106.

Stein, Stephen. 1992. *The Shaker Experience in America: A History of the United Society of Believers*. New Haven, CT: Yale University Press.

Stephen, Leslie. 1885. *Life of Henry Fawcett*. London: Smith Elder.

Taft, Philip. 1972. *Movements for Economic Reform*. New York: Octagon Books.

Taussig, F. W. 1911. *Principles of Economics*. New York: Macmillan. https://archive.org/details/principlesecono00unkngoog/page/n8/mode/2up?view=theater.

Tawney, R. H. 1920. *The Acquisitive Society*. New York: Harcourt Brace.

Taylor, Barbara. 1983. *Eve and the New Jerusalem: Socialism and Feminism in the Nineteenth Century*. New York: Pantheon Books.

Taylor, George Robert Stirling. 1919. *The Guild State*. London: George Allen & Unwin.

Taylor, Harriet. [1851] 1998. "Enfranchisement of Women." In *The Complete Works of Harriet Taylor Mill*. Jo Ellen Jacobs, ed. Bloomington, IN: Indiana University Press, 51–73.

Taylor, Sedley. 1884. *Profit-Sharing between Capital and Labour,* Six Essays. London: Kegan Paul, Trench. https://archive.org/details/profitsharingbet00tayluoft/page/n7/mode/2up.

Thistlewood, David. 1987. "A. J. Penty (1875–1937) and the Legacy of 19th Century English Domestic Architecture." *Journal of the Society of Architectural Historians* 46:4, 327–341.

Thompson, William. [1824] 1963. *An Inquiry into the Principles of the Distribution of Wealth, Most Conducive to Human Happiness*. London: Longman. Reprinted in New York: Augustus M. Kelley. https://archive.org/details/inquiryintoprinc00thomuoft/page/n25/mode/2up.

Thompson, William. 1826. "Objections to the Co-operative System, and Answers." *Co-operative Magazine and Monthly Herald* 1:7, 230–232.

Thompson, William. 1827. *Labour Rewarded: The Claims of Labour and Capital Conciliated: or, How to Secure to Labor the Whole Products of Its Exertions by One of the Idle Classes*. London: Hunt & Clarke. https://archive.org/details/laborreward edcla00thomuoft/page/n3/mode/2up.

Thompson, William. 1830. *Practical Directions for the Speedy and Economical Establishment of Communities, on the Principles of Mutual Co-operation, United Possessions, and Equality of Exertions and of the Means of Enjoyments*. London: Strange & E. Wilson.

Thompson, William and Anna Doyle Wheeler. 1825. *Appeal of One Half the Human Race, Women, Against the Pretensions of the Other Half, Men, to Retain Them in Political, and Thence in Civil and Domestic, Slavery: In Reply to a Paragraph of Mr. Mill's Celebrated "Article on Government."* London: Longman. https://books. google.com/books?id=bmJBAQAAMAAJ&pg=PR1&source=gbs_selected_pa ges&cad=2#v=onepage&q&f=false.

Thornton, William. 1869. *On Labour: Its Wrongful Claims and Rightful Dues; Its Actual Present and Possible Future*. London: Spottiswoode. https://books.google.rw/ books?id=0YkBAAAAQAAJ&pg=PP19&source=gbs_selected_pages&cad=2#v= onepage&q&f=true.

Torrens, Robert. 1819. "Mr. Owen's Plans for Relieving the National Distress." *Edinburgh Review* (October), 453–77. https://archive.org/details/sim_edinbu rgh-review-critical-journal_1819-10_32_64/page/454/mode/2up.

Trincado, Estrella. 2018. "The Debate between the Austrian School of Economics and the Cooperative Movement: The Assumption of Unequal Perception Among Agents." *Industrial History Review* 27:73, 81–103.

Trincado, Estrella and Manuel Santos-Redondo. 2019. *Economics, Entrepreneurship and Utopia: The Economics of Jeremy Bentham and Robert Owen*. London: Routledge.

Turner, Piers Norris. 2019. "John Stuart Mill on Luck and Distributive Justice." In *Routledge Handbook of the Philosophy and Psychology of Luck*. Ian M. Church and Robert J. Hartman, eds. New York: Routledge, 80–93.

Vargo, Gregory. 2020. *Chartist Drama*. Manchester: Manchester University Press.

von Mises, Ludwig von. [1922] 1981. *Socialism: An Economic and Sociological Analysis*. (J. Kahane, trans.) Indianapolis: Liberty Fund.

von Mises, Ludwig von. [1947] 1990. "Observations on the Cooperative Movement." In *Money, Method and the Market Process*. Richard Ebeling, ed. Norwell, MA: Kluwer Academic Publishers, 238–279.

Waithe, Marcus. 2006. "The Laws of Hospitality: Liberty, Generosity, and the Limits of Dissent in William Morris's 'The Tables Turned' and 'News from Nowhere'. *Yearbook of English Studies* 36:2, 212–229.

Watts, John. 1871. "What is Co-operation?" *Co-operative News* 1, 1–2.

Watts, John. 1872. "Co-operation Considered as an Economic Element in Society." *Co-operative News* 2, 50.

Webb, Catherine. [1892] 2020. "The Women's Guild and Store Life." In *Contemporary Thought on Nineteenth Century Socialism*. Vol. 2. *Socialism and Co-operation in Britain, 1850–1918*. Peter Gurney, ed. London: Routledge, 266–272.

Webb, Catherine. 1895. *The Machinery of the Co-operative Movement*. Manchester: Co-operative Union, Long Millgate. https://archive.org/details/machineryofcoope0 0webb_3.

Webb, Catherine, ed. 1921. *Industrial Co-operation: The Story of a Peaceful Revolution. Being an Account of the History, Theory, and Practice of the Co-operative Movement in Great Britain and Ireland*, 9th Ed. Manchester: Co-operative Union.

Webb, Catherine, ed. 1927. *The Woman with the Basket: The History of the Women's Co-operative Guild 1883–1927*. Manchester: Co-operative Wholesale Society's Printing Works.

Webb, Sidney. 1887. *Facts for Socialists*. London: Fabian Society. https://babel.hathitrust.org/cgi/pt?id=uc1.32106001098349&view=1up&seq=1&skin=2021.

Webb, Sidney. 1889. "The Historic Basis of Socialism." In *Fabian Essays in Socialism*. George Bernard Shaw, ed. London: The Fabian Society. https://archive.org/details/fabianessaysinso00fabirich/mode/2up.

Webb, Sidney and Beatrice Webb. [1894] 1907. *The History of Trade Unionism*. London: Longmans Green. https://archive.org/details/historyoftradeun00webb/page/n5/mode/2up.

Webb, Sidney and Beatrice Webb. [1897] 1902. *Industrial Democracy*. London: Longmans Green. https://archive.org/details/industrialdemocr00webbuoft/page/n7/mode/2up.

Webb, Sidney and Beatrice Webb. 1921. *The Consumers' Co-operative Movement*. London: Longmans Green. https://archive.org/details/consumerscoopera00webbuoft/page/n1/mode/2up?view=theater.

Whalley, H. 1930. *Jubilee History of the Denholme Industrial Co-operative Society Ltd., 1880–1930*. Manchester: CWS Printing Works, Longsight.

Wheeler, Anna Doyle. 1830. "The Rights of Women." *British Cooperator* 1:1, 12–15; 1:2, 33–36.

Wheeler, Anna Doyle (Vlasta pseudonym). 1833. "Correspondence from Vlasta." *The Crisis* 2:34 (August 24), 268–269.

Wheeler, Anna Doyle (Vlasta pseudonym). 1833. "Correspondence from Vlasta." *The Crisis* 2: 35 & 36, (August 31), 279–281.

Wheeler, Anna Doyle (Vlasta pseudonym). 1834. "Letter from Vlasta to Lord Hampden." In *Hampden in the Nineteenth Century; or, Colloquies on the Errors and Improvement of Society*. Vol. II. John Hinter Morgan. London: Edward Moxon, 301–325.

Williamson, Oliver. 1993. "Calculativeness, Trust and Economic Organization." *Journal of Law and Economics* 36:1, 453–486.

Williamson, Oliver and Sidney Winter. 1993. *The Nature of the Firm: Origins, Evolution and Development*. Oxford: Oxford University Press.

Winstanley, George. 1649. "The True Levellers Standard Advanced: Or, The State of Community Opened, and Presented to the Sons of Men." https://www.marxists.org/reference/archive/winstanley/1649/levellers-standard.htm.

Withers, Hartley. 1920. *The Case for Capitalism*. New York: E. P. Dutton.

Wollstonecraft, Mary. 1792. *A Vindication of the Rights of Woman with Strictures on Moral and Political Subjects*. London: Joseph Johnson.

Women's Co-operative Guild. 1896. *Report of Investigations into the Conditions of Women's Work, 1895–6*. London: Co-operative Women's Guild Central Committee. LSE Library Archives Special BP166795.

Women's Co-operative Guild. 1908a. "Summarised Report of the Women's Guild." In *The 40th Annual Co-operative Congress*. Manchester: Co-operation Union, 1–19.

Women's Co-operative Guild. 1908b. "A Co-operative Standard for Women Workers." Report of Annual Congress, June, 1908.

Women's Co-operative Guild. 1910. *Women Employees in Co-operative Stores and Factories*. London: Co-operative Wholesale Society. LSE Library Archives Special HD6/411.

Women's Co-operative Guild. 1915. *Maternity: Letters from Working Women*. London: G. Bell & Sons.

Woolf, Leonard. 1919. *Co-operation and the Future of Industry*. London: George Allen & Unwin.

Woof, Leonard. 1920. "Co-operation and Guild Socialism." *The Guildsman* (December), 3–4.

Woolf, Leonard. [1967] 1989. *Downhill All the Way: An Autobiography of the Years 1919–1939*. San Diego: Harcourt Brace Jovanovich.

Yeo, Stephen. 1995. *Who Was J. T. W. Mitchell?* Manchester: CWS Membership Services.

Yeo, Stephen. 2017. *A Usable Past, Volume 1, Victorian Agitator, George Jacob Holyoake (1817–1906)*. Brighton: Edward Everett Root.

INDEX

For the benefit of digital users, indexed terms that span two pages (e.g., 52–53) may, on occasion, appear on only one of those pages.

Tables and figures are indicated by *t* and *f* following the page number